Natural Human Rights

A Theory

This timely book by internationally regarded scholar of ethics and social/political philosophy Michael Boylan focuses on the history, application, and significance of human rights in the West and in China. Boylan engages the key current philosophical debates prevalent in human rights discourse today and draws them together to argue for the existence of natural, universal human rights. Arguing against the grain of mainstream philosophical beliefs, Boylan asserts that there is continuity between human rights and natural law and that human beings require basic, essential goods for minimum action. These include food, clean water and sanitation, clothing, shelter, and protection from bodily harm, including basic healthcare. The achievement of this goal, Boylan demonstrates, will require significant resource allocation and creative methods of implementation involving public and private institutions. Using the classroom-tested dynamic approach of combining technical argument with four fictional narratives about human rights, the book invites readers to engage with the most important aspects of the discipline.

Michael Boylan is Professor of Philosophy and Chair of the Philosophy Department at Marymount University. He is author of twenty-six books and more than a hundred articles. His monograph *A Just Society* (2004) was recently the subject of an edited volume featuring fourteen authors from eight countries entitled *Morality and Justice: Reading Boylan's "A Just Society."* He has served on professional and governmental policy committees and was a Fellow at the Center for American Progress and a program presenter at the Brookings Institution. He is an international figure who has been an invited speaker at a number of prominent universities outside the United States, including Oxford, Cambridge, Manchester, University College London, Trinity College (Dublin), University College (Dublin), the Sorbonne, the Katholic University of Leuven, University of Oslo, University of Copenhagen, Cologne University, Bochum University, Twente and Delft Universities, Valparaiso University (Chile), University of Sydney, University of Melbourne, Australian National University, and Charles Sturt University (Waga Waga, Australia). He is also a published novelist and poet.

Natural Human Rights

A Theory

MICHAEL BOYLAN

Marymount University, Virginia

CAMBRIDGE UNIVERSITY PRESS

CAMBRIDGE
UNIVERSITY PRESS

32 Avenue of the Americas, New York, NY 10013-2473, USA

Cambridge University Press is part of the University of Cambridge.

It furthers the University's mission by disseminating knowledge in the pursuit of education, learning, and research at the highest international levels of excellence.

www.cambridge.org
Information on this title: www.cambridge.org/9781107664210

First published 2014

A catalog record for this publication is available from the British Library.

Library of Congress Cataloging in Publication data
Boylan, Michael, 1952–
Natural human rights : a theory / Michael Boylan.
pages cm
Includes bibliographical references and index.
ISBN 978-1-107-02985-9 (hardback) – ISBN 978-1-107-66421-0 (pbk.)
1. Human rights – Philosophy. 2. Human rights – Cross-cultural studies.
3. Natural law. 4. Natural law – Philosophy. I. Title.
JC571.B6752 2014
323.01–dc23 2013041798

ISBN 978-1-107-02985-9 Hardback
ISBN 978-1-107-66421-0 Paperback

For my family: Rebecca, Arianne, Seán, and Éamon

Contents

Contents

Preface

I have fashioned this book as a symphony. There are several forms of the symphony, but in this depiction I have sought a literal and an artistic understanding of this word. *Sym-phonia* (συμφωνία) means bringing together various sounds or voices into a coherent presentation. So literally, the etymology refers to creating a harmony of voices, and since there are many voices in the cacophony of human rights discourse, I have taken it upon myself to present many of these voices and the patterns they convey and then to forge what I think is an account that best addresses critical problems: the melody of natural human rights.

The second meaning of the word refers to the artistic way I try to do this. My composition technique combines what I have termed "direct discourse philosophy" with "fictive narrative philosophy."[1] Direct discourse philosophy is what most people in the West think of when they consider philosophy. The materials are the claim (conclusion) and the reasons (premises that interact via an inferential logical structure). Most of this book is presented via direct discourse philosophy. However, there are a few variations to the themes via fictive narrative philosophy, as well. These come in the form of four original short stories that introduce each movement in the composition.

A musical symphony begins with an *overture*. This sets up the various themes that will be explored in the composition. In this case various inputs from the philosophical and political science literature are lightly set out in terms of background conditions in the current world affairs (Chapter 1). The overture presents the themes that will be developed.

---

[1] For further explication on the way direct discourse philosophy and fictive narrative philosophy work, see Michael Boylan and Charles Johnson, *Philosophy: An Innovative Introduction: Fictive Narrative, Primary Texts, and Responsive Writing* (Boulder, CO: Westview, 2010).

These themes include the traditions in the West and in China (Chapters 2 and 3) so that a more inclusive vision of the setting of human rights and natural law might be presented. In the process of setting out these histories, I have sought to give a more comprehensive shared community worldview account by melding direct discourse philosophy of various eras with glimpses of literature from that time. The addition of brief literary overviews works in counterpoint to the direct philosophy. This is a common practice among those who compose histories.

Next is the *adagio*. This is a rather more slowly moving time signature. In the very brief period of my life in which I tried composing classical music I would always pay attention to the adagio. It would reveal the essence of what was being put forth. Here as well, I examine what I feel are the principal theories that would justify human rights (Chapters 4, 5, and 6). Each is brought forward with its strengths and weaknesses. Obviously, I believe my own theory of agency-based human rights is the best choice. Therefore, I end the adagio movement with a strong presentation of my own version of natural human rights.

There is then an elision (Chapter 7) presenting my theory on how people actually accept new normative theories and the ontological commitments that various approaches entail. The elision leads to the *scherzo* (Chapters 8, 9, and 10), which is spritely and briefly sets out an application of the theory through three cases that both mirror the table of embeddedness's first three levels (basic goods level one, basic goods level two, and secondary goods level one) and are consonant with the three short stories that deal with the same problems: war rape, political speech, and LGBT rights. The scherzo moves quickly toward the ultimate resolution (cadence) in each instance.

In the *rondo*, the allegro pace continues the upbeat tempo and moves us toward summative resolution on how we think of political change and who is responsible for it.

Throughout, I engage each section with a short story that fits within the general plan of the table of embeddedness. I believe that this sort of presentation will resonate well with a wide range of readers and especially among those in the classroom (according to my coauthored empirical study).[2] Fiction connects with virtually everybody in presenting some essential characteristics of the problem at hand. In this symphony,

---

[2] "Using Fictive Narrative to Teach Ethics/Philosophy," coauthored with Felicia Nimue Ackerman, Sybol Cook Anderson, Gabriel Palmer-Fernandez, and Edward Spence, *Teaching Ethics* 12.1 (Fall 2011): 1–34.

there is a short story that is meant to represent what I call fictive narrative philosophy that presents another way to support the point of contention at hand.

Because of this innovative approach, I believe that this text can reach readers especially by

- presenting major modes of thinking about human rights
- setting out traditional ways that the West and China understood natural law (and the resulting human rights)
- examining the most prominent ways that human rights are justified within the current debate in the Western tradition
- arguing for an original position of natural human rights
- applying the apparatus to selected key problems relevant today
- introducing each major section with a short story that depicts a violation of human rights in line with the pedagogical structure presented

I believe this is a unique book that combines a variety of modes of conceptualizing human rights and provides an apparatus with which the reader can integrate the arguments into a worldview-challenging experience.

Acknowledgments

I would like to thank Jeff Reiman, Ethelbert Miller, Wanda Teays, Thomas Pogge, Bill Haines, and Rosie Tong (and the anonymous reviewers for the Press), who made many useful suggestions. I would also like to thank Beatrice Rehl, my editor, and all the production team at Cambridge. My family read and commented on my stories. Their comments improved the final product. Then there is my research team at Marymount: Tanya Lanuzo and Lynn McLaughlin, who assisted me in the monumental job of getting the best articles and books for my discussions. As always, I thank my wife, Rebecca, and my children for their intellectual acumen and loving support. None of this would happen without them.

PART ONE

CONCEPTUALIZING HUMAN RIGHTS

Overture

"The Spotted Butterfly"

Life is about suffering,
Hang on until it's over.
– Michael Boylan, "Existence 22/7"

It was almost three weeks since the end of the long rainy season. The ground was drinking in the water from the rains. In a small village, Gimbaya N'kufo was doing chores with her daughter, Mangeni. They were going down to the river to wash their clothes. Many people in the village criticized Gimbaya because she did her own washing. They said that the wife of the village chief should have someone else wash the clothes. But Gimbaya was a strong woman. Though slight in height, she had broad shoulders and had developed endurance because of her willingness to work.

It was important to wash clothes early in the day while the locusts were still singing their songs before the water went bad. People got sick when they washed their clothes later in the day. Gimbaya was able to wake up with the sun and do her duty. When she returned she prepared a meal and then attended to the education of her two children.

Life was good. Adaon, her husband, was a tolerant man and rarely beat her. He spent his days attending to people's complaints. It was not an easy task to be a village chief. Gimbaya was generally popular with the village women despite her meek demeanor. Some said she did not deport herself with sufficient pride for a woman of her station. On this day, after she had worked with her own children, a young unmarried woman in the village named Makemba Youlou came over to greet Gimbaya. "Makemba how is it with you today?"

This story is based on an interview I had with Sylvie Mugambe, a human rights worker from the Democratic Republic of the Congo, April 2009.

"It goes okay. But I feel strange like I feel near the beginning of the long rain."

Gimbaya went up to Makemba and placed her large hands on the young woman's shoulders. Makemba was short and slender. Her skin was a little more fair than was the norm in the village (some people said she had Tutsi blood in her). She wore her hair very short. Gimbaya gave the younger woman a squeeze with her hands that evoked a smile. "Why don't we sit down under that tree over there and I'll tell you a funny story about what Mangeni said to me not more than a few minutes ago?"

Makemba agreed and so they sat down together. A large spotted butterfly hovered overhead for moment displaying its daring pink patches of color against its black body. And Gimbaya began, "Well, Mangeni began her dream as if she were a fish!" Makemba laughed because 'mangeni' means 'fish.' "Well, Mangeni was swimming with her friends when she sees the shadow of a man wading. The man was carrying a spear" – at that moment Gimbaya was interrupted by the sound of gunfire. Four men (not of the village) had burst onto the scene. Gimbaya and Makemba scrambled to their feet. The men were large, stocky, and very dark skinned. They were also carrying machine guns.

Quickly they stormed to the center of the village. "Come on, we have to find Mangeni and Bonyeme." The two women tried to retreat into the trees in a looping motion toward Gimbaya's home. They didn't need to go far before Gimbaya saw her children. They cried, "Mommy!" Gimbaya tried to gesture to them to be silent, but it was too late. The attention of one of the gunmen was drawn their way. He was a young man not many years older than Makemba. As he approached Gimbaya could detect a deep scar under his left eye.

"Don't you move!" The accent was unmistakable: Hutu. "*You*, come over here." He was talking to Makemba. The young girl clung to Gimbaya who was holding her with her left arm. (Gimbaya's right arm was protecting her children.)

"Are you deaf? Get over here." Makemba was shivering with fright. Gimbaya's strong, large hands maintained their grasp. Gimbaya's attention was all on Scarface, so she didn't see that the entire village was lingering just out of view (including Gimbaya's husband, Adaon). The other three men were fanned out so that no one could come up to them from behind.

"Why have you come here?" asked Gimbaya in a strong, clear voice.

Scarface lifted his gun to the sky and discharged three rapid-fire rounds. "We're roaming about with a small army. Anyone who gets in our way will die. Do you want to get in our way?"

"Do you want food? We can give you some food and then you can be on your way. We want no fuss. We will give you what you want," Gimbaya's voice remained strong, but her tight grip on Makemba and on her children was causing the muscles in her arm to quiver. It was beyond her control. "We want that Tutsi girl."

"She's not Tutsi. She lives here. She was born here."

"She's Tutsi, bitch. Now you hand her over." Scarface was approaching Gimbaya.

"We'll give you food. We'll give you francs. Please, just don't hurt us."

Then Scarface lifted up his gun stock and knocked Gimbaya to the ground with a fierce blow to the side of her head. The village chief's wife tumbled to the ground. Her head was bleeding. Her children were crying and climbing onto her. The rest of the villagers watched behind trees. Adaon N'kufo, the village chief, began inching backward for his escape.

Scarface then ordered Makemba to the center of the common area. It was then, in front of everyone, that the stockiest of the group stripped and raped Makemba. But that wasn't all. Gimbaya was next. They picked up the dizzy woman and separated her from her children. As they stripped off her clothes, Makemba arose to try to help her friend.

Makemba was met with ten bullets to her face. She fell backward into the dust.

It was the middle of the night when Gimbaya found the road north. If nothing else worked, she'd try to walk to Uganda and her uncle Akiki. It was hard to walk. She was so very sore. But her children needed her. She hadn't eaten since morning. As the physical shock began to wear off, she strove to concentrate her thoughts. It didn't work. She had to keep moving until her legs would take her no further. Then Gimbaya and her two children lay down by the edge of the Kivu Lake, took a drink, and held each other for dear life.

The next morning Gimbaya awoke as a praying mantis was walking over her face. Her body ached. Her mind wouldn't go into its normal mode. She wasn't herself. But she had her two children. She knew the road led north so they got themselves up, drank some water, and kept their eyes out for some plants to eat. By the time the sun was high they had consumed several mini-meals.

Around mid-afternoon they met another woman on the main road north. She was coming from the west. Her name was Nabutungi Tsiba and she had a daughter, Abbo, who was about the same age as Gimbaya's own daughter, Mangeni. "Where are you going?" asked Gimbaya.

"To Goma at the north end of the lake; they have a place there for women like us."

Gimbaya didn't respond. But her memory was suddenly stimulated. She remembered her husband, the village chief, banishing her and her children from their home because she had become *unclean.* Adaon spoke with the authority of a mighty judge. There was only time to pick up a few things and put them in a blanket and be on their way. They had reached the main road by dusk.

"And what is this place like?" asked Gimbaya.

"They will take care of us: give us medical treatment, a new name, and a new life."

"I have a new name. The one I was born with, Uwakweh."

"That's a beautiful name," said Nabutungi.

Gimbaya smiled for the first time since she left her village. She reached out for the hand of Nabutungi. As she did so she saw that Mangeni and Abbo were also showing signs of friendship as they talked and patted the head of the younger Bonyeme.

It was a long walk. They had access to water in the lake and they ate plants (which were bountiful since the long rainy season had just recently ended). After a week, they made it to Goma. This would be a little difficult. Goma was so much bigger than anything they had ever experienced. It was the largest town in North Kivu.

"Excusez-moi, si vous voulez? Où est la maison des femmes?" asked Nabutungi. Gimbaya didn't speak French well. It was not spoken in her village. But she had learned a little when she was young and had visited her aunt for a year in Kindu. She felt fortunate that she had a sojourner who spoke the lingua franca.

The question had been posed to a rather rotund elderly lady who wore fancy blue-patterned clothes and a matching head scarf. The woman had smiled at them when they approached each other on the street, but after the question, her face became blank. All she did was point to the left. Then she hurried away.

After meandering for a while, they saw the ruins of a building. It had been a two-story wood-frame building. As they approached they saw a sign face down on the ground. Gimbaya picked it up. With the help of Nabutungi they discovered that the rubble was what was left of the women's center. Nabutungi hugged Gimbaya and they broke into tears. The children looked up at their mothers and also hugged each other and began to cry.

Then a very old lady with wrinkled skin, a wide mouth, and very thin lips approached them from across the street. "I seen you and been following you since Mrs. Big-stuff insulted you back there." The woman spoke in the local dialect.

"We have walked a long way, grandmother," began Gimbaya.

"I know you have. I still have eyes in this old skull of mine. And I have seen many other women, like yourselves, come here for help. The trouble started when certain men folk heard about the wonderful good that they were doing here. It was run by a young woman whose father was a retired college teacher. They lived at the end of town." The old woman's wide mouth dripped saliva on the right side as she talked. As the saliva began to drip to the ground she would pause and wipe it away with her left hand. "It wasn't those Hutus who are scourging our villages, but Congolese men themselves: the husbands and fathers of the victims." The old lady was speaking with strong emotion that caused her to cough. "Can you believe it? Their own kin: they despoil them again!" This time the coughing spasm required Gimbaya and Nabutungi to help the woman sit down on some rubble that looked secure. The children found a resting place close by. The women rubbed the old lady's back until she felt balanced. Then the old lady began again, "They came two weeks ago. They had bombs with them and they struck when the sun was high. They bombed the shelter and they also bombed the house. It was lucky that it was at mid-day because that's when all the women go down to the river to do their laundry. It was lucky that they did it in that order, because the sound of the bomb at the vacant shelter caused the college teacher to search after his daughter for their escape. He came and told the women what had happened and the group of them picked up their laundry and started walking."

"Where did they go?" asked Gimbaya.

"To Uganda – where else?"

"Yes – especially in the west near us. So many have traveled there."

The women thanked the old lady and offered to walk her home. Then the two mothers returned to gaze upon the wreckage of the women's shelter. Neither of them spoke. They were deaf to their own children playing. The two women in their long dresses stood tall; around them the children ran as if they were trees in a forest. Not a tear was shed, but the women both knew what they must do.

"We will walk to Kasese. My uncle told me that it sits on a grand lake – not as large as Kivu – but a calming spirit nonetheless. Akiki will take you and your daughter in and find a place for you. He is a good man."

Nabutungi gazed at her newfound sister and smiled. Then she picked up her load, and gathered the children. It was then that the women with wandering step and slow toward Uganda took their solitary way.

1

How Do We Talk about Human Rights?

Open the newspaper: how many times do you see the word "right" or "human right"? I tried this recently and found the word used in many different contexts from talking about politics and policy, to the activities of large corporations, to popular uprisings in the Middle East, to dissidents in China, to welfare economics, to affirmative action, to corporations as people, and even to youth sports uniforms: this in just one daily paper.

1.1 COMMON USAGE

Clearly we use the terms *right, rights, human rights,* and *natural human rights* in many different ways. One touchstone on English linguistic usage is the Oxford English Dictionary[1] that cites the usage of a word historically. When we look at the word "right" we find the same divergence that we saw in the newspaper:

1. A standard of conduct
2. A duty
3. To which is consonant with justice and goodness or reason – something morally or socially correct, just or honorable
4. Equitable treatment
5. The cause of that which is fair or morally correct
6. A judicial decision
7. Legal entitlement or justifiable claim (on legal or moral grounds)
8. An entitlement considered to arise through natural justice
9. Something that a person may properly claim

---

[1] *Oxford English Dictionary,* ed. James Murray, et al. (Oxford: Oxford University Press, 1971).

10. Political, civil, or liberties
11. Miscellaneous usages: map making, the Christian Service (rite), shoes, hunting, etc.

For the purposes of this book there will be aspects of 1–10 that will be set out in different ways. This is what it means to offer stipulative definition. However, there must be grounds for the stipulation. Otherwise we enter the realm of fantasy.

What we can see from the *OED* is that contained within *rights language* are the following: (a) a claim to some good; (b) the claim must be justified; (c) the grounds of the justification are either legal or moral; (d) the claim is so strong as to be an entitlement; (e) the entitlement claim is sometimes connected to natural justice; (f) the entitlement claim is fair and equitable; (g) rights are associated with duties.

These seven markers set out the way that 'right' (including but not limited to human rights) has been used in the English language from the earliest Anglo-Saxon documents onward. In the next two chapters this search will be expanded to include various historical usages of *human rights* and *natural human rights* along with allied concepts such as *natural law*. This exploration will also include some analysis of allied ontological tenets (as per the word "natural").

1.2 WESLEY HOHFELD

So what's so special about human rights? Wesley Hohfeld set these in context in Figure 1.1.[2] These fundamental opposites and correlatives set the context of Hohfeld's insightful analysis. When we think of the opposites, we envision different worldview perspectives. People come at life from different vantage points. These drive a conception of the social playing field where people live and carry out their lives. In the second category, correlatives, we have something like a Hegelian dialectic in which the conception of one side logically implies the conception of the other. The correlatives are tied together conceptually in a way that the opposites are not.

To get a handle on this in the context of this book, let's start with the notion of a *claim*. There are at least two senses of a claim: (a) a demand by some agent for some good; and (b) a demand that could be made on behalf of some agent whether that agent asked for it or not. For example,

---

[2] Wesley Hohfeld, *Fundamental Legal Conceptions* (New Haven, CT: Yale University Press, 1919): 36.

I. *Jural Opposites*

A. Rights v. No-Rights; B. Privilege v. Duty; C. Power v. Disability;
D. Immunity v. Liability

II. *Jural Correlatives*

A. Right v. Duty; B. Privilege v. No-Right; C. Power v. Liability;
D. Immunity v. Disability.

FIGURE 1.1. Hohfeld's Depiction of Rights in Context

a baby might have the claim right to nourishment in order to stay alive, but because the baby is pre-speech, he or she cannot enunciate the claim to anyone. Sure, the baby can cry. A cry means many things. It isn't specific. At least a crying baby declares to all in earshot that he or she is in need of *something*. If one were to be committed to (a), then he would be forced to say that there is no claim by the agent. And if (a) were the only way a claim right could be obtained, then the child has no claim right to whatever she was crying for: food, milk, change of diaper, or just to be held. However, by bringing (b) into the picture the focus moves away from what this child before me wants from her point of view, but rather what this child can legitimately claim in the context of what children, in general, would reasonably want. From this, it is the duty of the caregiver to ascertain whether the child needs food, milk, change of diaper, or just to be held. The (b) position operates from the generic point of view first and then particularizes the description to the individual at hand via a process that I have called *dialectical subsumption*.[3] In dialectical subsumption one begins with an individual and then goes back and forth between various generic categories in Hegelian fashion to determine just what category best fits the individual at hand. The process is very much like biological taxonomy.[4] In taxonomy, since there are no "perfect" cases, one must go back and forth with the specimen and insert boundary conditions to properly classify it. In the case of the laboratory, this can be time-consuming. Now in the case of a baby, decisions must be made in a very short interval. Nonetheless, this is what I assert happens: one has in his mind what babies need and then checks on whether one of these

---

[3] Michael Boylan, *A Just Society* (Lanham, MD: Rowman and Littlefield, 2004): 11–12.
[4] For treatments biological and nonbiological, see Kaesuk Yoon, *Naming Nature* (New York: Norton, 2009) and Judith Wilson, *Discovering Species* (New York: Columbia University Press, 1999).

factors is what *this* baby needs. When one hypothesis proves correct, then action is engaged.

This may seem rather artificial and long-winded to those who (like myself) have cared for infants. But I believe this is really the logical structure of how we recognize and respond to one sort of claims right.

Then there is the case of someone who is resigned to a sort of life and doesn't think much about it. For example, until 1920 in the United States women couldn't vote. I would conjecture that most women from the founding of the republic to the turn of the twentieth century were so engaged in their social roles that they didn't really think too much about whether they should vote.[5] Thus, these women didn't offer a claim in the sense of (a) listed previously. If a claim right is only to be understood as a claim in sense (a), then these women were not claiming a right to vote. Now, of course, after the turn of the century as the alliance with the temperance movement became popular, more and more women began *claiming* the right to vote.[6] This culminated in the Nineteenth Amendment to the United States Constitution in August 18, 1920. If a claims right is to be understood only via (a), then women in the United States had a right to vote only on August 18, 1920.

However, under the (b) interpretation of a claims right, the situation is rather different. Under the (b) position, a right may be claimed on behalf of some agent whether that agent asked for it or not. Thus, from the beginning of the republic onward someone who examined the question, "who should be allowed to vote in a democracy?" could examine relevant criteria (such as minimum cognitive ability to support voluntary action) and form a judgment via dialectical subsumption that women are properly subsumed into the category of those persons within a society who should have a right to vote. This conclusion does not depend upon any actual person crying out (as the baby did) for something. Even if everyone is silent, women still have a moral claims right to vote in a democracy from day one of the republic.

If the right is not recognized, then that says something against the republic. But how could women possess a right that they have not asserted?

---

[5] Two accounts that focus on particular figures show the split among women (and men) on suffrage. See N. E. H. Hull, *The Woman Who Dared to Vote: The Trial of Susan B. Anthony* (Topeka: University Press of Kansas, 2012) and Jennifer M. Ross-Nazzal, *Winning the West for Women: The Life of Suffragist Emma Smith DeVoe* (Seattle: University of Washington Press, 2011).

[6] For an account of how the temperance and suffrage movements worked together, see Holly Berkeley Fletcher, *Gender and the American Temperance Movement of the Nineteenth Century* (London: Routledge, 2007).

Many ask this question. It is a crucial question for those asserting natural human rights as opposed to conventional human rights. Those who advocate natural human rights believe that to speak of a claims right means simply that a right can be attributed to someone on the basis of his or her membership in *Homo sapiens*. As members of a species with certain characteristics, various rights can be independently attributed to everyone on the planet atemporally. Conventionalists, in contrast, will assert that rights become operational *only* when they are recognized by some political body: family, community, state, or some international agreement. This will be an important tension in this book: natural rights advocates versus conventional rights advocates (see Part Two).

A second notion of human rights relates to rights that are conferred to an individual in virtue of her particular social role. For example, in the United States, a governor of a state has the right to commute a prison sentence that has been given by the court. This sort of human right has been deemed by Wesley Hohfeld a *power*.[7] A power is a conventional right that attaches to either one's political or social station.

Rights that attach to one's social station were the only sort of right to which John Austin assented.[8] Indeed, since Jeremy Bentham declared human rights to be *nonsense on stilts* there was little interest among many nineteenth-century utilitarians in stand-alone human rights. This follows from the very formulation of moral duty under act utilitarianism as following the utilitarian formula. Every constructed, recognized right was provisional as such right flowed from social conditions of the present and could change as conditions changed.[9]

Hohfeld's third category is liberty rights.[10] Liberty rights are those rights that a person possesses naturally to act as he pleases ceteris paribus. Thus if person A is walking with person B and they see a five dollar bill on the ground five feet in front of them (and there is no obvious owner to the bill), then both A and B are at liberty to walk over and pick it up or even to dive forward to claim the prize. The latter behavior is rather aggressive, but nonetheless it is permitted under a liberty right. A liberty right is not a conventional right but a natural right.

---

[7] Hohfeld, *Fundamental Legal Conceptions*, 53–64.

[8] John Austin, *The Province of Jurisprudence Determined*, 5th ed. vol. 2, ed. Robert Campbell (London: John Murray, 1885).

[9] Jeremy Bentham, "Nonsense on Stilts," in *Jeremy Bentham: Rights, Representation and Reform*, in *The Collected Works of Jeremy Bentham*, ed. P. Schofield, C. Pease-Watkin, and C. Blamires (Oxford: Clarendon Press, 2003).

[10] Hohfeld, *Fundamental Legal Conceptions*, 47–50.

Finally, there are immunities and disabilities.[11] Immunities and disabilities ("no power") are correlatives. An immunity is a freedom from the legal power or control of another regarding a legal relation. This is often achieved by shifting the legal responsibility to another party. If this cannot be done and one is subject to real harm, then said victim can be described as being under a disability (lack of power to shift the harm elsewhere). These are descriptive—therefore, conventional.

Of these four categories of rights, the primary concern of this book is claims rights. Liberty rights will be subsumed under an understanding of claims rights, and powers and immunities and disabilities will be relegated to the realm of institutions and their separate operation.

1.3 HUMAN RIGHTS AND COMMON LANGUAGE CLAIMS FOR JUSTICE

"You can't do that. I've got a right!" This is a common claim. I have heard this refrain throughout my life. For example, when I used to volunteer at food kitchens for the poor, patrons would complain when the food was gone. We knew how much food we had to give. Tickets were made with numbers on them. After the numbers were exhausted we would tell the others lined up that there might be something left over, but we couldn't promise. We generally had about three hundred tickets and there would be fifty or so who would hang on in case there would be more food. Sometimes we would have enough extra slices of bread and gravy and some assorted carrot tops and other edible bits that we invited a few more in to finish what we had. But there was often resentment in this latter group. "Why don't we get the entire meal like the rest of them?" "Why do you promote women with children? Don't you know that some of these gals just find some kid so that they can move to the front of the line?" "I served my country in Vietnam and this is how they treat me: bread and gravy?" "Why can't we get a decent meal?"

Then I saw the thirty or so stragglers who walked away without even the bread and gravy. It's a tough life. When I was confronted openly about some good they wanted (in this case food), I was put on the spot to come up with a reply. Frankly, I didn't have a good answer. When someone makes an *overt request* (verbal or written) for some good, then we will call this a type-a claim for some desired good. The claim is open and made publicly. In this case the claim was for food. The reason I had no good

---

[11] Hohfeld, *Fundamental Legal Conceptions*, 60–63.

response to their overt request is that here we are in the richest country on earth and we can't even feed everyone? And then I thought about the fight that Mitch Snyder (Center for Creative Non-Violence) had with then President Reagan to lift the classified ban on the White House food refuse. All the good leftovers from presidential banquets and everyday meals would just rot away and be made into fertilizer when it could go to help those thirty who just had to walk away. Public pressure made the president rethink his position: that the White House garbage should be classified in the same manner that nuclear war secrets were classified. How would the USSR use this garbage to take over our country? This is one sort of common language claim about the human right to eat.

Then there is another sort of human right claim that gets implicitly expressed by those who are often marginalized in the process: children. The House of Ruth is a nonprofit charity that has as its mission the protection of women and children in situations of domestic violence. My wife and I have done some volunteer work at the House of Ruth in the past. The clients we saw were the children. Women came to the center because they had been abused by their husbands. The husbands may also have abused the children or sometimes the mothers had hurt them, themselves on a "violence down the food chain" mentality. The strongest hurts the second strongest who, in turn, hurts the third strongest. From my personal experience these were examples of *silent rights claims* (type-b). I didn't hear any of the language associated with these claims in the food kitchens. All I saw were grim, defeated faces. Type-b claims are not publicly enunciated by those in need, but can be logically deduced by their situation.

Most of the time, according to statistics on this, the women return to the men who beat them because they believe the line that tells them "you're no good; your only chance is if you stick with me."[12] These women and children do not enunciate that they have a right not to be beaten by their husbands. There are no strident exhortations of what they deserve, only the grim resignation to a fate of constant pain. In the common parlance this is still a muddied picture. Many consider the bedroom to be a private space that should not be violated by any outsider. From the beginning of our republic, there has been a tacit understanding that it's not so bad to beat your wife occasionally. The so-called rule of thumb

[12] Recent work on violence and the Stockholm Syndrome includes Chris Cantor and John Price, "Traumatic Entrapment, Appeasement, and Complex Post-Traumatic Stress Disorder," *Australian and New Zealand Journal of Psychiatry* **41**.5 (2007): 377–384, and Sinéad Rhodes and Fiona Jones, "Captivating Interest in Survival," *Psychologist* **22**.12 (2009): 1008–1009.

allowed a man to beat his wife with a stick no thicker than his thumb.[13] Such shared community worldviews as this have not been uncommon in the history of humankind. This is another sort of common language claim: protection from unwarranted bodily harm.

Another kind of good that people may claim (either type-a or type-b) is about liberty. Liberty is generally thought about in a positive and in a negative sense. In the positive sense A has liberty to do x just in case it is within the physical capability of A to do x. Mary has the liberty to walk up the stairs if her leg muscles, spine, and other somatic systems are working normally. We are constrained in our positive liberty by the characteristics given to us phylogenetically through our evolution to *Homo sapiens*. For example, as a human I cannot fly as a bird flies. We are not equipped to fly naturally as birds do. As such, we are constrained in positive liberty on how we come into the world (within some range due to effort or development).[14]

A second understanding of liberty is negative liberty. These are exterior constraints upon our ability to perform what we are positively capable of doing. For example, Mary may have the positive liberty to walk upstairs, but if there is a gunman at the top of the stairs pointing a rifle at her and telling her to turn around and go away or he will kill her, then despite Mary's positive liberty for climbing stairs, she is constrained by negative liberty from climbing the stairs.

In the odd case when there is an impediment against doing something that is already impossible to do – such as flying – then the positive analysis of liberty should trump the negative sense. For example, Jemal is standing on the green flapping his arms and a gunman comes up and asks him what he is doing, and Jemal says, "I'm going to fly into the air." The gunman then says, "If you leave the ground and fly into the air, then I will shoot you down much as I do ducks." Because Jemal will never leave the ground, the threat will never be actualized. In this way, positive liberty analysis should always precede negative liberty analysis.

Those who seek to use negative liberty to limit our potential agency generally fall into two groups: (a) protection against the state or large

---

[13] Though there is some dispute on the meaning of this adage (whether you can beat your wife with a stick as long as it is no fatter than your thumb), it is taken to be the centerpiece theme for the United States Commission on Civil Rights, *Under the Rule of Thumb: Battered Women and the Administration of Justice*, 2 vols. (Ann Arbor: University of Michigan Library, 1982).

[14] A classic general overview of some of these concerns can be found in Isaiah Berlin, *Four Essays on Liberty* (Oxford: Oxford University Press, 1969).

corporations; and (b) protection against interference by particular individuals concerning expression of actions in which we wish to engage. In the first instance, one's liberty to do such and such can be impeded by the actions of an overly restrictive government or large corporations. Governments often try to restrict the liberty to express oneself (cf. *Adagio:* "Double Talk" in Part Two of this volume). They feel threatened by the free flow of information. For example, at the writing of this book, officials in Iran are trying to control the Internet so that they might protect themselves from the free flow of information that has characterized the "Arab Spring–2011."[15] Governmental interference in prospective agency is perhaps the greatest instance of negative liberty in the world today. Most would declare these rights violations as unjust and thus unacceptable.

Large corporations can also present problems in the (a) group. For example, Facebook and Google are large corporations that gather a tremendous amount of information on us (we are not fully aware of much of what they collect). The way these corporations do this is by gathering enormous amounts of data on our behavior and then sharing this information with others with the intent of influencing our future conduct.[16] In the case of Facebook and Google, the point is about making money. If I discuss in an e-mail that I would like to travel to Germany, then when I go onto a social networking site or on my web browser I start finding ads about trips to Germany.

Many would say that for Google or Facebook to insert this information is innocuous enough and that users are free to purchase the products in the ads or not. Others see a darker problem – the many mistakes that arise in raw data mining.[17] A friend of mine, for example, gave a talk at Chico State University in California. On the university's website there was an advertisement of this philosopher's talk. However, on the next page of the university website was some description of Osama bin Laden (the mastermind of the 9-11-2001 tragedy). The data mining program that the Department of Homeland Security used linked the two together

---

[15] www.cbsnews.com/.../irans-leader-sets-up-internet-control-group.

[16] On general assaults of the new digital age on privacy, see Emily Christofides, Amy Muise, and Desmarais Serge, "Information, Disclosure and Control and Facebook," *Cyberpsychology and Behavior* **12**.3 (2009): 341–345; S. R. Peppet, "Unraveling Privacy: The Personal Prospectus and the Threat of a Full Disclosure Future," *Northwestern Law Review* **105**.3 (2011): 1153–1204.

[17] Concerning data mining and privacy, see V. Thavavel and S. Sivakumar, "A Generalized Framework of Privacy Preservation in Distributed Data Mining for Unstructured Data Environment," *International Journal of Computer Science* **9**.1 (2012): 434–441.

so that at the airport for his plane ride back my friend was detained for over two hours (making him miss his flight). He was also advised to hire a firm to clean up his online reputation if he ever wanted to fly outside the country and get back again. Mistakes such as this can cause people to lose their jobs or not to be hired or to be denied mortgage loans or any number of other difficulties. Most would declare these outcomes to be unjust.

Another sort of big business negative liberty that I know about first-hand concerns a trend in auto insurance to place GPS devices in all cars and to base auto insurance rates on actual mileage driven and whether one drives during rush hour (more accidents). The intent of this is positive: to encourage less automobile driving and thus help clean up the atmosphere. However, when I was serving on a U.S. Department of Transportation expert panel on this issue, we also explored possible side effects of all this newly acquired knowledge. For example, what if a married Mr. X wanted to meet his lover? In the divorce hearings, the GPS device would provide evidence of his being a philanderer. Some might say, hooray! Justice is done.

But once again, in the possibility of mistakes, the GPS might show an innocent person having been near to where a robbery or other crime was committed. This concomitant of location does not *prove* culpability. But with the GPS record, one might be judged guilty until proven innocent.

How might we constrain our action in the world if we thought that such mistaken *factual* data might be used against us because the context in such situations was limited by the technology? A GPS device does not say *why* someone was in a particular part of town, and a cyber-cookie does not disclose what one was doing, and data mining can put disparate data together and create a false positive. Most would declare the resultant situation unjust. All of these are instances of negative liberty that are relevant to discussions on natural human rights.

The penultimate example in this category of common language discourse on justice and human rights concerns what happens in conditions of natural disaster. Michael Sandel cites a case that occurred during Hurricane Charley that roared through Florida in the summer of 2004.[18] Gas station owners were selling a two-dollar bag of ice for ten dollars, and stores that normally sold gas-powered generators for $250 were now selling them for $2,000. Sandel quotes Charlie Crist, the attorney general

[18] Michael Sandel, *Justice: What Is the Right Thing to Do?* (New York: Farrar, Straus and Giroux, 2009): 3–5.

for Florida, as saying, "It is astounding to me, the level of greed that someone must have in their soul to be willing to take advantage of someone suffering in the wake of a hurricane."

This is a very good example of the common language relationship between justice and human rights. Many people are upset by the behavior of profiteering that is displayed in this example and others like it. They assert that when people are in a crisis mode, everyone should pull together, as a team effort, to try to get everyone the basics of life. For these people, the disadvantaged have some sort of right to whatever is minimally necessary to stay alive and the basis of such a claim lies in some sort of understanding of distributive justice.

Others see things rather differently. They would contend that in the United States we live in a largely capitalist economic system that is controlled by supply and demand. Whenever there is a spike in demand, those who are in the position to control the supply of the goods in question should be entitled to reap the rewards of the historical situation. This is a sort of Darwinian event in which the state of nature differentially rewards some parties at the expense of others. It's just the facts, ma'am.

There is real difference of opinion among many regular people on this question. What is not in dispute is that the situation highlights problems in rights and justice claims. This vacuum longs for some sort of justifiable practical response.

Finally, there is the case of the securities debacle of 2008. Investment banks and insurance companies created exotic investment instruments that were not financially sound. When the real estate market took a severe downturn, these highly leveraged products tanked and the so-called insurance edge on the derivative could not cover the exposure and the entire financial system of the G-8 nations (the eight most significant world economies: United States, United Kingdom, France, Germany, Italy, Japan, Canada, Russia) tilted toward collapse. This created the worst recession in the United States since the Great Depression of the 1930s. High unemployment and a national mortgage crisis resulted. People were angry. Some of the ways they expressed their anger had to do with their perception of human rights. They thought that when they bought stock through Bear Stearns their investments were safe. They felt that they had a right to a safe investment. Likewise, when they bought an insurance policy from AIG they felt they had a right to a secure company that was solvent and that they would be safe. They felt that this was a *right*. They didn't *deserve* to have their future at risk in what they thought was a highly regulated industry.

As it turned out, most of the panic in investments abated. Bear Stearns did go down, but not Goldman Sachs. AIG was bailed out by the U.S. federal government. However, there was great anger at the financial services industry that was perceived to have created the crisis through pressing the boundary between aggressive risk taking and fiduciary impropriety with other people's money. The highly compensated individuals heading this industry were excoriated by much of the U.S. public. Their greed created an unjust consequence that put in jeopardy what most people felt was their own right to invest in an honest, regulated market.

These are just samples of common usages of human rights and how they overlap with talk of justice.

1.4 RIGHTS AND DUTIES

The relationship between rights and duties is integral to discussing natural human rights. All rights claims are against someone or some group.[19] They are about a claim to some sort of good. The claim must be supported by an authoritative source – either a law or an existing institution that is itself in accord with the dictates of morality and justice.

Duties are responses to rights claims. The relationship between is tight correlation. All valid rights claims entail duties and vice versa. For purposes of clarification, I consider a rights claim either a claim that is made by some individual x or (more commonly) a claim that could be made by *any* x that is properly quantified. For example, a woman Laura might claim that as a citizen of the United States, for example in 1915, she had a right to vote that was not being recognized. This is an example of the *first* sort of *claiming*.

The more interesting *second* sort of claiming is that any woman in a democracy on earth either now or in the past or future has a right to vote whether she claims it or not. This sort of claim is an attributed claim based on the proposition: $\forall x \ \{(Px => Vx) \land (\forall y) \ (Wy => y = x)\}$. This translated means that for any x if x is a person, then x has a right to vote and that for any y if y is a woman, then that woman counts as a person, ergo, has a right to vote. If this analysis of a "claim" is correct, then it occurs at the group level – in the case of biological organisms, this means the species. The *claiming* is really a matter of *discovering* not unlike the sort of discovering that occurs in science. It would be odd to suggest that the equation "force equals mass times acceleration ($f = ma$)" was a

[19] E.g., Onora O'Neill, *Towards Justice and Virtue* (Cambridge: Cambridge University Press, 1991): ch 5, sect. 2.

claim that Newton just claimed for himself as the second law of motion.[20] Au contraire! He thought that he had discovered a truth about nature that really *was*. In the terms of modern philosophical epistemology it was asserted to be a realistic discovery about an independent realistic truth.[21] It is externalist and subject to intersubjective verification or falsification.[22] This is an important distinction in evaluating Newton, Einstein, or other key figures in the history of natural philosophy. I believe that the *claiming function* operates in the same way.

Human rights claims (whether anyone actually claims them, type-a or not, type-b) are capable of being attributed to groups on the basis of externalist criteria. This second sense of claiming (which I think is the primary sense for the justification of human rights) would make human rights both *real* and *natural*. More on this later.

[20] For an excellent overview of the significance of Newton's work, see Colin Pask, *Magnificent Principia: Exloring Isaac Newton's Masterpiece* (Amherst, NY: Prometheus, 2013).

[21] I am following the general account of externalist epistemology set out by Robert Audi, *Epistemology: A Contemporary Introduction to the Theory of Knowledge* (New York: Routledge, 2011).

[22] The literature on confirmation and falsification is quite large. Some classic articles include Moritz Schlick, "Positivism and Realism," trans. Peter Heath (1932–33), reprint *Moritz Schlick: Philosophical Papers II (1925–1936)* from *Vienna Circle Collection*, ed. Henk L. Mulder (Dordrecht: Kluwer, 1979): 259–284; Percy Bridgman, "The Operational Character of Scientific Concepts," in *The Logic of Modern Physics* (London: Macmillan, 1955): 1–32; Rudolf Carnap, "Empiricism, Semantics, and Ontology," in *Meaning and Necessity,* enlarged edition (Chicago: University of Chicago Press, 1956): 205–221; Karl Popper, *The Logic of Scientific Discovery* (London: Unwin Hyman, 1987 [1959]): 133–161; Hilary Putnam, "The 'Corroboration' of Theories" from *The Library of Living Philosophers,* vol. 14: *The Philosophy of Karl Popper,* ed. Paul A. Schilpp (LaSalle, IL: Open Court, 1974): 221–240; Thomas Kuhn, *The Structure of Scientific Revolutions,* 2nd ed. (Chicago: University of Chicago Press, 1962): 92–110; Bas van Fraasen, "To Save the Phenomena," *Journal of Philosophy* **73**.18 (1976): 623–632; Richard Boyd, "On the Current Status of Scientific Realism," *Erkenntnis* **19** (1983): 45–90; and Arthur Fine, "The Natural Ontological Attitude," in *Scientific Realism,* ed. L. Leplin (Berkeley: University of California Press, 1984): 83–107. More contemporary studies have greater focus on epistemological models and inductive logic (particularly statistics): Timothy McGrew, "Confirmation, Heuristics, and Explanatory Reasoning," *British Journal for the Philosophy of Science* **54**.4 (2003): 553–567; Laura Snyder, "Confirmation for a Modest Realism," *Philosophy of Science* **72**.5 (2005): 839–849; Aysel Dogan, "Confirmation of Scientific Hypotheses as Relations," *Journal for General Philosophy of Science* **36**.2 (2005): 243–259; John Lasee, *Theories on the Scrap Heap: Scientists and Philosophers on the Falsification, Rejection, and Replacement of Theories* (Pittsburgh: University of Pittsburgh Press, 2005); Christian Hennig, "Falsification of Propensity Models by Statistical Tests and Goodness-of-Fit Paradox," *Philosophia Mathematica* **15**.2 (2007): 1666–1692; and Kârin Nickelsen and Gerd Graßohoff, "In Pursuit of Formaldehyde: Causally Explanatory Models and Falsification," *Studies in History and Philosophy of Biological and Biomedical Science* **42**.3 (2011): 297–305.

Let's return to the subject of the correlative nature of rights and duties. First, there is a reciprocal relationship between duties and rights.[23] This relationship can be explained by the following sentence:[24]

I: "X has a Right against Y to Z in Virtue of P."

'X' is a person(s) and 'Y' is a person(s) and Z is a good (such as the liberty to vote, or to have adequate health care, or to maintain ownership of the automobile that is titled under your name, or to be able to purchase a new consumer product) and P is a legitimating moral institution (in the sense of the second sort of claim, described earlier).

This rights claim implies a correlative duty:

II: "Y has a Duty to provide X with Z in Virtue of P."

Let's consider a thought experiment and see how I and II might be used to formulate a solution.

THOUGHT EXPERIMENT 1.1

Charles Rudd is an African American living in the southern United States in the 1950s. His particular state has a poll tax one must pay and also a literacy test one must pass in order to vote. In the literacy test the applicant must demonstrate competence with complicated legal concepts often reserved for law schools. Another favorite as a literacy test was to ask an applicant, "How many bubbles are there in a bar of soap?" Of course, any answer given would be deemed *incorrect* (because there is no correct answer). The reasons for these two types of requirements are that the citizens of that state want to be sure that (in the spirit of the American Constitution) those voting are "properly qualified" to vote (really meaning they are (a) financially sound and (b) the right sort of people – racial, religious, gender, sexual orientation, etc.). Are these two requirements reasonable for the stated needs? Is there any other agenda? Do the sponsors of this sort of legislation fully understand their motives?

Thought Experiment 1.1 requires that we consider just what is intended in the legitimating institution. It is true that the Constitution of the United States as originally written did restrict voting to land-owning males. However, if one believes that the U.S. Constitution is an evolving document that can be amended and interpreted by the Supreme Court, then the sense is to open things up via the Thirteenth Amendment

---

[23] Hohfeld, *Fundamental Legal Conceptions*, 36–40, 65–67.
[24] This formulation originally comes from Alan Gewirth in Jeremy Waldron, ed., *Theories of Rights* (Oxford: Oxford University Press, 1984): 93. I have altered it somewhat for use in this volume.

outlawing slavery; the Fourteenth Amendment assuring equal protection of rights to all under the law; the Fifteenth Amendment that directly addresses the rights of African Americans as being upheld; and the Nineteenth Amendment that extends the right to vote to women. Clearly, the intent of these amendments (as interpreted by the Supreme Court) is to confer the privilege of voting to all citizens regardless of race or gender. If we understand the Constitution in this way, then we can assert that the import of I and II stated earlier is to say, "John or Kinshasa Doe has a right to vote against the Citizens of the United States in virtue of the Constitution of the United States and the Moral Principles upon which it stands." Now assume that Kinshasa Doe is an African American in a southern state in the 1950s where there were poll taxes and literacy tests that were given only to African Americans with the effect of denying these individuals their opportunity to vote.

The correlative duty statement would read: "The Citizens of the United States have a duty to provide John or Kinshasa Doe his or her voting privileges in virtue of the Constitution of the United States and the Moral Principles upon which it stands."

The Voting Rights Act of 1965 might be considered a moral response to this question. A law was passed that created safeguards against spurious devices (such as poll taxes and various "citizenship/civics" tests that served to deny universal suffrage).

THOUGHT EXPERIMENT 1.2

Lavinnia Jones is an African American living in Solace Senior Care Nursing home. Her son LeRoy is a mechanic at a small gas station. Lavinnia's social security (and some Medicaid) pays for her living at the nursing home. She has only a couple of dollars a month for spending money. LeRoy and his wife earn a thousand dollars over the poverty level. They live in a trailer with their two children. The Joneses have always taken civic pride in voting in national, state, and local elections. However, in their state there is a new voter ID law (identification law). To get such an ID a person needs to present a birth certificate and a proof of current address (such as mail received). To get a duplicate birth certificate costs $50 and to get the state ID costs another $25. Lavinnia would need about three years to accumulate this amount. LeRoy and his family struggle each month to pay bills. They don't go to movies. They don't buy alcohol. They just try to stay afloat. Neither Lavinnia nor her son's family will be able to vote under the new state voter ID law. It should also be noted that in the state where the Jones family lives there has never been a single documented case of voter fraud (people voting who were not citizens, or dead people voting, etc.). How is this case similar to and different from Thought Experiment 1.1? What rights and duties obtain?

At the time this book is being written, there is considerable debate on this question in the United States. Some claim that the two thought experiments are relevantly similar as to rights claims and duties while others point to the increasing requirements for documentation in society. For example, one person recently wrote to a newspaper saying that you have to have a passport to fly to Europe so why not have simple photo ID to vote? Others would reply that the Jones family would never have the money to fly anywhere – much less to Europe. Without the money for a car or a driver's license, their life expenditures are rather more modest. (A treat for this family might be a grocery store special on ice cream that suddenly makes it affordable. Even in the United States of America, the richest country on earth, there are millions like the Jones family who are one disaster away from homelessness.)

The former group would reply that one must show photo ID in the United States to buy cigarettes or alcohol. Why not treat voting on the same level? The reply would be that the Jones family doesn't smoke or drink and besides those photo ID laws are only applied (if ever) when the potential purchaser seems to be under age. Few people over the age of twenty-five are ever carded. There is a large class of people in the United States who have no "official government issued ID" nor do they have the need for one in their lives. In a study group at the Center for American Progress where I was a policy fellow between 2007 and 2009, the speculation was that virtually the entire lowest quintile of wage earners fit into this category. They are too poor to own a car and have no practical need for a photo ID: it's a luxury they cannot afford. If this demographic conjecture is correct, it would characterize around 60 million people – more than enough to make a significant electoral difference were their numbers largely suppressed in an election.

There are other examples of possible claims rights that are debated – such as the right to adequate health care. Can we say "John or Kinshasa Doe has the right to adequate health care against the Citizens of the United States of America in virtue of natural Moral Principles"? I have written in the past on this subject[25] suggesting that the answer is "yes," but it has been obvious that in the United States (at the writing of this book) this is a controversial position.

---

[25] Michael Boylan, "The Moral Right to Healthcare – Part Two," in *Medical Ethics*, 2nd ed., ed. Michael Boylan (Malden, MA: Blackwell, 2013); "Medical Pharmaceuticals and Distributive Justice," *Cambridge Quarterly of Healthcare Ethics* 17.1 (Winter, 2008): 32–46.

However, it is clear that the two examples given are of a different type from those that describe less essential goods, such as an automobile or a cellular phone. Can we say in the same way (as we did with voting rights) that "John Doe has a right to an automobile against the Citizens of the United States in virtue of a natural Moral Principle"? or "John Doe has a right to a cellular telephone against the Citizens of the United States in virtue of a natural Moral Right?" or "John Doe has a right to his own swimming pool against the Citizens of the United states in virtue of a natural Moral Right?" Certainly not. The type of good involved is different in kind.

At least we have established that rights, duties, and types of goods are related. What still needs to be explored is whether such rights claims follow from *natural* as opposed to merely *conventional* reasons.

A second issue is the question of *recognition* of rights/duties. Some authors such as H. L. A. Hart and John Austin have emphasized an examination of legal statutes and the general literature of the period as a way of addressing this issue.[26] They contend that without actual words for "right" or "duty" that are employed in the literature or legal statutes, there is no operational concept of 'right' or 'duty.'[27] If there is no "operational" right or duty, then the concept does not exist and it is not a legitimate category by which to judge societal/individual conduct.

Such arguments have also been made about Chinese culture in recent times.[28] The claim is that because there has never been a recognized tradition of human rights observance in China, then the individuals in China have no moral claim to such. This is based on the proposition that only publicly recognized rights are valid. This sort of claim asserts that the legitimatizing institution for human rights is a descriptive public agreement. Such a claim might fit very well within the contractarian approach or within the emotive/ethical intuitionist linguistic approach that sees ethics as a project of description. This sort of argument contends (quasi-operationally) that (a) if the literature and law statutes of the time (such as we have it) in some well-recognized society would support a duties/rights analysis, then such an attribution is appropriate; and (b) if the

---

[26] H. L. A. Hart, "Are There Any Natural Rights?" *Philosophical Review* **64** (1955): 176–177; John Austin, *Lectures on Jurisprudence,* 5th ed., ed. Robert Campbell (London: John Murray, 1883).

[27] See the essays by Beth Singer and Virginia Held in *Gewirth: Critical Essays on Action, Rationality and Community,* ed. Michael Boylan (New York: Roman and Littlefield, 1999): 13–28, 145–154.

[28] Singer and Held in Boylan, *Gewirth.* See also my discussion in Chapter 4.

actions of the people would support a duties/rights analysis, then such an attribution is appropriate.[29] But beyond such sociological or linguistic analysis there are no natural rights that belong to people, *as such*.

1.5 BEARING DUTIES

The last sort of conceptual issue to be explored in this initial chapter centers around those who want to examine the duty bearers: those who bear the duties in the correlative rights-duties formula set out previously. If "Y has a duty to provide X with Z in virtue of P," then one might profitably ask, "Who is Y, anyway?" In our voting rights examples it was "the people of the United States" or the citizens of a particular state (which sets particular voting regulations – subject to the 1965 Voting Rights Act that put certain states on a long probationary period for violating the duty to the nation as a whole). When the issue is legalistically framed, those states that have had a long history of violating the Fourteenth Amendment concerning voting ceded their absolute state sovereignty to the federal government. The federal government through the arm of the Justice Department took on the oversight role for future voting rights restrictions. At the writing of this book, at least two state voter ID laws that have been passed in these "probation" states have been rejected by the Justice Department on this ground. Other states that are not under such a federal overview (because they were not cited as being on probation) passed statutes that the federal government could not challenge, except in federal court as a violation of the Fourteenth Amendment. But these challenges are subject to judicial review. An appeals court must intervene for action to occur. This means that those states cited in the 1965 Voting Rights Act are proximately responsible to the Justice Department first and that those states not cited have their statutes intact subject to judicial review. The duty bearers in this situation (whether it be executive enforcement or judicial review) are institutional agents in the process.[30] As we transition to the practice/policy phase of this argument (Part Three), there will be an increasing need to delineate specific duty bearers within the *rights or the duty formulas* (set out earlier).

---

[29] This is a question of some dispute. See Singer and Reiman's comments in Boylan, *Gewirth*.

[30] Of course this landmark law has been severely affected by *Shelby County v. Holder* (2013) in which the United States Supreme Court changed the burden of proof from the state or local level to the U.S. Department of Justice. This may have the effect of gutting the practical force of the law.

However, the examination of the duty bearers must go further. To begin this exploration, one must first think about the organization of peoples in the world. At this moment in human history, the world is organized into large countries that, in turn, have suborganizational schemes. This is in contrast to earlier eras in human history in which very small organizational units were primary. The reason for this earlier organizational scheme was largely due to constraints on transportation and communication. When the horse, the boat, or human walking were the principal modes of transportation and communication, and if effective direct decision making required responses within a week (more or less), then the size of a community would be determined accordingly. I set out communities as being of two sorts. The first is the micro community in which everyone within the community could potentially meet and talk to everyone else in the community. The small sorts of effective communities that I mention here throughout human history and even in some parts of the world today are essentially micro communities. The second sort of human community is the macro community in which the flow of power is delegated (in one way or another) to rulers of the micro communities to act on their behalf in the shaping of larger policies.

Throughout most of the pre-nineteenth-century world, the actual effective unit of government (the micro community) was determined in how far one could travel in a week (more or less).[31] Confederations of various ruling fiefdoms could be called "states" and have a king or queen, but this secondary level of rule was very indirect and generally affected the monarch and the subrulers (dukes or warlords) who would pay the regent a fee (sort of protection money) for being a part of the confederation – the macro community. In this type of world, the duty bearers would be those real people living in the confines of a limited space (micro community) where they could conceivably mark their space by their own means of transport: by foot, horse, or boat. Thus, most on-the-

---

[31] The conjecture that communication and transportation played an important role in political organization has been a thesis that several have examined. For a small sampling of these, see Filippo de Vivo, *Information and Communication in Venice: Rethinking Early Modern Politics* (Oxford: Oxford University Press, 2009); Jurgen Habermas, *On Pragmatics of Communication* (Cambridge, MA: MIT Press, 2000); Hans J. Hummer, *Politics and Power in Early Medieval Europe: Alsace and the Frankish Realm, 600–1000* (Cambridge: Cambridge University Press, 2009); Jenni Nuttall, *The Creation of Lancastrian Kingship: Literature, Language, and Politics in Late Medieval England* (Cambridge: Cambridge University Press, 2011); and Jared Diamond, *Guns, Germs, and Steel: The Fates of Human Societies* (New York: Norton, 2005).

ground, practical duty bearing would be between people and families who knew each other. It would be clans looking out for each other.

As transportation and communication have developed, so did the knowledge about conditions around the world. The eighteenth, nineteenth, and twentieth centuries made progressively larger strides in this direction. In the post-Internet world there is really no excuse for anyone to be ignorant of the plight of virtually anyone living on earth.[32] For this reason, I supplemented my discussion of nationally based visions of justice in *A Just Society* (2004) with a cosmopolitan account in *Morality and Global Justice: Justifications and Applications* (2011).

The reason for these distinctions is to prompt the way we think about *duty bearers*. There is certainly a practical and a theoretical dimension here. In the practical dimension, if x (a person living in England) does not know that y (a person living in central Africa) even exists, then it is rather odd to think about x being a duty bearer to y. Using the *ought implies can* standard, before recent history, it was very difficult for x to know anything about y – much less that x owed y something. This practical dimension has driven some of the discussion on correlative duties to valid rights claims.[33] James Griffin thinks that many rights claims do not require a practically identifiable duty bearer – such as the duty to help victims of HIV/AIDS in Africa obtain anti-retroviral medication. Other claims – such as the right to world peace – are not comprehensible without some practically identifiable duty bearer.[34]

In the theoretical dimension, it makes no difference whether a duty bearer knows that he or she or some institution bears a duty. The duty is a duty if it is properly ascribed, regardless. It is based upon certain empirical facts about people and their lives in the context of what they are naturally entitled to claim. A justifiable duty that is not carried out due to ignorance or conscious choice is still a duty. However, it is rather Pyrrhic to say that x has a duty (either a person, a group of people, an institution

---

[32] This point is made by Julie Kirsch in supporting my position on Cosmopolitanism in "When Is Ignorance Morally Objectionable?" in *The Morality and Global Justice Reader*, ed. Michael Boylan (Boulder, CO: Westview, 2011): 51–64.

[33] For the position that there must be actually identifiable duty bearers, see Onora O'Neill, *Towards Justice and Virtue* (Cambridge: Cambridge University Press, 1991): ch. 5, sect. 2. Carl Wellman calls such instances *civil* rather than *human* rights in *Welfare Rights* (Totowa, NJ: Rowman and Allanheld, 1982): 181. Of course, a possible stand-in for duties can be public institutions: John Tasioulas, "The Moral Reality of Human Rights," in *Freedom from Poverty as a Human Right: Who Owes the Very Poor?* ed. Thomas Pogge (Oxford: Oxford University Press, 2007).

[34] James Griffin, *On Human Rights* (Oxford: Oxford University Press, 2008): 101–110.

(such as an NGO), a nation, or a multinational organization) if he or she or they are not aware of conditions on the ground (ignorance of the fact). The only question to be asked in this case is whether the ignorance is due to negligence or recklessness (what Aristotle called *asophrosume*).[35] If neither negligence nor recklessness is involved, then there is no culpability in not carrying out one's duty – because one is ignorant that he had a duty. Though there is no culpability, there is still a duty, but because of the caveat of ignorance there is no culpability among the duty bearers.

However, in today's world, as mentioned earlier, this can hardly be the case. With the Internet that is accessible to a very large portion of the world's population in some form (especially in the G-20 nations— geographically large and significant economies which are the G-8 plus South Africa, Mexico, Brazil, Argentina, China, South Korea, India, Indonesia, Turkey, Saudi Arabia, Australia and the European Union), people have an epistemological duty to make themselves aware of the plight of a significant portion of the world's population. This awareness that they are duty bearers should, with the proper personal worldview, give them motivation to action.[36]

Therefore, my response to the duty-bearer query is that the form for claims rights set out previously in every case requires specification of "against whom." This is specification of the duty bearer. This specification can be made against persons, groups of people, national institutions (such as NGOs), nations, or multinational organizations. Yes, duties need to be specified, but the duties exist regardless of whether those who bear the duties recognize that they must do them.

---

[35] Aristotle, *Ethica Nicomachea*, ed. I. Bywater (Oxford: Clarendon Press, 1920): VII.3–1146b 20–1149b 35. The key contrast here is with *akrasia*. *Asophrosune* is fully culpable and the paradigm for evil behavior while *akrasia* is less culpable.

[36] See my thoughts on personal worldview: Boylan, *A Just Society*; Michael Boylan, *Basic Ethics*, 2nd ed. (Upper Saddle River, NJ: Prentice Hall, 2009); and Michael Boylan, *Morality and Global Justice: Justifications and Applications* (Boulder, CO: Westview, 2011).

2

A Short History of Human Rights in the West

Why should anyone care about the history of how human rights have been recognized in the Western Tradition – or anywhere else for that matter? The answer goes to the heart of this inquiry: a theory of natural human rights. If as Charles Beitz suggests, it is the case that any useful understanding of human rights originated in 1948 with the United Nations' Universal Declaration of Human Rights, then the *legal approach* set out in Part Two of this volume becomes very plausible.[1] Others, like James Griffin, set the origins in the Enlightenment with foreshadowing in the Middle Ages. This mirrors the historical shift to the individual over against the community perspective. If the *interest approach* set out in Part Two of this volume is correct, then the historical transformation of attention to the individual perspective supports the sort of rights theory that the interest approach sets out. Finally, if my agency account is correct and if human agency is roughly the same throughout human history West and East, then I should be able to demonstrate background and related concepts throughout the human record on earth. To do this systematically would be a monumental task and beyond the scope of this volume. However, some important points can be sketched out with respect to the plausibility of these claims (a lower burden of proof). I address the Western tradition in this chapter and China in the next.[2]

[1] Charles Beitz, *The Idea of Human Rights* (Oxford: Oxford University Press, 2009): 13.
[2] Of course this leaves out a whole lot of the earth's population. I make these choices because first I come from the Western Tradition influenced from the beginning by Greek and Roman philosophy and second, among the so-called difficult cases, China is often brought up as a clear example against the sort of argument I am making. Begin here: some key texts that discuss this are A. W. Brian Simpson, *Human Rights and the End of Empire* (Oxford: Oxford University Press, 2004); J. H. Burgers, "The Road to San Francisco: The Revival of the Human Rights Idea in the Twentieth Century," *Human Rights Quarterly* **14** (1992): 447–477; Johannes Morsink, *The Universal Declaration of Human*

2.1 HUMAN RIGHTS AS A RECENT PHENOMENON

Kenneth Cmiel makes the historical claim that "prior to the 1940s, the term [human rights] was rarely used."[3] This links to an understanding of human rights as being involved in a practice in which "states are responsible for satisfying certain conditions in their treatment of their own people and that failures or prospective failures to do so may justify some form of remedial or preventive action by the world community or those acting as its agents."[4] When we focus upon the practice as Beitz sets out, Cmiel's claim is plausible. The center of interest in this respect is an international arena in which various nations try to get other nations to adhere to some sort of standard. This practice-based approach began with the Nuremberg Trials in which some of the more prominent Nazis were held accountable for their behavior during World War II. The impetus of the Holocaust helped re-form the defunct League of Nations into the United Nations. One of the very early documents in this newly formed organization was the Universal Declaration of Human Rights, which spawned considerable controversy when it was drafted. Some, like Hannah Arendt, believe that the outrage over the Holocaust has to be seen against an agreed background of what is appropriate and decent.[5] Under this assumption, the reaction to the Holocaust was a catalyst in the creation of the practice-based international approach to pressure particular nations to respect the negative right to exist without harassment, imprisonment, and death for the "crime" of being of a particular race, ethnic group, or religion. But this quickly broadened to a host of other *rights* including health and economic rights.[6]

In the 1950s, the scope of human rights ignited two separate movements: civil rights movements (concerning descendents of slaves and

---

Rights: Origins, Drafting, and Intent (Philadelphia: University of Pennsylvania Press, 2000); Mary Ann Glendon, *A World Made New: Eleanor Roosevelt and the Universal Declaration of Human Rights* (New York: Random House, 2002); Aryeh Neier, *The International Human Rights Movement: A History* (Princeton, NJ: Princeton University Press, 2012).

[3] Kenneth Cmiel, "The Recent History of Human Rights," *American Historical Review* **109**.1 (2004): 117–135, 117.

[4] Beitz, *The Idea of Human Rights*, 13.

[5] Hannah Arendt, *The Origins of Totalitarianism* (New York: Harcourt, Brace, Jovanovich, 1973 [1951]): 294.

[6] Certainly the body of writing since World War II has been enormous. For an idea of the work during the first wave of human rights talk, see Rex Martin and James W. Nickel, "A Bibliography on the Nature and Foundations of Rights, 1942–1977," *Political Theory* **6**.6 (1978): 395–413.

indigenous peoples) and decolonization movements to free countries from their colonial masters.[7] These movements were also a part of the human rights practice-based approach. The international community put pressure on colonial powers to grant independence to actual colonies or to neo-colonies such as Rhodesia (modern Zimbabwe), Zambia, Malawi, and South Africa. This international pressure sought home rule for these countries. The reason given was that individual autonomy (a human right) trumped the pretended paternalism that the colonial governments had asserted.

Thus, this first wave of post–World War II human rights talk incorporates discussion of matters of *civil and political rights* and *economic, social, and cultural rights*.[8] The theme was centered around national autonomy and articulated by writers from disparate parts of the world: Nigerian Mbonu Ojike stated, "The right to rule oneself is a natural right," and Ho Chi Minh quoted Thomas Jefferson's declaration of independence talk in asserting Vietnam's right to self-determination.[9]

There were some successes in the human rights practice-based approach: (a) the civil rights movement in the United States, Canada, Australia, and Western Europe; (b) the largely successful decolonization of various nations around the world – particularly Africa (the last holdout); and (c) the launching of concern about unempowered peoples such as women and children.

This large agenda expanded some, but then contracted as a second wave of human rights practice turned to the activity of nongovernmental organizations (NGOs) in the 1970s. Technocrats in these organizations were much more efficient in delivering services such as nutritional and

---

[7] The United States offers a model for civil rights movements in the 1950s and 1960s. See Danielle L. McGuire: *At the Dark End of the Street: Black Women, Rape, and Resistance* (New York: Vintage, 2011); Harry Hampton, Steve Fayer, and Sarah Flynn, *Voices of Freedom* (New York: Bantam, 1991). A few different ways of examining the fates of the world's indigenous peoples can be found in Noam Chomsky, *New World of Indigenous Resistance* (San Francisco: City Lights, 2010); Damien Short, *Reconciliation and Colonial Power: Indigenous Rights in Australia* (Farnham, UK: Ashgate, 2008); and Patricia Grimshaw and Andrew May, eds., *Missionaries, Indigenous Peoples and Cultural Exchange* (Eastbourne, UK: Sussex Academic Press, 2010). Finally, an excellent work on decolonization is Margaret Kohn and Keally McBride, *Political Theories of Decolonization: Postcolonialism and the Problem of Foundations* (New York: Oxford University Press, 2011).

[8] The anti-colonialism strain is stressed especially by Paul Gordon Lauren, *The Evolution of International Human Rights,* 2nd ed. (Philadelphia, PA: University of Pennsylvania Press, 2003): 251.

[9] Mbonu Ojike, *My Africa* (New York: John Day, 1946): 261, and Ho Chi Minh, "Declaration of Independence of the Democratic Republic of Vietnam," in Ho Chi Minh, *Selected Writings: 1920–1969* (Hanoi: University Press of the Pacific, 2001 [1973]): 53–56.

health support as well as agricultural assistance and job training.[10] This detailed assessment and response approach represented a deflationary definition of the practice as opposed to the grandiose vision of the first wave that sought to spread national autonomy and democracy around the world. The second wave wanted to identify exact needs and fulfill carefully and narrowly described terminal objectives.

A third wave can be identified that began at the end of the 1980s and the cessation of the Cold War. This wave once again expanded the purview of attention to women's rights, economic justice, and indigenous people's rights. The mood is often positive as it seems that dictators can be prosecuted and that sovereign immunity may be a thing of the past.[11] But this belies successive human rights abuses on the ground such as in Darfur, Kosovo, and Rwanda. One can wonder whether the backslapping over perceived progress is really justified. Surely there were successes: (a) decolonization occurred; (b) civil rights movements showed some success throughout the world; (c) some indigenous people's rights were recognized; (d) women's and children's rights were more widely recognized; and (e) NGO-targeted programs were largely successful within their given constraints. But Darfur, Kosovo, and Rwanda illustrate painful failures, as well.

Part of this difficulty may come from what some have called the *paradoxes of human rights*. The paradox occurs when one matches grand universal claims for a large number of human rights against a track record of practice that is far more modest than the theory. These disparities are not contradictions as such but illustrate that practice is not as expansive as the goals.[12] They call for cultural/political negotiation so that the practice can come closer to its stated goals.[13]

However, sometimes the gap between practice and stated goals faces further complicating factors. These may exacerbate the situation in cases involving racial and cultural tensions within a society. Sometimes these tensions inflate to genocide, which has been a touchstone for human rights practice since the Second World War.[14] Genocide often creates an opaque context in which the true horrors of its occurrence are not fully

---

[10] Jack Donnelly, "Recent Trends in U.N. Human Rights Activity: Description and Polemic," *International Organization* **35** (Autumn, 1981): 633–655, and Howard Tolley, *The U.N. Commission on Human Rights* (Boulder, CO: Westview, 1987).

[11] Lauren, *The Evolution of International Human Rights*, 241–298.

[12] Marilyn Young, Preface, in Jeffrey Wasserstrom, Lynn Hunt, and Marilyn Young, eds., *Human Rights and Revolutions* (Lanham, MD: Rowman and Littlefield, 2000).

[13] Robert Paul Churchill, *Human Rights and Global Diversity* (Upper Saddle River, NJ: Prentice Hall, 2006): 89–127.

[14] See Samantha Power, *A Problem from Hell* (New York: Harper, 2007).

recognized by the rest of the world until most (if not all) of the damage has been done.

These setbacks along with the 9/11/2001 terrorism tragedy in the United States made some commentators declare that the practice of human rights had been set back.[15] These premonitions came true to some extent as privacy rights were compromised with unauthorized surveillance, civilians were subjected to rendition, and torture was practiced to obtain strategic information.[16]

However, in a fast-moving world, even these setbacks seem to be temporary. The wide use of public communication devices available via smartphones and the Internet allows information to travel swiftly to the world via Twitter and other social networking media. This has proved to be a new tool that has instigated a *fourth wave* of human rights practice in the contemporary (post–World War II era). The display of communication (a bane to dictators everywhere) can be seen in the Arab Spring of 2011. The Arab Spring began in Tunisia when protesters demanded the removal of president Zine al-Abidine Ben Ali. The claims of the protesters were about the right to eat (the cost of food), political corruption, freedom of speech, and basic political rights. Then came Egypt, as thousands flocked to Tahrir Square in Cairo and elsewhere. Their demands were similar to those in Tunisia. Both sets of protesters were successful: the leaders of both countries fled. This was the first chapter of the Arab Spring. It was largely peaceful.

Then the citizens of other countries became involved: Bahrain, Yemen, Syria, and Libya. The leaders in these countries were not content to ride away into the sunset. They ordered their soldiers to fire live ammunition into the crowds and imprison the ringleaders. Many were killed. Colonel Muammar el-Qaddafi set out a bloody counterattack so brutal that it prompted a United Nations and North Atlantic Treaty Organization (NATO) military response. Eventually, Libya fell and Qaddafi was killed. At the writing of this book, the succession of governance in these countries is incomplete. The second chapter has been violent.

---

[15] Michael Ignatieff, "Is the Human Rights Era Ending?" *New Republic* **227** (2002): 18–19; Peter Mass, "How America's Friends Really Fight Terrorism," *New Republic* **227** (2002): 20–21; and David Luban, "The War on Terrorism and the End of Human Rights," *Philosophy and Public Policy Quarterly* **22** (September 2002): 9–14.

[16] For two different takes on the events of the Bush administration during the War on Terrorism, see Charles J. Ogletree Jr. and Nasser Hussain, eds., *When Governments Break the Law: The Rule of Law and the Prosecution of the Bush Administration* (New York: New York University Press, 2010), and *The 2010 Annual Report of the Council on Foreign Relations* (New York: Council on Foreign Relations, 2010).

The third chapter of the 2011–2013 Arab Spring continues as I write this book, with Syria at its focus. Bashar al-Assad is the autocratic leader. He is using the same sort of brute military force against his own people that his father employed in the Hama massacre that took 10,000 to 40,000 civilian casualties.[17] At this writing, the story in Syria is still being told – writ red in the blood of noncombatant civilians.

In Egypt, there was a counterreaction in 2013 to the 2011 nonviolent protest. This coup d'état by the military resulted in popularly elected President Mohamed Morsi being removed from power by General Abdul Fatah al-Sisi. The removal prompted protests but the army chose to use live ammunition to attempt to put down the rebellion. At the writing of this book, former pariah Hosni Mubarak was released from prison. The tide turned.

Other countries, such as Jordan, Oman, and Kuwait, also felt the pressure of these events and have made a few changes in response to mostly peaceful demonstrations (reminiscent of the Prague Spring in 1968). What seems clear to this author is that the description of human rights as a practice-based approach now must include the new media of smart cell phones along with the Internet to connect people together so that the knowledge chip moves away from the dictatorial autocrat and to the general populace (see Chapter 9). How this will play out in the future is anyone's guess. I do think that it is at least plausible that popular solidarity (necessary for any successful revolution) will be aided by the new communication devices – unless a counter technology emerges that shuts everything down.

What this section has tried to accomplish is to illustrate the way one might think about human rights if the origin is set as 1948 and the post–World War II era. It is distinctive that the practice of human rights advocacy by nations, international treaties, the United Nations, and NGOs has made a unique contribution during this era.

But is this the whole story? Stay tuned to the next two sections.

2.2 HUMAN RIGHTS IN THE ANCIENT AND MEDIEVAL WORLD

When we turn our attention to the ancient and medieval worlds, the question changes somewhat. The language is not explicit about natural human rights that attach to individuals but instead about the background conditions that validate understanding the human condition (considered

---

[17] See the Syrian Human Rights Committee, http://www.shrc.org/data/aspx/d5/2535. aspx (accessed May 1, 2012).

collectively and normatively) and nature (considered as a realm separate from and superseding human agreement). These two concerns can be depicted as the *natural law perspective*. This natural law perspective displays itself primarily via ethics/political/legal philosophy. But it can also be presented via natural philosophy (what we contemporaries call natural science). A few general comments can be made about both before pursuing in more detail some insights into the ancient world and then the medieval world.

The ethical/political/legal perspective is the broader of the two interpretations. The use of *phusis* or *natura* need not be excluded from god[s] in the ancient or medieval worlds. The two can be interchangeable as representing an ontological *other* that is cosmologically superior to the realm in which we exist. So what might this be like? On the interpretation that the ontological *other* is god[s] or principle[s], then either the *other* abides among us (à la Henry More or Alfred North Whitehead),[18] or the *other* exists somewhere else that is in immanent contact with *us*. The former could be consistent with atheist, agnostic, or deist traditions (since this other need not be anything more than real, regulative principles). For ease in discussion let us call this understanding *the realist assumption*. The latter interpretation is the more conventional response given by those in the Abrahamic religious traditions. For ease in discussion let us call this understanding *the theist assumption*. In either event, what is crucial is that a hierarchy of authority is created. Whether or not the laws exist as a second-order logical reality that governs us (without falling prey to the famous self-referential paradoxes) or in a reality that is separate and superior (in the sense of normative prescriptive governance), it can have the same effect (see Chapter 7). So to make things clear I take natural law in the ethical/political/legal realm to involve the existence of a justification for ethics, politics, and the law that is logically separate from and more authoritative than human constructions. This is the essence of the realist, naturalist position that this author endorses.

The natural philosophy perspective (concerning what we moderns call science) is narrower (and therefore simpler). It operates on the principle that the very existence of natural philosophy is defined as

---

[18] Both Whitehead and More situated God in this physical world. Whitehead's most general account of his process metaphysics can be found in Alfred North Whitehead, *Process and Reality* (London: Macmillan, 1929), and a summary of More's view of God as physical space can be found in Michael Boylan, "Henry More and the Spirit of Nature," *Journal of the History of Philosophy* **18**.4 (1980): 395–405.

when the gods leave.[19] Material principles (which become *mechanical* in the Enlightenment) take over. In this case the ontology becomes simpler. It must be the case that the natural laws abide among us (including all the natural actors and objects).

With these distinctions in mind, let us briefly consider natural law in the ancient world.

2.2.1 Natural Law in the European Ancient World

Because the questions about natural law are complex and because this is a very surface summary, we confine ourselves here to a few authors who have a substantial corpus of existent texts. We can begin with a brief examination of several key texts. First, there is Homer. In the *Iliad* there is a mixture of convention and natural law (here understood as being in accord with the gods). Achilles is angry with Hector because he killed Petroclus (who had been wearing Achilles' armor). In the conventional sense, Petroclus was wrong to wear another's armor. To others, this was a bull's eye that the ultimate hero of the battle was before them. He was fair game for Hector to encounter. But Achilles was enraged at the death of his friend/lover. He stormed back and not only killed Hector but defiled the laws of the gods (natural law) in dragging Hector's dead body around Troy. (Achilles also defiled the laws by leaving the corpse to be scavenged by wild animals.) This was a signature day in the narrative of the ancient Greek world. The noble (*kalon*) Hector is treated with disrespect that is shameful (*aischron*). The act is so egregious that Plato later makes reference to it in the *Gorgias* (473a–475d). The source of the *shame* was that the laws of the gods (natural law) were being violated.

This theme – that there are consequences for violating the laws of the gods – is developed in the *Odyssey* when Odysseus offends Poseidon and the other gods by not making proper sacrifice after the fall of Troy. Of course, the hubris that Odysseus portrays as he leaves the island of the Cyclops (a favorite of Poseidon) didn't help either. Both are instances of *pride*, which is the essence of sin in many of the world's religions (theistic natural law). By violating [theistically understood] natural law and inserting man's own achievements in its place, the *Odyssey* shows the conflict between natural and human law. Since the former should trump

[19] R. French, *Ancient Natural History* (New York: Routledge, 1994); contrast M. Beagon, *Roman Nature* (Oxford: Oxford University Press, 1992), and D. Lehoux, "Weather, When, and Why?" *Studies in History and Philosophy of Science* **35** (2004): 209–222.

the latter, and since Odysseus attempts to do the opposite, then his great journey and hardship are a cautionary tale of what happens when proper authority is ignored. In these first two cases, the schema is that there is a set of commands about how to act that is given by the gods. One learns about these commands through reading texts like the *Iliad* and the *Odyssey* (along with other canonical writers such as Hesiod, et al.). These texts are sung to the populace so that they can listen and integrate the messages. There are also the various temples with their priests and priestesses who transmit teachings based upon intuitionism. Individuals have a choice of obeying the natural law or not. Henrik Syse has called this sort of response the *objective* sense of natural law.[20] In the objective sense, natural law or natural rights are viewed as adjectives: "It is right of me to act in this way" as opposed to the *subjective* sense in which 'right' becomes a noun, "It is my right to act this way." This dichotomy is one way to examine the evolution of human rights. In the case of Homer and most of the ancient world, the prevalent sense is the objective sense of natural law/right.

A third literary case is in Sophocles' *Antigone*. After the Seven against Thebes attack failed (that was perpetrated by Polynices, son of Oedipus, who had exiled himself to Argos, married, and acquired connections), the other son of Oedipus, Eteocles (King of Thebes) gets into a fight with his brother. The result is that both brothers die. Eteocles is buried by the new king, Creon. This is done after the proper religious rites. But Polynices is not given these rites and his body is left to the dogs to devour contrary to religious law (reminiscent of Achilles' shameful treatment of Hector). Creon decrees that anyone tampering with the body will be killed (a rather extreme punishment in Greek times).

Antigone consults with her sister Ismeme. Ismeme wants to bend to Creon's decree. Antigone wants to defy it. Antigone sneaks in and performs certain purification rituals and puts some loose dirt atop her brother. This action is discovered by a Sentinel. He reports the whole thing to Creon, who is aghast as much by Antigone's partial acceptance of his decree (she didn't remove the body for full burial elsewhere) but not her *full* acceptance—she created a technical burial.

Antigone admits the crime. She confronts Creon with an argument that God's law supersedes the law of man. Creon demurs with an argument

[20] I am following Henrik Syse here on this distinction: Henrik Syse, *Natural Law, Religion, and Rights* (South Bend, IN: St. Augustine's Press, 2007): 5–6.

that is based upon the sovereign being regarded as the state. There is also an equivocation on 'honor' and 'loyalty.'

The language used here is crucial to understanding what is being intended. At line 943 Antigone says, "Look what I suffer, at whose command/ Because I respected the right."[21] The Greek word here is *eusebeo* – which more properly translates as respect for the gods (one of the two possible candidates for natural law). However, elsewhere there is more ambiguity: at line 538 Antigone uses *dike* (which means "just" and is the cognate of *dikaiosune* – "justice");[22] and at line 521 *euages* is employed that refers to being guiltless by being free of pollution. And in the most famous speech by Antigone at 450ff., she responds to Creon's charge that she disobeyed the laws of the state about the burial prohibition,

> For me it was not Zeus who made that order,
> Nor did that Justice who lives with the gods below
> Mark out such laws to hold among mankind.
> Nor did I think your orders were so strong
> That you, a mortal man, could over-run
> The gods' unwritten and unfailing laws. [450–455]

The two key terms here are *dike* [451] and *nomos* [455]. *Dike* we have just dealt with; *nomos* is a little more nuanced. It can mean "conventional" as well as "natural or general law."[23] In this context it is the latter sense that is implied. Thus, we have a clear case of our definition of a conflict between man's conventional law and the natural law. But we are still in the objective sense of human rights: Antigone may act or not based upon a supervening law that is sanctioned by the gods: *it is **right** for Antigone to act to observe the proper burial customs.* What this means in the history of human rights is that the subjective sense of human rights at this stage is only to recognize, decide, and act upon the natural law (to one's peril if he or she does not). One's subjective posture is to obey or be punished by the gods.

Another key text to examine in this context is Plato's *Euthyphro*.[24] The question posed by Socrates is whether some action is *hosion* (holy/pious/

---

[21] I am following David Grene and Richard Lattimore, translation, "Antigone" (Chicago: University of Chicago Press, 1954). For textual analysis I am following A. C. Pearson, ed., *Sophoclis Fabvlae* (Oxford: Clarendon Press, 1924).

[22] *Dike* like its root, *dikaios*, is opposed to *adikaios*, giving it a more abstract connotation; cf. Herodotus I. 96 and Aeschylus, *Agamenon*, l. 1604.

[23] For the latter sense, see Aristotle, *Politics* 1292a7 and Plato, *Theaetetus* 173d.

[24] The text I use is *Platonis Opera*, vol. 1, ed. John Burnet (Oxford: Clarendon, 1900); translations are my own.

good) by itself or because the gods love it. I reconstruct the central second argument as follows:

ARGUMENT 2.1: THE RELATION OF BEING *HOSION* AND BEING *"LOVED BY THE GODS"*
Euthyphro Argument #2

1. Antithesis: *hosion* is what is pleasing to the gods – Assertion/ 9e 1
2. The active and middle tenses of a verb are different – Fact/ 10a 5
3. [The middle tense implies a state of being] – Fact
4. All states of being imply a prior action that creates that state of being – Assertion/ 10b 5
5. The prior action causes posterior results, that is, states of being – Assertion/ 10c 6
6. The middle tense of a verb implies a state of being that was caused by a prior action – 1–4/ 10c 8
7. Something that is in "the state of being loved" is in the middle tense – Fact/ 10d 1
8. Something in "the state of being loved" implies a prior action that put it into that state – 5,6/ 10d 4
9. [*hosion* is the only action that might qualify as being related to the gods loving something] – Assertion
10. Something is in "the state of being loved" because it is pious – 7, 8/ 10d 6–8

_____

11. Thesis: The antithesis (*hosion* is what is pleasing to the gods) ought to be rejected – 10, 1 {Note that this assumes the antithesis to be asserting a causal connection}
   or 11. That which is a causal consequent cannot be identical to its causal antecedent – Fact/ 10e 2–5

_____

12. Thesis: The antithesis (*hosion* is what is pleasing to the gods) ought to be rejected – 10, 11, 1 {Note that this assumes the antithesis to be asserting an identity relation}

The argument can be understood as a causal or identity argument. Both versions are set out. Plato intends in either that any action or event is *hosion* or *anosion* according to the intrinsic characteristics that it possesses and not extrinsically through its instrumentality to the gods (or to anyone else, for that matter). This assertion of the intrinsic quality of virtue is a major feature of natural law theory. It backs up our earlier texts against the backdrop of changeable perspectives (*Euthyphro,* argument one: 6e10–8a10).

It is also important to note that Plato's discussion of the just soul can be writ large to be applicable to the state as in the *Republic* in which the three parts of the human soul are compared to the three classes of peoples who live in the state in a one-to-one correspondence: *epithumos* = the common man; *thumos* = the managers and military; and *sophia* = the rulers.[25]

Among Plato and Aristotle it is important to introduce another term for examination: *phusis* (nature). Sometimes *phusis* is understood as a regular ordering of nature.[26] Along this line is the contrast to *tuche* (chance).[27] Some natural events occur because they are part of a causal structure. Aristotle understood the causes to be fourfold. They represented regularity in nature that also bordered upon an active power:[28] *Nature does nothing in vain.* This was a description of how one might understand the workings of biomedical science in the ancient world. It had the status of a biological natural law that influenced natural philosophers from Aristotle to Galen and beyond.[29] Along with this are other *natural laws* such as bilateral symmetry, no animal part has two natural functions, efficiency in "the more and the less," and so on. These biomedical generalizations (laws) were essential for the debate on ancient biomedicine.[30] What they contribute to our investigation is a support for the realist assumption under the nonactive understanding of nature and the theist assumption under the active understanding of nature.

Phusis is also used by Aristotle in the ethics/political/legal category in the *Politics* by saying that man is naturally a political animal (*o anthropos phusei politikon zoon,* 1253a 2–3). The sense of nature is an inherent part of who we are as people.

[25] Compare *Republic* IV (personal) to *Republic* III (sociological).

[26] Plato, *Republic* 444[d] and *Gorgias* 488[b]; cf. Democritus Fr. 176.

[27] Plato, *Laws* 889[b], and Aristotle, *Politics* 1253[a]3, and of course *Physics* II.1 193[b]23 ff.

[28] Aristotle, *Metaphysics* 1014[b] 16, *De Caelo* 271[a] 33, *Meterologica* 381[b]5, et passim. See also my discussion in "Galen on the Blood, Pulse, and Arteries," *Journal of the History of Biology* 40.2 (2007): 207–230, and Michael Boylan, "Aristotle's Biology," entry in *The Internet Encyclopedia of Philosophy* (2004); cf. to my forthcoming book *The Origins of Ancient Greek Science: A Philosophical Study of Blood* (London: Routledge).

[29] These historical connections have been made by me in "Galen's Conception Theory," *Journal of the History of Biology* 19.1 (1986): 44–77, and Boylan, "Galen on the Blood, Pulse, and Arteries."

[30] See my entry on Galen in *The Internet Encyclopedia of Philosophy* (2004).

Another key input from Aristotle is his theory of virtue ethics set out in the *Nicomachean Ethics*. In this work, Aristotle creates a theory that identifies character as the goal of ethics. This character is built upon habits that are formed first through parents training their children and then through the state that creates laws in the place of the parent. Obviously, there is an element of free choice in the process. One can choose to reject the habits that are suggested by the parents and then by the state. But Aristotle does not really critically evaluate the character traits themselves: justice, wisdom, self-control, courage, et al. He assumes that everyone would agree that a man with these character traits would be judged to be excellent (*arête*). That is, he is assuming that his doctrine of the mean (*EN* II.5–6) would be acceptable along with his list of virtues. This implies a connection to a realist conception of both the doctrine of the mean and the excellences (virtues) themselves. Under this reading Aristotle is compatible with the natural law ethical tradition.

These brief citations along with the notes set out the plausibility that the ancient Greeks had and applied notions of natural law both in their popular culture (as represented in their literature) and in their philosophy – both ethical/political/legal as well as natural philosophy.

Then there are the Stoic philosophers. Most people who want to examine natural law in the ancient world start here. I, myself, did the same thing at the beginning of my philosophical career.[31] This is because the Stoics are very explicit on their use of natural law in both the senses that we are exploring. In the case of Seneca's *De beneficiis*, an elaborate system of social duties is set out based on what is noble (*noblis*) or base (*turpius*) in the giving and receiving of benefits – whether they imply a tangible duty (*officium*).[32] The giving and receiving of benefits is asserted to be descriptive of the human condition and so fitting into the ethical/political/legal bucket.

Marcus Aurelius discusses in several places the various key senses of natural law in *Meditations*: Nature constructs via form and matter: IV.21; the universe is a living being: IV.40; and nature is known by reason: III.9; IV.29; V.8; vVII.11; VIII.41.[33] In these instances nature is separate from humankind and is a regulative entity (the realist if not the theistic standpoint). But these references show several key ways that the stoics used nature.

---

[31] Michael Boylan, "Seneca and Moral Rights," *New Scholasticism* 53.3 (1979): 362–374.

[32] Seneca, *Moral Essays*, vol. 3., trans. J. W. Basore (Cambridge, MA: Harvard University Press, 1935).

[33] Marcus Aurelius, *Meditations*, trans. Robin Hard (New York: Oxford University Press, 2011).

Another strong advocate of natural law is Chrysippus. He extends the extent of law as a "standard" (*kanon*) to separate the just from the unjust.

> [Law] ought to be in charge of what is morally good and bad, and a ruler and guide (*hegemona*), and in this respect [it ought] to be a standard of what is just and unjust, and, for all naturally political animals, [it ought] to command what must be done and prohibit what must not be done.[34]

This passage is interesting because it relates law as a guide to human conduct. It is the ultimate arbitrator to human whims about what is proper or not. It also reinforces Aristotle's notion that humans are naturally political animals. The "naturally" here can be an active normative force. What should or should not be done is *not* merely an agreement among men.

Elizabeth Asmis follows this by saying that "Chrysippus' definition of human 'impulse' indicates that this guidance exists in each human being as a psychological force. In his book *On Law* he is also said to have written: 'The impulse (*horme*) of a human being is reason (*logos*) commanding (*prostakitikos*) him to act.' As a 'commanding' force reason acts as law."[35] If the (natural) Law exists in all humans as an inherent impulse, then all have access to the natural law via reason. This reinforces the standard by which vulgar human legislatures enact obligations and prohibitions with penalties. There is a separate standard by which human legislation can be judged, and that is the natural law.

Cicero in *De legibus* declares:

> But in our present investigation we intend to cover the whole range of universal Justice and Law in such a way that our own civil law, as it is called, will be confined to a small and narrow corner. For we must explain the nature of Justice, and this must be sought for in the nature of man; we must also consider the laws by which States ought to be governed.... Law is the highest reason, implanted in Nature, which commands what ought to be done and forbids the opposite. This reason, when firmly fixed and fully developed in the human mind, is Law. And so they believe that Law is intelligence, whose natural function it is to command right conduct and forbid wrongdoing. (*De legibus*, I.v.17–19)[36]

---

[34] Hans von Arnim, *Stoicorum Veterum Fragmenta in Four Volumes* (Leipzig: Teubner, 1903–1924): 3.314; trans. Elizabeth Asmis in "Cicero on Natural Law and the Laws of the State," *Antiquity* **27**.1 (2008): 1–33.

[35] Asmis, "Cicero on Natural Law," 11.

[36] Cicero, *De re Publica and De Legibus*, ed. and trans. Clinton Walker Keyes (Harvard, MA: Harvard University Press, 1928). Unless otherwise noted I will follow Keyes's translation.

This Book One passage begins by discussing a characteristic of the discourse as *universal* Justice and Law (*universi iuris et legume*). These are not, therefore, the laws that are passed in legislative bodies but realistically or theistically grounded principles. The conventional law that is passed by governments is the civil law that is confined to a small corner. It is inferior to the natural law and to natural justice. For a specification of natural law and natural justice one must turn to the nature of man. A separate exercise is to determine how the states should make their laws. This second exercise begins with recognizing natural law through the exercise of human reason. Through such scrutiny one can detect the Law which is the highest reason implanted in nature (*lex est ratio summa insita in natura*). Because of this position the natural law can command duties both positive and negative (obligations and prohibitions). And because the Law binds to all human society and is based on one Law (which is known by right reason), the Law will understand as a command either obligation or prohibition (*est enim unum ius, quo devineta est hominum societas, et quod lex constituit una; quae lex est recta ratio imperandi atque prohibendi*);[37] there is the further implied imperative to bring everyone over to the correct natural law. This connects remotely to the contemporary interest in human rights post–World War II to bring others over to the collective view of what should be recognized as a human right.[38]

This natural Law (now normatively encompassing both the ethical and judicial) is imbued in the very logical structure of reason. I follow Elizabeth Asmis and Phillip Mitsis that Stoic law (in general) and Cicero (in particular) prescribe not only right actions but also intermediate appropriate actions.[39] The upshot of this is that the sort of rationality required to view the natural law correctly need not be perfect in all respects but can be more generally accurate. The effect of this is to widen the access to the dictates of natural law to a greater number of people. This will have a rather democratic effect.

---

[37] Cicero, *De legibus*, I. xv. 42.

[38] For example, Beitz, *The Idea of Human Rights*, 1, 152–160. It should be emphasized, however, that Beitz takes an anti-realist contractarian position rather than the natural law position discussed here.

[39] Asmis, "Cicero on Natural Law," 13–14; Philip Mitsis, "Natural Law and Natural Right in Post-Aristotelian Philosophy. The Stoics and Their Critics," in *Aufstieg und Niedergang der römischen Welt*, ed. W. Haase and H. Temporini (Berlin: Walter de Gruyter, 1994): II.36.7: 4812–4850. An opposing view is taken by Paul Vander Waerdt, "Philosophical Influence on Roman Jurisprudence? The Case of Stoicism and Natural Law," in *Aufstieg und Niedergang der römischen Welt*, ed. W. Haase and H. Temporini (Berlin: Walter de Gruyter, 1994): II.36.7: 4851–4900.

A second passage from *De legibus* says, "I shall seek the root of Justice in Nature, under whose guidance our whole discussion must be conducted" (I.vi.20). Again, this passage shows the path of authority. The most authoritative source for ethics, justice, and the law lies in nature. The way to access the dictates of nature, as we have seen, is via reason.

The way to understand "Nature" here leans toward the theistic, "Nature has likewise not only equipped man himself with nimbleness of thought but has also given him the senses, to be, as it were, his attendants and messengers" (I.viii.26). Nature in this context is an active agent.

Next, I will bring attention to the following argument. Cicero considers whether justice may only be set out by law and national customs (cf. Chapter 4). He rejects this approach:

> But if Justice is conformity to written laws and national customs [only], everything will be tested by the standard of utility, and anyone who thinks it profitable to him will, if he is able, disregard and violate the laws.

> It follows that Justice does not exist at all, if it does not exist in Nature, and if that form of it, which is based upon utility, can be overthrown by that very utility itself. And if Nature is not to be considered the foundation of Justice, that will mean the destruction [of the virtues on which human society depends]. (I.xv.42–43).

It is clear to Cicero that proper civic law in its best sense cannot be distinguished from naturally based justice and ethics: all are intertwined. The authority for each of them is that they are all grounded in nature so that, in the best possible worlds, civic laws will be identical to Laws of Nature.[40] (Those that are not identical cannot be valid civil law but must be directed (*diriguntur*), i.e., set straight by natural law.) Well, what is to be made of such an identity? For one, as has been said earlier, it has a basis in realistic or theistic natural authority. But second, the identity claim also speaks to the longevity of the law. Since realistic or theistic understandings of *ius* or *lex* are set forever, then the identity hypothesis would make proper human law eternal as well – or at least long lasting (since the human input is logically contingent). Both Girandet and Dyck recognize the importance of this feature of Cicero's depiction of the

---

[40] This aligns me with Asmis contra the Platonic interpretation of Turnebus, in F. Creuzer and G. H. Moser, eds., *M. Tulli Ciceronis de legibus libri tres, cum Adriani Turnebi commentario ejusdemque apologia et ominum eruditorum notis* (Frankfort: E. Typ. Broeneriano, 1824), and P. L. Schmidt, *Die Abfassungszeit von Ciceros Schrift ber die Gesetze* (Rome: Centro di Studi Ciceroniani, 1969).

natural law as underlying his own code of law.[41] As Asmis says, Cicero's laws have "a contingent durability."[42]

At the end of the day in the Ancient European world the various words that might be translated as 'right' or 'law' relate to a standard that is realistically or theistically based. As said earlier, this attaches to the average man on the street in what Henrik Syse calls the objective sense of rights.[43] Under this analysis, the objective sense of right amounts to the use of the term in a primarily adjectival sense: "It is right of me to express this belief." In the objective sense of *right*, it is an existent set of truths that are out there for me to correspond to or not (correspondence theory of truth). When I do, then my fidelity to them confers truth and validates my ethical/political/legal connection to something *other*. This act of predication is adjectival in its force.

In contrast to the objective sense of right is a subjective sense of right such that it is a good that the subject possesses: "I have a right to express this belief." Here *right* transforms from an adjectival predication to one of possessing a noun. This latter move (for the most part)[44] does not exist in the Ancient European World. But this seems central to our contemporary understanding of human rights. How and in what way we get to the subjective attribution of rights is the subject matter of the next subsection.

2.2.2 Natural Law in the European Medieval World

The European medieval world was built upon the European ancient world. It began as a commentary on the ancient world and evolved its own canon that incorporated disputations on theology and its applications in both natural philosophy and in ethical/political/legal philosophy. The worldview perspective of the ancient world that sought to emphasize community was often fragmented as this historical era was beset with warfare. Learning was largely confined to some monasteries and some convents, which themselves were subject to attack and sacking. Thus one theme of this era was about maintaining a fragile connection

[41] K. M. Giradet, *Die Ordnung der Welt: Ein Beitrag zur philosophischen und politischen Interpretation von Ciceros Schrift De legibus* (Wiesbaden: Franz Steiner, 1983): 83, and A. R. Dyck, *A Commentary on Cicero, De legibus* (Ann Arbor: University of Michigan Press, 2004).

[42] Asmis, "Cicero on Natural Law," 25.

[43] Syse, *Natural Law, Religion, and Rights*, 109–110; cf. Fred Miller, *Nature, Justice, and Rights in Aristotle's Politics* (Oxford: Oxford University Press, 1995).

[44] I would still contend that in Seneca's *De Beneficiis*, this subjective sense occurs.

to community in the face of the awful insecurity of marauding bands that could pillage and destroy a region in order to exact future tribute or simply to disrupt the general order.

"The Wanderer" and "The Seafarer" are two very prominent Anglo-Saxon poems that set out these themes in sharp relief. The schism between the individual and the community is set out at the beginning of "The Wanderer."[45]

> "Often the solitary man happens upon
> Mercy and grace amidst his sorrows
> Though he's been forced by fate
> To steer across the icy-cold waters
> Of many seas in his forced exile." [5]
> So said the wanderer who recalled
> Hard, cruel wars and the deaths of lords.
> "Often I have had to mourn in solitude—
> Morning cares carried again and again. There is
> No one on earth to whom I dare reveal my heart [10]
> Openly. For I know that verity of life
> That it is indeed a noble virtue
> To hide one's intellect and to lock-up feelings
> In a treasure chest despite one's inclination.
> A weary heart cannot oppose inevitable fate." [15]

The form of the poem is clear: a community that had existed (in accord with natural law) has now been obliterated. The natural order (in the objective sense) has been forsaken, forcing the outcast to endure harsh weather and painful wanderings (another sense of nature). What does this mean? One answer is that it brings the *individual* into relief.

> Anyone who has given careful thought
> To this creation and its depraved existence [90]
> Often is haunted by the many massacres
> In times past that scream forth,
> "Where are the horses and the heroes that rode them?
> Where is the generous lord? Where are the drinking tables?
> Where the joys of the festive pleasure hall?"
> Alas for the bright cup, the armed comrade,
> And the lord's glory. That day is over. [95]
> It has faded into the night as though it had never been.
> The splendid high wall, with its paintings of wild serpents,
> Stands as memorial to that precious troop of men.

[45] Geroge Philip Krapp and Elliott van Kirk Dobbie, eds., "The Wanderer" and "The Seafarer" in *The Exeter Book* (New York: Columbia University Press, 1936): 134–136; 143–146; translations are my own.

> It was the gore-stained spear and terrible fate [100]
> That took those heroes away. And now,
> Storms pummel these rocky cliffs.

The old ways are gone. It is a death knell. Nature has turned from mutual contentment according to a code [covenant] to bitter struggling. But still the narrator must carry on. Likewise, in "The Seafarer" the protagonist faces bitter disappointment as he must find his individual way in the midst of horrendous conditions.

> When hail fell hard, I heard naught save the savage sea.
> The song of the wild swan I have made my own.
> The cacophony of sea fowl was my soul music [20]
> The gulls' constant drone was my mead hall mirth.
> Storms crashed cragged cliffs; terns turned icy wings
> The sharp beaked eagle shrieked in agony.
>
> No patron had I to soothe and succor my spirit. [25]
> Those whose comfort defines their lives
> With pride inflated by wine can little *understand*
> Since they abide in the kind comforts of city-life,
> Safe from terror and danger.
> I have oft suffered, weary from duties above the brine. [30]
>
> Black nightshade; northern snow
> Frost held the land; hail pelted down
> Ice Kernels and yet now my heart's desire
> Drives me forward to mount towering
> Waves: the salt water's play. [35]

It is the wild sea that is so relentless. It will be an intellectual predecessor to the *state of nature* that is the subject of the Enlightenment authors. Here there is a paean of agony from the individual set out *alone* against nature bereft of the social structure that had been there before. Seen on its own terms, the prospect is very bleak – at best. And then, as a nod to the past, the poet invokes the theistic natural law at the end:

> Blessed is the meek man for to him shall come heavenly grace.
> Because his faith is rooted in God's power
> The Creator will make fast the moor line of his spirit.
> A man's self-control flows from his strength of mind. [110]
> He must hold firmly to that through honest dealings
> And a pure heart. He should live by moderation
> In all his dealings (be they friend or foe).
> No man would wish his friend to burn
> On an earthly pyre or in Hell's fire. [115]
> Yet fate is mightier than these: it is the Lord's inscrutable plan for us all.

Ponder first where to find a permanent home
And then consider from whence we came
So that we may pass into Eternal Blessedness, [120]
Wherein is the place of life within God's abode.
Hope is above all. Thanks be to the Almighty
Who has saved us by the Resurrection of the wondrous Prince,
Our Lord, who *is* without end— forever and ever.
Amen.

This stark reality of a life framed by war and violence is not to be diminished as the objective natural law perspective comes under scrutiny: if there is a good and loving God, then why (if one obeys the rules) is there so much sorrow and pain (especially if one has upheld his part of the covenant)? This is the first chink in the received chain that moves the orientation (to a small degree) toward the individual and his own choices in the process of gritty survival.

As the Middle Ages progressed past the millennium, there are other visions that seek to reinforce community and its possibility via war conducted under an acceptable, just model (reinforced by virtue/natural law). The Arthurian legends of Chrétien de Troyes, Thomas Mallory, and the writer of *Sir Gawain and the Green Knight* all emphasize the knight of virtue who can chop your head off, but only under the conditions of virtue: the knightly code (natural law). Still further, Dante Alighieri tries to reinforce what he takes to be theistic natural law with his *La divina commedia* in which the three metaphysical realms – hell, purgatory, and paradise – are set out as rational/just in a way that is reminiscent of Cicero's description of the natural law being above civic laws. In this case, people who might have been (wrongly) successful in this life are punished in the next in hell – including even Pope Boniface VIII and Pope Nicholas III!

The literary representation of the contemporary community worldview in the later Middle Ages (12th century onward) was much more positive than the early period cited previously. And yet, still the influence of the cracks and fissures was not lost – after all, it was during this period that the Crusades were undertaken (1095–1272). The consequences of which were as severe as the marauding of the early medieval period.[46]

---

[46] For more background on the violence and warfare of medieval Europe, see R. W. Southern, *The Making of the Middle Ages* (New Haven, CT: Yale University Press, 1961); Niall Christie, *Noble Ideals and Bloody Realities: Warfare in the Middle Ages (History of Warfare,* vol. 37) (Leiden: Brill, 2001); and Michael Prestwich, *Armies and Warfare in the Middle Ages: The English Experience* (New Haven, CT: Yale University Press, 1999).

Among philosophers of this era the words that connect to rights include *libertas, potestas, facultas, immunitas dominium, iustitia, interesse,* and *actio.* Charles Reid claims that all these words in the medieval corpus can (depending upon context) be construed as 'right' (in the objective sense).[47] Up until and including Aquinas (1225–1274) medieval philosophy continued to see rights in the objective sense via natural rights and law as perfected by the Stoics. This is evident by a quick look at Thomas's treatment.[48] He makes a distinction between eternal and temporal law. Though he quotes Augustine here, the distinction harkens back to Cicero's understanding of the distinction between natural and civil law. For his explanation of authority Thomas uses an analogy:

> Now, in every [natural event] there are primary movers and secondary movers. The latter derive their efficacy from the former. This is the same in government: the king directs his [barons] who in turn direct their [vassals]. In this way a state's purposive action flows from the king through his lesser administrators. This is also true in art [within the art guild]. The master of the guild directs other craftsmen, from the journeymen to the apprentices (who work with their hands).... the activities of the bureaucracy follow the eternal law.

In this passage the authority of the commanding force of the law comes from God. Because God exists in eternity, this sort of command is demonstrative of eternal law. However, when we ask how this eternal law is to be known by people, the question turns.

> Isidore asserts that the natural law is common to all nations. My view is this: man is inclined to the natural law. This includes all objects to which man is rationally drawn and guides his action in the world. [Aristotle] in the *Physics* says that there are two sorts of predication: (a) generic, and (b) specific. This corresponds to the distinction between theoretical and practical reason. Theoretical reason deals with that which cannot be otherwise [that is, necessary deductive conclusions] about universals. Practical reason deals with the realm of the contingent: human action. This means that when we make a transition from the universal principles common to many species, the application to the particular often encounters less exactness.

Because men are inclined to the natural law and because it is open to rational inspection and discovery, people have access through reason to a set of principles that cover all aspects of life from natural philosophy

[47] Charles J. Reid, "The Canonistic Contribution to the Western Rights Tradition: An Historical Inquiry," *Boston College Law Review* **33** (1991): 37–92.

[48] Thomas Aquinas, *Summa Theologica,* I–II, q93, a2; q93a3; q94, a4 (Rome: Typographia Forzani, 1894); translations are mine.

(Aquinas was keen on Aristotle's interest in biology) to the ethical/political/legal. This is very similar to the Stoics described earlier. Then Aquinas introduces another interesting distinction between understanding at the genus level (universals that yield necessary deductive conclusions) and understanding at the species level (sorts of real-world problems that are messy). Though there is absolute certainty at the genus level, there is some contingency at the species level and a fortiori even more at the level of individuals. This messiness has to do with the individuation of the lofty principles. Though it may be the case that the generic principles are absolute, in terms of application the options available may be something less. This is reminiscent of Elizabeth Asmis and Phillip Mitsis's interpretation of the intermediate appropriate actions in Cicero. In each instance there is a nod toward a subjective sense of right in the very particularity of actual decision making.

The search for the "missing link" to a subjective understanding of human rights that is generally understood as such within the intellectual and popular communities is still elusive. Here are a few of the top contenders.

First, there is Marsilius of Padua (1275–1342) who in *Defensor pacis* presented two meanings of *ius:*

> In one signification, therefore, 'right' (*ius*) is the same as law (*lex*), divine or human.... In a second way, 'right' is predicated of every human act, power, or acquired disposition that issues from an imperative of the human mind, be it internal or external, immanent or transitive upon some external thing or an aspect of it ... in conformity with rights so-called in the first signification.[49]

It is this second sense of 'right' that appeared in the fourteenth century that made a significant step forward in the recognition of the subjective meaning of right. It also connects the two approaches such that the possession of the noun-understanding of right is given authority by the objective (adjectival) sense of natural law. This interpretation is strained, but there is something going on about *power*. When we think of power and human action together we arrive at a notion of human agency. As will be made evident in Chapter 6, I believe this to be a crucial distinction (as developed later). Though this is in the main a small break from

[49] *Marsilius of Padua: The Defender of the Peace,* trans. Annabel Brett, Cambridge Tests in the History of Political Thought (Cambridge: Cambridge University Press, 2005). This passage was first brought to my attention by Alan Gewirth as I was updating an article we co-authored: "Marsilius of Padua," co-written with Alan Gewirth, entry in *The Encyclopedia of Philosophy,* 2nd ed., ed. Donald M. Borchert (Farmington Hills, MI: Macmillan, 2006).

Aquinas, Cicero, and the other Stoics who emphasized (for the most part) merely the objective sense, it will be, I believe, a central feature of the strongest justification for human rights.

Along this same line is Jean Gerson (1363–1429) who contends that *ius* per se belongs to all people. *Ius* is connected to potential actions and this predication allows potential actions to occur: "a right is an immediate faculty or power pertaining to a thing according to the dictate of right reason."[50] In this way *ius* was a noun possessed by an agent (any agent), but the Stoic condition of *according to right reason* still obtains. However, the fact of its being a possession (faculty or power) means that we are moving toward an understanding of *ius* subjectively.

Brian Tierney also mentions Konrad Summerhart (1455–1502) in this regard as distinguishing *ius* as law and *ius* as power (that could be applied individually): "In another sense *ius* is taken to be the same as a power as when we say a father has a right (*ius*) as regards his son, or a king as regards his subjects and men have a right (*ius*) in their things and positions."[51] Clearly, this is another small step toward viewing rights as subjectively owned.[52]

William of Ockham (1287–1347) moved the bar forward toward subjectively owned rights regarding property rights and political rights that an individual possesses to permit human action.[53] Also to be noted in this transition period are the Spanish neo-Scholastics such as Francisco Suárez (1548–1617; intellectual leader of the school of Salamanca)

[50] Jean Gerson, *De vita spirituali animae*, vol. 3, 141: "ius est facultas seu potestas propinqua conveiniens alicui secundum dictamen rectae rationis," from Jean Gerson, *De vita spirituali animae*, in *Oeuvres complètes*, ed. P. Glorieuvx, vol. 3 (Paris: Palémon Glorieux, 1965). This connection is also made by Brian Tierney, *The Idea of Natural Rights: Studies on Natural Rights, Natural Law and Church Law 1150–1625* (Atlanta: Scholars Press, 1997): 248, and Annabel S. Brett, *Liberty, Right, and Nature: Individual Rights in Later Scholastic Thought* (Cambridge: Cambridge University Press, 1997): 126.

[51] Brian Tierney, *The Idea of Natural Rights: Studies on Natural Rights, Natural Law, and Church Law, 1150–1625* (Atlanta, GA: Scholars Press, 1997): 109. Tierney is citing Konrad Summenhart, *De contractibus licitis atque illicitis Tractatus* (Venice: Francesco Ziletti, 1580): I.1.1.

[52] When the point about power includes some sense of voluntarism, then Duns Scotus (1265–1308) can also be brought into the mix, as per Syse, *Natural Law, Religion, and Rights*, 52–62. When these powers to individually act come into contact with God's plan (as per a form of *predestination*), then the Calvinist approach also is a step toward the subjectivist approach – see John Witte, *The Reformation of Rights: Law, Religion, and Human Rights in Modern Calvinism* (Cambridge: Cambridge University Press, 2008).

[53] Here I am following Michel Villey's assessment of Ockham, "Une qualité du subjet, une de ses facultes, plus précisément une franchise, une liberté, une possibilité d'agir," from "La Genèse du Droit Subjectif chez Guillaume d'Ockham," *Archives de la Philosophie du Droit* 9 (1969): 97–127.

who moved the analysis toward moral psychology in his analysis of *ius* as power (*potestas*) or liberty (*libertas*).[54] This rested principally upon an analysis of self-mastery such that each human's share of nature was the same; thus if [objective] rights were invested in nature, and if nature belongs to all humans collectively, then each human has an equal share to them [subjective rights].

There is *not* a single line of causal moments that can account for the change from the community approach in the ancient and early medieval world that emphasized natural laws and natural rights that were objectively understood as applying to all on some sort of principle of subsumption (much like the laws of Newtonian motion aspired to generally apply to all cases) to a subjectively understood private possession of said rights. There are many conjectures. Each of them probably contains a modicum of truth. But what is important is that at the end of this historical era, there were significant schisms in the exclusive objective rights paradigm. Ultimately, I believe that it is not the case that the objective understanding of rights was discarded in favor of subjective possession, but rather that a new understanding of rights was beginning to emerge that was seen as an emanation of the previous worldview.

However, entering into this gradualist approach is Dutch jurist Hugo Grotius (1583–1645). He writes in the "Prolegomena" to *De jure belli et pacis* that the impelling desire for a peaceful social life that is responsive to rational judgment must also reflect "the law of nature that is the nature of man."[55] What Grotius means by this is an endorsement of the realistic hypothesis instead of the theistic hypothesis. Grotius wants to consider an understanding of natural human rights that is not connected to God (*etiamsi daremus non esse Deum*).[56] Such a move appalled

---

[54] Regarding Ockham, see Syse, *Natural Law, Religion, and Rights*, 62–84, and regarding Suárez, see Erik Akerlund, "Suárez's Ideas on Natural Law in the Light of His Philosophical Anthropology and Moral Psychology," in *The Nature of Rights: Moral and Political Aspects of Rights in Late Medieval and Early Modern Philosophy,* ed. Virpi Mäkin (Helsinki: Philosophical Society of Finland, 2010): 165–196.

[55] Hugo Grotius, *De jure belli et pacis*, Prolegommena, trans. Francis W. Kelsey et al., 2 vols. (Oxford: Oxford University Press, 1925): II, 11–13. For a discussion of Grotius's and John Selden's role in shaping the more individualistic notion of human rights apart from natural law, see Richard Tuck, *Natural Rights Theories* (Cambridge: Cambridge University Press, 1982): 58–100. Tuck's strategy is to put these influences before Hobbes, who is Tuck's critical synthesizer.

[56] For a fuller discussion of this, see James Saint Leger, *The "Etiamsi Daremus" of Hugo Grotius: A Study in the Origins of International Law* (Rome: Pontificium Athenaeum Internationale, 1962).

Samuel Pufendorf as "an impious and idiotic theory."[57] This is because (according to Pufendorf) it would mean that God was not interested in the affairs of men (the Deist hypothesis).

From our contemporary perspective Grotius's move to eliminate the theistic worldview (if only as a hypothesis) marked a radical change amid the gradualism within the ancient and medieval worldviews. If we are to conceive of natural law and natural rights away from an objective sense grounded in God (at least heuristically), then the playing field has changed and it is time for the Enlightenment.

2.3 HUMAN RIGHTS AS CENTERED IN THE ENLIGHTENMENT

Another answer to the question about the origin of human rights ties human rights thinking to the Enlightenment and its emphasis upon individuals over and against a more communal view.[58] There are different ways to do this. On the one hand, we can think of the individual versus the community problem from the contemporary perspective.[59] This is instructive to understand the logical dynamics of these two ways of constructing a shared community worldview that makes experience in the world comprehensible. Approaches to human rights are different when one takes the communal perspective rather than the individual perspective. As someone who has written that the *proper* perspective is in the middle, I think it is instructive to think about life at the extremes. At the communal perspective was the ancient world paradigm. The natural law was understood objectively and applied via subsumption to the community. Under the theistic understanding of this, a covenant was formed such that adherence meant continued prosperity. However, this worldview was fractured in the medieval world. Post-Grotius the theistic

---

[57] Samuel Pufendorf, *De jure naturae et gentium. Libri Octo. Lib. II. Cap 3. 19*, trans. C. H. and W. A. Oldfather, 2 vols. (Oxford: Oxford University Press, 1934): II, 215.

[58] Key proponents of the origin of human rights from the modern era (seventeenth–eighteenth centuries) include Leo Straus, *Natural Right and History* (Chicago: University of Chicago Press, 1953), and C. B. Macpherson, *The Political Theory of Possessive Individualism: Hobbes to Locke* (Oxford: Oxford University Press, 1962).

[59] For an introduction to authors advocating the endpoints in the liberalism (individualism)/communitarianism (general will) continuum, see John Rawls, *A Theory of Justice* (Cambridge, MA: Harvard University Press, 1971); Alan Gewirth, *Reason and Morality* (Chicago: University of Chicago Press, 1978): v; Michael J. Sandel, *Liberalism and the Limits of Justice*, 2nd ed. (Cambridge: Cambridge University Press, 1998); and Amitai Etzioni, *Rights and the Common Good: The Communitarian Perspective* (Belmont, CA: Wadsworth, 1994). In *A Just Society* (Lanham, MD: Rowman and Littlefield, 2004): 123–133, I argue for a view midway between these poles.

understanding of natural rights was replaced, at least by hypothesis, by the realistic worldview.

This subsection highlights the individual perspective as it is a recognized part of the European Enlightenment Project (seventeenth and eighteenth centuries, also known as Modern Philosophy). Michael Oakeshott's philosophy of individualism and his connection to Hobbes is surely one way to understand the move to the individual during this time period.[60]

John Milton's *Paradise Lost* is an insightful contemporary example of this worldview change of emphasizing the individual against the given common order. The poem was published in 1674 after the return of Charles II. The English Civil War from 1642, when Charles I raised the standard, to the Royalist surrender in 1646, to Charles's beheading in 1649 created a very tumultuous era. In 1660 (two years after the death of Cromwell), Charles II ascended to the throne and various institutions in the country were reinstated (though not without the stamp of intervening change). Milton's poetic masterpiece stands within this backdrop that might be simplified by saying that the long-standing traditional order was overturned for a time and then reinstated, but not without difference. Even completely unconnected events such as the London fire of 1666 took on apocalyptic dimensions because of the tumultuous context.

If we look at *Paradise Lost* with these considerations in mind, then the Book One declaration of Satan (who is often the spokesperson for the new Enlightenment, post-Grotius individualism) is important:

> ... Here at least
> We will be free; th'Almighty hath not built
> Here for his envy, will not drive us hence:
> Here we may reign secure, and in my choice
> To reign is worth ambition though in hell:
> Better to reign in hell, than serve in heaven.
> [BK 1, 259–264]

Individual freedom is asserted against the established communal combine of church and state. Satan is the figure who sets out these thoughts. (Milton can make Satan say whatever he (Milton) wants because *who is going to credit the thoughts of Satan?* He can even explore Grotius since

---

[60] Michael Oakeshott, "Introduction to *Leviathan*," in *Hobbes on Civil Association* (Berkeley: University of California Press, 1975): 15–28. For discussions to situate this, see Paul Franco, "Michael Oakeshott as Liberal Theorist," *Political Theory* **18**.3 (1990): 411–436, and Michael Boylan, "Michael Oakeshott," entry in *The Encyclopedia of Philosophy*, 2nd ed., ed. Donald M. Borchert (Farmington Hills, MI: Macmillan, 2006).

Satan gives no authoritative credence to God).[61] Further, when Satan uses logic with Eve in Book IV, Milton is still on firm ground in his politically sensitive time because *who is going to credit the thoughts of a woman – especially Eve?*

> From thir own mouths; all is not theirs it seems:
> One fatal Tree there stands of Knowledge call'd,
> Forbidden them to taste: Knowledge forbidd'n?
> Suspicious, reasonless. Why should thir Lord
> Envy them that? Can it be a sin to know,
> Can it be death? And do they only stand
> By ignorance, is that thir happy state
> The proof of thir obedience and thir faith?
>   [BK IV, 513–520]

This argument by Satan sets out an Enlightenment argument: individuals have a [right] to pursue knowledge by themselves and act accordingly. The existing communal establishment (the Roman and English Catholic churches) sought to keep obedience, as such. This is the community enveloping the individual. The church's stance against the Bible and services in the vernacular are part and parcel to this holdover from the medieval worldview. If the individual has rights to learn and to know, then it cannot be responsible for the actions of the church (because the church will decide for the community and all must accept its verdicts). But what if the regular people, who are literate, can read the texts themselves and make up their own minds? This is a change from the ancient community worldview that had been hanging on during the tumultuous Middle Ages. The church in Europe saw this as a threat to the established worldview; thus it reacted against those who sought to bring this about (e.g., William Tyndale who was killed for translating a portion of the Bible into the vernacular). Satan's words to Eve have an effect. If ignorance and blind allegiance are the only way to lead a life, then is such a life worth living? These questions only make sense when one presumes the individualist stance.

Then Satan comes to Eve while she is asleep. Squatting like a toad (IV, 800) Satan sets out a scenario for Eve to imagine eating the apple – down to the last detail (V, 83–93). The result was fantastic. She attained knowledge and power from her individualistic action. Milton (who supported

---

[61] In this reading of Milton (not the only way), he is set on the direction of the contemporary trilogy of the Golden Compass (Philip Pullman, *Golden Compass Trilogy* [New York: Knopf, 2006]): the theistic account is overly oppressive so that fighting against the established church and God (itself/himself) becomes an act of human rights expression.

the Republicans in the English Civil War) may here be using Satan as a sort of Oliver Cromwell figure who presided over what turned out to be (in the end) a losing effort. But that is beside the point of whether the principle is correct. Finally, in book eight Milton sets himself as at least sympathetic to Copernican astronomy (Copernicus being another individualistic figure who stands up against the Establishment, albeit on his deathbed). Adam and Raphael are in a discussion about the heavens (the central topic of Book Eight).

> Whether the Sun, predominant in Heaven,
> Rise on the Earth, or Earth rise on the Sun;
> He from the east his flaming round begin,
> Or she from west her silent course advance
> With inoffensive pace that spinning sleeps
> On her soft axle, whilst she paces even,
> And bears thee soft with the smooth air along –
> Solicit not thy thoughts with matters hid.
> [Bk VIII, 159–167]

Raphael takes the *save the phenomena* approach, but the case is not set out with conviction. Thus, careful Milton (on the wrong side during the Restoration) is perhaps here showing his sympathy to the cause of the individualistic new Astronomers.

In the end, *Paradise Lost* stands as an important text that unites the history of upheaval in seventeenth-century Britain along with the Enlightenment thought about politics and science – especially concerning the new elevated place of the individual.

Another way to think of this historical worldview change to the individual in a historicized sense would be Michel Foucault's account of historical change. Foucault attempts to map historical *epistemes* (epochs of epistemic certainty) that are separate and distinct from one another.[62] In the pre-Enlightenment world the role of the individual was frequently subsumed into larger types (thus blurring the modern type-token distinction). Foucault cites the example of the Chartres Cathedral construction. In this episteme, Foucault contends that there is a submergence of the individual to the group effort. The case of Chartres seems to bear this out. As it is, we know nothing about the architect, or any key individual

---

[62] Michel Foucault, *Les Mots et les Choses* (Paris: Gallaimard, 1966). Leo Strauss also emphasized a change in direction with the advent of the Enlightenment (modern philosophy) but he couches his argument more on a fragmented worldview (from the more unified ancient and medieval worldviews) – *Natural Right and History* (Chicago: University of Chicago Press, 1953).

responsible for the project (save for the clerics who approved it). What counted was the work completed for *Gloria dei* and not some particular individual. The author is invisible.[63]

The medieval painting guilds constitute another example. What counted was the completed artifact. Who did what and how was secondary. The only modern counterpart, Foucault suggested, might be the newspaper in which people often move their eyes directly to the story as if there were no byline.[64] We look to the story as the artifact and do not inquire about the author.

As we saw in the last two subsections, this ideal (as set out in literature and philosophy of the period) was more consistent in the ancient European world and was beginning to decay in the medieval European world. Thus, I take Foucault's comments to be about an aspirational receding goal that was in the process of falling apart.

Others make similar claims from the perspective of historicized sociology and anthropology – such as Geoffrey Hawthorne and Louis Dumont.[65] The upshot of this line of analysis is that a plausible case can be made that there was a historical change away from the submergence of the individual (for the most part) to an exultation of the same. When the center of attention is the individual himself, then it is logically necessary that an accompanying examination of the proper attributes that should be attached to each person might also come under special scrutiny. One such attribute might be individual human rights. This is because it falls under what a person might plausibly claim for himself.

As we have seen earlier, Wesley Hohfeld has identified eight fundamental ways that an individual might claim a right or a liberty.[66] If the modern age (seventeenth to eighteenth centuries) also included a mixture of argument on what ought to be the case concerning natural human rights along with a move to practicality,[67] then these might

---

[63] Michel Foucault, "What Is an Author?" trans. Josué Harari, in *The Classical Tradition,* 3rd ed., ed. David H. Richter (Boston: Bedford/St. Martins, 2007): 904–914.

[64] Michel Foucault, "The Archeology of Knowledge," in *The Archeology of Knowledge and the Discourse on Language,* trans. A. M. Sheridan Smith (New York: Pantheon, 1972).

[65] Geoffrey Hawthorne, *Enlightenment and Despair* (Cambridge: Cambridge University Press, 1987), and Louis Dumont, *Essays on Individualism* (Chicago: University of Chicago Press, 1992).

[66] Wesley Hohfeld, *Fundamentals of Legal Conception* (New Haven, CT: Yale University Press, 1919): 35–64; cf. John Finnis, *Natural Law and Natural Rights* (Oxford: Clarendon Press, 1980): 199–205.

[67] Strauss, *Natural Right and History,* 174, 177; he's talking about the influence of Machiavelli here; cf. my encyclopedia article, "Niccolo Machiavelli" entry in *The Encyclopedia of Philosophy,* 2nd ed., ed. Donald M. Borchert (Farmington Hills, MI: Macmillan, 2006).

be characterized (though perhaps too simply) as attaching themselves to Locke and to Hobbes, respectively. The thought experiments about the state of nature conceive of a pre-social moment in which the individual has the full complement of natural rights. (Though it could also be conceived of as a post-social moment after society falls apart as per "The Wanderer" and "The Seafarer.") In either case, a posit concerning human nature is necessary. With a cooperative person, Locke's account is more plausible; with a competitive vision, Hobbes's seems best. The end result of both is that a state is formed from different motives. For Locke, the sovereign is the general populace exercising their collective individual rights while for Hobbes there are numerous simultaneous implicit individual contracts that cede power to the king in return for personal protection from unwarranted bodily harm.[68]

In either case, this marks a change from the theologically abstract worldview centered on natural law that characterized the ancient and medieval writings to one that is more concretely oriented and proximately concerns a collection of individuals and what they properly should be able to claim. The story is less about the nature of things as such (with people being subsumed as they can be) to one that begins with people as the primary focus.[69]

Spinoza also fits in here. Jonathan Israel quotes Spinoza as distancing himself from Hobbe's monarch and the forfeiting of certain natural rights when one joins the state: "When his friend Jelles enquired in 1674, what was the basic difference between his political philosophy and that of Hobbes, Spinoza answered that it 'consists in this that I always preserve the natural right in its entirety,[70] and hold that the sovereign power in a state has a right over a subject only in proportion to the excess of its power over the subject; this is always the case in the state of nature.' Thus in place of Hobbes's assigning a contracted overriding power to the sovereign, Spinoza leaves the citizen with his natural right intact."[71]

So to summarize this subsection so far, the focus on the individual in a fictional state of nature creates a cauldron whereupon the flavor that individual rights might acquire was concocted: either an *inalienable*

---

[68] Boylan, *A Just Society*, 128–129.

[69] James Griffin, *On Human Rights* (Oxford: Oxford University Press, 2008): 29–30, depicts this as the "bottom-up" as opposed to the "top-down" perspective; cf. to his situating of Samuel Pufendorf as influencing Locke, 11. Samuel Pufendorf, *On the Law of Nature and Nations,* trans. C. H. Oldfather (Oxford: Oxford University Press, 1934): 201.

[70] Baruch Spinoza, *Letters,* trans. Samuel Shirley (Indianapolis, IN: Hackett, 1995): 258.

[71] Jonathan I. Israel, *Radical Enlightenment* (New York: Oxford University Press, 2001): 259.

natural right that cannot be forfeited by any action of the agent *or* an *alienable* natural right that could be traded in commerce with the sovereign aspirant (backed up by the divine right of kings). In either event, this is different from the first subsection of this chapter because there is general agreement that the predication of R (rights) to x (any particular individual) – that is, Rx (x possesses R) – is justified either via God or via Reason. It does not originate from an agreement, but in the second case it can be traded away for the guarantee of peace and security. We might term these writers (Spinoza, Locke, Hobbes, and Pufendorf) as being in the first group of modern philosophy writers who describe a theory of natural human rights that focuses on individualism in its presentation.

Another way to examine natural rights in the Enlightenment is through an examination of another worldview change: the scientific revolution of the seventeenth century. The most significant change in the scientific revolution was an interest in seeing science (especially astronomy) mechanically on its own terms. This meant jettisoning the doctrine of *saving the phenomena* that characterized ancient and medieval astronomy.[72] Since the empirical charting of planets in the zodiac did not match the theory presented (geocentric universe), the alterations that had been used to square theory and observation often relied upon ad hoc assumptions that were outrageous. Retrograde motion and variant speeds were not consistent with the neo-Ptolemaic geocentric account. The ad hoc changes required to save the theory from aberrant observations were drastic. The epicycle and the equant point were just two additions needed to square the explanandum with the explanans.[73]

The reason for the extraordinary measures taken by these ad hoc additions to the standard neo-Euclidean account was to satisfy certain teleological metaphysical needs. If the earth were the center of the universe, then the uniqueness of the earth would be maintained. Having the earth as unique supports the received reading of the Genesis account of creation. In creation God gave the earth the central position in the

---

[72] Two articles that properly modify my rather sweeping claim are Bas van Fraasen, "To Save the Phenomena," *Journal of Philosophy* **73**.18 (1976): 623–632, and Hilary Putnam, "Explanation and Reference," in *Conceptual Change*, ed. G. Pearce and P. Maynard (Dordrecht: Reidel, 1973): 199–221. In both cases the authors argue that sometimes it is rational to add ad hoc hypotheses to an existing theory rather than to radically change things. If the existing theory is only slightly wrong, then a slight change might be the best move to make.

[73] A very good account of this in the light of worldview change has been made by Thomas S. Kuhn, *The Copernican Revolution* (Cambridge, MA: Harvard, 1957): 48, 57, 61.

whole universe (though Genesis never says this – it was the established interpretation of the wider sensibility). This position also gave central emphasis to the uniqueness of the sacrifice of Jesus of Nazareth on the cross. The single action on earth would be sufficient for the entire universe. (When in the latter part of the seventeenth century the heliocentric hypothesis was front and center among the intelligentsia, Henry More speculated that this might mean that there was more than one inhabited planet in the universe and that Jesus would have had to hop onto each one to be crucified in order to save that planet.)[74] The entire ability of the Bible to speak as a document of physical cosmology had to be maintained for its explanatory power to be at its strongest. Thus, the reason for employing the standard neo-Euclidean account was teleological. The end was squaring with the Bible and with its aforesaid role: purveyor of all truth (including science). The scientific revolution – particularly the heliocentric hypothesis – called all this into question. Powerful individuals had a vested interest in stopping it. But they failed to do so.

With the publication of *De revolutionibus orbium coelestium,* the cogency of the received account was called into question. The laws of nature were to be *discovered* and not *imposed upon* the phenomena.[75] When one spoke of *laws of nature* they were the rules that existed apart from humans that controlled the way the planets moved and later (with Newton) the way ordinary objects moved. Since the ancient Greeks, mathematics had been used to predict the motions and positioning of the planets and stars.[76] It is what caused the disconnect between *explanans* and *explanandum.* But ancient mathematics could not describe motion properly. Calculus was necessary for that. At the end of the day, ancient science was essentially qualitative and this allowed for it to be part of an overarching structure that teleologically subsumed physical science.[77] In the seventeenth century, the final cause was exchanged for the efficient cause. This process of *discovering* the laws of nature gave a different slant to natural laws and how they might relate to natural

---

[74] I cite More on this in Michael Boylan, "Henry More and the Spirit of Nature," *Journal of the History of Philosophy* **18**.4 (1980): 395–405.

[75] Nicolaus Copernicus, *De revolutionibus orbium coelestium* (Nurenberg: Johannes Petreius, 1543), bk. 1.

[76] Arpad Szabo, *The Beginnings of Greek Mathematics* (Dordrecht: D. Reidel, 1978), and Ian Mueller, *Philosophy of Mathematics and Deductive Structure in Euclid's Elements* (Cambridge, MA: MIT Press, 1981).

[77] Biomedical science was somewhat different: Michael Boylan, *Method and Practice in Aristotle's Biology* (Lanham, MD: UPA/Rowman and Littlefield, 1983).

human rights: natural human rights might also be subject to discovery in a similar way.[78]

The net result of the scientific revolution to human rights is to make the discussion more empirically concrete and separate from a teleological approach. Hume, for example, eschewed the contractarian basis for human rights (as being less empirically concrete) because the theory requires a level of consent that has never existed in Britain. Consequently, the "state of nature" thought experiment that includes the contractarian basis for human rights is empirically unproven. Since the empirically concrete method requires actual plausibility through historical records instead of philosophical speculation, Hume instead opted for a political philosophy (including implicit duties) that was buttressed upon the virtues of fidelity, allegiance, and justice.[79]

Kant also followed this trend. In the *Rechtslehre* he enhances his freedom formula from the *Grundlegung* to one of more explicit external freedom

---

[78] One account of this process was given by Daryn Lehoux, "Laws of Nature and Natural Laws," *Studies in History and the Philosophy of Science* **37** (2006): 527–549.

[79] This is Hume's argument from "Of the Original Contract," in *Social Contract*, ed. Ernest Barker (London: Oxford University Press, 1947): 147–166.

1. Assume that there was an original social contract – Assertion
2. A father does not bind his son by the father's promise – Assertion
3. More remote filial relations also do not bind the present population – 2
4. If there were an original contract, it was long ago – Fact
5. The original contract does not bind the present population – 1–4
6. Britain and Ancient Athens are the most extensive democracies in human history (as per the middle of the eighteenth century) – Assertion
7. There is little actual consent in either Britain or in Ancient Athens – Fact
8. [Locke bases his consent model upon democracies] – Assertion
9. There must be more than consent that legitimizes a government – 6–8
10. Consent theories also say that those who don't like a society can just leave it and by a person's staying he gives tacit consent to the rules of society (a social contract) – Assertion
11. Many (if not most) people in a society cannot (in a practical and realistic sense) leave a society if they don't like it – Assertion
12. The model of social contract based upon tacit consent is flawed and should be rejected – 10,11
13. Original contract theories and tacit consent contract theories are not adequate to legitimize a government – 5, 9, 12
14. Moral duties have two sources: (a) natural inclinations that carry no sense of obligation, e.g., a parent's love of his children, (b) moral duties divorced from natural inclination, e.g., fidelity, allegiance, and justice – Assertion
15. Without fidelity, allegiance, and justice a state cannot operate well – A
16. Duties as per 14-b are really the foundation of the state – 14, 15

---

17. Moral duties disconnected from natural inclination such as fidelity, allegiance, and justice ground the legitimate state, not a social contract – 13, 16

that, in turn, presents an argument for positive and negative duties that aspire to be scientifically based because they take in the post-Newtonian world as a standard by which to measure their achievement. For Kant this meant creating a quasi-mathematical model by which negative and positive duties might be characterized within a rubric of their being either logical or illogical (the ultimate justification for the two forms of the categorical imperative).[80] Any duty would be ascertained on the basis of its being logical or not given the background conditions that Kant provides. At the conceptual level at which it is presented in the *Grundlegung* the results follow rather mechanically. For application, *Die Metaphysik der Sitten* and *Metaphysischen Anfangsgründe der Rechtslehre* come back midway toward applying his generic standards to *types* of applications.

Thus, this second section of this treatment of human rights in the seventeenth and eighteenth centuries in Europe has been influenced by the scientific revolution and its transition from final to efficient causation. Intersubjective rigor based upon the epistemological standards of the evolving natural science (both through Humean mitigated skeptical empiricism and through Kant's transcendental synthesis of the rational and the empirical) rules the day. At this point, more than abstract conceptual argument is needed to establish the existence of duties and the rights that they imply.

Much of the intervening period, between the latter philosophers of the eighteenth century and the post–World War II world at which this chapter began, was concerned with distancing itself first from theism and then engaging a debate about realism itself. The understanding of human rights continued to vacillate from its being nonsense on stilts to its having some actual appeal. Part of this was tied up with the steady decolonization of the post–World War II era. But the status of these claims was confused as invocations of intuitionism in the face of the grim reality of the Holocaust overshadowed authors who wanted to use reason to construct either a conventional or realistic edifice to support human rights – natural or otherwise.

CONCLUSION

At the beginning of this chapter the question was posed concerning whether a historical exploration could help us decide which theory of human rights was plausible: the legal basis, the interest basis, or the agency

---

[80] My view on how the two forms of the categorical imperative work can be found in Boylan, *Basic Ethics,* 176–182.

basis. The good news is that it has. The bad news is that it has! Each of
the three theories and their historically necessary antecedents has been
shown to be plausible. The post–World War II era has certainly shifted
international understandings about human rights in a way that is largely
unprecedented (thus supporting the legal approach). The modern era
did make some dramatic changes regarding the status of the individual
and the recognition of the subjective approach to human rights (thus
supporting the interest-based approach). Finally, the ancient and medieval perspectives have robust theories of natural law and natural rights
(largely objectively understood) that support a universalist approach so
necessary to the agency-based approach. Though the plausibility of each
has been established, we still have more descriptive groundwork to go
through before looking at the justifications for each theory.

I have chosen to focus on one paradigm case of China. This is both
because China is often brought forth as an exception to Western ideas
about human rights and because almost one out of every five people on
earth lives there. For a brief view of some of these concerns from the historical cultures of China, turn the page. Our brief history will soon come
to a conclusion.

3

A Short History of Human Rights in China

It happens with some regularity. There is a newspaper report about a dissident who is arrested for questioning a public policy of the People's Republic of China (PRC). The incidents do not always turn out the same way. For example, there is the case of Hu Jia, a human rights and AIDS activist who also criticized China's hosting of the 2008 summer Olympics. Hu was arrested on April 3, 2008, and released June 26, 2011. While he was in jail his wife (another human rights activist) and daughter were held under house arrest. They disappeared the day before the opening ceremonies for the Olympics.[1]

There is also the case of Liu Xiaobo who was arrested in June 2009 for inciting subversion of state power because of his participation in the *Charter 08* manifesto on human rights: freedom of expression, democratic elections, and private enterprise (that was meant to coincide with the sixtieth anniversary of the United Nation's Universal Declaration of Human Rights). He was found guilty and sentenced to eleven years in prison. This was his fourth incarceration. On October 8, 2010, Liu was awarded the Nobel Peace Prize, an honor he was personally not allowed to accept.

Another story with a different ending concerns Chen Guangcheng, a blind activist who protested China's policies on family planning including forced sterilizations and forced abortions. Chen's activities were largely in rural China, but he still drew the attention of the authorities and was put into prison with a four-year sentence in 2006. After his release in 2010 he was placed under house arrest until his dramatic escape on April 22, 2012. His journey to the U.S. Embassy in Beijing, then to a hospital to

---

[1] August 9, 2008, *USA TODAY,* http://www.usatoday.com/news/world/2008-08-09-china-human-rights_N.htm?csp=34 (accessed May 29, 2012). Some unconfirmed reports say that mother and daughter have now been released.

protect his wife and children made world headlines. The event was on the eve of Secretary of State Hillary Clinton's visit to the country for high-level meetings. Chen was allowed to leave the country with his family on a temporary student visa to study at New York University. This seems like a potential happy ending, but it may not work out that way.[2]

Then there was the case of Internet spying in China. Using data-mining techniques, officials identified key words and questioned suspects. Words such as "Tiananmen Square" in your e-mail could cost you a visit by the security police.[3] It could also cost the individual a term in jail.

Cases such as these have caused Western NGOs such as Human Rights Watch and Amnesty International to advocate that the United Nations in concert with Western powers put pressure upon China to reform their human rights policies, for example, on PRC forces in Tibet 2008–2010.[4]

But this is not the end of the story. China (and some international scholars) asserts that such demands amount to cultural imperialism. China asserts that it has its own historical cultural tradition and it has developed a different sensibility regarding human rights. The West should respect this.

This debate affects the basic theme of this book: the existence and application of universal natural human rights. If the legalists are correct, then they will assert that the historical development of Chinese understanding of and operationalizing of human rights principles are the result of negotiated treaties that may be connected to trends in international trade: like globalization.

If the interest advocates are correct, then they will point to Chinese tradition, which sets out a similar concept of rights, as a human interest that exists among other interests.

Finally, if the agency advocates (such as this author) are correct, then there will have to be a demonstrated tradition that supports a connection between morality, worldview, and any conception of human rights (or stand-ins like natural law).

---

[2] As I am writing this section, Chen's nephew was arrested on charges (related to Chen's activity) that could result in the death penalty. This would create a sad double ending. Michael Ireland, "Chen Guangcheng's Nephew Could Face Death Penalty," *ASSIST News Service*, 24 May, 2012, http://www.assistnews.net/Stories/2012/s12050097.htm (accessed May 25, 2012). Also, David Batty, "Chen Guangcheng's Brother Goes Missing after Fleeing to Beijing," The Guardian Online, May 26, 2012, http://www.guardian.co.uk/world/2012/may/26/chen-guangcheng-brother-missing?newsfeed=true (accessed May 27, 2012).

[3] See http://www.hrw.org/reports/2006/china0806/3.htm (accessed May 25, 2012).

[4] *I Saw It with My Own Eyes: Abuses by Chinese Security Forces in Tibet, 2008–2010* (New York: Human Rights Watch, 2010).

To explore this question further we must return to a brief survey of various philosophical and literary expressions on these topics.

3.1 THE CLASSICAL PERIOD: SUN TZU, CONFUCIUS, AND MENCIUS

When we look briefly at the Classical Period in China we do so with a laser beam toward certain virtues and worldview tenets that will help us ascertain a sort of starting point in our quest to sketch a quick portrait of traditional values and understandings about the world. It will be apparent that the model of virtue ethics supplemented by communitarianism will be important in this exhibition. Such a combination can connect Aristotle to Confucius. My intent here is similar to the one in Chapter 2: to indulge in very broad overviews based upon very select passages.

3.1.1 Sun Tzu (Sunzi)

The first author we examine in the Classical Period is Sun Tzu. In his text, *The Art of War,* Sun Tzu constructs more than a manual of warfare.[5] Rather, what is primary is that he is setting out a normative worldview within a competitive environment. Here are seven famous quotations from the book.[6]

1. "The supreme art of war is to subdue the enemy without fighting."
2. "Supreme excellence consists of breaking the enemy's resistance without fighting."
3. "A leader leads by example, not by force."
4. "Keep your friends close, and your enemies closer."
5. "If your enemy is secure at all points, be prepared for him. If he is in superior strength, evade him. If your opponent is temperamental, seek to irritate him. Pretend to be weak, that he may grow arrogant. If he is taking his ease, give him no rest. If his forces are united, separate them. If sovereign and subject are in accord, put division between them. Attack him where he is unprepared, appear where you are not expected."

---

[5] Though the explicit content of the book is about how to be successful in warfare, the book has been more often explored metaphorically as a guide to virtue in a competitive environment.

[6] Sunzi (Sun Tzu), *The Art of War,* ed. John Minford (New York: Viking, 2002). Following are the citations for each section: #1, #2, and #4 are in Chapter 3, "Strategic Offensive"; #3 is in Chapter 9, "On the March"; #5 and #7 are in Chapter 1, "Making of Plans; #6 is in Chapter 6, "Empty and Full."

6. "Be extremely subtle even to the point of formlessness. Be extremely mysterious even to the point of soundlessness. Thereby you can be the director of the opponent's fate."

7. "When one treats people with benevolence, justice, and righteousness, and reposes confidence in them, the army will be united in mind and all will be happy to serve their leaders."

Quotation #1 is about striving for an end without striving (or appearing to strive – *wu wei*). This is an important part of the classical Chinese worldview. It has to do with staying within oneself and not overreaching. One seeks one's ends within a larger context that breeds restraint and balance.

However, this does not mean that one forgoes his goals (#2). The goals of purposive action are still there, but the best strategy for success is not necessarily bold externalist action that all can see and confront. Rather one must find ways of subterfuge to indirectly gain the day. To add onto quotation #2 one might say that it is even more perfect to defeat one's enemy without a battle and without the enemy aware that he has been defeated!

Quotation #3 is about exemplars. One way of teaching others is through one's own actions. When one is in a position of authority (here the general, but the point transfers to the state and the family), he should demonstrate virtue and humanity (*ren*) in his actions. This is a duty of leaders. It is their source of power over others for the general good.

In Quotation #4, the theme of subterfuge emerges again. One cannot act effectively for the common good without adequate information. By keeping one's enemies close, one can surreptitiously gather strategic data that can aid one in out-maneuvering one's foe (either on the battlefield or in life). If one is successful in garnering such information and using it effectively to one's own advantage, then the leader can defeat his opponent without a fight.

Quotation #5 describes a reactive strategy. The main idea is to use the momentum of your opponent against himself. Such an approach will require self-control to wait and assess the enemy. How does he present himself to the world? How can you use that presentation against him? Behind this dictum is the notion that our strengths are also our weaknesses. Once the man of authority assesses the character or behavior of his opponent, then that expression of character will be provoked to its extreme. At the mean, the trait may be effective, but taken to the extreme it will be a weakness. Once again, you allow the opponent to defeat himself (given a certain manipulation of the environment).

Inscrutability is the essence of quotation #6. If information about a competitor is essential to his efficient demise, then why would one want to supply information about oneself? The less the opponent knows about you, the more he will have to *guess* rather than *know*. This state of affairs puts the general in a better situation: he knows detailed information about the opposing general, but the reverse is not the case. Supposing that when one *knows* x he has better information than one who *opines* about x, and if information is the key to efficient success, then q.e.d. one should strive to be inscrutable.

In the last quotation, the moral character of the leader is set out. This reveals a very interesting dynamic. Not only is the general/leader an emblem for his army/people as a means of education, but also his character represents the group. Since a group is rather an amorphous concept because it is a heterogeneous collection, the best way to predicate attributes to the group is by reference to the general/leader. This becomes a shorthand way of discussing the group. Such and such army has an attribute – such as disciplined and hardworking – because their general possesses these traits. Part of the identity of the group comes from its leader. Thus we are the army of Sun Tzu (since he is the general). In the same way one can say that we are the industrious people of Emperor X (because Emperor X is known to be industrious). The character of the leader is important when one assumes both (a) a communitarian perspective, and (b) a causal connection between leadership and the community (in modern Western jargon – a transformational leader).

There are certainly more pithy aphorisms that are embedded in *The Art of War*, but these seven set out some aspects of normative worldview from the sixth century BCE that resonate throughout the Classical Period.

3.1.2 Confucius

Most of the secondary literature on the classical roots for Chinese explorations of human rights has focused upon Confucius and *The Analects*. Like *The Art of War*, the presentational style of *The Analects* (circa 500 BCE) is one of short, pithy instances of wisdom. It falls under the global genre of aphorisms or wisdom literature. Confucius wrote in a time roughly contemporaneous to that of Sun Tzu so that their views can be compared and contrasted without multi-century disparities.

One way into thinking about what Confucius is presenting in *The Analects* is a theory of virtue ethics that can be compared to Aristotle's *Nicomachean Ethics* and *The Politics*. As we briefly set out in Chapter 2, Aristotle's virtue ethics theory is compatible with natural law theory (a theory akin to natural rights). Without this connection to natural law, one would have to categorize Aristotle as a moral relativist. Since Aristotle is decidedly *not* a relativist regarding the rest of human knowledge, and since he believes that his ethical maxims represent the best of common opinion (*endoxa*), it would be peculiar to take him to be a moral relativist.

Thus, if Confucius is taken to be engaged in the same sort of project as Aristotle (a virtue ethics in which virtue is connected to action that flows from the character of a good man who has acquired good habits nurtured by his parents and his government) and if Aristotle's account is consistent with a natural law account, then so is the account of Confucius.

If we extend this reasoning somewhat to express the status of the responsibility for the acquisition of these character virtues as *duties* and that these imply first-order moral rights, then virtue ethics connects to a theory of ethically based first-order rights.[7]

One of the criticisms against virtue ethics as an ethical theory has been that it does not tell you *what to do*.[8] Deontological theories and utilitarian theories uniquely do this on a universal scope. Virtue ethics concentrates upon individual character that leads to choice that flows from that character.

In the case of Confucius, the context of this choice involves harmony (*he*) and filial sensibility (*xiao*) which leads to humanity or humanness (*ren*). Youzi (Confucius's student) puts it:

> It is a rare thing for someone who has a sense of filial and fraternal responsibility to have a taste for defying authority. And it is unheard of for those who have no taste for defying authority to be keen on initiating rebellion. Exemplary persons concentrate their efforts on the root, for the root having taken hold, the way (*dao*), will grow therefrom ... filial and fraternal responsibility ... is the root of humanness (*ren*). (*Analects* 1.2)[9]

---

[7] This is the argument of May Sim, "Rethinking Virtue Ethics and Social Justice with Aristotle and Confucius," *Asian Philosophy* **20**.2 (2010): 195–213.

[8] Maurice Cranston, "Human Rights, Real and Supposed," in *The Philosophy of Human Rights,* ed. Morton E. Winston (Belmont, CA: Wadsworth, 1989): 128.

[9] These are the words of Youzi (Confucius's student): Sim, "Rethinking Virtue Ethics," 198–199.

Initiating rebellion is to go against harmony (*he*). Harmony, by its very definition, includes a group dynamic: acting in concert. There cannot be a harmony of one! Thus, if harmony is a central concept, then a communal understanding is assumed as primary. If harmony is one of the virtues, then one will not achieve *ren* via disharmony (including the putting forth of oneself against the established moral order). The way to harmony is to observe ritual propriety (*li*). One seeks to find harmony within the established order. This requirement is intended to modify one's personal inclinations when they come into conflict with community standards. For ease in discussion, let us call this *communitarianism*.

Though there are other virtues such as courage (*yong*), wisdom (*zhi*), appropriateness in action (*yi*), and truthfulness (*xin*), et al., *li* is a second-order command that sets out the prescription for personal and shared community worldview. This extends even beyond the rituals of common life to a metaphorical expression in music (*yue* –musical harmony).

In this way Confucius, like Aristotle, adopts a sensibility that identifies various traits of character (that are honored by the community) as the basis of being a moral agent. And like Plato, Confucius views the small relations as proportional to large relations – writ large: individual subordinated to family :: family to state/ therefore individual is subordinated to the state (see also Chapter 2).

It is the community that is primary. But how is this to be understood? Some assert a particular political dimension to *ren* that is supported by Shirong Luo.[10] The question to be addressed here is whether *ren* is a particular virtue – one that primarily applies to rulers (or to people aspiring to be rulers) or whether *ren* is a general virtue. Those who represent the first camp are like D. C. Lau who habitually translates *ren* as 'benevolence' (understood in situational contexts) and Shirong Luo who emphasizes the connection to *li* (ritual practice) in relation to its instrumentality to being a good political person (anyone who is in or aspires to be in the policy-making part of the government).[11]

Those who represent the second camp like Arthur Waley represent *ren* as 'goodness.' He contends that *ren* "in the *Analects* means 'good' in an extremely wide and general sense."[12] Roger Ames and Henry Rosemont Jr. say that "*ren* is one's entire person: One's cultivated cognitive, aesthetic, moral and religious sensibilities as they are expressed in one's ritualized

[10] Shirong Luo, "The Political Dimension of Confucius' Idea of Ren," *Philosophy Compass* 7.4 (2012): 245–255.

[11] Confucius, *The Analects,* trans. D. C. Lau (New York: Penguin Books, 1979).

[12] Confucius, *The Analects,* trans. Arthur Waley (New York: Everyman's Library, 2000): 22.

roles and relationships."[13] I am persuaded by the generalists, therefore; I am inclined to support their position. The generalists – particularly Ames and Rosemont – overlap with my own work on normative worldview and will thus provide a bridge between ethical theories East and West.[14] (It should be noted that there are others who move in both camps such as Wing-tsit Chan who reads *ren* this way: "As a general virtue, *jen* [*ren*] means humanity, that is, that which makes a man a moral being. As a particular virtue it means love.")[15] In this way, it is both a general virtue that is instrumental to being human and a particular virtue: love.

Let's look at the supporting text for this (*The Analects* 12.22):

> Fan Ch'ih asked about benevolence. Confucius said, "Love your fellow men."
>
> Fan Ch'ih asked about knowledge. Confucius said, "Know your fellow men." Fan Ch'ih did not comprehend. Confucius said, "Elevate the honest above the wrong doers, and the wrong doers can be made honest."
>
> Fan Ch'ih retired. He went to see Tzu Hsia and said, "A while ago, I asked the Master about knowledge and he said, 'Elevate the honest above the wrong doers, and the wrong doers can be made honest.' What did he mean?"
>
> Tzu Hsia said, "His words are rich in meaning. When Shun had all under heaven, from many he elected to elevate Kao T'ao and so those who were not benevolent were kept afar. When T'ang had all under heaven, from many he elected to elevate Yi Yin and so those who were not benevolent were kept afar."[16]

Under the generalist reading of *ren* it can mean some particular general disposition – such as abstract benevolence or humanity. It can also be a stand-in for particular instantiations of the same. What makes this passage interesting to me is its insistence that the community (state) needs to enforce the rules of morality for them to have social consequence. By elevating those who show *benevolence* through love and *knowledge* via justice, the moral character of the community is maintained and all who live in the community will prosper. However when we translate this into rights language (as per Chapter 1) it is a little unclear. First, who is the owner of the right and who is the duty holder? One could make a case

---

[13] Confucius, *The Analects,* trans. Roger T. Ames and Henry Rosemont Jr. (New York: Ballantine Books, 1998): 49.

[14] Michael Boylan, *A Just Society* (Lanham, MD: Rowman and Littlefield, 2004); Michael Boylan, *Morality and Global Justice* (Boulder, CO: Westview, 2011).

[15] Wing-tsit Chan, ed. and trans., *A Source Book in Chinese Philosophy* (Princeton, NJ: Princeton University Press, 1963): 40; cf. also to Sim, "Rethinking Virtue Ethics."

[16] Confucius, *The Analects,* trans. William Cheung (Hong Kong: Confucian Publishing, 1999): 12.22.

that it was the law-abiding individual against the community or that it is the community against the law-breaking individual. The text can support either reading equally. Since the legal stand-in for the community is the ruler (and those who work for him in the government), this passage could certainly take on a political dimension.

There are some other key passages along the same line:

Fan Ch'ih asked about benevolence. Confucius said, "At home, be courteous. At work, respectful. In dealing with people, be loyal. Such must not be abandoned, even when among the Yi and Ti [small units of measurement]. [13: 19]

Tsu Chang asked Confucius about benevolence. Confucius said, "The ability to enact the five everywhere under heaven is benevolence." Asked to elaborate, Confucius said, "Courtesy, tolerance, trustworthiness, quickness, and generosity. With courtesy there is no mockery. With tolerance there is support from the people. With quickness there is merit. With generosity people can be employed willingly." [17: 6]

Yen Yuen asked about benevolence. Confucius said, "To discipline self to fulfill the rites is benevolence. The day when self-discipline fulfills the rites, all under heaven would be with benevolence. Indeed, the practices of benevolence originate from self and not from others!" Yen Yuen said, "May I ask for more details?" Confucius said, "Do not look at what is not in accordance with these rites; do not listen to what is not in accordance with the rites; do not speak when it is not in accordance with the rites; do not act when it is not accordance with the rites." Yen Yuen said, "[I], though not quick, will attempt to do things accordance with these words." [12: 1]

Each of these three passages gives different understanding of benevolence (*ren*). They contrast with the 12:22 passage in that there is a political slant in 12:22 that is only picked up in 17:6 a bit in the last line: *people can be employed willingly*. However, Mencius pointed to 12:22 and the *ai ren* reference – to love others, and Mencius seems to think that among these passages it is the most authoritative. If Mencius is correct, then it would give support to the more general understanding of *ren* (which I support). Using 'love' (an emotive term with broad implications) would be a major step in being able to connect Western and Eastern wisdom literature. However, there are detractors to this move – such as Shirong Luo who contends that the context demands an understanding of the subject and objects of 'love.' Shirong Luo points to the fact that in the 13:19 passage there are several specific virtues mentioned instead of the general reference to 'love.' I am not put off by this. Just because there is a general term that can cover all the virtues (call it love) does not disqualify there being specific instantiations of the same. The Western philosopher/theologian Saint Augustine of Hippo made the same move when he declared, "Love and do what you will."[17] One can assert a universal statement about a general trait and, at the same time, believe that in differing contexts *love* will require you to exhibit particular virtues – such as ritual propriety (*li*), appropriate conduct (*yi*), and promise keeping (*xin*). Indeed, I will take *ren* to be a general virtue that is akin to a general understanding of *humanness* or even as *goodness*.[18]

What I take the input of *The Analects* to be is that we have a text that espouses a version of virtue ethics that seems roughly consistent with Aristotle's *Nicomachean Ethics* – especially if we grant that *ren* is understood to be a general trait (much like Aristotle's *arête* – dispositionally understood) and not a particularized single trait that is only designed to make one a good ruler. It is at least plausible that it applies to all humanity encompassing many other particular virtues. If this is correct, then Confucius is espousing an ethics that involves duties that apply to all based upon a realistic, natural ontology.

3.1.3 Mencius

Mencius wrote in the fourth century BCE. He was a defender of Confucius against movements that sought to usurp the sage (e.g., Mozi and Yang Zhu). Mencius also presents a virtue ethics program (like Confucius). The four principal virtues are *ren* (humanness/ benevolence), *li* (ritual observance), *yi* (propriety), and *zhi* (wisdom). Mencius has a positive view of human nature and includes a use of *ren* as affective concern.

I would like to highlight three passages that will advance our exploration of the human rights tradition in China. The first selection comes in an interchange between Kao Tzu and Mencius.

> Kao Tzu said, "Human nature is like the *ch'i* willow. Dutifulness is like cups and bowls. To make morality out of human nature is like making cups and bowls out of the willow."
>
> "Can you," said Mencius, "make cups and bowls by following the nature of the willow? Or must you mutilate the willow before you can make it into cups and bowls? If you have to mutilate the willow to make it into cups and bowls, must you, then, also mutilate a man to make him moral? Surely it will be these words of yours men in the world will follow in bringing disaster upon morality."[19]

---

[17] Saint Augustine of Hippo, in Jacques Paul Migne, ed., *Patrologia Latina* (Paris: Garnieri Fratres,1844–1855): vol. 35, 2033.
[18] Confucius, *The Analects*, trans. Edward Slingerland (Indianapolis, IN: Hackett, 2003): 202.
[19] D. C. Lau, *Mencius* (Harmondsworth, UK: Penguin, 1970): Book 6, A:1.

The two positions at stake are: (a) whether man is so depraved as to be a willow that has no intrinsic strength (in contrast to the cup and bowl, which by their functional design must be stiff and strong), or (b) whether man intrinsically is good and to see him otherwise is to mischaracterize and mistreat him. Mencius is on the latter side.

For our exploration of human rights, this distinction is important. In my 2004 book *A Just Society*, I open the book with this first sentence, "All people by nature desire to be good." I bring this same sensibility into this project. Mencius and I are on the same side here.

Inasmuch as Mencius has been a significant influence upon Chinese historical personal and community worldview, this creates a common starting point that will be important in the eventual theory that is generated.

Another interesting point to note is the use of natural metaphors in making the point of what a human is. The elevation of 'nature' here in this historical context provides some connection to the Western tradition's use of the same term. In the West, *nature* became ambiguous in its ontological status in the seventeenth century. It could be a nature that just happens-to-be on a case-by-case basis. In that instance, one might expect that a sort of ethical relativism would hold sway. However, if there were some common cause that undergirds nature (even as machine-like), then relativism would be out of the question. To better understand the point, let's turn our vision to natural laws – such as the modern laws of physics. Is it the case that $E = mc^2$ or $F = ma$ are only applicable in Europe (where they were set down)? Most of us would say, "No." The reason for this is that the source for these laws is set outside ourselves. We *discover* these truths. This is what naturalistic realism is all about as an ontological claim (see Chapter 7).

A text that can lend some light on Mencius' views on this comes from 4A: 7:

> In good years the young men are mostly lazy, while in bad years they are mostly violent. Heaven (*tian*) has not sent down men whose endowment differs so greatly. The difference is due to what ensnares their hearts.

Denis Hsin-an Tsai takes passages like this to indicate that the invocation of Heaven (*tian*) is an indicator of a universalism in Mencius's thought that is built upon Confucian virtues.[20] This is similar to the tack taken by the Ancient Greeks, Stoics, and medieval Christian philosophers: if

---

[20] Denis Hsin-an Tsai, "On Mencius' Choice," *Philosophical Review* (Taiwan) **10** (1987): 137–175. This thesis is also countered by James Behuniak Jr., "Naturalizing Mencius," *Philosophy East and West* **61**.3 (2011): 492–515.

the source of virtue is Divine, and if the Divine is omniscient and the Creator, then a natural realism follows, q.e.d.

This source applies to the cardinal virtue: *ren*. In 4A:11 Mencius says:

> Benevolence (*ren*) is the heart of man, and rightness his road. Sad it is indeed when a man gives up the right road instead of following it and allows his heart to stray without enough sense to go after it. When his chickens and dogs stray, he has sense enough to go after them, but not when his heart strays. The sole concern of learning is to go after the strayed heart. That's all.

This passage (and others like it) seems to create an 'idealism versus realism context.' The ideal person follows his heart (which is inclined to good behavior) – others do not. The prescription is to follow what is imprinted on all people's hearts: to cultivate (through ritual behavior) and express their humanity through what is already within them (and, by extension, within all people throughout the world).[21] Since we do not live in a perfect world, it would be rather utopian to leave it at that. Every day we see people doing bad things. The causal account for this is that the so-called Mencius doctrine of *extending affection*[22] (*tui en*) is presented within a context that allows for a remedial doctrine that will bring people back if their own lives have gone astray. This happens by another person extending his natural goodness to those in need or in the case of 4A:11, by using one's mind as stimulated by study of the sages – particularly Confucius – to bring oneself back to his natural state. A positive duty is raised to extend goodwill (rationally and affectively)[23] to others in need. However, the form of the positive duty is not explored. Two situations might obtain: (a) the positive duty is to do *charity* to others who have no *right claim* against the Good Samaritan; or (b) the positive duty is attached to a *right claim* that can be attributed to the person in need. The latter would be most beneficial to the case that I would like to construct, but unfortunately the text is silent on this matter.

But one crucial question, given the exhortation of natural goodness and its ontological grounding in heaven, is the authority of the Confucian

---

[21] The balance between realism and affective acceptance is set out in the context of just war theory by Kim Sungmoon, "Mencius in International Relations and the Morality of War," *History of Political Thought* **31**.1 (2010): 133–156. This is just one more instance in which Mencius can be seen to support a universalist theory of justice – in this case, just war theory.

[22] This doctrine is discussed by Qingping Liu, "Is Mencius' Doctrine of 'Extending Affection' Tenable?" *Asian Philosophy* **14**.1 (2004): 79–90.

[23] I discuss these two senses of the goodwill in Boylan, *A Just Society*, 34–43.

virtues. Are they relative to whatever political regime happens to be in power? The answer comes at 4A:16.

> Mencius said, "There are honors bestowed by Heaven, and there are honors bestowed by man. Benevolence, dutifulness, conscientiousness, truthfulness to one's word, unflagging delight in what is good – these are honors bestowed by Heaven. The position of a Ducal Minister, a Minister, or a Counselor is an honor bestowed by man.... Men of today bend their efforts towards acquiring honors bestowed by Heaven in order to win honors bestowed by man and once the latter is won they discard the former. Such men are deluded to the extreme, and in the end are sure only to perish."

The relative virtues belong to the realm constructed by humans. These man-made honors that are cherished by many truly have no *real* (Heavenly) value. They are, instead, purely conventional. Only the heavenly virtues have real, absolute worth. If one were to make the further extension that Cicero does, then we would say that Heavenly generated virtues and duties trump those created by man, conventionally. This establishes an ontology in which realistically based virtues and duties trump conventionally generated virtues and duties.[24] If these readings are correct, then Mencius can also be brought on board as supporting universal moral principles based upon a realistic, naturalistic ontology.

These universal moral principles apply equally to those in power as well as the common man. Mencius discusses the case of a man who is not given his proper share of the realm's resources because the ruler has hoarded it all for himself.

> To speak ill of those in authority because one is not given a share in such enjoyment is, of course, wrong. But for one in authority over the people not to share his enjoyment [gross revenues] with the people is equally wrong.[25]

Since the origins of moral law are separate from any individual (because they come from Heaven), they apply to all – even the ruler. Such depictions from these classical Chinese authors are reminiscent of those the Stoics set out in Chapter 2 as they grounded political rulemaking in natural law within a community context. Confucius and Mencius are engaged in a very similar project.

---

[24] This connection of Mencius to universal principles is supported by Philip Ho Hwang, "An Examination of Mencius' Theory of Human Nature with reference to Kant," *Kant-Studien: Philosophische Zeitschrift der Kant-Gesellschaft* **74** (1983): 343–354.

[25] *Mencius*, trans. D. C. Lau (New York: Penguin, 2005): B:4; cf. 5B:9 in which it is mentioned that a bad ruler cannot be removed by the people but only by ministers with royal blood. This would disallow revolution – including Mao Zedong's revolution.

3.1.4 Literature from the Classical Period

As we did in Chapter 2, another way to understand the shared community worldview concerning the market basket of concepts related to human rights (many of which were set out in Chapter 1) is to look at literature contemporary to the philosophers in question. For example, in the Classical Period, one example of the predisposition to a collective sensibility over the individual can be found in Sima Qian's story about the first emperor of the Qin dynasty (221–206 BCE). This emperor had many great accomplishments: he built the Great Wall of China, unified China, commissioned an army of life-sized terra cotta soldiers, and other deeds. But he shunned the collective advice of others – preferring to go it alone. He was given to vanity, seeing himself as exceptional and preeminent in history. This was a reason for his individualism. This individualism caused him to shun advice that might have saved him from committing various errors – such as the slaughter of 460 scholars both as a warning of his power and as a sign that he did not need the advice of even the most learned. He also ordered the burning of all books that were produced outside of the state of Qin (thus moving away from a collective Chinese understanding to one that favored the single Qin province).

> The First Emperor was greedy and short-sighted, confident in his own wisdom, never trusting his meritorious officials, never getting to know his people. He cast aside the kingly Way and relied on private procedures, outlawing books and writings, making the laws and penalties much harsher, putting deceit and force foremost and humanity and righteousness last, leading the whole world in violence and cruelty. In annexing the lands of others, one may place priority on deceit and force, but insuring peace and stability in the lands one has annexed calls for a respect for authority. Hence I say that seizing, and guarding what you have seized, do not depend upon the same techniques.
>
> Qin put an end to the Warring States period and made itself ruler of the empire, but it did not change its ways or reform its system of government, which shows that the means employed to seize an empire differ from those needed to guard it. Qin tried to guard it alone and single-handed, and therefore its downfall was merely a matter of time.[26]

The normative language used in the passage is meant to show critical judgment against the First Emperor because he displayed negative traits: he was greedy, short-sighted, confident in his own wisdom against the

---

[26] Sima Qian, *Records of the Grand Historian: Quin Dynasty*, trans. Burton Watson (Hong Kong: Research Center for Translation, Chinese University of Hong Kong, and Columbia University Press, 1993).

wisdom of his counselors and the people (i.e., he adopted hard individualism). This hard individualism caused him to commit crimes against the people. He may have been a successful warrior, but he was not successful in peace: his individualism led to his downfall.

Another popular ancient text is from *The Book of Songs* (1027–771 BCE).

> Ye locusts, winged tribes,
> How harmoniously you collect together !
> Right is it that your descendants
> Should be multitudinous!
> Ye locusts, winged tribes,
> How sound your wings in flight!
> Right is it that your descendants
> Should be as in unbroken strings!
> Ye locusts, winged tribes,
> How you cluster together!
> Right is it that your descendants
> Should be in swarms!
>
> The peach tree is young and elegant;
> Brilliant are its flowers.
> This young lady is going to her future home,
> And will order well her chamber and house.
> The peach tree is young and elegant;
> Abundant will be its fruits.
> This young lady is going to her future home,
> And will order well her chamber and house
> The peach tree is young and elegant;
> Luxuriant are its leaves.
> This young lady is going to her future home,
> And will order well her family.[27]

This poem also deals with the shared community worldview. By focusing upon locusts, the poet links the community worldview to the natural worldview. This suggests that the community approach is really true. It applies throughout nature. By metaphorical extension, it must also apply to humans. It is important to view how the action of the community is depicted. "Harmony" of the wings in flight as an auditory sensation indicates the Confucian virtue of harmony. If the activity of the locusts were not natural, then one might expect cacophony. But this is not the case. A pleasing harmony results – showing that communal effort in concert is good (and because it is *natural*, it is also true).

[27] From *Zhong hua xue yi she*, in *The Chinese Classics*, 4 vols. (London: Trübner, 1875–1876); available online in Chinese and English from the University of Virginia at http://etext. lib.virginia.edu/chinese/ (accessed on June 1, 2012).

In the second stanza, floral phenomena are directly linked to human virtue. The elegance and beauty of the peach tree flowers arrest a young lady. Interaction with beauty is a good per se. But the flowers of a peach tree promise of fruit to come – as the young lady is also thinking of her own future home. A beautiful flower (here understood as the person of virtue) will bring forth good peaches (here understood as a well-ordered family). To be well ordered is to be "naturally ordered." Again, since nature is assumed to be realistically true and divulging truths to be discovered, one's proper interaction with and assessment of nature is pivotal in her path to virtue (universally sanctioned). These texts connect to my depiction of the shared community worldview imperative (Chapter 6) and can be used in a universalist, natural theory of human rights.

3.2 NEO-CONFUCIANISM (POST-CLASSICAL PERIOD)

The post-Classical neo-Confucian period in China can range greatly. Some scholars put the range into five periods: (a) The Five Masters of the Northern Sung Dynasty (960–1127); (b) Chu Hsi [Zhu Xi], (1130–1200); (c) Wang Yang-Ming [Wang Shou-Jen] (1472–1529) through the end of the Ming Dynasty (1368–1644); (d) Tai Chen (1723–1777); and (e) Advocates of Chu's and Wang's thought in the twentieth century in Fung Yu-lan (1895–1990) and Hsiung Shih-li (1895–1968).[28]

Stephen C. Angle[29] sets out two eras of neo-Confucians: Early (Song Dynasty, 960–1279, and Yuan Dynasty, 1279–1368) and Later (Ming dynasty, 1368–1644, and Qing dynasty, 1644–1911). In any event, the point is this long period of time is characterized by those supporting the positions and worldview of Confucius and Mencius against rival worldviews of Daoism and Buddhism (see the next subsection). For simplicity, let us concentrate on two thinkers: one from the earlier period and one from the later – Chu Hsi [Zhu Xi] (1130–1200) and Wang Yang-Ming [Wang Shou-Jen] (1472–1529). We briefly examine each in order.

[28] Carsun Chang, *The Development of Neo-Confucian Thought*, 2 vols. (New Haven, CT: College and University Press, 1963); William Theodore de Bary and Irene Bloom, eds., *Principle and Practicality: Essays in Neo-Confucian Practicality* (New York: Columbia University Press, 1979); William Theodore de Bary, *Neo Confucian Orthodoxy and the Learning of the Mind-and-Heart* (New York: Columbia University Press, 1981); William Theodore de Bary, *The Message of the Mind in Neo-Confucianism* (New York: Columbia University Press, 1989); and William Theodore de Bary, *Learning for One's Self: Essays on the Individual in Neo-Confucian Thought* (New York: Columbia University Press, 1991).

[29] Stephen C. Angle and Marina Svensson, *The Chinese Human Rights Reader* (London: M. E. Sharpe, 2000): xvii; cf. Stephen C. Angle, *Sagehood: The Contemporary Significance of Neo-Confucian Philosophy* (Oxford: Oxford University Press, 2012).

Chu Hsi (Zhu Xi) is a pivotal figure. His interpretation and defense of Confucius and Mencius (against the inroads of Daoism and Buddhism) is reminiscent of Thomas's work defending Aristotle and the early Church Fathers. In his work *A Treatise on Jen* [*Ren*][30] he says:

> If we can truly practice love and preserve it, then we have in it the spring of all virtues and the root of all good deeds. This is why in the unceasing effort in the pursuit of *jen*. In the teachings (of Confucius, it is said), "Master oneself and return to propriety." This means that if we can overcome and eliminate selfishness and return to the Principle of Nature (*T'ien-li*, Principle of Heaven), then the substance of this mind (that is *jen*) will be present everywhere and its function will always be operative. (*A Treatise on Jen*, I)

As in Confucius, the principle of nature and heaven stand as a realistic standard upon which one's cultivation of *jen* [*ren*] is constructed. If one goes into another direction, then one will turn to egoism, the default position of people who accept no moral values. A worldview that is focused upon the self and its gratification is viewed as corrupt. This is important to our investigation because it parallels in many ways the Stoic sensibilities as well as those of Aquinas. If these are foundational to the emergence of a particularized recognition of natural human rights (within a community context) in the West, then the same background conditions also exist within roughly contemporaneous time frames in the East (viz., in China).

Regarding Mencius's claim that human nature is basically good, Chu Hsi says:

> The fact that whatever issues from the Way [*dao*] is good may be compared to water always flowing downward. Nature is simply nature. How can it be described in words? Therefore those who excel in talking about nature only do so in terms of the beginning of its emanation in silence, as when Mencius spoke of the Four Beginnings (of humanity, righteousness, propriety, and wisdom). By observing the fact that water necessarily flows downward, we know the nature of water is to go downward. Similarly, by observing the fact that the emanation of nature is always good, we know that nature involves goodness. (*A Treatise on Ch'eng Ming-Tao's 'Discourse on Nature'*)

Chu Hsi comes to a similar conclusion as Mencius, but it is by a principled, factual path. When one observes nature, she can see its factual

---

[30] Wing-tsit Chan, trans., *A Sourcebook in Chinese Philosophy* (Princeton, NJ: Princeton University Press, 1963).

characteristics. These characteristics gain traction only when we add the posit that nature is good (ceteris paribus). This adds a normative dimension. By fiat, it posits value. Value is not derived from fact (as in the "fact-value" problem), but it is justified by the principle of Heaven that is understood by the philosopher (via intuition and observation) to be true. Thus, since people are an emanation of nature (just like falling water), and since nature is good (intuited to be true because of the principle of Heaven), then we know that people are also good. Since this process is materially grounded in the Four Beginnings, it takes on a more objective observational force that saves it from circularity. In this more convoluted way, Chu Hsi affirms Mencius in a qualified manner.

What is not qualified is that Chu Hsi is a moral realist. There is something that *is*. This gives legitimacy to these pronouncements on *ren*, *li*, and *t'ien-li* (the principle of Heaven). This entity is the Great Ultimate. The Great Ultimate is the grounding of *what is*. It is foundational to a realistic understanding of the world (normatively and epistemologically). Though it would be a misstatement to call this *God* (as understood in the West because it has no characteristics of personality or action), it still is a principle of *what is*. A further passage elucidates the ontology of this attribution further:

> The Great Ultimate is merely the principle of heaven and earth and the myriad of things. With respect to heaven and earth, there is the Great Ultimate in them. With respect to the myriad of things, there is the Great Ultimate in each and every one of them. Before heaven and earth existed, there was assuredly this principle. It is the principle that "through movement generates the yang." It is also this principle that "through movement generates the yin." (*Sayings on the Great Ultimate,* 11: 49:8b–9a)

This passage asserts in no uncertain terms that the Great Ultimate, which is the ontological source of making real everything that exists, transfers this reality hereditarily through the various emanations that follow: Great Ultimate => Heaven => Yin-Yang (the foundational complementary principles of the cosmic and material forces that are only approximately connected to the feminine and masculine). The various gradations of primal source to its expression in empirical reality is similar to Vedic writings in Hinduism.[31] Chu Hsi asserts a realistic vision that promotes a general

---

[31] Compare to "The Creation Hymn" in *Rig Vedas,* trans. Wendy Doniger (New York: Penguin, 2005): 10.129.

vision among his readers of what it means to be virtuous. This vision also applies universally to all through an immanent, practical mechanism of balance: yin-yang.

What we find from Chu Hsi is a shared community worldview that contains a vision of collective virtue in accordance with an ontological structure that gives it *authority:* this is the way things are. In a deep way everything flows from a separately existing reality that *is.* This structure connects Chu Hsi to Confucius and Mencius in much the same way as Aquinas was connected to Aristotle and the Stoics. A natural law paradigm has been created that legitimates a set of principles that supersede agreed upon laws set out by some emperor.

In the case of Wang Yang-Ming [Wang Shou-Jen] (1472–1529) there is more specification on the nature of the community and its ontological status.

> The great man regards Heaven, Earth, and the myriad things as one body. He regards the world as one family and the country as one person. As to those who make a cleavage between objects and distinguish between the self and others, they are small men. (*Inquiry on the Great Learning*)[32]

The great man here is one of learning – the sage or approaching the sage. This is the point of view of one who knows. If everything is really *one,* then everything is connected. The nature of this connection is not set out in a way we might expect from Leibnitz or Whitehead who took pains to argue for an ontology of monism. What is clear is the claim that a personal worldview that does not include a comprehensive, relational context is deficient.[33]

> This means that even the mind of the small man necessarily has the humanity that forms one body with all. Such a mind is rooted in his Heaven-endowed nature, and is naturally intelligent, clear, and not clouded. For this reason it is called "clear character."

The community of humans and all other existing things are united and have real, systemic interaction. This community perspective owes its foundations to nature that is heaven-created. This perspective is consistent with the ancient and medieval Western perspective (as per Aristotle,

---

[32] Wang Yang-Ming, "Inquiry on the Great Learning," in *A Sourcebook in Chinese Philosophy,* ed. and trans. Wing-tsit Chan (Princeton, NJ: Princeton University Press, 1963).

[33] I have argued for an analogous worldview standpoint with reference to environmentalism: "The Self in Context: A Grounding for Environmentalism," in *Environmental Ethics,* ed. Michael Boylan (Malden, MA: Wiley-Blackwell, 2013): 14–24.

the Stoics, and Thomas). Moving away from the community is a false standpoint that can result in being off-centered (cf. Buddhist *dukkha*).

> Hence, if it is not obscured by selfish desires, even the mind of the small man has the humanity that forms one body with all as does the mind of the great man. As soon as it is obscured by selfish desires, even the mind of the great man will be divided and narrow like that of the small man.

Hard individualism is a false worldview. Even in a great man it will lead to problems. In a real way it is the way of all evil: excessive individualism. Everyone should adopt a version of the community worldview as primary and as helping to form the personal worldview.[34]

This goal is set out by Wang Yang-Ming:

> Only when I love my brother, the brothers of others, and the brothers of all men can my humanity really form one body with my brother, the brothers of others and the brothers of all men. When it truly forms one body with them, then the clear character of brotherly respect will be manifested. Everything from the ruler, minister, husband, wife, and friends to mountains, rivers, spiritual beings, birds, animals, and plants should be truly lived in order to realize my humanity that forms one body with them, and then my clear character will be completely manifested, and I will really form one body with Heaven, Earth and the myriad of things ... the nature endowed in us by Heaven is pure and perfect ... selfish ideas ... obscure the law of right and wrong.

All people should accept their relational nature. This creates a brotherhood of all. From the ruler to the lowly: all are connected into a communal union. The presence of extreme individual dissenters creates an inauthentic worldview perspective. This offends Heaven and Nature. People should strive to fit into the communal whole. To do otherwise is to fail in one's moral duty.[35] Just like Mencius, Wang Yang-Ming asserts that this monism applies to all – even the autocratic ruler. As a steward of the realm, the selfish ideas of the ruler are just as bad as anyone else's. Monism is thus a way of expressing universalism in the context of a natural moral realism.

The ancient and medieval writers in China assert many of the same tenets as their counterparts in the West: a natural law grounded in Heaven that applied to all in a community context. Where the West veered off this course was in the late sixteenth and seventeenth centuries with writers like Hugo Grotius (1583–1645) who was only a century or so later than Wang Yang-Ming. And Grotius, among others, was part of a movement in Europe that changed two parts of the Western paradigm: community to individual

---

[34] For a fuller description of these dynamics see Chapter 6.
[35] This is not too dissimilar to Hegel in *The Philosophy of Right* – particularly in his discussion of the relative value of *Moralität v. Sittlichkeit* in Boylan, *A Just Society*, 7.

and theistic to natural account. Wang Yang-Ming and Chu Hsi could agree somewhat on the latter development (because of nuanced understandings of Heaven) but not on the former. China's development in roughly the same historical era is marked by its remaining communitarian.[36]

3.2.1 Literature from the Post-Classical Period

There is also a literature that supports total self-effacement through the embracing of the Zen idea of *mu* (emptiness that still has significance). The translation of the *Diamond Sutra* into Chinese, *jīngāng bōrěbōluómìduō jīng* (around 401 CE) was very influential. In a famous passage from the *Diamond Sutra* the narrator contrasts two novices. The first novice seeks by discipline and good habits (rather Confucian) to obtain *nirvana* (being awake and in harmony – not in *dukkha*, off-centered because of desire). The first novice, Shen Hsiu writes a poem on the wall:

> Our body is the Bodhi-tree,
> And our mind a mirror bright.
> Carefully we wipe them hour by hour
> And let no dust alight.[37]

This epigram was supposed to bring awe and approval to Shen by his teachers who felt that he was on the verge of awakening because he was so worthy. But Shen was confronted by a senior elder who told him that he, Shen, had missed the boat. Shen then stepped back, puzzled.

The narrator of the story is the lowly son of a recently deceased bureaucrat, who had been dismissed from his position in the government. After his father's death the son moved to a Zen monastery near Canton. In his social position the narrator is at the bottom of the social scale (a child of a dismissed bureaucrat). He is observed by the other novices as an outcast. He is illiterate and asks permission to read his poem from memory. There is some grumbling, but the elder says, "Do not despise a beginner." So the outcast novice dictates his own stanza:

> There is no Bodhi-tree
> Nor stand of a mirror bright.
> Since all is void,
> Where can the dust alight?

---

[36] Note that the use of "communitarian" in the ancient and medieval realms is generally at a midpoint between hard communitarianism and hard individualism (to be discussed later in the chapter). I use the term here because the ancient and medieval sentiments of both Europe and China are similar until the shift toward hard individualism in the West during the seventeenth century.

[37] *The Diamond Sutra*, trans. A. F. Price (Boston: Shambhala, rpt. 2005): ch. 1.

The illiterate social outcast brought awe and attention from his teachers and the elder. It was clear that he was already *awake* (had achieved nirvana).

The importance of this passage in conveying worldview is that it sets out (a) that there is another cultural tradition that takes abnegation further than the Confucians: hard work and diligence may not be enough to lead a choice-worthy life; and (b) that the classes set out by Confucius can be superseded by sincere and authentic seeking. This is an important tenet in thinking about the way one views the individual in Chinese tradition. Here the role of intuition (championed by Wang Yang-Ming) is a means to gaining Truth by the individual, who as a result is put forward. The illiterate novice is meritorious by *wu wei* (supplemented by sincere and authentic searching). The community of the monastery, the persistence of the novice, and intuitive insight are the keys to successfully becoming awake to the reality of *mu*.

3.3 THE EIGHTEENTH AND NINETEENTH CENTURIES

Stephen C. Angle has written persuasively on how concepts of human rights have passed from the West into China. This subsection sketches out a few of these claims as they relate to the nineteenth century. Much of this history, according to Angle, was trying to align Chinese terms with technical terms from Europe.

Angle claims that one starting point arose when English merchants began trading opium in China during the end of the eighteenth century and the struggle to open ports for trade (and the so-called Canton System).[38] This new complexity in dealing with the British East India Company created the need for knowledge about European trade laws including the compilation of many documents from maps, to aspects of diplomacy, to rules of negotiation – and *even* selections of Emmerich de Vattel's *Le Droit des gens* (*The Law of Nations*) a book on international law published in France in 1758. Translators literally had to scour the Chinese language for the proper terms for "rights" in connection with commerce. Peter Parker, an American missionary, and Wei Yuan, a writer on statecraft, tried their best, but their efforts were largely inconsequential for the literature on *rights*.

In 1862 another American missionary, W. A. P. Martin began a translation of Henry Wheaton's *Elements of International Law*. This work

[38] Stephen C. Angle, *Human Rights and Chinese Thought* (Cambridge: Cambridge University Press, 2002): 104.

proved more influential as the most common word to translate "rights" is *quan*. "Natural Rights" are rendered *ziran zhi quan*, "property rights" are *zhangwu zhi quan*, and so on. This trend continues to other practical books such as the Chinese compendium, *General Laws of the Myriad Nations*. Here the term for rights becomes *quanli*. Martin's breakthrough was made by connecting to classical texts, like Mencius.[39] The motive was to put these foreigners into a familiar shared context. These projects show that terms for various aspects of the word "right" already existed in China back to the classical sources (albeit set in slightly different contexts – though not altogether different, as shown previously). Thus, 'rights' cannot be thought to be entirely pressed upon China from the West. The Chinese have a tradition of rights that rests within a communitarian context (though not a hard communitarian context). This context somewhat alters the strict expression of human rights via the parameters of that communitarian and natural law context.

Angle argues that the next wave of East-West interaction in China occurred as the result of China's need to be able to better negotiate trade deals with the West. Angle cites Li Hongzhang who set out *liquan* as "a transitional concept which in his hands begins to be transformed from 'economic control' toward something closer to 'economic rights.'"[40] In this case it is the Chinese who are asserting economic rights against the Europeans. This can have a populist ring as per the earlier writer Han Tan (1637–1704) who said, "The less money coined by the government, the more the people will use their own counterfeit money to benefit themselves. Economic control (*liquan*) will be dispersed among the masses."[41] Thus, the enforcement of *liquan* is shuffled over to the Customs Office as it interacts with colonial powers as they infuse legal concepts with normative force. This represents an advance from the so-called *value-free* legal positivism of nineteenth-century Britain.

The idea of assigning rights principally to individuals does not exist in this context according to Angle. But conceptual changes continue to creep in. For example, Yan Fu's translation of Huxley's account of social Darwinism uses *quanli* to translate "rights." And in 1904 Yan used *quanli* in his translation of Edward Jenks's *A History of Politics*.[42] Though China lacked a decided move toward individualism in this dynamic debate on *quanli* (during the eighteenth to nineteenth century), *still* the natural

[39] Angle, *Human Rights and Chinese Thought*, 108–110.
[40] Angle, *Human Rights and Chinese Thought*, 111.
[41] Angle, *Human Rights and Chinese Thought*, 113.
[42] Angle, *Human Rights and Chinese Thought*, 139.

law classical and medieval neo-Confucian discussions overlap considerably with the traditions of the pre-seventeenth-century West for a genuine dialogue about natural human rights.

3.4 LANGUAGE ANALYSIS AND THE DEBATE TODAY

The emphasis in the last subsection is on the force of rights being connected to economic rights, also known as economic power against foreign colonial powers. This perspective is from a country that has been abused by the powerful military of European colonialism. This is the form of a negative right against those who have forced unfair trade contracts and addicted a portion of the populace to opium. The reality of China in this time period is to emphasize the meaning of *quan* as power. It is the power of the community against other foreign communities that used force to subjugate a people for the colonial nation's own benefit. These power dimensions affect the interplay between East and West on the meaning of rights as intended by both shared community worldviews.

The alignment language games of the last two hundred years are still alive today. Angle presents an imaginary contemporary dialogue between two students, Ms. Wang (a senior at Beijing University) and Mr. Smith (an American student).

> Wang says, "*Ren ren dou you shengcun quan*" [which she translates as] "All people have a right to subsistence." Smith immediately denies this, asserting "People do not have a right to subsistence." Wang is mystified, wondering in English, "But isn't this absolutely central to what 'rights' are? Are we even talking about the same things?"[43]

The two students then quarrel on whether human rights are about food, clothing, shelter, or a more literal understanding of *li* as rights and *quan* as power. Wang understands a notion of positive rights while Smith's understanding is based on a bias toward negative rights only (noninterference with liberty). I believe Angle's imaginary dialogue sets up a very important quarrel about human rights that transcends the East–West dialogue. Are human rights fundamentally about noninterference with liberty in a very narrow sense of the U.S. Bill of Rights' First Amendment? Or are they something more like the United Nations Universal Declaration of Human Rights, a more comprehensive document that includes positive welfare rights as well?[44]

---

[43] Angle, *Human Rights and Chinese Thought*, 28–29.
[44] Angle, *Human Rights and Chinese Thought*, provides numerous examples from the founding of the Republic of China to the People's Republic of China.

The contemporary debate on China and recognition of human rights is often set out with two sides: (a) China fails to see the objective reality of natural human rights and should be brought around, and (b) China is a victim of imperialism by the West for not accepting its version of human rights. There is some truth to both of these positions. Let's examine the arguments for each.

First is that China fails to see the objective reality of natural human rights and should be brought around. It is true that China has a rich natural law tradition that emphasizes sharing the wealth among all those in the community (state) from the ruler to the government to the common people. We have seen how Mencius specifically calls out rulers who try to hoard money for themselves. This flows from a more comprehensive sense of welfare rights being primary. However, this communitarian standpoint occasionally veers to hard communitarianism. Under hard communitarianism, individual liberty is principally defined in terms of how the individual can best help the community to survive. And though welfare rights are very important (see Chapter 6) they are not exhaustive. China needs to accept a concept of individual rights akin to the First Amendment to the U.S. Constitution.

> Congress shall make no law respecting an establishment of religion, or prohibiting the free exercise thereof; or abridging the freedom of speech, or of the press; or the right of the people peaceably to assemble, and to petition the Government for a redress of grievances.

These basic liberty rights owe their genesis to the individualistic turn of the Western tradition in the sixteenth and seventeenth centuries. The communal vision in the West was also altered via the Reformation and the move to an individual's statement of conscience over that of the guardian of communal authority:

> Unless I am convicted by Scripture and plain reason – I do not accept the authority of popes and councils, for they have contradicted each other – my conscience is captive to the Word of God. I cannot and will not recant anything, for to go against conscience is neither right nor safe. Here I stand. I can do no other. God help me. Amen. Martin Luther before the *Diet of Worms*, April 17, 1521[45]

---

[45] For a discussion, see the classic, Charles Beard, *Martin Luther and the Reformation in Germany until the Close of the Diet of Worms* (Cornell, NY: Cornell University Press, 2009 [1889]). A comprehensive historical treatment can be found in Robert Fossier, ed., and Sarah Hanburg-Tenison, trans., *The Cambridge History of the Middle Ages: Volume III, 1250–1520* (Cambridge: Cambridge University Press, 1986) and a short accessible treatment in Peter Marshall, *The Reformation: A Very Short Introduction* (Oxford: Oxford University Press, 2009).

Perhaps China did not have a Grotius or a Luther during that post-medieval time period, but that is not the case in the twentieth century. In Stephen Angle's 2000 reader he presents articles that demonstrate a very active debate on individual human rights. In the following subsection on contemporary Chinese fiction, this consciousness is also prevalent in the general worldview. Thus, the claim that China has not had a prominent spokesperson for individualization of human rights no longer holds weight (see the next subsection on literature).

The second response is whether China is the victim of Western imperialism. This sort of argument works in various ways. Most of them raise the issue that China (unlike the West) did not recognize a movement to emphasize individualism over communitarianism in its expression of natural law and the rights that flow from them. Some brief review of the current literature finds that some writers assail the West as imperialists in the colonial tradition who tried to change China to fit the image of the West.[46] Others make a similar case based upon cultural constructivism.[47]

There is some truth in these claims, but in order to discern *how much* truth, one must examine the consequences of such a position: moral relativism. In order to do this, we must distinguish between two senses of relativism.[48] The first is legitimate cultural relativism. This mode considers differences in cultural practice that have no ethical impact. For example, table etiquette, marriage customs, dress customs, and others generally fall into the first category. Religious practices are also protected (so long

---

[46] Among those who take this position or one close to it are Michael Ignatieff, *Human Rights as Politics and Idolatry,* ed. Amy Gutmann (Princeton, NJ: Princeton University Press, 2001); Robert Deacon, "Human Rights as Imperialism," *Theoria* **50**.102 (2003): 126–138; and Randall Peerenboom, "Human Rights, China, and Cross-Cultural Inquiry: Philosophy, History, and Power Politics," *Philosophy East and West* **55**.2 (2005): 283–320.

[47] Louis Althusser, "Ideology and Ideological State Apparatuses," in *Lenin and Philosophy, and Other Essays* (New York: Monthly Review Press, 1971): 127–186; Antonio Gramsci, *Selections from the Prison Notebooks,* trans. Quintin Hoare and Geoffrey Nowell Smith (London: Lawrence and Wishart, 1971); Stuart Hall, "The Local and the Global: Globalization and Ethnicity," in *Globalization and the World System: Contemporary Conditions for the Representation of Identity,* ed. Anthony King (Binghamton, NY: Macmillan, 1991): 19–39; Jing Yin, "The Clash of Rights: A Critical Analysis of News Discourse on Human Rights in the United States and China," *Critical Discourse Studies* **4**.1 (2007): 75–94; Kate Nash, *Cultural Politics of Human Rights: Comparing the U.S. and U.K.* (Cambridge: Cambridge University Press, 2009); Arvind Sharma, *Are Human Rights Western?* (Oxford: Oxford University Press, 2006); and Chengqiu Wu, "Sovereignty, Human Rights, and Responsibility: Changes in China's Response to International Humanitarian Crises," *Journal of Chinese Political Science* **15** (2010): 71–97.

[48] I discuss this issue in more detail in Michael Boylan, *Basic Ethics,* 2nd ed. (Upper Saddle River, NJ: Prentice Hall, 2009): ch. 3.

as they don't include practices that are independently immoral – such as ritual murder, somatic mutilation, or exploitation of others).

The second sense is not relative. If there is a cultural practice that deprives people of the basic goods of agency (level one or level two), as such, it is unethical (see Chapter 6). This is absolute (universalism): its authority crosses cultures and historical eras. Regarding this later sense of absolutism, it has been shown that the classical and neo-Confucian writers in China agree. This is based upon the "heaven-based" connection. These Chinese thinkers did not believe that heaven covered only them. It was universal. Thus, the debate on this score is not about whether there is ethical relativism or absolutism. Rather, it is about which *absolutist theory* is correct? If there is considerable overlap between the Western and Chinese traditions (as I have suggested there is), then we are in a place to engage the universalist debate. It is not the West versus China. Rather, it is which *universalist* theory is correct?[49]

3.4.1 Contemporary Literature

Two contemporary expatriate Chinese novelists offer rich worldview examples of the individualistic understandings of human rights that stand in contrast to hard communitarianism in China today. In the first case, Gao Xingjian in *Lingshan* (Soul Mountain)[50] sets out a tale where none of the characters are named. The narrator uses the pronouns "I" and "You" to refer to himself. This is meant to be an effacement of the individual during the Cultural Revolution in which the author (much like the protagonist) was falsely declared to have lung cancer. It is set forward whether the *cancer* is really an affliction of the state in a complementary symmetry: the narrator was diagnosed with a cancer he didn't have and the state is not diagnosed with a cancer it *really* has.

The narrator is an official writer licensed by the state. He even has an identity card with a forgery-proof stamp. This reinforces the official *inauthentic* community worldview standpoint. In this quest the narrator becomes "a searcher of archeology," "an anthropologist interested in

---

[49] Western writers on universalism regarding human rights include Alan Gewirth, *The Community of Rights* (Chicago: University of Chicago Press, 1996); Henry Shue, *Basic Rights* (Princeton, NJ: Princeton University Press, 1980); Robert Paul Churchill, *Human Rights and Global Diversity* (Upper Saddle River, NJ: Prentice Hall, 2006); Jack Donnelly, *Universal Human Rights: In Theory and Practice* (Ithaca, NY: Cornell University Press, 2003); and James Griffin, *On Human Rights* (Oxford: Oxford University Press, 2008).

[50] Gao Xingjian, *Soul Mountain*, trans. Mabel Lee (New York: HarperCollins, 2000/ first published as *Linghan*. Taiwan: Linjing Chubanshe, 1990).

folk songs," "a novelist wanting to write a novel," "a man wanting to find his roots – his own childhood and the childhood of his nation," and "a seeker after the truth of Taoism and Buddhism." These various personae allow the reader to see the narrator as different people all connected by a single worldview. At the center of this worldview is the notion of the quest: the search for the possibly nonexistent *Lingshan* (Soul Mountain). This is symbolic of the soul of the Chinese people (cf. the role of Heaven in the classical and neo-Confucian figures).

The general drift of the stories works like this. The narrator comes to several remote villages by bus or on foot and a number of things happen. At one, he shows his identity card and is given reverence by the town leaders (who in the backs of their minds must be suspicious that he is an agent of the Red Guard and the old Cultural Revolution purification movement). At another, the narrator comes in unnoticed and meets a young woman and has sex with her. Either before or after sex the author tells a story. The stories are often about women who have been abandoned by their men or families or have been "undone." The result is often gang rape, suicide, or exile. Life is hell for women.

Then there are the instances in which the narrator (pretending to be a collector of folk songs) meets people who try to keep the old traditions alive. They are suspicious of the narrator at first, thinking he may be after them in a cultural purge (not unknown in the recent past). These episodes result in an immersion in the local customs and a situated view of truth.

Then there are instances in which the narrator (pretending to be a historian or archeologist) seeks ancient relics and the keepers of these relics (often indistinguishable from the holy men and women).

Finally, there are the instances of interaction with religious monks and nuns (one of which has sex for a couple days with the narrator). These scenes are always incomplete. Is this a koan? It is perhaps for this reason that the narrator (author?) begins to insert himself in espousing religious truth. This begins very late in the book (Chs. 52, 54, 58, 66, 70, 72, 76, 77, and 81). Chapter 74 is one of the most striking in the book. In that chapter the narrator finally comes upon religion in the interior of a mountain (perhaps his quest?). It is a Taoist temple built inside an obscure mountain so that it is completely unseen. The narrator comes by this temple in the middle of the night on a narrow path that has beaten down his physical strength. He is met by a spiritual man who lets him sleep on a wooden bed (no mattress). In the morning the narrator leaves and finds the main road again. On that road he sees a young child abandoned and crying. The narrator picks up the child and tries to calm it, but then realizes the obligation that might befall him so he takes the child back to the spot where he found it. The child is asleep, and the narrator leaves the child alone.

Many of the stories of this book end up with people being left alone. This may be the ultimate message of the book: the state (the honored community of history) should leave people alone to find their own personal journey.

The second literary example is Dai Sijie, *Balzac and the Little Chinese Seamstress.*[51] It is 1968 and Mao, the Great Helmsman of the Chinese Revolution, has launched a campaign that profoundly altered the country. The universities were closed and young intellectuals (boys and girls from high school) were sent into the countryside to be "reeducated" by common peasants. Luo and his friend were likewise sent to a small village. When they arrive, the village leader searches through their things. He finds a violin in the narrator's belongings. He doesn't know what it is. They are about to burn it when Luo offers for the narrator to play it. He does. They ask the name of the song. The narrator says, "Mozart ..." This doesn't sound so good since it could be a mark of foreign bourgeoisie. But the quick thinking Luo says, "Mozart's Thinking of Chairman Mao." All of a sudden the art form is all right. It is politically correct.

The boys go through hard labor. They soon find a way to avoid some of it by retelling the village people various movie plots. All the movies have Communist themes. The boys are given time off to go to the larger neighboring village to watch another movie, and then return to tell its story to the people of the small hamlet.

Soon the boys meet Four-Eyes, another boy being reeducated. His mother has found a way for him to return home: to record rural songs/poetry and then to return to the city and to put them into a poetry journal to talk about the strength of the peasant. But Four-Eyes is a prig and cannot get the miller (the man who knows the most of these rural artists) to talk. Luo and the narrator make their pilgrimage and pretend to be emissaries of Beijing. It works. In return Four-Eyes lends them a book by Balzac translated into Chinese. The book transforms the boys' lives.

The boys on their travels to the neighboring village meet a teenaged girl who works as a seamstress for her traveling tailor father. The boys are attracted to the girl and begin telling her stories to "educate" her. She falls for Luo and soon begins a sexual relationship that leads to her getting pregnant.

[51] Dai Sijie, *Balzac and the Little Chinese Seamstress,* trans. Ina Rilke (New York: Anchor, 2002/ first published as *Balzac et la petite tailleuse chinoise.* Paris: Gallimard, 2000).

Meanwhile Four-Eyes' mother comes to the village and takes her son home – but not before the narrator and Luo steal the trunk holding forbidden books. The books are forbidden because they will corrupt the soul away from the moral puritanism of Communism. The boys read all the books over and over. They tell the stories both to the little seamstress and to her father, who visits the boys in the hamlet on his travels. Once the village head himself listens all night long outside the house on stilts (that houses the boys), and he threatens to turn them in unless they fix his tooth. In a gruesome scene, the tailor allows Luo to use his sewing machine as a dentist's drill to fix the tooth and then to put melted tin into the tooth. It works and the boys have an easier time after that. In an indirect sense, it is the art of the narrative that fills the cavity of pain.

Meanwhile, Luo's mother is allowed to go back to her and Luo's former home in the city. Luo decides to pay her a visit. While he is gone, the narrator looks after the little seamstress. She's pregnant by Luo and the narrator goes through the dangerous task of getting her an illegal abortion. Luo returns, but the little seamstress has left for the city. She arranged everything officially without telling the boys or her father. She says that Balzac changed her life and told her, "a woman's beauty is a treasure beyond price."

The boys return to their house dejected and burn all their books.

Like Gao Xingjian's book, the generating event in Dai Sijie's book is the Cultural Revolution. This is the most extreme form of communitarianism: hard communitarianism. Under this form, the community is the primary unit. It exists naturally. The individuals that make up the community have the right to find out how they can successfully contribute to the mission of the natural unit (the community). For any individual to move outside the natural unit is to undermine the mission of the community and such behavior has to be suppressed. Hard communitarianism is judged by Dai Sijie's presentation to be *unnatural* since everyone follows it only because it is backed up by force. The villagers try little tricks to get around its punitive rules.[52] This is one indicator that hard communitarianism is not natural but an artificial device of dictators. The other indicator is the place of *art*. Both the music of the violin and the thousand and one stories told emphasize the authentic standpoint of the artist who as an individual sets out his or her unique vision to the world. This is not hard individualism, because the artist must find an audience to share and

---

[52] Cf. Ha Jin, *Waiting* (New York: Vintage, 2000) in which the protagonist is able to get around the state-mandated one-child only policy by careful scheming and a bit of luck.

react to the art. If this is the real natural worldview, then Four-Eyes is a corruptor of art and stands for Helmsman's hard communitarian mentality. It is a tragedy that hard communitarianism wins.

3.5 A FINAL ANALYSIS OF HUMAN RIGHTS IN CHINA

It is an impossible project to capture comprehensively almost four thousand years of Chinese civilization concerning human rights in a brief chapter. There is tremendous selectivity, but perhaps the notes will point the intrepid reader a way to investigate further. The focus of this last subsection is to offer a few brief observations on the interaction between the contemporary expression of the heritage of Western ideas on human rights and Chinese ideas on human rights so that we might go forward to examine various ways to justify human rights – including this author's preferred version.

The key issue on the table is whether China has enough overlap with Western tradition that a philosophical discussion on a universal vision can authentically be engaged. Randall Peerenboom has set out several key issues in this regard to evaluate these claims:[53] (a) What is distinctive about China's human rights discourse? (b) What are the limits in cross-cultural inquiry? (c) What are the limits of tolerance? (d) What role does abstract philosophy play? (e) To what extent does politics obscure cross-cultural dialogue? (f) What are the benefits of human rights discussions? (g) Has an emphasis upon human rights promoted or lessened human misery? (h) Should utopian language replace practical discussions?

These are very important questions. They move us toward the anti-realist notion of ongoing negotiation about what human rights practices should be observed in the same frame of mind as "what tariff policies should we recognize right now?" This will amount to the legalistic approach to human rights (Chapter 4). It is important in this discussion to distinguish the debate on what *ought to be the case* based upon valid arguments presented in the court of reason and *strategies on how to bring natural rights to the table.*

The first phase relates to the metaphysical status of the claim, namely, whether we are seeking after truths that *really exist* or those that are only *conventionally accepted* (like the tariff policies). If the former is correct, and if free speech were one of those natural rights, then one might

---

[53] Randall Peerenboom, "Human Rights, China, and Cross-Cultural Inquiry: Philosophy, History, and Power Politics," *Philosophy East and West* **53**.2 (2005): 283–320, 284–285.

confront a situation in which country x did not allow free speech. The response would be that country x was wrong in not allowing free speech, F. The person or country leveling the charge against x would be, in the first case, dependent upon the strength of his argument to convince a rational audience of the truth of his contention. Now some might say that in the international arena reason does not hold sway and is a utopian fancy. I take such charges seriously since I have advocated for what is practically possible – what I call aspirational.[54] However, those not so charged may be more open to consider and debate the truth of the claim (that citizens of any country should have the right of freedom of speech, ceteris paribus). We can call this venue the international court of opinion. It is here that academics (philosophers and other public intellectuals) have a real opportunity to make a difference in international opinion. For example, at the writing of this book, the scientific community has played this role in the general acceptance of global warming as an outcome of human activity. Though there are still some dissenters, the academics have had real influence. And in some subregions in the world (such as the European Union) there have been some real policy changes as a result.

This leads us to the second phase: how to move from conviction to strategies on how to bring natural rights to the table. In this phase, one transitions from questions about *truth* to questions about *tactics*. One could imagine a situation in which countries a, b, c, … m, all agreed that x should adopt F. They say that each of us has adopted F: Fa, Fb, Fc … Fm. Because we have all adopted F as the result of an argument q, and because q is true, x should adopt F as well. However, it is unlikely that such an approach will work (see Part Three). At this juncture countries a–m will have to adopt negotiating tactics that will be very similar to those of the anti-realists who skip the first phase (because they don't believe it to be accurate – see Chapter 7) and move directly to this stage of the process.

Some very practically minded folk would then ask, if both sides end up at a negotiating table using the same tactics to bring x around, then what is the sense of the first phase at all? To many this is axiomatic. These pragmatists care only about the outcomes and generally use ethical intuitionism to come to their particular understanding of normative value. At the end, they get to the negotiating table faster. Does this render the first phase irrelevant? This will be the subject matter of Part Two. Stay tuned.

---

[54] I discuss this distinction in ch. 7 of Boylan, *A Just Society*.

JUSTIFICATIONS FOR HUMAN RIGHTS

Adagio

"Double Talk"

Those who in private life behave well towards their parents and elder brothers,
in public life seldom show a disposition to resist the authority of their superiors.
– The Analects of Confucius[1]

Hu Shi was worried. He didn't like the way his e-mail went last night. Hu was sitting in the kitchen waiting for his wife. He had set out the food: youtiao for him and zongzi for her (she was, after all, from Shanghai). They each had a cup of warmed milk that was cooler by the minute. He looked at his watch, waiting. Time was a rigid commodity just now for Hu. He looked again at his watch and then reached for his warm twisted, juicy dough stick and took a bite.

It was early November and even now the weather was turning cold. Their little kitchen had a black table in the middle with four chairs: two for Hu and his wife and two for company. They had a new stainless steel refrigerator that had been the gift of his father (who worked in a procurement agency concerned with foreign trade).

Hu Shi was thinking about the e-mail exchange with his father last night. Hu Li, his father, was very factual in his communication (he had to be because of the pervasive graft in the procurement agency). However, whenever he wanted to broach a sensitive subject, Hu Li would invoke one of the many fairy tales that he had spun when Shi was a child. Hu Li would then alter those familiar tales to take on a double meaning. The cover story was that he was creating material for the time when Hu Shi and his wife Ding Chaoxing might have their own child and so make father Hu Li a grandfather. "My future grandson would love this version of Hok Lee and the Dwarfs" or some other tale.

[1] *The Analects of Confucius*, trans. Arthur Waley (New York: Vintage Books, 1938), Book One. I would like to thank William Haines who read this story and corrected some errors.

But this was a front. Hu Li wanted to communicate with his son about sensitive topics in a safe way. To this end they had stand-ins for forbidden topics or people. For example, the panda was really "Liu Xiaobo." Whenever something happened to the panda, it was really a comment about Liu Xiaobo, who had authored *Charter o8* (a manifesto on human rights, which many brave souls have covertly signed onto). Hu Shi's elder brother, Hu Gang, was also a part of this charade. Hu Gang was officially a civil engineer, but he too was involved in the *Charter o8* Movement. However, Liu Xiaobo had been rewarded for his authorial efforts with an indefinite jail term, so the father and his two grown sons knew that caution was essential.

Hu Shi knew that as a philosophy professor in the Research Center on Marxism at Beida (Beijing University) he was under constant scrutiny. He had a position that many would kill for and was, even now, up for a promotion to deputy director. Such a post would give him academic power. His personal goal could also be met: that he and Ding Chaoxing might have a child. Everything was within his grasp. Was he dreaming? And it was all about to happen – soon.

Then Ding Chaoxing came straggling down for breakfast. Her long hair was scraggly, and she was blinking her eyes hard.

Hu Shi sprung up and went to her, "Are you okay?"

She gave him a look. Hu Shi knew what it meant: snoring again. Ding Chaoxing was always a heavy sleeper. She claimed that the only thing that would wake her was Hu Shi's snoring. This was an assertion that Hu Shi fervently denied! But he had been there before.

"The milk is getting cold," said Hu Shi.

"Then we'll heat it up again," responded the wife who was still wearing a red clingy housecoat and was running her fingers (like a comb) through her hair. She continued to blink sleep from her eyes.

"But we've got to get to the University," replied her husband looking down at his wife.

"You've got a lecture at eleven. I don't lecture until one. You're free to go whenever you want to." Ding Chaoxing pivoted away, sat in her chair, and started eating her food. When you sit down it doesn't matter if you're rather short – there's a sort of equality there.

Then Hu Shi got up and put his own milk in the microwave to reheat it. While Hu Shi was waiting the sixty seconds on the beverage reheat mode, he mentally returned to his e-mail disquiet. There was to be a talk in the early evening ostensibly about the changes in Buddhism in the seventeenth century in the History Building, but then concurrently a small number of people were to meet surreptitiously at a lower-level conference room to discuss a pamphlet on *Charter 08* vis-à-vis revising government policy and creating a set of individual rights along the lines of the U.S. Bill of Rights. The group was all academics, but some had parents or brothers who held high positions in the government or in the Communist Party (which was generally the same thing).

BING! The milk was ready. Hu Shi brought his milk back to his chair. Ding Chaoxing was humming some sort of song to herself (food had a way of waking her up in a hurry). When Hu Shi sat down she turned and watched him drink his warmed milk. The two ate their breakfast in silence.

When they had finished Ding Chaoxing took her dishes to the sink. Then she turned to her husband, "So do you want to ride with me to University or not?"

"Sure I do."

"Then let's race to get ready."

The pair was a tag-team alternating grooming activities in the bathroom and their bedroom as the space for each was rather limited.

When they were ready and had placed rubber bands on their pant legs, they mounted their bicycles and headed for the Zhongguancun Bell on the way to the southeast gate of Beida. As they rode Ding Chaoxing would take the lead and Hu Shi would follow behind. He loved to watch his wife and her superior bicycling skills. He would imitate her form from behind even as he kept mentally returning to the e-mail of the night before. It was a continuous tape that kept replaying until he had locked up his bike in front of the Research Center on Marxism.

"Hello, Professor Hu," the voice was a familiar one. It was Jiang Menglin, his doctoral student. His Cantonese accent always made Hu Shi smile.

"Hello, Menglin. Did you want to talk to me?"

"As a matter of fact, I do – if you have a spare moment."

"Well, I'm giving a lecture in twenty minutes,"

"I could meet you this evening, sir, after your institute meeting."

"I can't meet then, I've got *another meeting*! But, hey, if it's short, you can follow me to my office and we'll talk on the run."

"Yes sir." Jiang Menglin was a chubby, robust young lad. He walked with Hu Shi about a half-pace behind his mentor.

"So what is it that you want, Jiang?"

"I'm having some trouble with historical materialism. I guess I really don't understand it as I should, because it seems anachronistic."

Hu paused on the stairs and looked at his student. Then with his free hand Hu took off his glasses and rubbed them on his coat sleeve before putting them on again.

"Professor?"

Hu Shi smiled. "I just wanted to see whether I understood you properly. Everyone has trouble with historical materialism particularly when buttressed by functional explanation. Most of the writers in the West try to get around this difficulty by rejecting the problem out of hand. But that isn't good enough. Understanding the contradictions (whether real or apparent) is essential for your project. Come up to my office and I'll lend you a book that argues that functional explanation creates, by elaboration, background conditions that solve the typical conundrums associated with historical materialism."

Hu Shi then set out again. When they got to his office he pulled down a slender volume bound in thin brown paper. He handed it to his student, "Here, look at this for a week. Make an appointment, and we'll discuss it. It is essential to your work. Without this or something like it historical materialism is a failed concept."

Jiang Menglin nodded his head in a short bow and left. He headed toward the west gate. When he had exited the university grounds Jiang headed toward a pharmacy shop. The doctoral student took out a cigarette, lit it and waited. In the space of five minutes he saw a car pull up across the street. The windows of the car were tinted so that people from the street could not easily see inside. Jiang Menglin threw away his butt and hustled over to the car and into the car's back seat.

The other occupant in the back seat was middle-aged fat man who looked Mongolian. He had narrow eyes and very wide, high cheeks. He sported a pencil moustache. The car started away from the university. The Mongolian looking man was smoking a Turkish cigarette.

Jiang Menglin stared at the man and waited.

When they had traversed several blocks the older man asked, "So what have you found out?"

"Well, I did what you said. I read the hacked e-mails of professor Hu and they don't make too much sense to me."

The rotund man blew his smoke directly at Jiang Menglin. Then he took the cigarette out of his mouth and moved it toward Jiang Menglin's face. "Have you ever been burned by a cigarette?"

"No sir, Mr. He Lin, sir." Jiang tried as hard as he could to show no emotion.

He Lin then pulled the cigarette away from the younger man's face and laughed. "Ha! I wouldn't burn you on the face: too obvious. You'd be useless as a DSD informant if I did that. Everyone would know."

"Yes, Mr. He Lin, sir."

"Tell me how you interpret this story about the spider and the silk worm? Isn't this a children's tale about how the silk worm works for the People's Republic of China (since he dies for his country and his silk goes to help clothe the people) while the spider is a selfish capitalist (since his silk is only an elaborate trap to capture insects that he takes for his own pleasure)? Then there is this *panda* that comes in. After that, both the spider and the silk worm have a right to do what is natural to them. I have never heard of this version of the story. Is it something that they teach at the university?"

"No sir. We do not study children's stories at the university. I am learning Marxism for my doctoral degree." Jiang Menglin watched as He Lin finished his cigarette and put the stub into the silver tray on the arm rest.

"And then the e-mail we sent you said that the *panda* would gather a council so that all the animals in the forest might feel free to discuss their differences."

Jiang Menglin tried to smile, but it turned into a grimace.

He Lin leaned over and grabbed the young man by his coat collar and fixed his grip so that the young man felt pressure against his trachea. He Lin's thumbs rested on Jiang Menglin's larynx.

The gasping philosophy student managed, "I think it means that Hu Shi is going to convene a meeting of dissidents. He's probably a counter-revolutionary." Jiang Menglin gagged some while He Lin loosened his hold just a bit.

"When is this meeting?"

Jiang Menglin's mind was racing to say something. He was afraid of what might happen if he didn't say anything. "Tonight, after the institute meeting."

"Where?"

"I don't know. Follow him. That's the best I can say."

The DSD operative released his grip on the boy. He Lin rubbed his hands as if the act of touching Jiang Menglin was to touch filth. Then He Lin smiled with a dash of irony. "Stop the car," He Lin ordered the driver. The vehicle came to a gradual halt. "Is that all you have to say?"

"Well, professor Hu Shi said that Marxism was nonsense."

"When did he say this to you?"

"Today. Just before our rendezvous."

"Shit. I don't care about Marx. I care about traitors." He took out another Turkish cigarette and tapped it on the palm of his hand. "You get out. Your information better be good."

He Lin lowered the window so that he could watch the young man walk away. It was a slow gait that veered back and forth tentatively into the crowd. Then He Lin lit his cigarette and shut the window.

After the institute meeting Hu Shi walked over to the History Building where the evening lecture was to occur. But Hu attended another meeting in the basement. The meeting was about *Charter 08*. Various speakers talked about what it might mean for the country if the constitution were to be amended. Shing Yue (a history professor) suggested that Liu Xiaobo could be interpreted via Confucian duty. Hu Shi said that might be a stretch and thought that a Marxian interpretation would better fit the document. There was also some discussion on how *Charter 08* might be seen as a logical step in the People's Revolution. The meeting ended at nine. Then Hu Shi met Ding Chaoxing and they went to dinner. It had been agreed that if things had gone well at the department meeting that they would eat at a nice restaurant and if badly, they'd go to a "stand-up" place.

Things had gone well!

As they sat across the table from each other. Hu Shi gave Ding Chaoxing the details of his promotion to deputy director of the research institute. The appointment would be effective after the New Year and would mean a 30 percent increase in salary. The couple gazed at each other with the sublimity of the future sparkling in their eyes.

Hu Shi was sitting in the kitchen waiting for his wife. He had set out the food: youtiao for him and zongzi for Ding (she was, after all, from Shanghai). They both had a cup of warmed milk set out that was cooling rapidly by the minute. Today, she was not too late. There would be no problem bicycling to the campus in time for an 11AM lecture. The banter was gone. Instead, they talked about how they would decorate their place with their new income, and how they might fashion a nursery for their future child. Except for time constraints of going to work, the couple was ready to start *that process* immediately! The couple looked longingly at each other, and Hu Shi reached for her hand and started to say something and then stopped. The clock chimed. They both laughed.

Duty first. Time to dress. Time to depart. They put the rubber bands on their pant legs, got their bikes, and headed for the door. It was a bright

November day. Ding Chaoxing mounted her bike and looked back for Hu Shi. He was just getting his leg around when four husky policemen appeared from nowhere, grabbed Hu Shi and kicked his bike over.

Ding Chaoxing started screaming when one of the police pulled a gun and pointed it at her. She understood and stopped. They took her husband away from her. They put him into a dark blue van and drove off.

The diminutive history professor looked at Hu Shi's bike lying on the ground: the front wheel was twisted up. She dismounted her own bike and stood it against the wall of the apartment building while she returned her husband's bike to their flat. When she returned, her own bike had been stolen. On the ground was her backpack with her lecture notes and her university papers strewn on the pavement. Ding Chaoxing shut her eyes for a moment. Then she opened them and said aloud to no one, "What does it matter: A bicycle? A husband?" She shut her eyes once more and opened them again without a tear. But then a drop hit her nose. She looked up to the sky. It was beginning to rain. She shook her head and sighed. Chaoxing walked alone to the campus in the rain.

4

Legal Justifications

Part Two of our exploration examines what I take to be the principal approaches to justifying human rights: legal justifications, interest justifications, and agency justifications. There are others that we won't explore – such as religious justifications. Some authors (though primarily in one category) also work in another category, such as Joseph Raz, whom I characterize primarily in the interest category even though he has done much work in the legal category as well. To make sense of these dualizers, I concentrate mostly on the justification rather than the application of human rights. (For a discussion of applications, see Part Three.)

Part Two ends with an analysis of the role that ontology should or should not play in our understanding of human rights. It is certainly a key concept that is largely ignored in contemporary discourse on human rights.

Chapter 4 examines the proposition that human rights are best understood as the result of legal justifications. Those who are attracted to this position will also be those who are most drawn to the presentation in Chapter 2 on the recent history of human rights. In this chapter some of the philosophical consequences of this position are examined in the light of the proponents of this position and this author's critique of the same.

4.1 LEGAL JUSTIFICATIONS

Those advocating legal justifications are immediately confronted with a problem when they seek to move from the national to the international arena. They are very different. Are they even analogous? Do they make sense or are they bound in some inherent contradiction? Are they sufficient to justify a general theory of human rights?

To answer such questions, let us begin with the simpler arena of the nation-state and see what characteristics it exhibits. To explore these dynamics let's look at two examples from the United States: (a) women's de jure right to vote, and (b) African Americans' de facto right to vote.

This exposition takes on the shared community worldview that is nationally based (sometimes called municipally based). These legal systems are minimally defined as *governmental orders backed up by threats.* In democracies the orders come in the form of laws that are considered and agreed upon by a legislative body elected by some portion of the population designated to choose the lawmakers. The sovereign (here understood as that institutional entity at the apex of authority) is the people's representative.[1] In the United States there is shared sovereignty among the legislative branch (that enacts the rules), the executive (enforcement) branch, and the legal (highest review of the rules) branch. In an autocracy the monarch/dictator is the sovereign.

For clarification in understanding this dynamic let us agree on a distinction between first- and second-order rules and meta-foundational rules.[2] A first-order rule is the rule-making function. It concerns the process of making rules in the society and the scope of the intended obligations. A second-order rule addresses shortcomings in first-order rules considered by themselves: uncertainty, static character, and inefficiency. By employing rule-remedies to these shortcomings, second-order rules create a richer sense of a legal system. They answer the uncertainty defect with a rule of recognition. The static character is handled by rules of change. Finally, the inefficiency problem is addressed by rules of adjudication (and the creation of a court system).[3]

A meta-foundational rule concerns the higher order authority that the legislators or sovereign use to justify the rules that are set out.[4] This justification can be an abstract moral principle or an appeal to a historical community worldview with its attendant institutions and the procedures that can bring about rational understanding and consensual

---

[1] As such, the people (in a democracy) are sovereign. However, their interests in macro communities must be advanced by institutions that are directly or indirectly politically accountable.

[2] H. L. A. Hart makes a similar distinction in *The Concept of Law* (Oxford: Oxford University Press, 1961): 208–231, 255–257. I have changed the terms from primary and secondary rules to first- and second-order rules to try to alleviate confusion. Though there is some overlap in Hart's and my distinctions, I have modified his distinctions substantially for my own purposes.

[3] Here I am following Hart closely.

[4] My understanding of foundational rules departs radically from that of Hart.

acceptance of first- and second-order rules in the given domain (e.g., the state or the world). Those who advocate a positivist understanding of law on the model of John Austin will take rules (such as those dealing with rights) to be answered, in cases where the statute is ambiguous, first from British common law and in cases in which it is still undetermined, to Britain's adopted parent, the Roman Empire.[5] Like Hegel, Austin holds that meta-foundational authority lies in history: precedent.

Whether one grounds law in morality or in the historical community (shared community worldview, authoritative texts, past legislative enactment, or judicial precedent), it is assumed that meta-foundational rules exhibit more authority than first-order rules. This is because meta-foundational rules condition first-order rules and not vice versa. Observance must be maintained via specified sanctions (including moral suasion administered socially).

With respect to first- and second-order rules, in democracies the people, in principle, can change the laws through the political process. The way they do it sets out the statute itself and the way it is brought about enhances rule recognition (the most important second-order rule). In autocracies the people, in principle, can change the law through violent or nonviolent revolution. Rule recognition comes from putting people in jail or killing them.

For the most part (in democracies) popular movements ground their desires for first-order rule change in morality-based appeals. But this need not be the case. One might say that he wants a rule changed from advocating A to advocating B from a principle of personal self-interest or because it fits in with the group self-interest in some way construed. In either event, first-order rules are changed only on the basis of arguments from a meta-foundational rule vantage-point.

Since most of our examples take place in the United States (a democracy) we highlight this governmental perspective here. In the United States, the women's suffrage movement began in the middle of the nineteenth century. From 1832 onward it did not really gain traction. It wasn't until the suffrage movement linked up with the abolitionist movement that sufficient political momentum made the Seneca Falls Convention in 1848 possible. Suffragists like Elizabeth Cady Stanton and Lucretia Mott teamed up with abolitionists such as William Lloyd Garrison and

---

[5] John Austin, *Lectures on Jurisprudence,* 5th ed., ed. Robert Campbell (London: John Murray, 1885).

Frederick Douglass to try to energize a national movement.[6] They were unsuccessful. Other tactics were needed.[7] The movement sought another partner. Enter the prohibitionists. Together they won the day so that on June 4, 1919, the Senate followed the House, which had ratified the constitutional amendment a year earlier, and the amendment went to the states; they promptly began ratifying it until Tennessee on August 18, 1920, put it over the top and it became law eight days later. Women won the right to vote in the United States on August 26, 1920. When my late mother was born (1917) women could not vote in the United States. The UK followed suit in 1928, Canada declared women to be people (and thus able to vote) in 1929, and at the writing of this book women still cannot vote in Bhutan, Lebanon, Brunei, Saudi Arabia, and the United Arab Emirates.

The essence of this story is that 51 percent of the U.S. population (women in a biologically statistically normal sample space) was denied the right to vote by law. In order to alter this, the law had to be changed. In one sense (a strictly legal one on the first-order rule model) women in the United States did not have the right to vote before 1920. But what about the meta-foundational moral sense? Did they always have a right to vote except that the society did not recognize this moral right? If meta-foundational rules are interpreted merely as the history of the shared community worldview, then the answer is, "No!" Women did not possess a meta-foundational right to vote. This position is called the *emergent rights* position of human rights: particular human rights exist only when there is a society that recognizes that right.[8] However, if the meta-foundational rules are interpreted as moral principles, then the question is an open one subject to the particular moral theory that is brought forward. In Chapter 6, I contend that women have always had this right. It was simply a right that was not recognized (a failure of second-order rules) by the given society. Such an omission is to any society's discredit.

---

[6] Two accounts of this dynamic are Ellen Carol Dubois, *Feminism and Suffrage: The Emergence of an Independent Women's Movement in America 1848–1869* (Ithaca, NY: Cornell University Press, 1999), and Jean H. Baker, *Sisters: The Lives of America's Suffragists* (New York: Hill and Wang, 2006).

[7] To get a feel for these sorts of tactics, see the interactive book Kerrie Logan Holihan, *Rightfully Ours: How Women Won the Vote* (Chicago: Chicago Review Press, 2012).

[8] For a fine defense of this position, see Beth Singer, *Operative Rights* (Albany, NY: State University of New York Press, 1993), and Paul Gordon Lauren, *The Evolution of International Human Rights: Visions Seen* (Philadelphia: University of Pennsylvania Press, 1998).

The second example concerns de facto voting privileges for African Americans in the United States before 1965. Here, the situation is a little more complicated. After slavery was abolished by the Thirteenth Amendment to the United States Constitution, and the Fourteenth Amendment overruled the *Dred Scott* case that denied African Americans equal protection under the law and made them full citizens (including the right to vote), it would seem that the problem was solved by rules enacted by a reasonably democratic process. Thus, de jure African Americans had the right to vote. But then under the so-called Jim Crow laws, various obstructions to vote were set up, especially in the states that had formed the Confederacy in the Civil War. These obstructions (affecting second-order rule recognition, change, and adjudication) included charging people large sums to vote (relative to their means) and including unanswerable questions in a literacy test, such as how many bubbles are there in a bar of soap? Though African Americans had the legal right to vote, the practice in these locales was rather different. In some southern states a sizable population was disenfranchised. Like the women's suffrage movement, political change did not occur without demonstrations. From the filing of the lawsuit *Brown v. Board of Education*, 347 U.S. 483 (1954), to Rosa Parks's refusal to sit at the back of the bus (1955) to the founding of the Southern Christian Leadership Conference by Charles K. Steele and Fred Shuttles (1957) and the stalwart work of many others (Martin Luther King Jr., John Lewis, Ralph Abernathy, et al.), a political process was engaged that used the *worldview overlap and modification* strategy to create a normative worldview transformation in mainstream America.[9] The result was the 1964 Civil Rights Act and the 1965 Voting Rights Act.[10] The political process in the United States proved successful. Though de jure rights had been obtained almost a century before, they were not uniformly enforced de facto. The enforcement of the law is a major part of the "sanctions" portion of the rule of law. Unless the rule is enforced with the threat of penalty, there really is (in fact) no law. This was the situation at the time especially in the cited states: Alabama, Alaska, Arizona, Georgia, Louisiana, Mississippi, South Carolina, Texas,

---

[9] I describe this process in Michael Boylan, *A Just Society* (Lanham, MD: Rowman and Littlefield, 2004): 10–14. I use the case of Martin Luther King Jr., in particular, as a paradigm of this process.

[10] There are a number of good accounts on this transformation – many of them citing first-person narratives. Two rather focused, balanced discussions come from Bruce J. Dierenfield, *The Civil Rights Movement*, rev. ed. (Boston: Longman, 2008), and Sara Bullard, *Free at Last: A History of the Civil Rights Movement and Those Who Died in the Struggle* (Oxford: Oxford University Press, 1994).

and Virginia. These states were put under federal supervision regarding voting restrictions.

Though this case is different from the first example of women's suffrage (because in that case there was never a de jure right) it is similar in the way that it could persuade institutions to allow the vote to those who had been denied it. And similarly, this de facto charge to obey existing law again suggests the question of whether African Americans had the right to vote only after the 1965 Voting Rights that required enforcement of existing law or whether African Americans *always* had this right but it was simply not observed (a failure in second-order rules). As in the case of women's rights, I argue in Chapter 6 that it is the latter: a moral principle acting as a meta-foundational rule that should have been observed by legislators. They were wrong not to do so. The legal approach to justifying human rights has a hard time with examples such as this. This is why it is not my choice for grounding human rights.

4.2 PROBLEMS WITH INTERNATIONAL LAW

Even if the legal approach is not sufficient to ground human rights (as I contend), we cannot ignore the legal approach. This is because in the practical sphere, rights are recognized and enforced within the context of legal systems. Since the question of natural human rights is not bound by nations, we are forced to extend our discussion of the legal context for human rights to the international sphere. The realms of international law and cosmopolitan moral rights are very contentious. Let us address these in order.

First, there is the issue of international law. What is international law? If law, in its simplest form consists of *governmental orders backed up by threats,* then we have to ask these questions: (a) who issues the orders, and (b) who enforces the threats (and what authority is brought forth to ensure second-order rule recognition)?

In the first case the orders generally come either from the United Nations or from bilateral or multilateral treaties. So long as they are negotiated in a fair manner recognizing all parties involved, one can assume that at some minimum level (appropriate to the international community) the orders set out represent the will of a significant number of nations who are stakeholders (those who in some way are affected by the proposed rule).

In the second case, since we have no mechanism of international sovereignty, the model of the sovereign making the rules and backing them up with sanctions goes out the window.[11] Both international models work on voluntary sanctions. This is a severe practical problem, and because the legal model is only about a practical solution, it is another challenge to this approach. However, it is a challenge that we have to meet in practical implementation. The reason is *that it is all we have* in the realm of action. However, in the meantime what really happens is that if a state is significantly upset over the activities of another state, they go to war. The enforcement mechanism is the threat of war.

Now these days, war is a many-faceted thing. I have shown elsewhere that interstate wars are on the decline in a significant way.[12] In its place are regional intrastate conflicts with outside surrogates giving support (from guns, to aerial support, to boots on the ground) and the advent of drones and cyber warfare.[13] This new face of war has played out through the Arab Spring of 2011. In most of those instances, the *support surrogate role* allowed Western countries to supply the insurgents. In Libya this was extended to providing air support to the rebels (by participating NATO nations) to counter Qaddafi's use of his own air force to bomb the rebels. Again, the surrogate role was successful and Qaddafi was killed and replaced. A second wave of the Arab Spring involves Syria. At the writing of this book, the support surrogate role has taken the form of weapons supplies, food, and medical assistance – especially over the border in Turkey. If Bashar Hafez al-Assad escalates the war, there is a threat that NATO forces and the Arab League may step up their involvement.

In Afghanistan and elsewhere (such as Somalia), drone warfare has been the stick of choice to sanction those who wish to engage in international terrorism. In Iran (vis-à-vis their nuclear program and the intelligence that they are violating the international prohibition on creating

---

[11] Some, like Hart, believe that there is a logical contradiction in a national sovereign becoming a nonsovereign to some realm of international authority. Either the state chooses when and how it will voluntarily agree to allow itself to pay a fine or otherwise accept punishment or it ceases to be a state. A voluntarily accepted punishment hardly fits the notion of law set out previously. For a discussion, see Hart, *The Concept of Law*, 215ff.; Glenn Negley, "Values, Sovereignty, and World Law," *Ethics: An International Journal of Social, Political, and Legal Philosophy* **60** (1950): 208–214; Thomas May, "Sovereignty and Internal Order," *Ratio Juris* 8.3 (1995): 287–295; and Jean Cohen, "Whose Sovereignty? Empire v. International Law," *Ethics and International Affairs* **18**.3 (2004): 1–24.

[12] Michael Boylan, *Morality and Global Justice: Justifications and Applications* (Boulder, CO: Westview, 2011): ch. 13.

[13] I most recently discussed this in a speech at Oxford's Institute for Ethics, Law, and Armed Conflict on November 8, 2011. A podcast of this speech is available at www.elac.ox.ac.uk/podcasts/.

new nuclear states), cyber warfare has been the weapon of choice to enforce the prohibition.

But warfare is not a proper sanction to an arena that seeks to cultivate the rule of law. This is because war is capricious and can be driven by extreme internal factions. The rule of law requires (in its best conception) a mechanical subsumption of rule recognition, discovery of offense by an entity that has been given that legal power, and punishment within set confines of proportional retributive harms. These conditions for the rule of law are generally absent from the model of warfare. To put law enforcement into the hands of military generals or a fear-prone populace is to invite a state-of-nature krateristic approach. "Kraterism" is what I call the might makes right approach (after the ancient Greek word for power). Such a situation inherently promotes vigilante anarchy and thus cannot stand as a reasonable model for "international law."

A better model for sanctions is multilateral economic penalties. These can be effective if enough nations sign on but can be rendered useless if one major player decides to go its own way (and undercut the effect of the sanctions). The economic embargo against South Africa in the 1970s–1980s was successful in bringing about the end of apartheid and the election of Nelson Mandela on May 9, 1994.

However, as this book is being written, many cases of trade embargoes are not as successful – such as those against Iran (vis-à-vis its nuclear weapons program) and Syria (in its efforts to quash internal protest). What makes the multilateral economic penalties so appealing is that they use diplomatic devices to represent the stick (sanction). There is something about the rule of law that seeks to use as little violence as possible in bringing about its ends. But to do so, there has to be virtually unanimous consensus among the G-20 nations for them to be effective, and there must be complete unanimity among the G-6. This display of the second-order *rule of change* gives authority to *rule recognition*. The future of international law lies here.

In the third case, since there is no long-standing shared-community worldview – or even an extended community worldview[14] – the "historical community" answer is not really an option. If we put war off the table because *kraterism* is always the course of last resort (and because appeal merely to self-interest is internally incoherent considered generally), and if we put laws based upon the historical community off the table

---

[14] The extended community worldview imperative seeks to address communities beyond our ken – such as those described by Peter K. Unger, *Living High and Letting Die* (Oxford: Oxford University Press, 1996); see my discussion in Boylan, *Morality and Global Justice*, 25–27.

(because there is no viable cosmopolitan historical community), then what we are left with is the question of how to justify cosmopolitan moral rights. I have been drawn into this controversy because my 2004 book on justice (*A Just Society*) took a nationalist or statist perspective. I did this because I was following Hart's analysis of the amorphous character of international sanctions (a critical part of any operational legal system).[15] However, I believe that the critical answers to these questions must come from a searching discussion among the nations of the world about what counts as a moral right and how it can transfer into something resembling the sort of emerging quasi-legal system set out previously. The prescription is essential for second-order international rules to develop. This is a tough assignment, and I believe that only natural human rights will fit the bill to provide the sort of justification that will get the ball really rolling. Read on to see why I think this to be the case.

4.3 META-FOUNDATIONAL RULES AND LEGAL JUSTIFICATIONS FOR HUMAN RIGHTS

Without a doubt, the Universal Declaration of Human Rights is a historically significant document (coming as it did at the end of World War II, during which horrific evil occurred in the Holocaust and in the acts of the Japanese army, such as the rape of Nanking). Atrocities often bring about different reactions. How are we to understand these reactions? It is characteristic of the legal justification of human rights that debates are engaged about fashioning a change that might prevent the latest horrific event from happening again. Different intuitions are engaged with the hope that some policy response might emerge. Various writers who support the *emergence position* on human rights often take the post–World War II moment as the baptism of modern sensibilities about human rights.[16] The worldview behind the emergent theories is that human rights are not "natural" nor do they follow from "natural law." Rather, they are human constructions that are based on conscience or on intuitions that are elicited by horrific actions. There are two worldviews behind the emergent

---

[15] See my precise response in "A Reply to My Colleagues," in *Morality and Justice: Reading Boylan's 'A Just Society,'* ed. John-Stewart Gordon (Lanham, MD: Lexington Books, 2009): 179–220.

[16] See Charles Beitz, *The Idea of Human Rights* (Oxford: Oxford University Press, 2009), 1, 13–14; Kenneth Cmiel, "The Recent History of Human Rights," *American Historical Review* **109**.1 (2004): 117–135, 117–118; and J. H. Burgers, "The Road to San Francisco: The Revival of the Human Rights Idea in the Twentieth Century," *Human Rights Quarterly* **14** (1992): 447–477.

hypothesis. The first worldview is consistent with one version of the post-modern suspicion that there are no abiding truths in history.[17] This can come in the thick or thin variety. In the thick variety, epistemology amounts to a particular way of framing for the sake of achieving certain practical ends (part of the narrative one is living by). Some versions of pragmatism can also resemble this (even when they aspire to be externalist).[18] The focus is upon the result to be achieved. This is not too far removed from the "save the phenomena" move in the history of science that Kuhn and others have discussed.[19] When one concentrates upon the end – such as a particular policy end – then one works retroactively to create enabling conditions to allow that policy to happen. For example, one might wish to deny women the right to have an abortion and so create enabling conditions for this public policy that involves a definition of personhood at the first cell division of pregnancy and to subsume the status of the pre-blastula into the laws covering the murder of persons living in the world.[20] The government, under this account, should step in and interfere with a person's liberty to have an abortion.

In another case, the same person might not want universal health coverage as a public policy entitlement. In this account, the prior conditions might be that the individual does not want to be forced to pay taxes for someone else's health coverage (in the case of single payer or

[17] For some broad overviews of post-modernism and understanding history, see Jörn Rüsen, "Jacob Burckhardt: Political Standpoint and Historical Insight on the Border of Post-Modernism," *History and Theory* **24**.3 (1985): 235–246; David Jasper, "Violence and Post-Modernism," *History of European Ideas* **20**.4–6 (1995): 801–806; Perez Zagorin, "History, the Referent, and Narrative: Reflections on Postmodernism Now," *History and Theory* **38**.1 (1999): 1–24; and Louis Mink, "Postmodernism and the Vocation of Historiography," *Modern Intellectual History* **7**.1 (2010): 151–184.

[18] The project of pragmatism along with naturalized realism can ironically take this sort of turn. For some of this discussion (which is very wide ranging), see Albert Hofstader, "The Myth of the Whole: A Consideration of Quine's View of Knowledge," *Journal of Philosophy* **51** (1954): 397–416; Henry Frankfurt, "Meaning, Truth, and Pragmatism," *Philosophical Quarterly* **10** (1960): 171–176; John Capps, "Dewey, Quine, and Pragmatic Naturalized Epistemology," *Transactions of the Charles S. Peirce Society* **32**.4 (1996): 634–668; and Thomas Mormann, "A Place for Pragmatism in the Dynamics of Reason?" *Studies in the History and Philosophy of Science* **43**.1 (2012): 27–37.

[19] I am thinking here of Thomas S. Kuhn, *The Copernican Revolution* (Cambridge, MA: Harvard University Press, 1957): ch. 2 and the general argument of Paul Feyerabend, *Against Method* (New York: Verso, 1975).

[20] The most extreme case that I have read asserts that personhood begins even before the biological parents have sex! See http://www.huffingtonpost.co.uk/2012/04/13/arizona-abortion-law-2012-pregnancy-fetus-ultrasound-late-term-abortion-20-weeks-jan-brewer_n_1422853.html and http://thenewcivilrightsmovement.com/pregnancy-begins-2-weeks-before-conception-now-the-law-in-arizona/politics/2012/04/13/37993.

government-run models) or to be forced to purchase health insurance in the open market (the approach of the U.S. Affordable Healthcare Act, 2010). In the case of health care the individual claims that he does *not* want the government to step in to interfere with a person's liberty to take care of his own health *just the way he wants to.*

It is often the case that one and the same person holds that the government *should* and *should not* interfere with individual liberty of action on important choices in anyone's private life. Why should this apparent contradiction be allowed? The answer from the thick form of post-modernism is, "Why not?" One seeks various ends for practical reasons. Each end requires its own background story and so it goes. Different background stories tag onto different policy options that both support and deny human rights. Since these post-modernists are neither coherentists nor correspondence theory advocates, no problem ensues.[21] There may be some reason that a particular collection of policy ends is chosen, but there need not be; the thick theory does not require it.

The thin form of post-modernism creates a background condition of cultural history that both buffers sudden changes and offers a direction for the evolution of new standards that flow from popular movements: a sort of dialectical process that resists quick change but can affirm *proper* modifications at the same time. This sort of direction follows from one reading of Hegel's *Philosophy of Right.*[22] Hegel believes that the *Sittlichkeit* in its historical development better describes the way we should view rights and ethics than *Moralität* because it is more concrete and particular than the "empty formalism" of Kant.[23] These represent the two modes of justifying meta-foundational rules set out earlier.

---

[21] For a discussion of this issue within a large context, see Michael Boylan, *The Good, the True, and the Beautiful* (London: Continuum, 2008), part two.

[22] G. W. H. Hegel, *Grundlinien der Philosophie des Rechts,* ed. Hansgeorg Hoppe (Frankfurt: Suhrkamp, 2005): section 135.

[23] The contemporary particularist objection comes from Jonathan Dancy, *Ethics without Principles* (Oxford: Clarendon, 2006); cf. Joseph Raz, "The Trouble with Particularism," *Mind* **115**.457 (2006): 99–120 and Mark N. Lane and Olivia M. Little, "Defending Moral Particularism," in *Contemporary Debates in Moral Theory,* ed. James Dreier (Malden, MA: Blackwell, 2006). The second objection comes from G. W. F. Hegel, *Werke,* vol. 8, *Grundlinien der Philosophie des Rechts,* ed. E. Gans; trans. T. M. Knox, *Hegel 's Philosophy of Right* (Oxford: Clarendon Press, 1942), section 153, pp. 90ff. See also Allen Wood's explanation of this critique in "The Emptiness of the Moral Will," *The Monist* 72 (1989): 454–483. For a defense of Kant on this point, see Marcus Singer, *Generalization in Ethics* (New York: Athenaeum, 1961): 279–295, and David Cummiskey, *Kantian Consequentialism* (Oxford: Oxford University Press, 1996): 47–50. For a compromise opinion, see Christine M. Korsgaard, "Ethical, Political, Religious Thought," in *Creating the Kingdom of Ends* (Cambridge: Cambridge University Press, 1996): 14–16.

Under this thin theory, one assumes a direction of history that is continually self-justifying. For example, advocates of this position might point to the U.S. Supreme Court's *Bowers v. Hardwick*, 478 US 186 (1986), that upheld Georgia's sodomy law as being situationally "true" for that snapshot in time as measured by the standards of legal realism that says the law should mirror the commonly held views/standards on morality. In 1986, those community views held homosexuality to be a voluntary choice that the mainstream (heterosexual community) viewed as a perversion. When in 2003 the shared community worldview changed, so did the court's position on homosexual activity. In *Lawrence v. Texas*, 539 US 558 (2003), the court reversed itself and struck down the anti-sodomy laws. This change in interpreting the law represented an advance in recognizing the rights of homosexuals to act in accord with their biological orientation. The court changed because popular attitudes changed. Why did popular attitudes change? From the perspective of the thick or thin versions of post-modernism, the answer is made in *descriptive* terms dealing with how gays and lesbians are depicted in popular media and public polls. No definitive *reason* can be given. It is very Heraclitan: *things are changing all the time; one must be attentive and align oneself to the river's flow.*

4.4 CONTRACTARIANISM AS A SUPPORT FOR LEGAL RIGHTS

The second worldview behind the emergent hypothesis follows from the first and asserts a contractarian view of rights and morality. John Rawls and Charles Beitz offer examples on how this sort of procedure works. Rawls's argument runs this way:[24]

ARGUMENT 4.1: RAWLS'S CONTRACTARIAN JUSTIFICATION FOR LEGAL RIGHTS

1. [These conditions of (a) there being a reasonable starting point for liberal societies to provide rightly based stability; (b) an advancement toward democratic peace; and (c) a social contract that ties together our considered political convictions and moral judgments jointly would justify the argument for the law of peoples for liberal societies] – Assertion[25]

2. [A reasonable utopia should be the goal for the law of peoples] – Assertion

---

[24] John Rawls, *The Law of Peoples* (Cambridge, MA: Harvard University Press, 2001).
[25] My reconstruction of logical arguments in this book follows the rules I set out in *Critical Inquiry: The Process of Argument* (Boulder, CO: Westview, 2010).

3. 'Reasonable' means that (a) it relies on socially feasible pluralism, and (b) it recognizes primary goods and basic liberties – Fact (Rawls, *The Law of Peoples*, pp. 12–13)

4. 'Utopia' means that (a) the society is constitutional; (b) liberties are assigned a special priority; (c) all citizens are given at least minimal primary goods; (d) the principle of reciprocity is manifested – Assertion (p. 14)

5. A 'reasonable utopia' employs (a) a political conception of justice; (b) political and social institutions; (c) a commitment to a consensus of compatible comprehensive doctrines; and (d) a reasonable amount of tolerance – Assertion (pp. 15–16)

6. The law of peoples satisfies conditions mentioned in premises #3–5 – Assertion (pp. 14–16)

7. [The law of peoples satisfies the goal of a reasonable utopia] – #2–6

8. Liberal peoples are (a) under a constitutional government; (b) united by common sympathy; and (c) have a dual moral nature (a sense of justice and a conception of the good) – Assertion (pp. 23–24)

9. Liberal peoples consider themselves first as states and then internationally – Assertion (p. 26)

10. [The process of law-making internationally is analogous to that of law-making nationally] – Assertion

11. National law-making requires an original position imposing five essential features: (a) the original position models the parties as representing citizens fairly; (b) it models them as rational; (c) it models them as selecting from among available principles of justice those to apply to the appropriate subject, in this case the basic structure; (d) the parties are modeled as making these selections for appropriate reasons; and (e) the parties select reasons related to the fundamental interests of citizens as reasonable and rational – Assertion (pp. 30–31)

12. International law-making requires an original position imposing three additional points: (a) parties are situated symmetrically and thus fairly; (b) parties are rational and guided by fundamental interests of democratic society; and (c) parties are subject to a veil of ignorance properly adjusted for international terms – Assertion (p. 32)

13. The process that liberal peoples engage in when making international law should contain the two original positions – 8–12

14. The two original positions along with the character of liberal peoples imply the traditional principles of international justice: (a) peoples are free and independent, and their freedom and independence are to be respected by other peoples; (b) peoples are to observe treaties and undertakings; (c) peoples are equal and are parties to the agreements that bind them; (d) peoples are to observe a duty of nonintervention; (e) peoples have a right of self-defense but no right to instigate war for reasons other than self-defense; (f) peoples are to honor human rights; (g) peoples are to observe certain specified restrictions in the conduct of war; (h) peoples have a duty to assist other peoples living under unfavorable conditions that prevent their having a just or decent political and social regime – Assertion (p. 37)

15. [The traditional principles of international justice are highly plausible and provide stability for the right reasons] – Assertion

16. The second original position (a reasonable starting point) is highly plausible and provides stability for the right reasons – 7, 8, 13, 14, 15

17. There are three sorts of international organizations: (a) trade; (b) bank lending; and (c) a quasi-legislative group (like the United Nations) – Assertion (p. 42)

18. The organizations cited in #17 provide stability for the right reasons (as opposed to the stability formed out of fear) – Assertion (pp. 43–44)

19. To create real peace, societies have to disavow extending their territories and ruling over other nations and to accept the peace hypothesis: (a) all just democratic societies should accept their political institutions, their history, and their achievements: this acceptance makes their peace more secure; (b) to the extent that societies satisfy (a), they will be less likely to go to war except in self-defense – Assertion (p. 49)

20. One is inclined to accept the conditions of the principles in premise #19 if they possess the five features of a just society: (a) fair equality of opportunity; (b) a decent distribution of income and wealth; (c) society as an employer of last resort; (d) basic health care for all; (e) public financing of elections – Assertion (p. 50)

21. Liberal societies will be just and satisfied by fulfilling the conditions in #20 – Assertion (pp. 50–51)

22. Liberal societies advance democratic peace by meeting the conditions of a satisfied society – 17–21 (pp. 50, 51–54)

23. Public reason requires reciprocal debate from the standpoint of being an "as if" legislator – Assertion (p. 56)
24. [Debating from the standpoint of liberal people "as if" they were legislators unites various sections of society] – Assertion
25. The social contract understanding of the law of peoples coherently ties together our considered political convictions and moral judgments – 8, 23–25 (pp. 54–57)

------

26. The law of peoples is sound and justified for liberal peoples – 1, 16, 22, 26 (p. 58)

Under Rawls's theory applied internationally, decent societies that fall short of liberal societies should be tolerated, but benevolent absolutist societies and outlaw societies should be changed. The force of this argument follows from the second form of the original position along with public discourse.

Much has been said about the national or statist standpoint of Rawls's 1971 argument from *A Theory of Justice*. Documents such as the Universal Declaration of Human Rights or the Helsinki Accord have an international scope. Thus, if our purview in human rights discussion were *only* about what we do within the contexts of nations, then it would seem that they would be inadequate to handle what the present age demands. For this reason, Rawls follows his earlier work (*A Theory of Justice*, 1971) with one that has an international scope (*The Law of Peoples*, 2001). Here, Rawls introduces criteria to achieve a reasonable utopia. These criteria are grounded in his conception of a liberal society. Only a liberal society can achieve this goal. The criteria listed in premises 19 and 20 set out these conditions that allow for a second original position to go forward. This original position is not the same as the original position of his earlier work because it has more exacting outcomes. Those arguments were set against the nationalist version. Objectors to *A Theory of Justice*'s original position focused upon (a) the veil of ignorance since it makes such unreasonable expectations upon the parties involved that it fails in its avowed goal to illustrate pure human nature because no real persons can ever be situated in a veil of ignorance – it is a thought experiment about a possible world that is not and cannot be ours;[26] and (b) the

------

[26] I have called such moves "the thought experiment fallacy." It occurs when one creates a possible world that is unlike our own in essential ways. Then the practitioner poses and solves a problem in that possible world and seeks to apply the conclusion to our own world. See Michael Boylan, *The Good, the True, and the Beautiful* (London: Continuum, 2008): 211–213.

mini-max view of rational decision theory is flawed because it presents a skewed view of rationality that does not account for a wider view of individual preference assessment according to a multi-variable model that may (for example) include gambling.[27] These alleged shortcomings are only accentuated here when applied internationally. Sen makes a similar point against Rawls when applied broadly.[28] He claims that Rawls's contractarian bias limits the desired contrast between Rawls's own theory and utilitarianism (thus excluding capability theory). When seen in the perspective of the agency approach to justifying human rights (as I depict capability theory), then Sen and I are in agreement in our criticism of Rawls's contractarianism to justify the argument made earlier.

Another proponent of a different sort of contractarianism is Charles Beitz. Beitz's argument runs this way:[29]

ARGUMENT 4.2: BEITZ'S CONTRACTARIAN JUSTIFICATION
FOR LEGAL RIGHTS

1. Agreement theories conceptualize human rights as standards that are objects of agreement among members of different cultures whose moral and political values are dissimilar – Fact (Beitz, *The Idea of Human Rights*, p. 73)
2. There are two main sorts of agreement theories: (a) common core, and (b) overlapping consensus – Assertion (p. 74)
3. Common core advocates exclude rights to democracy, religious toleration, legality for women, and free choice of a marriage partner because these protections are not found in every country – Fact (p. 75)
4. Common core advocates also exclude rights that incur too heavy duties – such as physical and mental health – Fact (p. 75)
5. Common core advocates frequently refer only to the major societies in the world (to the exclusion of others) – Fact (p. 75)
6. Common core agreement theories are deficient – 2–5 (p. 75)
7. Overlapping agreement consensus comes from John Rawls – Assertion (pp.76–77)

---

[27] Advocates of gambling generally claim that there is an *intrinsic* payoff in trying for one's ideal profession (for example). Even if the recent Ph.D. in philosophy from a top school cannot get a job in his field and ends up selling insurance, he may consider that earning the degree may have been worthwhile: the gamble contains an intrinsic value. Outcomes analyses only (that are generally part of game theory simulations) are not sufficient to describe worldview self-fulfillment.

[28] Amartya Sen, *The Idea of Justice* (Cambridge, MA: Harvard University Press, 2009): ch. 2.

[29] Beitz, *The Idea of Human Rights*, 73–95.

8. Human rights theories are supposed to be critical norms to judge or to revise national laws – Assertion (p. 78)

9. If actual consensus is the standard, then the existence of a racist society might agree with genocide, but this is to get agreement and justification backward – Fact (p. 78)

10. Actual consensus agreement theories should be rejected because they mix up agreement and justification – 6–9 (p. 78)

11. One way to rectify the problem in #10's problem is to put conditions upon deliberation that would be used in international agreement à la Bernard Williams[30] that a regime is legitimate if most people obey the law from a justified belief and not out of a fear of punishment – Assertion (pp. 78–80)

12. Abdullahi An-Na'im[31] sets out pragmatic grounds that support consensus theories (since without consensus there will not be compliance) – Fact (pp. 80–81)

13. The Helsinki Declaration is an example of a swap: USSR gets recognized boundaries for Eastern Europe and in return accepts the existence of certain human rights – Fact (p. 82)

14. An-Na'im's approach is to create a trade-off discussion of this (Helsinki) sort to spur moral development around the world (thus satisfying the objections to actual consensus) – 10–13 (pp. 82–83)

15. The American Anthropological Association's Executive Board in 1947 was skeptical about the Universal Declaration of Human Rights concerning the issue of paternalism – Fact (pp. 83–85)

16. Appeal to some common worldview assumptions can create a climate wherein actual agreement is replaced by progressive convergence – Assertion (pp. 86–88)

17. All agreement theories possess this dilemma: (a) human rights are supposed to provide reasons for action to members of every culture to which human rights apply, and yet (b) human rights as an international doctrine cannot be seen as actually shared among the world's main political/moral cultures; thus, it is not an object of agreement – Assertion (p. 88)

18. Premise #17 implies that either human rights must be a small subset of possible rights (the ones agreed to) or give up agreement as a basis of rights – Assertion (p. 88)

---

[30] Bernard Williams, "Human Rights and Relativism," in *In the Beginning Was the Deed* (Princeton, NJ: Princeton University Press, 2006): 62–64.

[31] Abdullahi A. An-Na'im, "Universality of Human Rights: An Islamic Perspective," in *Japan and International Law: Past, Present, and Future*, ed. Nisuke Ando (The Hague: Kluwer Law International, 1999): 315.

19. An alternative to #18 is to move away from actual agreement to possible emergent agreement that might evolve – 15–18 (p. 88)
20. This possible emergence is called progressive convergence – Fact (p. 88)
21. Progressive convergence is supported by Charles Taylor's "unforced consensus,"[32] An-Na'im's "evolutionary interpretation,"[33] and Joshua Cohen's "justificatory minimalism"[34] – Assertion (pp. 88–89)
22. Progressive convergence relies on what is reachable from a particular worldview stance (e.g., An-Na'im's progressive reform in Islam from passages in the Quran, p. 92) – Fact (p. 90)
23. This reachability can be enhanced by Bernard Williams's "sound deliberative route"[35] – Assertion (pp. 90–91)
24. If human rights are reachable from a worldview, then action to enforce human rights in a society in which that worldview was widely accepted would not be objectionable – Assertion (pp. 92–93)
25. A doctrine of human rights should express a toleration appropriate to a wide range of moral and religious worldviews: this is another aspect of "reachable from" – Assertion (p. 93)
26. [Progressive convergence of worldviews is the best form of agreement theory] – 1, 2, 6, 10, 19–25
27. Progressive convergence risks circularity unless we apply sympathetic imagination – Assertion (pp. 94–95)

---

28. Though progressive convergence via sympathetic imagination is the best agreement interpretation, it still falls short of the [utopian] goal that human rights should be recognizable as common concerns among all the world's cultures – 26–27 (p. 95)

Beitz's argument is forceful. It operates on a more concrete level than does Rawls's. The first part of the argument sets out the contrast between common core and overlapping consensus (which leads to progressive convergence with the addition of boundary conditions and the sympathetic

---

[32] Charles Taylor, "Conditions of an Unforced Consensus on Human Rights," in *The East Asian Challenge for Human Rights,* ed. Joanne R. Bauer and Daniel Bell (Cambridge: Cambridge University Press,1999): 124–144.

[33] Abdullahi A. An-Na'im, *Toward an Islamic Reformation: Civil Liberties, Human Rights, and International Law* (Syracuse, NY: Syracuse University Press, 1990): 179.

[34] Joshua Cohen, "Minimalism about Human Rights," *Journal of Political Philosophy* **12** (2004): 201, 202.

[35] Bernard Williams, "Internal Reasons and the Obscurity of Blame," in *Making Sense of Humanity* (Cambridge: Cambridge University Press, 1995): 35.

imagination). This is not too far removed from my own argument about the way everyone confronts novel normative theories.[36] I call my version *overlap and modification*. The direction is to how people can change their worldviews when confronted by an alternative that shares features of the former view. This is certainly a much more productive approach than that of the common core advocates who elicit either coinciding and amplification or dissonance and rejection.

Then there is the setting of the key issue in premise #10 about the difference between agreement and justification. I do concur that this is a central failing in contractarian theories.[37] However, Beitz believes that he can overcome this difficulty by presenting a version of contractarianism that he calls progressive convergence. What this really amounts to is a strategy for conflict negotiation in which the worldviews of the parties are taken into account as they search for common ground to agree on some common endpoint (human rights, for example). It can be anything such as environmental protection, tariff treaties, fishing rights, and so on. These are sound principles of negotiation, but they are not *distinctive* of human rights. A contrast can be made here to Robert Paul Churchill who also puts forth a theory of rights negotiation but in the context of a naturalistically grounded justification scheme.[38] Churchill's stance is that there is a difference between negotiation among a diverse group with vested interests (cross-cultural negotiation) and one's own justification standpoint regarding human rights. I support Churchill here. We can accept something like progressive convergence as a negotiation strategy without buying into it as a mode of justification. My own preference for justification is set out in Chapter 6.

What I find problematic about contractarian or agreement theories as justifications for human rights (or for morality) is that they are so invested in asserting that people acting within some constraints (such as Rawls's notion of rationality within the original position #1 or #2 or Beitz's belief in constructive dialogue that will lead to progressive convergence) will generate a normative conclusion. What is there about agreement that yields positive normativity? There are many agreements that are made that are strikingly immoral as Hegel and Marx have set out

[36] Boylan, *A Just Society*, 11–124.
[37] Michael Boylan, "Worldview and the Value-Duty Link," in Michael Boylan, ed., *Environmental Ethics* (Upper Saddle River, NJ: Prentice Hall, 2001: 180–196 [rpt. Wiley-Blackwell, 2013]): 11–12, 36–37.
[38] Robert Paul Churchill, *Human Rights and Global Diversity* (Upper Saddle River, NJ: Prentice Hall, 2006): ch. 3.

(the master-slave dialectic and the stages of alienation within industrial society).[39] What *agreement* produces is a voluntary pact between people or between institutions/countries. But agreements can be *bad*. The 1939 Nazi-Soviet Non-Aggression Pact was an agreement that was voluntary – but the ends for which it was conceived were evil. There are countless other examples like this.[40]

Those who hold contractarian theories often reply that the sorts of contracts that I am trotting forth are not *authentic* contracts. By "authentic" they really mean that they are contrary to morality that is being brought in by the back door. Unless, they mean anti-real, non-natural intuitionism, they are involved in begging the question. If they *do* mean anti-real, non-natural intuitionism, then they have seceded from the realm of intersubjective discourse. In this vacuum, only power is left. The power players engage in treaties with lesser states while they seek to exact terms favorable to their own advantage according to their shared community worldview.

This may be descriptively correct on how much progress has been made in human history, but it is hardly a defensible normative position because it is merely kraterism. The world needs something better.

4.5 WHAT CAN THE LEGAL PERSPECTIVE TELL US ABOUT HUMAN RIGHTS?

What this chapter has argued is that the legal perspective is important inasmuch as it wants practically to implement an international or cosmopolitan legal system. Through *overlap and modification* or *cross-cultural negotiation* or *progressive convergence* the practical task of second-order rule recognition will be essential for any progress in achieving an operating legal system (even of the most basic variety). As argued earlier, the most important element of this practical implementation will require an independent system of sanctions that cannot be vetoed if one of the G-6 nations is uncomfortable with the outcome.

---

[39] On the master-slave dialectic from Hegel, see G. W. F. Hegel, *The Phenomenology of Mind*, trans. J. B. Baillie (London: G. Allen and Unwin, 1931): 228–240, and on Marx, see Karl Marx, "The Economic and Philosophical Manuscripts," in Karl Marx, *Early Writings*, trans. T. B. Bottomore (New York: McGraw-Hill, 1963): 120–134, 147–157.

[40] In Boylan, *Morality and Global Justice*, 10–11, I cite the case of Wolf Sullowald, a former butcher who enters into a contract with an Austrian to be killed on an Internet site, butchered, and eaten. By all accounts the arrangement was agreeable to both sides – and there were witnesses. This is an extreme example of the defects in contractarianism as the foundation of ethical theory.

Obviously, this is a huge hurdle to surmount. At present the voluntary acceptance of sanctions amounts merely to a negotiating tool for some other policy initiative. There is never an acceptance of real penalty that is against national interest among the most powerful nations of the world. Until there is, international/cosmopolitan law will be largely utopian: an artful, meaningless charade.[41]

One of the reasons for pessimism for the project of meaningful international/cosmopolitan law respecting human rights lies in the justifications that have been employed. This chapter has argued that anti-realist theories such as ethical intuitionism and contractarianism really devolve into *kraterism*. In this way, they are not helpful in getting people past the barriers that have held back progress. This is because they are aligned with mere self-interest, adding to a political discussion that is devoid of any realistic or naturalistic moral input. What I'm going to suggest is that instead we need another foundation with different moral approaches that do possess realistic and/or naturalistic moral input. I've limited the choice to two: interest-based theories and agency-based theories. Let's see if they can do any better in the area of justification.

---

[41] My approach has always been that utopian solutions violate the fourth category of the personal worldview imperative, namely, that they can be actualized in the world – even if the task is rather difficult (aspirational). See Chapter 6. Thus, on the continuum of (a) practical now; to (b) aspirational; to (c) utopian, we should stop at (b) and go no further. It is my contention that the legal justification for human rights is hopelessly utopian and therefore ought to be rejected.

5

Interest Justifications

This chapter examines the interest justification for human rights. Though there are numerous practitioners who take this approach, I have chosen to concentrate on two who I think are emblematic. One of two candidates comes from an anti-realist perspective and the other from a naturalist perspective. To get a handle on this distinction, let us agree that among the realistic theories that can be put forward some are (a) natural-realm only (that is, their truth can be derived from an examination of natural phenomena and that is where their truth resides); (b) natural and real in some ontological realm that is non-natural (that is, their truth can be derived from an examination of natural phenomena) and – as a matter of fact – they correspond to truths that exist independently; and (c) real only in a realm that is non-natural (that is, they exist in an independent realm that exhibits a one-to-one correspondence with the natural world in such a way that the one affects the other). Examples of (a) include Alan Gewirth, Philippa Foot, James Griffin, Amartya Sen, and Martha Nussbaum. Examples of (b) include myself, John Locke, and Immanuel Kant. An example of (c) is G. E. Moore.

Joseph Raz, the first proponent of interest justification I will examine, is an anti-realist. The import of this classification is set out in Chapter 7.

For now, we examine what the *interest-based* theorists contend and their respective strengths and weaknesses.

5.1 THE INTEREST-BASED APPROACH

Two key proponents of the interest-based approach (from very different perspectives) that I have chosen to examine are Joseph Raz and James Griffin. Both deal with some notion of human interest as contained in human welfare – in some sense. However, the way they approach welfare

is different. Why is *interest as welfare* of sufficient interest that it would
ground human rights? The reason is that it assumes that humans have a
conception of what they minimally want out of life and how that "minimal level" might be increased to something approaching a "flourishing level." This grounding of rights is really a grounding of expectations
about what it means to be human in some fundamental sense. How do
we arrive at our concepts of what it means to be human? Are the concepts
given to us naturally or are they socially constructed? What if I, as a heterosexual male, decided that I needed a wife for me to be at a minimal
level? What about more than one wife? There are certainly societies that
have fostered this polygamous attitude. What about home ownership? In
the United States this was so ingrained in the national consciousness that
politicians allowed banks to issue mortgages on very reduced financial
criteria, a practice that became a contributing factor in the 2007 housing crisis that hit the United States and Europe.

One could go on with this. One obvious counterresponse is that when
someone brings forth a suggestion for an interest (such as a swimming
pool) objectors will say that it is not a *minimum interest*. But when minimum
is defined by fidelity to a conception of a desirable life, what is to stop
Amanda Wingfield (in *The Glass Menagerie*)[1] from declaring that minimum
interest is "seventeen gentleman callers"? This general question will hang
over both presentations of the interest justification for human rights.

5.2 THE ARGUMENT OF JOSEPH RAZ

The first approach to be discussed comes from Joseph Raz. His position
begins with these four key assertions:[2]

- "X has a right" if and only if X can have rights, and, other things being
  equal, an aspect of X's well-being (his interest) is a sufficient reason
  for holding some other person(s) to be under a duty[3]
- An individual is capable of having rights if and only if either his
  well-being is of ultimate value or he is an "artificial person" (e.g., a
  corporation)[4]

---

[1] Tennessee Williams's play *The Glass Menagerie* opened at the Playhouse Theater, March
   31, 1945. A current edition with an introduction by Robert Bray was published in New
   York by New Directions, 1999.
[2] Joseph Raz, "The Nature of Rights," in *The Morality of Freedom* (Oxford: Clarendon Press,
   1986): ch. 7, 165–192.
[3] Raz, "The Nature of Rights," 166.
[4] Raz, "The Nature of Rights," 166.

- Rights must be specified by the object that one is said to have a right to[5]
- Rights are grounds of duties in others[6]

From this it is clear that "X has a right" refers to an individual (or a particular artificial individual)[7] who makes a claim for some object that is of ultimate value. Something of ultimate value cannot be waived because it possesses some perceived intrinsic value. Presumably this intrinsic, ultimate value is perceived via intuition since there is no mechanism for giving it identity. However, this leads us to the problem discussed in the last section: various people might intuit different objects as being of ultimate value. Though the terms have switched from "minimum value" to "ultimate value," the conundrum remains the same. This is important because the result of this intuition will ground a duty in others. It is entirely different to say that food, freedom, a new car, or a swimming pool is of ultimate value.

But perhaps the problem here is on the level of specificity. It may not have been Raz's intent at this stage to focus upon particular objects but rather a more general concept.

General rights statements do not entail statements of particular rights that are instances of it (e.g., the general right to free expression does not allow libel)[8]

This goes against my depiction of the one-to-one correlation of rights and duties that I set out in Chapter 1. Raz signals out Richard Brandt to attack for this particular tenet.

ARGUMENT 5.1: RAZ ON RICHARD BRANDT

1. Richard Brant says, "X has an absolute right to enjoy, have or be secured in Y" means the same as "It is someone's objective overall obligation to secure X in, or in the possession of, or in the enjoyment of Y, if X wishes it"[9] – Fact (Joseph Raz, *The Morality of Freedom*, p. 170)[10]

---

[5] Raz, "The Nature of Rights," 166.

[6] Raz, "The Nature of Rights," 187.

[7] The 'ultimate value' conundrum only gets harder when you consider a corporation within the context of a capitalist economy. What rights may a corporation claim? A fair market by which to do business (that is enforced by government regulators)? A stable currency? Some limit on the amount of regulation? This is a difficult question that seems question-begging, at best.

[8] Raz, "The Nature of Rights," 170.

[9] Richard Brandt, *Ethical Theory* (Englewood Cliffs, NJ: Prentice Hall, 1959): 438.

[10] Brandt, *Ethical Theory*.

2. Premise #1 suggests that for every right there is a corresponding duty – Fact (p. 170)[11]
3. Many rights ground a number of duties (instead of a single duty) – Assertion (p. 170)
4. Some rights (such as the right to self-protection) do not imply any duties against anyone (except negative rights not to harm, e.g., not to rape, not to assault, and not to imprison) – Assertion (p. 171)
5. A right of one person is not a duty to another person but rather the ground of a duty – Assertion (p. 171)
6. There is no closed list of rights and duties such that there is a one-to-one correspondence between the lists – Assertion (p. 171)

----

7. [Rights and duties, strictly speaking, are not necessarily correlative] – 1–6

What is interesting in Raz's analysis is that he seems to be suggesting that ultimate value may have various logical levels of expression (depending upon how actually *ultimate* the value is). Some may ground a single duty (low level of abstraction) while others ground many rights to multiple objects (high level of abstraction). Again the question is how one is to decide what is the appropriate level. The answer must be intuition (since no other justification is brought forward).

It is also important to note that rights are not carte blanche. The right to self-protection is constrained by negative duties not to engage in the unprovoked assault of others just as the right to freedom of expression does not include the right to libel. This is a question of framing the scope of the right. But how does one do this? Much of the argument proceeds as if we all know. This is reminiscent of Potter Stewart's dictum that he would know pornography when he saw it (and presumably the rest of us would, too – in exactly the same terms).

I think what Raz wants to get at is that rights and duties are prima facie in and of themselves because they will come into conflict with other rights and duties. However, Raz doesn't set it out that way (more on this in Chapter 6 when I set out my preferred version of this dynamic).

And then in premise #5 Raz talks about the *ground* of a duty instead of a direct one-to-one right-duty relation. A ground is a more general term that seeks specific explication. What is the mechanism for moving from

----

[11] Brandt, *Ethical Theory*.

a *ground* to a *specific explication?* The only answer to be given is ethical intuitionism.[12]

Certainly one could argue against Raz here to say that this difficulty between rights at various levels of generality might be adjudicated by changing the rules of primacy among terms. What if the rights were dependent upon the status of the goods that they entitle (as I argue in Chapter 6)? This would change the focus of the discussion and mute Raz's attack on Brandt.

Raz's argument continues. It develops as follows:

ARGUMENT 5.2: RAZ ON WELL-BEING AS GROUNDING DUTY

1. If an individual has a right, then a certain aspect of his well-being is a reason for holding others to be under a duty – Assertion (Joseph Raz, *The Morality of Freedom*, p. 172)

2. Rights are a (part of) the justification of many duties but only to the extent that there are no conflicting considerations of greater weight – Assertion (p. 172)

3. In many cases involving institutions, duties must be imposed by those in power – Assertion (p. 172)[13]

4. For example, political participation in England is a right, but there is no corresponding duty for the government institutions to facilitate this, except by making conditions available for people to make informed judgments – such as in a free press – 1–3 (p. 172)

5. There is a right to promise based on the promisor's interest to be able to forge special bonds with other people (it is qualified since small children and some mentally deranged people lack it – and it cannot be based on immorality: one's right to promise does not include the right to perform immoral acts) – Assertion (p. 173)

6. This right to promise also includes an obligation: if a person communicates an intention to undertake by that very act of communication a certain obligation, then he has that obligation – Assertion (p. 173)

7. People should be able to bind themselves if they wish – Assertion (p. 173)

---

[12] Readers can view my rather schematic explication of ethical intuitionism in Michael Boylan, *Basic Ethics,* 2nd ed. (Upper Saddle River, NJ: Prentice Hall, 2009): ch. 8.

[13] Raz argues for this in "Legal Rights" in *Oxford Journal of Legal Studies* 4 (1984): I, and "The Internal Logic of the Law," *Materiali per Una Storia della Cultura Giuridica* 14 (1984): 381.

8. The power to promise and the obligation to keep promises they make is in everyone's interest – 5–7 (p. 173–174)

9. The right to promise involves a duty on the part of the promisee not to interfere with the promise-maker's ability to execute the promise or his ability to carry it out – Assertion (p. 174)

10. The right to make a particular promise is derivative of the general right to promise, and two kinds of conditional promises are (a) a promise made conditional on an action by the promisee (e.g., "I will give you ten pounds if you give me this book"), and (b) a promise made conditional on a promise to be given by the promisee (e.g., "I will give you ten pounds if you promise to give me the book") – Assertion (p. 174)

11. The right and obligation relation between promise-maker and promisee is really a right to enter into agreements – A (p. 175)

12. Each person has an interest in being able to create voluntary bonds with other people – Assertion (p. 175)

13. Each person has a *pro tanto* interest that promises made to him be kept – 9–12 (p. 175)

14. Artificial persons (like corporations) have the capacity for rights inasmuch as they have the capacity to be assigned duties – Assertion (p. 176)

15. The *reciprocity thesis* says that only members of "the same moral community" can have rights – Fact (p. 176)

16. Rights are nothing but the ground of duties – Assertion (p. 176)

----

17. If duties observe a reciprocity condition and can be had only toward members of the same moral community, then the same is true of rights – 4, 8, 13–16 (p. 176)

This is an essential argument in Raz's interest-based position. In this argument he declares in premise #1 that a certain aspect of an individual's well-being (the ultimate interest) is a reason that others should be put under a duty. Is this a positive duty to provide that person with that object that would be in his interest? Or is it merely to get out of the way (like most negative duties)? In a later argument on equality Raz finds that "most egalitarian theories (that are linked to non-diminishing and insatiable principles) go against the principle of happiness and therefore ought to be rejected."[14] This argument goes a ways to providing the specificity of just what might count as an identifying mechanism for

[14] Raz, "The Nature of Rights," 243–244.

acceptable interests: they should be diminishing and satiable (e.g., when a person who is hungry eats some food, he is sated, and if you give him any more food to eat, the added effect follows the law of diminishing returns). Thus, providing basic goods of minimum welfare would satisfy these criteria and thus offer a mechanism for legitimate interest. This might provide the identification criteria for a legitimate interest that I have been requesting. Let's look at the rest of the argument and see.

In premises #5–#13 Raz puts forth an institutional moral right to promise. This right is considered to be of ultimate interest because Raz is showing his anti-realism penchant for contractarianism. This is one positivist way to construct a base for moral rights as we saw in Chapter 4. It is also primary to legal positivism (Raz is a dualizer here). If there were no right to promise with the expectation that the whole institution of promise-making (under appropriate guidelines) might underlie the moral understanding of human rights, then there would be no human rights (since the anti-realist cannot appeal to anything aside of social practice). This is an important issue. It requires a brief exploration of the social practice justification.

There are certainly some proponents of social practice. They often cite Wittgenstein's comments on social use fixing linguistic meaning. This is because "meaning is use." Wittgenstein begins his *Blue Book* by asking the question, "What is the meaning of a word?"[15] This has been often expanded by commentators to include "What is the meaning of a sentence?"[16] This sounds like the structure of what I have depicted as level-one intuitionists *grasping truth*.[17] It is a similar set of questions, but the results are much different. Because here, the *meaning is* determined by its 'use' (*Gebrauch*), or 'employment' (*Verwendung*), or 'application' (*Anwendung*). Meaning is seen in the context of the rules of the language game and those rules, by themselves, "hang in the air."[18] They only become rooted in actual cases. This creates a public basis for meaning. There can be no private language (sec. 269, 275). Therefore, the sort of experience that the intuitionists describe (an introspective, reflective assertion of 'what is') is *meaningless*. This is because introspective, reflective acts are both intangible and indescribable. They require a public

[15] Ludwig Wittgenstein, *Das blaue Buch: Eine Philosophische Betrachtung.* Hrsg. von Rush Rhees, G. E. M. Anscombe and G. H. von Wright (Frankfurt: Suhrkamp, 1970).

[16] This expansion, however, is controversial.

[17] Boylan, *Basic Ethics*, ch. 8.

[18] Ludwig Wittgenstein, *Philosophical Investigations*, ed. G. E. M. Anscombe, Rush Rhees, and G. H. von Wright ; trans. G. E. M. Anscombe (Oxford: Blackwell, 1953), sec. 198.

context to give them significance. This is because "to signify," means "to signify => to someone." Ergo, the nature of signification and meaning is public. If my earlier conjectures about Raz using ethical intuitionism to justify key sections of his argument is correct, then this move to social practice creates a contradiction (if we accept Wittgenstein's analysis).

The social practice foundation is a descriptivist posture. If there is no independent existence of truth, then the *true* is only what people say it is. The cultural/societal context determines it all. If we return to Chapter 3, then we would be deeply committed to a general relativism – also the robust boundaries demarcating these contexts within larger social and linguistic groups fall prey to overlapping standards. Overlapping standards cause ambiguity and resulting confusion. For example, one might point to the Middle East as a social/religious/linguistic area that has overlapping standards due to this dynamic. To describe this further, let's turn to a thought experiment.

THOUGHT EXPERIMENT 5.1: LOYALTY AS THE HIGHEST VIRTUE[19]

As the head of school in a college located in Beirut, Lebanon, you are faced with a troubling situation. You are expelling a student, Ahmed X, from the university for selling drugs. The expelling of Ahmed X upsets the militias that are in your neighborhood. Your contention is that you are the chief officer in charge of the mission of the college. Selling drugs or any other illegal activity is prohibited. Their contention is that, "sure" selling drugs is bad, but you have to stack this against Ahmed's support of the local militia and the larger Hamas group. Ahmed's support demands a reciprocal demonstration of *loyalty,* which outweighs the *crime* of Ahmed's drug sales (considered by the militia and the general community to be a mild-middle offense). Ahmed should be readmitted to the university so that he might get his degree and continue on with the cause. You believe in both the mission of the university as an academic institution and in the causes represented by the militia and the larger group, Hamas. Which imperative should trump?

From the point of view of ethical noncognitivism, if the culture in Lebanon values loyalty above all other virtues, then the various sentences that talk about value will put loyalty at the top. The crime of drug sales (to willing buyers) is considered to be a mild-middle offense. In the trade-off within this cultural context, loyalty wins. All the observer can do is to learn more exactly about how this is the case and fall in line.

[19] This is based upon an actual case related to me by Raja Nasr of Marymount University in Arlington, Virginia.

Noncognitivism has a basic meta-ethical position of parsing sentences into (a) sentences about fact – the so-called empirically based cognitive uses of language; (b) sentences about linguistic meaning within a social context; and (c) sentences about instrumental value that are noncognitive and are set within various social constructs and intuitively justified (at level two) by citizens within some society.

An example of sentences of the first type is this: "The boiling point of water at sea-level is 100 degrees Centigrade." These sentences talk about the empirically observed nature of the world and are empirically falsifiable. An example of sentences of the second type is this: "Murder in the United States is wrong." An example of sentences of the third type is this: "Don't murder." The first sentence is about a state of affairs and can be falsified. The second describes a linguistic/social context – the language game within a particular context. There are linguistic and social constructs that are only quasi-factual in a social science sense because they describe a moving target. The third sentence is a command that is set out to persuade an audience. It is not factual. It only reveals the level-two intuitionism[20] standpoint of the speaker. The speaker has a "con" attitude about murder.

Since Raz is intent on maintaining a noncognitivist version of contractarianism based upon the various social constructs (as his examples suggest), he will fall prey to the relativist consequences of such a position. It should be clear that he readily admits this in his premise #15 in which he claims that artificial persons (such as corporations) derive their duties from existing communities. This falls under a contractarian notion of *reciprocity*. Raz puts forth the *reciprocity thesis* that says only members of "the same moral community" can have rights.[21] The reason Raz gives is that only the same moral community can rely on its internally accepted understanding of what is good. I call this community dynamic the shared community worldview. It is a collection of the communal understandings (as vague as this can be with larger communities) of what is factual and normatively correct about the world.[22] Among noncognitivist contractarians there is a possibility that another moral community might sanction

---

[20] I depict level-two intuitionism as a meta-level immediate acceptance of principles that guide action and not actions themselves; see Boylan, *Basic Ethics*, ch. 8.

[21] Raz, "The Nature of Rights," 176.

[22] I distinguish between micro communities in which a committee of the whole is still possible and the entire community can gather and discuss these shared factual and normative understandings (probably around 500 people), and macro communities in which indirect representation becomes necessary; see Michael Boylan, *A Just Society* (Lanham, MD: Rowman and Littlefield, 2004): 102–105; 113–115.

different rights. What the noncognitivism background condition ensures (to this contractarian position) is that there will be *no universal human rights* unless the world becomes one single community!

At best, a single world community seems implausible. At worst, if it did come to pass, it would amount to a travesty in international imperialism – whether the one culture comes from the West or the East.[23]

In the end we are left with an interest-based approach that intends that "The special features of rights are their source in individual interest and their peremptory force, expressed in the fact that they are sufficient to hold people to be bound by duties; thus, rights have a distinctive and important role in morality."[24] This abstract structural force is supported both by ethical intuitionism, noncognitivism, social practice, and contractarianism, which have different (sometimes contradictory) agendas. The consequence of this combination is of lowering the scope of coverage to particular distinct communities that may (and probably will) vary worldwide. Our ending question is whether this is all we can claim in the human rights discussion.

5.3 THE ARGUMENT OF JAMES GRIFFIN

Another proponent of the *interest-based* justification to human rights is James Griffin. Griffin differs considerably from Raz because Griffin is a naturalist. He bases his understanding of naturalism in his personhood account.

ARGUMENT 5.3: GRIFFIN ON PERSONHOOD AND INTEREST

1. Human rights are human inasmuch as they protect one's personhood – A (Griffin, *On Human Rights*, pp. 32–33)
2. Personhood minimally contains (a) autonomy and (b) liberty – Assertion (p. 33–37)
3. Minimal provision (practicality) is necessary for human existence (*mutatis mutandis* for agency) – Fact (p. 37)

---

4. Human rights concern agency via an interest in autonomy, liberty, and minimal provision [along historical precedents] – 1–3 (pp. 33–37)

---

[23] My shared community worldview imperative contends that diversity is essential. This counters any designs of a common world culture; cf. Boylan *A Just Society*, ch. 5.
[24] Raz, "The Nature of Rights," 192.

Unlike Raz's interest model that is reducible to claims about welfare, Griffin argues for a position that sets out a model that is based upon being a person in the world. The "interest" that we all have is in becoming and maintaining our personhood. This is not a statement about welfare, though it includes welfare. Primarily, the justification is in providing whatever is necessary to become and maintain personhood. This entails creating a list of goods where everything is on the same level – including personal security, a voice in the polis (political autonomy), free press, freedom to worship, a right to basic education, and minimum welfare provision.[25] This is not about *flourishing*; Griffin believes in a right to pursue happiness but not in a right to happiness itself.[26] It is all about what it means to be a person: autonomy, liberty, and minimum provision. Concepts such as agency flow from personhood but are not primary.

The heart of Griffin's unique approach comes about in his Chapter 6 argument against David Hume.

ARGUMENT 5.4: GRIFFIN ON BASIC BELIEFS AND HUMAN INTERESTS

1. In Hume's "taste model of value judgment" there are facts (found in the world) and values (subjective matters of taste) – Fact (Griffin, *On Human Rights*, p. 111)

2. Facts are true or false (objective) while values are neither true nor false (subjective) – Fact (p. 111)

3. Hume's 'actual preferences' should be dropped for 'rational preferences' [a desire is rational if it persists despite all relevant natural facts][27] – Fact (p. 112)

4. Rawls's example of the man who counts blades of grass is a telling counterexample to Brandt[28] – Assertion (p. 112)

5. [Rational preferences could disprove Hume's model, but stricter grounds are needed] – 1–4

6. 'Appropriate reaction to desire' is a good emendation for rational desire (and it comes about via an analysis of 'preferences') – Assertion (pp. 112–113)

7. 'Appropriate' is to be understood as Wittgenstein's 'a form of life' – Assertion (p. 113)

8. 'A form of life' situates a community worldview as being true; cf. Donald Davidson's notion that we cannot interpret language unless

[25] James Griffin, *On Human Rights* (Oxford: Oxford University Press, 2008): 33.
[26] Griffin, *On Human Rights*, 34.
[27] Richard Brandt, *A Theory of the Good and Right* (Oxford: Clarendon Press, 1979): 10.
[28] John Rawls, *A Theory of Justice* (Cambridge, MA: Harvard, 1971): 432–433.

we have certain beliefs and attributes common to the object in question as situated into a rich social context – Assertion (p. 113)

9. The basic beliefs of Wittgenstein and Davidson talk about a concern with basic human interests – Assertion (p. 114)

10. Basic human interests allow us to factually say we've accomplished something in life to make it worth living[29] – Assertion (pp. 113–116)

11. [Basic human interests can form a common profile of accepted values that can be socially tested] – 6–10

12. Claims about biological and nonbiological interests can be true or false – Assertion (p. 116)

13. Recognition that some interests are part of the profile of accepted values is "something in the world" – Fact (p. 118)

14. These recognitions can be judged as being correct or incorrect vis-à-vis whether they promote legitimate human interests and this judgment of value is "*independent of the process of coming to regard it as such*" (p. 119), that is, it has a character via human nature – Assertion (p. 119)

15. "Meeting an interest" is parallel to *x soothes an irritation* – Assertion (p. 120)

16. Inference to the best explanation is a well-established logical principle in philosophy – Fact (p. 121)

17. Wittgenstein's "a form of life" is the best explanation for understanding some accomplishments as being life fulfilling and a judgment about an ointment being soothing – Assertion (p. 122)

18. [Both judgments in premise #17 are factual] – Assertion

19. [Moral realism accepts that there are moral facts even if they are mind-dependent] – Assertion

────────

20. Moral realism is correct, and Hume is wrong – 5, 11, 12–19 (pp. 122–124)

Hume is often taken to be the poster boy for the anti-realists. This is because of the hard distinction between statements of fact and statements of value (that are merely tastes grounded in a cultural milieu). These tastes are conditional and anti-real. But Griffin and this author think that Hume's understanding of *fact* is too narrow.[30] There is not a

---

[29] An example of Griffin's list is on p. 114 of Griffin, *On Human Rights*.

[30] Griffin, *On Human Rights*, 35–36. An interesting discussion of some of the issues involved from the position of a former advocate of the fact/value distinction can be found in the title essay of Hilary Putnam's book, *The Collapse of the Fact/Value Dichotomy and Other Essays* (Cambridge, MA: Harvard, 2004).

hard dividing line between fact and value. For Griffin, the basic approach is to point to the factual human interests (to become a person) and these interests are met (or not) as that individual lives her life in the world. Naturally, within those factual interests are robust values.

There are some real overlaps between Griffin and myself in this regard. In my personal worldview imperative (set out in Chapter 6) I am also keen on viewing the way a person *becomes* as very important. My approach will differ from Griffin's, but we both hold that the process of human actualization is crucially important to human rights and the entire moral enterprise.

A critical premise in the above argument is #3. The move from 'actual preferences' that are possibly based upon emotions and desires to 'rational preferences' (using Brandt's criteria) provides an operational, rationally based approach. This move ultimately undermines Hume because the emotionally based desires are not needed to generate a preference. 'Preferences' are necessary to an interest-based model, so that by grounding preferences in reason, Griffin satisfies the possible Humean objection.

But more is needed. One could have a rational preference (that clears Brandt criteria) for counting blades of grass in various people's lawns (Rawls's example). And though this eccentric soul is aware that no one is interested in his results and that there is no identifiable practical use in his findings, still there is nothing that violates logic in his enterprise. This seeming counter-example to Brandt's criteria does not cause us to throw out the criteria but merely to tighten them: enter Wittgenstein and Davidson.

In premises #6-#9 'rational preferences' is emended to 'appropriate rational preferences.' The 'appropriate' comes from Wittgenstein's notion of 'a form of life,' which in this case refers to an environment in which our language can meaningfully develop and in which it can be judged to be intelligible.[31] This *form of life* mirrors my notion of *personal worldview* within the context of *community worldview*. Both work interactively to allow the conditions of meaning and intelligibility to emerge.

Davidson brings forth a similar insight. We cannot interpret others unless we make certain assumptions on what attitudes and beliefs we have in common with them.[32] If Davidson is correct in this claim, then skepticism about the ability of communities to come to meaningful

---

[31] Ludwig Wittgenstein, *Philosophical Investigations* (Oxford: Blackwell, 1953), sect. 1–38, 136–156, 167–238 – esp. on the concept '*a form of life*': 19, 23, 241.

[32] Donald Davidson, "Psychology as Philosophy" (237) and "Mental Events" (222), in *Essays on Actions and Events* (Oxford: Clarendon Press, 1980).

agreement about shared values and beliefs is unfounded. This dynamic corresponds to my notion of *the common body of knowledge* that I hold to be essential to the information flow of rational argument for the purpose of discussion and agreement within the shared community worldview in a way that can be tested.[33]

At premises #14–#19 Griffin takes what has gone before to move to a clearly stated position of moral naturalism. 'Recognition of interests' is supported by 'a profile of accepted values in the world.' Of course, this seems to raise the issue of *why* the profile was accepted. Griffin's response is whether the values promote legitimate human interests and this judgment of value is *independent of the process of coming to regard it as such*, that is, it has a character via human nature. This is not a mere posit but is connected to whether these values, in general, make life work better for the person and for other persons living in the world. Again, this is a factual question (on our robust understanding of *factual*). In this way judgments about human interests can be correct or incorrect (119). Thus, being correct here is analogous to the concept of an ointment that is applied to a skin irritation either soothing it or not. The dynamics of the ointment and skin operate at one level and the person's recognition of the effect operates at another level. The holistic result is integrated as one. "Meeting an interest" is like this holistic dynamic that is situated within the particular form of life at hand. Both are factually based illocutionary statements that offer support to naturalistic truths that go against Humean anti-realism.

This is a powerful argument and one that grounds human interests within a naturalistic conception of personhood that has the potential to argue strongly against moral relativism or ethnocentrism.

5.4 PROBLEMS WITH THE INTEREST-BASED APPROACH

Though there are many important insights provided by the interest-based approach and some significant overlaps with my own agency approach (that is set out in the next chapter), there are clear reasons why I think the interest-based approach does not quite fit the bill. Let's look at my assessment of Raz and Griffin separately.

In the case of Joseph Raz, interest is set out in terms of welfare. Thus, his interest-based methodology will rise and fall along with welfare as a master value upon which to base morality. My analysis of this sort of

---

[33] Boylan, *A Just Society*, ch. 5.

project follows Tim Scanlon.[34] Scanlon sets out three uses of well-being: (a) the basis of individual decision making (1st person); (b) the basis of a concerned benefactor's action (3rd person); and (c) the answer to the "why should I be moral?" question.[35] Well-being (a) is experientially made known to us subjectively. Sense (b) is generally understood as "fulfilling desire."[36] However, mere *desire* is not sufficient for fulfilling rational choice (cf. Griffin's take earlier).

But perhaps mere desire can be amended to *rational desire as grounding a preference for some good* and in this way be brought forward as a ground for well-being.[37] However, Scanlon asserts (and I agree) that the good is not dependent upon preference (informed desire) but the reasons that make it worthwhile.[38] Just because I have a rationally grounded preference for some good does not confer the realization of that good to include my well-being. Again, Rawls's grass-blade counter comes to mind. I may have a rational desire to count the blades of grass (due to personal aesthetic or horticultural reasons) but these reasons do not confer value on the activity. And only worthwhile rationally grounded preferences count as increasing my well-being. But in order to determine what is *worthwhile* I must import a separate moral principle derived from some other source than "interest" or "well-being" (otherwise one would be involved in a circular argument).[39] The only candidate that one could bring forward (based upon the text) is ethical intuitionism. However, I think Raz's well-being-interest approach is intended to give more substance to his justification of human rights than the rather amorphous ethical intuitionism approach.

Many rational desires, such as scientific investigation or Aristotelian goodness-based friendships are not directed toward increasing well-being. In the case of science one may be driven to discover some truth that can be personally and generally painful (such as the trajectory of an asteroid that will shortly collide with the earth killing millions of people). Further, one of the basic tenets of scientific inquiry is that it is disinterested. To take an interest and thus increase well-being takes the investigator away from the objective mental state that is the goal of

[34] T. M. Scanlon, *What We Owe to Each Other* (Cambridge, MA: Harvard University Press, 1998).
[35] Scanlon, *What We Owe*, 108.
[36] Scanlon, *What We Owe*, 113.
[37] Scanlon, *What We Owe*, 116.
[38] Scanlon, *What We Owe*, 119.
[39] This last twist of the argument moves away from Scanlon.

researchers.[40] Similarly, this is the case with Aristotle's goodness-based friendships.[41] It follows from the way Aristotle sets up the three forms of friendship – utility-based, pleasure-based, and goodness-based – that the goodness-based cannot be for the sake of increasing well-being, nevertheless; Aristotle argues (and I agree) that the object (goodness) is the highest of the three forms of friendship.

Therefore, joining forces again with Scanlon, I would contend that though rational aims and well-being share some connections, the former does not determine the latter. Further, well-being, as such, is without limits. One can always imagine a higher state of well-being.[42] This creates a boundary problem for well-being. Morality is a science, which, by necessity, must have constrained boundaries.[43] Therefore, well-being is an inappropriate grounding for morality, and if well-being is synonymous with *interest*, then there can be no interest-based grounding for morality and a fortiori for human rights.

Well-being can also make one selfish. This was the first sense of well-being mentioned. If one goes through life concentrating on how he will increase his own well-being, then the focus becomes upon the self-only. This solipsistic disposition, I have termed *the egg carton approach*.[44] Egg carton individuals live in geographical communities, but just like eggs in a carton, they aspire to touch no one. There is no sense of social community. Some proponents of individual human rights are like this. They concentrate upon the individual to the exclusion of the community. By sidestepping this perspective they become *free riders* who live for themselves and indulge themselves in a fantasy that they have achieved whatever they have *all by themselves with no help from anyone*. Since no one has helped them, why should they help anyone else? Becoming an egg carton free rider is a real risk in the well-being (or interest) approach. Thus, Scanlon's first sense of well-being when applied to Raz is shown to be flawed when used as a general support of morality and human rights.

---

[40] See my essay, "Ethical Limitations on Scientific Research," in *Scientific Freedom*, ed. Simona Giordano, John Coggon, and Marco Cappato (London: Bloomsbury, 2012): 149–161.

[41] Aristotle, *Ethica Nicomachea*, ed. I. Bywater (Oxford: Oxford University Press, 1894): 1156a 7–1156b 4; 1156b 31.

[42] Cf. Scanlon, *What We Owe*, 129.

[43] Note here my definition of morality as the science of the right and wrong in human action (Boylan, *Basic Ethics*, 3). This reflects my ethical realism position, see Chapter 7.

[44] Boylan, *A Just Society*, 115–116.

In the second, third-person, sense of well-being, the perspective shifts from the decision maker to that of a good friend or parent.[45] These individuals (benefactors) have different reasons for why x should or should not do y. The well-being component may shift from what will directly benefit x (as selfishly understood) to what might make x flourish (were he to do y). This may also include wider contexts such as family, community, country, and others. The benefactor is acting according to what she sees as X's well-being (and thus in his interest). But this can become dicey when classical cases of paternalism present themselves. Benefactor A (say a parent) may say to her son X (who wants to be a playwright) that a career as a lawyer is steadier and a better use of his talents. Mother may try to use her influence and any strings she still has attached to X in order to dissuade him from Y (trying it out on Broadway) in order to do Z (becoming a corporate lawyer). Mother may be correct if one gauges success on being able to support oneself financially. From a statistical viewpoint ceteris paribus, Mother may be right in her assessment that her son chose doing Z over Y. If X is really interested in his well-being (gauged by statistically probable outcomes), then he should choose Z over Y.

But there may be more to the picture than that. Paternalism (as we have seen in the burgeoning number of essays in medical ethics)[46] has

[45] Scanlon, *What We Owe*, 134.

[46] This is a very large literature in health care ethics. For an introduction to some of these issues, see George J. Annas, "The Emerging Stowaway: Patients' Rights in the 1980's," in *Value Conflict in Health Care Delivery*, ed. Bart Gruzalski and Carl Nelson (Cambridge, MA: Ballinger, 1982): 89–100; H. A. Bassford, "The Justification of Medical Paternalism," *Social Science and Medicine* **16**.6 (1982): 731–739; Tom L. Beauchamp, "The Promise of the Beneficence Model for Medical Ethics," *Journal of Contemporary Health Law and Policy* **6** (Spring 1990): 145–155; J. Berger, "Paternalistic Assumptions and a Purported Duty to Deceive," *American Journal of Bioethics* **9**.12 (2009): 20–21; D. R. Buchanan, "Autonomy, Paternalism, and Justice: Ethical Priorities in Public Health," *American Journal of Public Health* **98**.1 (2008): 15–21; James F. Childress, *Who Should Decide? Paternalism in Health Care* (Oxford: Oxford University Press, 1982); James F. Childress and Mark Siegler, "Metaphors and Models of Doctor-Patient Relationships: Their Implications for Autonomy," *Theoretical Medicine* **5** (1984): 17–30; Lee Coleman, *The Reign of Error* (Boston: Beacon Press, 1984); Gerald Dworkin, *The Theory and Practice of Autonomy* (Cambridge: Cambridge University Press, 1988); T. Hope, D. Springings, and R. Crisp, "Not Clinically Indicated: Patients' Interests or Resource Allocations," *British Medical Journal* **306** (1993): 379–381; L. A. Jansen and S. Wall, "Paternalism and Fairness in Clinical Research," *Bioethics* **23**.3 (2009): 172–182; A. A. Kon, "Silent Decisions or Veiled Paternalism? Physicians Are Not Experts in Judging Character," *American Journal of Bioethics* **7**.7 (2007): 40–42; Florencia Luna, "Paternalism and the Argument from Illiteracy," *Bioethics* **9**.3/4 (July 1995): 283–290; Mary B. Mahowald, "Against Paternalism: A Developmental View," *Philosophy Research Archives* **6**.1386 (1980): 340–357; Rosa Pinkus, "The Evolution of Moral Reasoning,"

some severe drawbacks in the welfare game. In the example, Mother may be acting on how she thinks her son will enjoy the greatest well-being. However, part of that might involve Mother's personal worldview (which might be different from her son's). Mother's values might not translate into a prescription that will really maximize *his* well-being (given his personal goals and aspirations). Instead, Mother may be an instrument of imperialism and her paternalism (maternalism?) can become tyranny. Because of this real possibility, the third person well-being approach also fails.

Finally, there is the first-person view of the "why should I be moral?" problem (Scanlon's third sense).[47] This could be answered by indicating how well-being is connected to being moral such that satisfying the first gives an answer to the second. But this is tricky because this sense of well-being requires one to justify moral principles on grounds that presuppose what people are entitled to (for their well-being). But surely this is circular: (a) one should be moral because it enhances one's well-being (one's interest); (b) enhancing one's well-being is in everyone's interest; (c) acting in everyone's interest is what defines morality because well-being is a master value for morality.

Because all three senses of well-being are shown not to be foundational for justifying morality (a fortiori human rights), the well-being tack should be rejected as the justification for human rights.

In the case of James Griffin, interest is grounded in personhood. From the outset, I should admit that this version of the interest-based approach is closer to my own than Raz's. From 5.3 it should be clear that it is in everyone's interest to become a person who performs actions over time that makes his or her life significant. This approach owes much to Aristotle's notion of potentiality and actuality as applied to some individual's own life. This requires the individual to take pains about creating himself or herself via his or her application of autonomy and liberty (given some adequate set of provisions). This is a prescription for self-fulfillment. The enthymemic argument here is that it

Medical Humanities Review **10** (Fall 1996): 20–44; Daniel Sulmasy, "Managed Care and the New Paternalism," *Journal of Clinical Ethics* **6**.4 (Winter 1995): 324–326; Mark R. Wicclair, "Patient Decision-Making Capacity and Risk," *Bioethics* **5** (April 1991): 91–104; Henrik Wulff, "The Inherent Paternalism in Clinical Practice," *Journal of Medicine and Philosophy* **20**.3 (1995): 299–311. Meg Zomorodi and Barbara Jo Foley, "The Nature of Advocacy vs. Paternalism in Nursing: Clarifying the 'Thin Line,'" *Journal of Advanced Nursing* **65**.8 (2009): 1746–1752.
47 See Scanlon's discussion, *What We Owe*, 137–138.

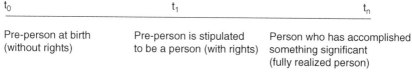

t_0	t_1	t_n
Pre-person at birth (without rights)	Pre-person is stipulated to be a person (with rights)	Person who has accomplished something significant (fully realized person)

FIGURE 5.1. An Aristotelian Reading of Griffin's Personhood

is in every person's interest to become fulfilled. The goal is really this. One becomes fulfilled by performing (and recognizing) an activity over time – such as parenting (for example). If one puts in significant time as a father or mother and the offspring develops into a position where she or he is also on the verge of doing something significant, then who could ask for more? One is complete. There are no other rights or duties involved.

Though I am very sympathetic to this paradigm (especially the ends envisioned), I think there is some confusion in setting these out as a justification for human rights. At some point in time, t_1 a young person ('people' become 'persons' all at once for Griffin) seeks to act in such a way that she is moving toward becoming the kind of person she desires to be (having accomplished something significant) at t_n. At this later state the earlier person (who was largely potential) *becomes* something more: an actualized person who has fulfilled some plan of life that she values.

While there is much to admire in this Aristotelian reading of Griffin, there is also much to question. First, is it appropriate to use the potential-actual continuum upon persons when using it is forbidden on pre-persons (young children and fetuses)?[48] Why does it become suddenly all right to use this model when it was explicitly denied earlier? Griffin's answer is by stipulation.[49] To be fair to Griffin, he does not use the words "actuality" and "potentiality" as he describes his process of self-fulfillment, but those are the functional effects. Since the valued state of personhood grants moral rights and dignity,[50] the mechanics of the process are important to explore. And these mechanics are rather unclear *without* the Aristotelian interpretation. If Griffin were open to the Aristotelian interpretation the situation might look like Figure 5.1.

Under the rendition of Figure 5.1 the pre-person at t_0 is pure potentiality. The baby is entirely dependent upon the caregiving of the parents.

[48] Griffin, *On Human Rights*, 87.
[49] Griffin, *On Human Rights*, 94–95.
[50] Griffin, *On Human Rights*, 87.

But there comes a time when the pre-person gains enough of a vision of life (autonomy) and is given sufficient liberty and provisions that she can begin her journey toward achieving something significant in her life.

But the Figure 5.1 account works only if Griffin will allow potentiality between t_0 and t_1, but this is something he does not want to do (presumably because he does not wish to get tied into that aspect of the abortion debate). But you don't have to give up a thorough potentiality-actuality account to create a permission for abortion. I have created just such an argument via my worldview account.[51]

Another possible problem is that a pre-person does *not* gain enough of a vision of life (autonomy) – say, because he lives in a totalitarian society and does *not* have sufficient liberty and provision because the totalitarian society is very poor. North Korea comes to mind as a contemporary example. Would that mean that the pre-person never has a t_1 moment that confers personhood? Might these poor souls trudge through life continually as pre-persons? Émile Zola depicted French coal miners in this way in his 1885 novel *Germinal*. *Homo sapiens* who are oppressed in this way might struggle through life and never obtain personhood – much less become fully realized persons. But aren't these just the sorts of individuals who need human rights the most – in order that they might achieve their t_1 moment? And further, what is the ontological account of these pre-persons? What are they? What are the mechanics of the transformation?

What is lost here is a continuous account of the person from birth onward. Instead, we have a *something* that mysteriously becomes a person at some point in time by stipulation. This is foggy developmental psychology. And since *almost* everything rides on personhood for Griffin, this observation is a severe drawback to his personhood account. The *almost* caveat comes from his secondary interest justification, which he calls *practicalities*.[52] This is really similar to my shared community worldview imperative. It modifies some individual rights when seen in a community context. Along with certain understandings of human nature Griffin thinks that some minimum level of "existence conditions" must be maintained. These are not rooted in time or place but exist in virtue of being *Homo sapiens* (though not necessarily a person). This minimum

---

[51] Michael Boylan, "The Abortion Debate in the 21st Century," in *Medical Ethics,* ed. Michael Boylan (Upper Saddle River, NJ: Prentice Hall, 2000): 289–304; 2nd ed. Wiley-Blackwell (Oxford: Wiley-Blackwell, 2014): 203–217.

[52] Griffin, *On Human Rights,* 37–38.

level would allow Zola's coal miners to stay alive, but not much else. It can create a two-tiered system in which interests are justified via person-hood interest (those who have reached the t_1 moment) or via practical interest (those who have not reached the t_1 moment). The former are accorded more robust rights claims: autonomy, liberty, and provision to actualize these while the latter are merely accorded minimum provision to stay alive (because they cannot effectively use autonomy and liberty in Griffin's sense – they have not had their t_1 moment). The practicalities tack saves Griffin from being Thomas Malthus, but does not save him from the Zola objection.

A second problem in conceiving of the pre-person (as spontaneously becoming a person)[53] is that its foundation is rather arbitrary. If we are to base human rights on the nature of a dignity-deserving individual, then the relevant mechanics of that person need to be set out more completely. Why should this individual deserve rights? Griffin quotes Kant on dignity (i.e., uniqueness) and then offers a modification show-ing our "exercise of our personhood – that is, our autonomously and, no doubt, repeatedly choosing paths through life and being at liberty to pursue them – as in itself an end the realization of which characteristi-cally enhances the quality of life."[54] This is formulated into a teleological account that lends credence to my Aristotelian reading of Griffin. But if we embrace the teleology, then we need a more substantial understand-ing of how the person comes-to-be. This is logically prior to his rights or his betterment in life.

Finally is the issue of why the three foundational rights – autonomy, liberty, and provision (welfare) – should be on a par. Depending upon how one defines personhood – via action theory or via personal identity of the agent in time[55] – the triad may shift with one or the other being more important. If action theory is chosen then it would probably run (a) Provision, (b) Autonomy, and (c) Liberty. One needs provision to commit minimal action. Autonomy allows a greater range of action, and negative liberty expands this even further. When one shifts to internalist

---

[53] Remember, Aristotle was also keen on spontaneous generation – though in a different sense; *Metaphysics* 1032a, 13–30.

[54] Griffin, *On Human Rights*, 36.

[55] The personal identity theory that is internalist tracks with that style of epistemology. A few of the difficulties with this approach in any realistic context are addressed by Sven Bernecker, "Davidson on First-Person Authority and Externalism," *Inquiry: An Interdisciplinary Journal of Philosophy* **39**–1 (1996): 121–139. For an account of the action theory approach, see the next chapter (Chapter 6).

theories of mind, then provision (including relative quiet) is sufficient to become a person (given that the individual follows a reliablist program). It seems to me that Griffin leans toward the action theory account – though he doesn't set it out as such. I believe that the action-theory interpretation of his account makes it stronger (and is consistent with the Aristotelian interpretation). The "interest" would deflate into simply the conditions for effective action. This is the approach that I advocate. Next up are the action-theory accounts.

6

Agency Justifications

This chapter sets out what I believe to be the best justification for human rights: agency justification. The strategy of this justification is in one way or the other about enabling people to carry out purposive action in the world. We have moved away from contractarian agreement (legal justifications) and interests (welfare or personhood) to a debate about what are the conditions necessary for agency. These goods are necessarily subject to a rigorous level of empirical justification and so the authors in this chapter should be required to accept some form of ethical naturalism. That is, the only concern is whether nature can tell us what conditions are necessary for action. Various versions of ethical naturalism are discussed in the following chapter.

Since the justification apparatus for my theory of natural human rights is largely set out here, my discussion of two other approaches – capability theory (Sen and Nussbaum) and minimum agency theory (Gewirth) – will be succinct. I fill up the rest of the chapter with my own approach.

6.1 CAPABILITY THEORY

The capability approach is one sort of agency justification. The two principal proponents of this approach have been Amartya Sen and Martha Nussbaum. To get a handle on this, one has to understand what is meant by *capability*. Among the several senses that are put forth, the central concern is that of *opportunity*.[1] By opportunity one can mean several things. Two prominent senses are (a) providing certain minimum goods that are generally necessary for action, and (b) providing *whatever* it takes to put a person into a position in which he or she can freely make choices about

[1] Amartya Sen, *The Idea of Justice* (Cambridge, MA: Harvard University Press, 2009): 231.

his or her life. In two different contexts, Sen rejects the first approach in favor of the second. The reason for this is that Sen believes that public policy supporting opportunity will vary according to national circumstances. Instead of offering universal criteria for capability, he believes that the resolution of this problem occurs via debate that engages national public reason. That debate will reject insufficient proposals such as those that measure poverty on a single factor – such as income. In his book *Inequality Reexamined*, Sen[2] argues that social choice is not accurately represented under this approach. This is because first, the income measure of poverty ignores the various strata of poor people (which are critical to consider). Sen argues that at different levels, specially tailored strategies are necessary to enable capability.[3] Second, Sen argues that though there is general agreement on what constitutes diminished capacity, the same cannot be said about goods designed to meet basic needs (cf. the discussion of Raz's interest theory in Chapter 5). Poverty is (a) an acknowledgment of deprivation, and (b) a matter of identifying the focus for public action (the first is more descriptive while the latter is primarily normative).[4] Since diagnosis logically precedes prescription, the descriptive acknowledgment must be made to ascertain why the prescription (in terms of goods) is necessary. Thus capability (or the lack of it) is the logically prior concern. Because this assessment is largely factual, there should be general agreement, at least in principle, on what the problem is.

However, it is not always a simple process. For example, *hunger* might seem to be an easy case. However, as Sen has argued in several venues, if a person is hungry because he is involved in a religious fast or because she is a graduate student in economics with a limited stipend from the department, then these two instances are voluntary and cannot be compared to someone who is hungry because she is a single mother with two children, little education, and few marketable skills.[5] Utility or low-income analysis does not capture this dynamic. Capability analysis does. This is because capability analysis is rather like capturing the "typical" suffering individual in various categories. This is much like modal averaging (as opposed to mean averaging and median averaging that are used in utilitarian calculations). In modal averaging one seeks to identify particular profiles of various strata of the general population to be examined. The focus is upon constructed individuals who represent the

---

[2] Amartya Sen, *Inequality Reexamined* (Cambridge, MA: Harvard University Press, 1992).
[3] Sen, *Inequality Reexamined*, 103–105.
[4] Sen, *Inequality Reexamined*, 107.
[5] Sen, *Inequality Reexamined*, 114.

profile that is different from other profiles and has sufficient number of individuals to warrant public policy focus. Because this sort of modal depiction is what capability analysis is all about, its advocates argue that it is superior to utility calculations (of which Sen is an antagonist).

In *The Idea of Justice*, Sen broadens his analysis along the same lines.

ARGUMENT 6.1: SEN ON THE INDIVIDUAL FREEDOM APPROACH

1. Various economic measures of happiness are connected to rather static aggregate devices such as national income (following William Perry, seventeenth century) – Fact (Sen, *The Idea of Justice*, p. 226)
2. Aggregate devices miss the plight of subgroups, for example, African Americans have mortality rates comparable to second and third world countries – Fact (p. 226)
3. Other overgeneralizations include Asians being inclined to living under tyranny while the West is freedom loving – Fact (pp. 227–228)
4. The individual freedom approach allows (a) more *opportunity* for the individual to pursue her objectives; (b) enjoyment of the *process* of choosing and its importance per se – Fact (p. 228) [cf. the example of Kim who wants to stay at home on a Sunday afternoon (choice a) and the intervention of thugs who either throw Kim in the gutter (choice b) or enforce Kim's staying at home (choice c) – (a) and (c) have the same opportunity aspect (though rather narrow) while (c) differs in process from (a)]

    ───

5. [The individual freedom approach is superior to the aggregate and generalization approach] – 1–4

This argument emphasizes an individual approach to human rights. In premise #4 Sen shows his interest in *individual freedom* as the driving force in this process. This is a theme that he repeats in *Development as Freedom*, "Freedom is a principal determinant of individual initiative and social effectiveness; it is good primarily because it enhances the ability of individuals to help themselves."[6] This is characteristic of the Sen/Nussbaum approach. The community and econometrics that are oriented in the direction of group dynamics are derided in favor of policies that are individually oriented.[7] This is a question of strategy that can work both

───

[6] Amartya Sen, *Development as Freedom* (New York: Alfred A. Knopf, 1999): 19.
[7] According to Sen's modal typology.

ways. For example, Rosemarie Tong has argued forcefully that in cases of public policy involving the health of typical citizens the individual approach (the clinical approach) is often less effective than the group approach (public health).[8] Getting Americans to stop smoking was a failure under the clinical approach but found real traction under the public health approach beginning in the late 1960s. The same dynamic occurs today with obesity. The current policy of treating the problem as an individual matter between patient and doctor (the clinical, individualistic approach) has been failing miserably. The problem is getting worse. This author is personally involved with an alternative public health project that meets the criteria that Tong sets out.[9] Based on this personal experience, I can see certain problems that are better served under a model that targets groups and not modally constructed typical individuals.

The point here is that when the aim is to increase happiness or public capability, sometimes policy measures need to be tailored toward heterogeneous group dynamics rather than some statistically composite individual that one constructs in order to meet her needs. This speaks to the more general bias that the capability approach evinces to the individual against the community. As the reader will see later in this chapter, I think there needs to be a balance between these two concerns. The shift to a decidedly individual approach, with opportunity fostering *individual liberty* (also known as the individual preference approach)[10] as the only driving force, is limited. This is only half of the project.

Sen recognizes this sort of attack. His response is the following:[11]

ARGUMENT 6.2: SEN'S REPLY TO THE "INDIVIDUALISM APPROACH"
1. A common attack against capability theory is that it exalts individuals over communities – Fact (Sen, *The Idea of Justice*, pp. 244–245)
2. Communities can be understood as individuals living within the domain of social influences – Assertion (p. 245)

[8] Rosemarie Tong, "Taking on the Big Fat," in *Public Health Policy and Ethics*, ed. Michael Boylan (Dordrecht: Kluwer/Springer, 2004): 39–58.
[9] I have been involved with a group of orthopedic surgeons and public health personnel in a project called "Movement Is Life: Addressing Musculoskeletal Health Disparities." The group has been active in pilot projects in poor populations both urban and rural to fight musculoskeletal problems often caused by obesity. The strategies mentioned by Tong are being applied in this project.
[10] The import of viewing liberty as the expression of individual preferences (a backdoor to one form of well-being) is made by H. E. Baber, "Worlds, Capabilities and Well-Being," *Ethical Theory and Moral Practice* **13**.4 (2010): 377–392.
[11] Sen, *The Idea of Justice*.

3. The community perspective often improperly creates an analogy between individuals in their thought processes and communities as well as leveling a dominant identity upon the individual – Assertion (pp. 246–247)
4. Dominant identities are oppressive to the individual – Assertion (p. 247)

_____

5. The common attack against capability theory fails – 1–4 (pp. 244–247)

Sen's counter-rebuttal is that communities have no actual character. This is rather like Gilbert Ryle's famous thought experiment on *where the real Oxford is.*[12] Ryle sets out a person visiting Oxford asking to see the *real* university. This individual would be asking an empty question were he to visit the Bodleian, the various colleges, the Ashmolean Museum, the Sheldonian Theater, and view the dons and students walking about – and *still* ask to see the real Oxford. For Ryle and Sen. this is all Oxford is. There is no *esprit de corps* (or in my terms, shared community worldview). Sen is too dismissive of communities. Though they exist differently than do individuals (more on this in the next chapter), I contend that the properties of the community really *exist*, though they do so in a different ontological fashion than the individual. Sen's dismissiveness of communities follows from his reluctance to engage the question of ontology.[13] This dispute will be engaged in the next chapter.

Second, Sen claims that the community perspective is oppressive. This can be true only if the individualistic perspective is repudiated. What I have argued elsewhere[14] is that there should be a balance between individual and community perspectives (as in Figure 6.1). Sen seems to think that the only alternatives are X versus Z. I think this misses the real contribution of both that are necessary for a balanced moral approach in social/political philosophy. I argue that Y is the best perspective.

Extreme individual perspective	Balanced perspective	Extreme community perspective
X	Y	Z

FIGURE 6.1. The Individual Perspective versus the Community Perspective

[12] Gilbert Ryle, *The Concept of Mind* (London: Hutchinson, 1949): 11–24.
[13] Sen, *The Idea of Justice*, 41–42.
[14] Boylan, *A Just Society*, ch. 6.

A final problem that I find with Sen is his emphasis on abstract out-comes of opportunity/liberty that he calls capability. My objection is somewhat along the lines of Hegel's famous criticism of Kant.[15] It is one thing to say that we want to advance human agency because we want all human agents to be capable of exercising their liberty. Who would disagree?[16] To his credit, Sen does offer a few concrete proposals when he focuses on health care, general women's rights to education, and to birth control. He focuses in particular on the Kerala Province in India and within Costa Rica.[17] These macroeconomic policies are based on the microeconomic-essentialist model that the modal averaging technique creates.

One leaves Sen searching for *more*.[18] A few scattered goods that help to enable capability are fine for an appetizer, but a thorough groundwork for public policy demands more. Martha Nussbaum takes up some of this slack with her table of central human capabilities (Table 6.1).

[15] G. W. F. Hegel, *Werke,* vol. 8, *Grundlinien der Philosophie des Rechts,* ed. E. Gans; trans. T. M. Knox, *Hegel's Philosophy of Right* (Oxford: Clarendon Press, 1942), Section 153, p. 90ff. See also Allen Wood's explanation of this critique in "The Emptiness of the Moral Will," *The Monist* 72 (1989): 454–483. For a defense of Kant on this point, see Marcus Singer, *Generalization in Ethics* (New York: Athenaeum, 1961): 279–295, and David Cummiskey, *Kantian Consequentialism* (Oxford: Oxford University Press, 1996): 47–50. For a com-promise opinion, see Christine M. Korsgaard, "Ethical, Political, Religious Thought," in *Creating the Kingdom of Ends* (Cambridge: Cambridge University Press 1996): 14–16.

[16] One author who disagrees is Mozaffar Qizilbash, "Sugden's Critique of the Capability Approach," *Utilitas: A Journal of Utilitarian Studies* **23**.1 (2011): 25–51. Qizilbash sets out Sugden's suggestion that the abstract nature of capability analysis allows it to be applied in a manner that is paternalistic (thus restricting individual liberty). Nussbaum's approach here fares better. The author recognizes that both Sen and Nussbaum under-stand this possibility and attempt to ameliorate it.

[17] Sen (*Inequality Reexamined*) states that in Kerala (a province of India) there is (compared to the country as a whole) higher literacy (91% v. 52%), higher female literacy (87% v. 39%), and also a low female to male ratio (meaning that female babies aren't killed) (p. 127). In Kerala there is a much lower level of real income than in the rest of India, however; the life expectancy is 70 versus 57 years (there is also a lower infant mortal-ity rate) (p. 126). He also mentions Costa Rica in the context of mortality figures. It is his conjecture (and I agree) that populations that live longer are probably happier. Among comparable poor countries, those with cultural and institutional capabilities live longer (e.g., the gross national product (GNP) per person in South Africa is $2,470; Brazil, $2,540; Gabon, $2,960; Oman, $5,220; compare with China, $350 and Sri Lanka, $430). Mortality rates in the first group of countries are 53–66 years old versus 70 for the poorer. Also, in Costa Rica (at $1,780 v. USA $20,910) life expectancy is 75 versus 76 years! (pp. 125–128). China, Sri Lanka, and Costa Rica have communal health care, basic education, and other cooperative social factors (p. 126).

[18] This issue about an abstract account of free preference over an account that presents real, tangible goods is a source of some controversy, with Thomas Pogge coming out against Sen in favor of defined goods from a Rawlsian perspective: (*cont. on p. 156*)

TABLE 6.1. *Nussbaum's Central Human Functional Capabilities*

1. Life – Being able to live to the end of a normal-length human life and to not have one's life reduced to a life that is not worth living.

2. Bodily Health – Being able to enjoy good health that includes (but is not limited to) reproductive health, nourishment, and shelter.

3. Bodily Integrity – Being able to move about freely, in addition to having sovereignty over one's body, which includes being secure against assault, including sexual assault, child sexual abuse, domestic violence and the opportunity for sexual satisfaction and choice in reproductive decisions.

4. Senses, Imagination, and Thought – Being able to use one's senses to imagine, think, and reason in a "truly human way"– informed by an adequate education. Furthermore, having the ability to produce self-expressive works and engage in religious rituals without fear of political ramifications. Being able to have pleasurable experiences. Being able to search for life's ultimate meaning in one's own way and not to be subject to unnecessary pain.

5. Emotions – Being able to have attachments to things and people outside of ourselves; this includes being able to love others, grieve at the loss of loved ones, and be angry when it is justified. Not to have one's emotional development arrested or blighted by traumatic events of abuse or neglect.

6. Practical Reason – Being able to form a conception of the good and critically reflect on it in the process of setting out a plan for one's own life.

7. Affiliation

A. Being able to live with and show concern for other human beings, empathize with (and show compassion for) people, and have the capability of justice and friendship. Institutions help develop and protect forms of affiliation through the fostering of social/political institutions that have these capabilities as their stated outcomes along with freedom of assembly and political speech.

B. Being able to have self-respect and not be humiliated by others, that is, being treated with dignity and equal worth. This entails (at the very least) protection against discrimination on the basis of race, sex, sexual orientation, religion, caste, ethnicity, and nationality. In work, this means entering relationships of mutual recognition as ends.

8. Other Species – Being able to have concern for and live with other animals, plants, and the natural world.

9. Play – Being able to laugh, play, and enjoy recreational activities.

10. Control over One's Environment

A. Political – Being able to effectively participate in the political choices that affect one personally. This includes the right of political participation, free speech, and association.

B. Material – Being able to own property (real and portable property) on an equal basis with all other members of society, not just formally, but materially (that is, as a real opportunity). Further, to have the ability to seek employment on an equal basis as others, and the freedom from unwarranted search and seizure.

Source: This is my paraphrased reconstruction of the central capabilities from Martha C. Nussbaum, *Women and Human Development* (Cambridge: Cambridge University Press, 2000): 78–80.

There is much in Nussbaum's table that I find fulfills the latter criticism that I have leveled against Sen. By breaking out a series of capacities (the "being able"), she identifies outcomes that would characterize a society whose citizens enjoyed human capability. This is a big step forward, but it is still not enough. Two steps that would improve this chart would be (a) a tighter connection to the supporting theory; and (b) a better sense of hierarchical ordering in the chart. To her credit, Nussbaum goes a step toward each of these objections. In the first case, she takes an Aristotelian *endoxa* approach of reporting common opinion: "The list represents the result of years of cross-cultural discussion and comparisons between earlier and later versions will show that the input of other voices has shaped its content in many ways. Thus it already represents what it proposes: a type of *overlapping consensus* on the part of people with otherwise different views of human life."[19] As I mentioned in Chapter 1, such public dialogue in the cosmopolitan arena will be necessary for any practical policies to be put into place. I also believe that public dialogue within various communities and between communities is a necessary precondition to establish the shared community worldview. However, where I differ from Nussbaum, Sen, and Rawls in this regard is that dialogue alone (even directed dialogue) is not enough. This generates merely contractarianism: what people agree to is given force by the very agreement alone. This is an anti-realist approach that I have addressed earlier. Instead, I would contend that this essential dialogue needs to take place within a moral structure of natural human rights supported by the sincerity and authenticity criteria set out below.

Second, since it is unlikely that this set of capability candidates is of equal weight, it would be useful to set out a triage hierarchy. Nussbaum also agrees that the capabilities are not of equal weight: "Some items of the list may seem to us more fixed than others. For example, it would be astonishing if the right to bodily integrity were to be removed from the list; that seems to be a fixed point in our considered judgment of goodness. On the other hand, one might debate what role is played by literacy in

Thomas Pogge, "Can the Capability Approach Be Justified?" *Philosophical Topics* **30**.2 (2002): 167–228. Sandrine Berges defends Sen against Pogge: Sandrine Berges, "Why the Capability Approach Is Justified," *Journal of Applied Philosophy* **24**.1 (2007): 16–25. Rutger Claassen and Soran Reader support a listing of goods that is compatible with my table of embeddedness: Rutger Claassen, "Making Capability Lists: Philosophy versus Democracy," *Political Studies* **59**.3 (2011): 491–508, and Soran Reader, "Does a Basic Needs Approach Need Capabilities?" *Journal of Political Philosophy* **14**.3 (2006): 337–350.
[19] Martha Nussbaum, *Women and Human Development* (Cambridge: Cambridge University Press, 2000), 76.

human functioning, and what role is played by our relationship to other species in the world of nature."[20] Though she admits that some capabilities are more "fixed" than others, there is no clear dynamic to compare competing claims. Without this hierarchical dynamic, it still seems that we are dealing in an "all-or-nothing" dynamic: either a capability is *in* or *out*. But this seems wrong to me. In public policy discussions, there is generally a more gradated set of priorities so that hard decisions can be made based on the nuanced principles of triage. Because the list was originally generated in a Rawlsian public reason domain, and because public agreement is variable and changeable, this seems to be an intractable difficulty.

In the end, there is much to admire in the capability approach. First, it is an agency justification that focuses on enabling action. Second, it aspires to create a table of practical capabilities that make more concrete the abstract principles of the system. However, because the theoretical foundations are either based on intuitionism, aporetic economic analysis, or contractarianism, this author is left wanting more from an agency theory: enter Alan Gewirth.

6.2 THE ARGUMENT OF ALAN GEWIRTH

Alan Gewirth provides a strong naturalistic argument that aspires to offer a dialectically necessary principle that all people have the generic rights to freedom and well-being. He does this in two forms: a direct and an indirect form. In my opinion, the indirect is the stronger form, however; the one that is most often discussed is the direct form. It runs as shown in Table 6.2. Premise #7 is a version of the Principle of Generic Consistency: *Act in accord with the generic rights of your recipients as well as yourself.*[21] The indirect version of the argument emphasizes more the act of *claiming* and what is entailed by that speech act.[22] It is

---

[20] Nussbaum, *Women and Human Development*, 77.

[21] From Alan Gewirth, "The Arguments for the Principle of Generic Consistency," in *Reason and Morality* (Chicago: University of Chicago Press, 1978): 135.

[22] The "Indirect Version" of the argument is my interpretive reconstruction of Gewirth's argument that I discussed with him at the conference I held in his honor at Marymount University in 1997. He accepted this as not distorting his vision. I note that the most respected Gewirth scholar in the world, Deryck Beyleveld, does not use indirect reconstructions of Gewirth in Beyleveld's masterful work, *The Dialectical Necessity of Morality: An Analysis and Defense of the Principle of Generic Consistency* (Chicago: University of Chicago Press, 1992).

1. Antithesis: "I" (some possible objector to Gewirth) claim that some PPAs do not have a moral claim right to freedom and well-being – Assertion
2. Action is essential to being human (i.e., is a part of one's human nature) – Fact

my opinion that the goal of *dialectical necessity* is best advanced by creating an imaginary situation in which someone theoretically denies freedom and well-being for himself (Stage II). When this is shown to be prudentially flawed, the next scene has Mr. X claiming freedom and well-being for himself, but denying it to Ms. Y (Stage III). How can one

3. In order to act (i.e., to be a PPA), I (or anyone else) must have some modicum of freedom and well-being – Fact

4. In order to act effectively (meaning "at an approximately level starting line"), I (or anyone else) must have a fuller sense of freedom and well-being (beyond biological minimums; relative to the "starting line" in each society) – Fact

5. All people must claim the rights for themselves of that which is essential to their human nature – Fact

6. All people when confronted with acting minimally versus effectively will choose to act effectively – Fact

7. All people must claim for themselves (prudential only) the rights of freedom and well-being (in the fuller sense) – 2, 6

8. "I" or anyone else can recognize the prudential sense of premise #7 – Fact

9. It is rational to assume that "I" am no different from anyone else in a relevant sense concerning the foundations of action – Fact

10. To deny to others that which I claim for myself (viz., freedom and well-being), when the basis of attribution is premise #7, is to assert that I am an exception to the general rule or that others are to be excepted from the general rule; is to fail to recognize basic facts of deductive and inductive logic, namely, the basic principles of class inclusion (whether seen deductively [an instance of the universal quantifier] or inductively [as a "cogent" feature that will allow said attribution]) – Fact

11. All people to be fully *Homo sapiens*, must accept the dictums of rationality (a minimum sense of deductive and inductive logic – which includes some informal understanding of the universal quantifier) – Assertion

12. The universal quantifier does not permit exceptions to a properly constructed generalization nor does induction allow a special status for any members of a properly described sample space – Fact

13. Premise #7 is a properly constructed generalization about what rights must be claimed by everyone – Assertion

14. To believe in exceptions for myself (or anyone else) from a universal statement covering all people (when "I" am no different from others) is to be irrational – 8–13

15. To deny others the freedom and well-being which I claim for myself is to be irrational – 7, 14

16. I cannot (or anyone cannot) deny to others the freedom and well-being (in the fuller sense) that I claim for myself – 15, 11

17. Moral rights are those rights that apply to every PPA – Assertion

18. To admit to a universal claim right (which applies to every PPA for freedom and well-being) is to admit to a moral right to freedom and well-being – Assertion

19. "I" (or anyone else) must claim that all PPAs have a (moral) claim right to freedom and well-being – 16–18

_____

20. Thesis: "I" or anyone else, that is, every PPA has a (moral) claim right to freedom and well-being – 1, 19

TABLE 6.2. *The Direct Version of the Argument*

Stage I

A Prospective Purposive Agent (PPA) claims the following:

1. I do (or intend to do) X voluntarily for some purpose, E. By virtue of making this claim, the PPA rationally must consider that (claim) in logical sequence.
2. E is good.
3. My freedom and well-being are generically necessary conditions of my agency.
4. My freedom and well-being are necessary goods.

Stage II

By virtue of having to accept premise 4, the PPA must accept the following:

5. I (even if no one else) have a claim right (but not necessarily a moral one) to my freedom and well-being.

Stage III

By virtue of having to accept premise 5 and on the basis of premise 1, the PPA must accept the following:

6. Other PPAs have a moral right claim to their freedom and well-being. If this is the case, then every PPA rationally must claim, by virtue of claiming to be a PPA.
7. Every PPA has a moral claim right to freedom and well-being.

From Alan Gewirth, "The Arguments for the Principle of Generic Consistency," in *Reason and Morality* (Chicago: University of Chicago Press, 1978): ch. 3. This reconstruction comes from Michael Boylan, Introduction to *Gewirth: Critical Essays on Action, Rationality, and Community* (Lanham, MD: Rowman and Littlefield, 1999).

accept the former and deny the latter? Gewirth's answer was that only a Callicles or his reading of Nietzsche could move in this direction. The enthymeme here is that Callicles (a stand-in for Gorgias) and Gewirth's interpretation of Nietzsche didn't hold that all people are essentially (with respect to prospective purposive action) equal. Thus, with this worldview perspective one could generate (without contradiction) a position in which someone could claim freedom and well-being for herself without admitting that others could legitimately claim the same thing. In a 1998 visit to the United States Holocaust Museum that I made with Alan Gewirth (whose birth family were immigrant, nonobservant Russian Jews), we discussed the philosophy behind the Nazis and their attitudes toward the Jews they were murdering and how they could have done such a thing if the PGC were descriptive instead of just being prescriptive.

Gewirth responded that the background condition for PPAs was that they possessed *and followed* the basic principles of deductive and inductive logic. Thus, those who did not were not PPAs and were really out of the system. Callicles and Nietzsche (philosophical stand-ins for the Nazis according to Gewirth) were beyond the pale. Since they considered only a small number of people as deserving (the privileged 1%?),[23] they disagreed with the background condition of all people being equally deserving qua PPAs. If all people are not equally deserving as PPAs, then the argument fails.

However, I don't think it's that simple. Gewirth was right to exclude the 1 percent of the population who think of themselves as Tom Wolfe's *masters of the universe*.[24] Surely, if we accept the Aristotelian doctrine of *epi to polu* (for the most part), then Gewirth is entitled to his conjecture about everyone being equal and that virtually everyone would factually agree to this. For an empirical hypothesis, proving the null set in only 1 percent of cases is very good in inductive logic. I agree with Gewirth here. We cannot set out moral theories on the basis of eccentric slivers of the population – even if the slivers are very recklessly powerful. To say that these masters of the universe wannabes are simply mistaken is the normative tack to which I also agree.

What the direct and indirect arguments for the PGC offer (that other previous arguments presented in this book do not offer as a justification for human rights) is a hard, logically based argument set upon the natural conditions of human agency: freedom and well-being. This is a plus for Gewirth.

What I find lacking in Gewirth's argument for the PGC is that he frames it from the vantage point of some (any) particular agent's claim for freedom and well-being (FWB). The level of logical discourse is the individual. Because the individual has no particular parameters attached (aside from possessing some minimum competence in inductive and deductive logic), Gewirth thought he could invoke Universal Generalization

[23] This reference to the 1 percent is meant to refer to the very privileged. Around the Western world, between 2011 and 2012 there were protests by those identifying themselves as the 99 percent who sought economic justice. For a theoretical discussion of these issues, see Joseph Stieglitz, *The Price of Inequality: How Today's Divided Society Endangers Our Future* (New York: Norton, 2013).

[24] The reference is to Tom Wolfe's depiction of Wall Street bankers during the 1980s who made a lot of money and considered themselves to beyond supermen – they were gods! *Bonfire of the Vanities* (New York: Bantam, 1988).

and move from PPAj => C_p FWBj to $(\forall_x)$ {PPAx => C_{mr} FWBx}["If John is a Prospective Purposive Agent then John has a claim$_{prudential}$ for freedom and well-being"; to "For any person if that person is a Prospective Purposive Agent, then that person has a claim$_{moral-right}$ to freedom and well-being."] Most attacks that have been made against Gewirth arise at just this point.[25]

Gewirth could have avoided these attacks had he justified his analysis of action at the level of the species instead of creating a fictive voice of some randomly selected individual (cf. my own approach in The Moral Status of Basic Goods, later in the chapter). However, what he would sacrifice in such a move would be the dialectical necessity that only occurs in the fictive role of a claimant and objector. On balance, I think Gewirth made the wrong choice.

Gewirth sets out the universe of goods as three sorts: basic, nonsubtractive, and additive.[26] Basic goods are fundamental to action. Nonsubtractive goods are goods in one's possession. Additive goods are goods that one wishes to obtain. Basic goods have the most moral relevance. Next come the nonsubtractive goods that are more important than additive goods (though the reason for this last priority seems tied again to an implicit libertarian understanding of work and property). Basic goods are determined by the PPA relative to her view of her own agency. When *Reason and Morality* was first published, this individual focus made it a favorite among libertarians. However, this subjective track opens Gewirth to the same arguments I made against Raz's interest approach. This applies to Gewirth's depiction of basic goods as well as his presentation of well-being. By ignoring the community dynamic he is also subject to the argument I made against Sen. It is a flaw in the picture of rights that Gewirth draws.

Gewirth realized that the libertarian understanding of his theory was contrary to his intent. So he tried to modify his position by creating his own kingdom of ends in *The Community of Rights* (1998).[27] By creating the supportive state (that operated according to the PGC) he tried to bring political discourse into the picture as defining just what the basic

---

[25] For a review of many of these attacks and the reply from a sympathetic Gewirthian voice, see Beyleveld, *The Dialectical Necessity of Morality*.

[26] Gewirth, "The Arguments," 53–58.

[27] Alan Gewirth, *The Community of Rights* (Chicago: University of Chicago Press, 1998). An attack on whether this really works comes from Beth J. Singer in Michael Boylan, ed., *Gewirth: Critical Essays on Action, Rationality and Community* (Lanham, MD: Rowman and Littlefield, 1999): 145–154.

goods might be. This is also the approach of Sen. Also, like Sen, Gewirth leaves his definition of freedom rather abstractly set out. However, as I argued earlier, this leaves too much to chance. The theory remains hanging in the air.[28] This is an especially forceful shortcoming given the role of Gewirth's tight logical argument for the PGC. What would be preferable would be for Gewirth to have created a chart of rights either on the plan of Nussbaum or of my own table of embeddedness (Table 6.3). What would be even better would be for that chart to follow naturally from the theoretical grounding of the central principle of morality and a fortiori of human rights.

A final shortcoming to Gewirth's account is that he does not address what he thinks is an adequate understanding of personhood. The reason for this derives from his original ambiguity between depicting *some random* individual – for example, John, mentioned earlier – and trying to move by Universal Generalization to *any* individual. Certainly, *any* individual may legitimately be rather faceless. But that cannot be the case for John (who lends the aspired-for dialectical necessity). For the most part, what we are left with is a reason machine that has the requisite minimal facility in deductive and inductive logic.

When Gewirth read the first edition of my book *Basic Ethics* and my own personal worldview imperative (with its emphasis upon both the rational and emotional good will), his response was to send me his latest (and what proved to be his last) book *Self-Fulfillment* (1998).[29] This book aspires to indirectly discuss what is the optimum model of personhood by focusing on the way to live the most choice-worthy life. The approach sets out two ways to become self-fulfilled: via aspirational fulfillment and via capacity fulfillment. These are tempered by a morally based account of human rights that acts as border of restraint upon the tendency of both sorts of fulfillment (especially the capacity fulfillment) to overreach.[30] This is similar to the concern I raised in the previous chapter about the first-person account of well-being as a pivotal interest to support human rights.

In the end, the rational human machine lives on in Gewirth's writing. It severely limits his personhood account.

---

[28] Donald Regan makes a similar point in Boylan, *Gewirth*, 45–70.

[29] Alan Gewirth, *Self-fulfillment* (Princeton, NJ: Princeton University Press, 1998). I might remark in passing that Gewirth had begun a book for my *Basic Ethics in Action* series. It would have been an accessible monograph on the relationship between morality and human rights claims.

[30] Gewirth, *Self-fulfillment*, 215–217.

6.3 THE ARGUMENT OF MICHAEL BOYLAN

In this last section of the agency justification chapter, I present my own approach. It is this approach that I believe sets out the most plausible justification for natural human rights. I have waited to present my approach only after a general survey of cultural and historical contexts and other thinkers who I think have emblematically approached the problem from my tripartite analysis of legal, interest, and agency justifications for human rights. The reason for this is that I believe my theory of natural human rights resonates within both the European tradition and the Chinese tradition (an example of a high ancient civilization that is non-Western and often a point of controversy). I invite the reader to refer back to ways that these thinkers approached natural human rights and also to reflect forward to my own account. A short orientation of my direction is that natural human rights are based upon theories of morality and justice (cf. Chapters 2 and 3). Thus the symphony of natural human rights is set upon themes of morality and justice.

6.3.1 The Personal Worldview Imperative

Among the writers I've presented in this book, James Griffin shows the most concern for personhood as a critical factor in presenting a justification of human rights. I share Griffin's interest in the role of a rounded individual (who is more than a rational machine) in the construction of an adequate justification for human rights. My own personhood account begins with various criteria that the sincere and authentic agent ought to employ in a self-reflective effort toward personal renewal and development. By *sincerity* I mean someone who puts forth an individual commitment toward using his highest capacities to examine the questions raised concerning his understanding of facts and a commitment to the values in his life via the personal worldview imperative. By authenticity I mean a person who engages in her sincere quest via a reliable process that she has consciously and reflectively chosen via the rational and emotional good will. This book recommends the structure of the personal worldview imperative as a general guide.

An imperative is a command. These first-order meta-ethical principles[31] are presented as fundamental requirements for all *Homo sapiens*. These

---

[31] I want to be clear in the way I use "meta-ethical." Instead of the restricted meaning of second-order ethical claims I make a more general contention of meta-ethical as referring to those principles that are necessary to address normative ethical theories. This

commands require personal reflection from an acquired standpoint that I call *the common body of knowledge*. From the common body of knowledge the individual is confronted with social background conditions about what the group believes are facts and values about the world. These background conditions cannot be accepted *tout cort* but should be examined by the individual using other current and historical background conditions (and the agent's own critical imagination) to create the conditions under which the personal worldview examination can proceed. We have visited this terrain in Chapter 5, discussing Wittgenstein and Davidson in the context of Griffin's discussion on the forms of life.

For my purposes, the common body of knowledge is a social background condition that allows all discourse to proceed. This process begins with a speaker and an audience (that is, a speaker in a social context).[32] The speaker wishes to make observations, discuss, or argue for a particular position. The way that the speaker interacts with his audience depends partially upon some body of understandings about facts and values in the world. This common sensibility exists between the speaker and the audience. For example, if I were to address an unknown audience without any idea who these people were, it is very possible that I would not effectively communicate with them. This is because people exist in a context. The context is a social ethos and it creates a rubric that modifies who we are and how we might behave. There are many levels of how this ethos acts to set up rigorous standards or practices.[33] They begin with the very language itself. Through much of the world, the tongue we use to express ourselves is a political statement that can garner support or make enemies. Evidence for this rests in the ways that conquered peoples (such as the Irish, Indians, Angolans, Jews, and others) make it the first order of business after liberation to resuscitate their historical languages and to make them the official mode of discourse.[34]

includes all of what is often termed meta-ethical and expands its purview to other methodologies that are logically prior and necessary for the construction of normative ethics. For a simplified version of my views in this respect, see Michael Boylan, *Basic Ethics,* 2nd ed. (Upper Saddle River, NJ: Prentice Hall, 2009): 7–9.

[32] I am not intending the comprehensive social basis of inductive/abductive knowledge advocated by Charles Sanders Pierce (e.g., Justus Buchler, *The Philosophical Writings of Pierce* (New York: Dover, 1955): 160–164), but rather a more modest claim that I have outlined in greater detail in Boylan, *A Just Society*, ch. 5.

[33] Here I am following Alasdair MacIntyre, *After Virtue: A Study in Moral Theory* (London: Duckworth, 1985): 190.

[34] Linguistic imperialism goes hand-in-hand with political oppression. Two anthologies that support this point (albeit in different ways) are Florian Coulmas, ed., *Linguistic Minorities and Literacy: Language Policy in Developing Countries* (New York: Mouton, 1984), and

The choice of language (that at first might seem like a rather transparent medium) is really filled with various meanings that affect the communication flow between speaker and audience. The language links itself to the history of a people and in that way is a purveyor of those aspects of the ethos that resonate from the community's heritage.

Second, each language has its own strategy of expression. This strategy can alter the manner in which the observation, discussion, or argument is understood. Whereas I do not agree with those who are linguistic determinists,[35] I still hold that language is not a mere transparent vehicle of universal thinking.[36] I think that it does not leave "everything as it is" as Wittgenstein would say.[37] Instead, the *manner* and *strategy* of expression affect the content of what is expressed. This does not mean that people who think in different languages cannot communicate, but it does mean that the communication is not without some (perhaps crucial) perturbation.

Thus, language is an essential element in communication both because it conveys many cultural, political, and historical elements of the country's ethos, but also because the very mechanical exposition of language affects the content to some degree.

After language, there are other important factors that affect the interrelationship between any given speaker and his audience. These include (but are not limited to) etiquette, the political and cultural facts that describe the audience, religious preference and practice, and all the other mores and folkways of a given people.

The common body of knowledge is not about epistemological relativism. Instead, it is a statement about the understanding of *things and attitudes on the ground.* Each agent must engage in some critical appraisal of the common body of knowledge before undergoing the guided reflection commanded by the personal worldview imperative. The standpoint of the personal worldview imperative assumes a critical evaluation of these background conditions via reliable epistemological criteria.

Lenore A. Grenoble and Lindsay J. Whaley, eds., *Endangered Languages: Language Loss and Community Response* (Cambridge: Cambridge University Press, 1998).

[35] The extreme case of this point of view are those who expose linguistic determinism. The most prominent proponent of this thesis is Benjamin Lee Whorf, *Language, Thought, and Reality,* ed. and with introduction by John B. Carroll (Cambridge, MA: MIT University Press, 1966; rpt of 1956).

[36] An example of this position would be Aristotle in *De Interpretatione,* 16a 3ff., "Spoken words are the symbols of mental experience and written words are the symbols of spoken words. Just as all men have not the same writing, so all men have not the same speech sounds, but the mental experiences, which these directly symbolize, are the same for all" (E.M. Edghill, tr.).

[37] Ludwig Wittgenstein, *Philosophical Investigations,* 3rd ed., trans. G. E. M. Anscombe (New York: Macmillan, 1971): I, sec. 124.

After establishing a sound epistemological stance the agent is ready to delve into her own conception of what is good as well as how she should fit into a geographical community. As a matter of developmental fact, humans go through various searching examinations (the timing of which are often socially determined). For example in the United States most individuals engage in intense soul-searching during adolescence, moving away from the family either into college or to a job, getting married, getting fired, experiencing the death of family members, divorce, serious disease or accident, long-term unemployment, and the prospect of death. For others there are often less intense examination processes associated with their religious traditions (Lent for Christians, Ramadan for Muslims, and Yom Kippur for Jews). In popular society, many undergo some reflection around birthdays, anniversaries, and the New Year. In my discussion with those of other cultures, it seems to be the same. Personal reflection is scheduled into our very lives (with more opportunity among those with more time for leisure).[38]

There are thus two meta-levels of the command issued forth by the personal worldview imperative: (a) that common introspection is engaged on a regular basis with sincere and authentic reflection undertaken at key intervals in life; and (b) that the reflection should proceed in a structured manner. The structure of the command mode means that these exercises are not optional. We all are enjoined to enter into this sort of reflection to be sincere and authentic people living on earth.

The first of these theoretical devices is the personal worldview imperative:

> All people must develop a single comprehensive and internally coherent worldview that is good and that we strive to act out in our daily lives.

As noted earlier, one's personal worldview is a very basic concept, containing all that we hold good, true, and beautiful about existence in the world. There are four parts to the personal worldview imperative: completeness, coherence, connection to a theory of the good, and practicality. Let's briefly say something about each.

First is *completeness*. Completeness refers to the ability of a theory or ethical system to handle all cases put before it and to determine an answer based upon the system's recommendations. This is functionally achieved via the good will. The good will is a mechanism by which we decide how to act in the world. The good will provides completeness to everyone who develops one. There are two senses of the good will. The first is the

---

[38] Aristotle, *Metaphysica*, ed. Werner Jaeger (Oxford: Clarendon Press, 1957): 981b, 12–24.

rational good will, which means that each agent will develop an understanding about what reason requires of us as we go about our business in the world. Completeness means that reason (governed by the personal worldview and its operational ethical standpoint) should always be able to come up with an answer to a difficult life decision. In the case of ethics, the rational good will requires engaging in a rationally based philosophical ethics and abiding by what reason demands. Often this plays out practically in examining and justifying various moral maxims – such as maxim alpha: "one has a moral responsibility to follow through on one's commitments, ceteris paribus." This maxim is about promise-making. One could imagine someone, call him Luke, going through the process of sincerely and authentically trying to define and justify moral maxims via reason and a chosen ethical theory. Imagine that college student Luke has accepted maxim alpha. Imagine also that Luke has asked Jennifer out to a big social event at his college. Jennifer accepted, but then one week before the event, Monique (a student whom Luke greatly prefers to Jennifer but never approached because Luke had thought she was out of his league) calls up Luke and asks *him* to the school event. Luke had made a prior promise to Jennifer. But Luke really would prefer going with Monique. What should Luke do? The rational good will (as Luke, himself, has developed it via maxim alpha) says that Luke should carry through with his promise to Jennifer since there is no conflicting moral issue that would invoke the ceteris paribus clause in the maxim. For Luke to act otherwise would be an instance of denying completeness based upon the rational good will. Luke should keep his promise to Jennifer.

Another sort of good will is the *affective* or *emotional good will*. We are more than just rational machines. We have an affective nature, too. Our feelings are important, but just as was the case with reason, some guidelines are in order. For the emotional good will, we begin with sympathy. Sympathy will be taken to be the emotional connection that one forms with other humans. This emotional connection must be one in which the parties are considered to be on a level basis. The sort of emotional connection I am talking about is open and between equals. It is not that of a superior "feeling sorry" for an inferior. Those who engage in interactive human sympathy that is open and level will respond to another with care. Care is an action-guiding response that gives moral motivation to assisting another in need. Together sympathy, openness, and care constitute love.

In the previous case on promise-making, Luke wouldn't be about making and justifying moral maxims such as maxim alpha. Instead, Luke would be developing his capacity sympathetically to connect with other people. If Luke sympathetically connected with Jennifer, his caring response would guide him toward maintaining his promise to Jennifer because to do otherwise would sever the sympathetic connection. Luke would not be acting like a loving person to do otherwise. Likewise, he would like to connect to Monique's offer by acknowledging how happy it made him and how he would very much enjoy seeing her in the future (in another venue). This sort of affective good will comes from one-on-one personal connections that elicit caring responses. The affective good will is every bit as comprehensive as the rational good will.[39]

When confronted with any novel situation, one should utilize the two dimensions of the good will to generate a response. Because these two orientations act differently, it is possible that they may contradict each other. When this is the case, I would allot the tiebreaker to reason. Others demur.[40] Each reader should consider her own response to such an occurrence.

A second part of the personal worldview imperative is *coherence*. People should have coherent worldviews. This also has two varieties: deductive and inductive. Deductive coherence speaks to our not having overt contradictions in our worldview. An example of an overt contradiction in one's worldview would be for Sasha to tell her friend Sharad that she has no prejudice against Muslims and yet in another context she tells anti-Muslim jokes. The coherence provision of the personal worldview imperative says that you shouldn't change who you are and what you stand for depending upon the context in which you happen to be.

Inductive coherence is different. It is about not adopting different life strategies that work against each other. In inductive logic, a conflicting strategy is called a sure-loss contract.[41] For example, if a person wanted to be a devoted husband and family man and yet also engaged in

---

[39] Since the affective good will comes from the completeness condition of the Personal Worldview Imperative, the conditions of the imperative also apply to this sort of philosophical love that I have set out. Some detractors think that you cannot order love (as I have done). I give a response to this argument in Michael Boylan, "Duties to Children," in Michael Boylan, ed., *The Morality and Global Justice Reader* (Boulder, CO: Westview, 2011): 385–404.

[40] This is particularly true of some feminist ethicists. See Rosemarie Tong, "A Feminist Personal Worldview Imperative," in *Morality and Justice: Reading Boylan's A Just Society*, ed. John-Stewart Gordon (Lanham, MD: Lexington/Rowman and Littlefield, 2009): 29–38.

[41] The phrase "sure-loss contract" comes from the notion of betting houses. Say you were betting on the finals of the World Cup: Brazil versus Germany. If you gave 5–1 positive odds for each team, then your betting house will go out of business. A positive assessment of one team requires a complementary negative assessment of the other; failure to observe this rule results in a sure-loss contract.

extramarital affairs he would involve himself in inductive incoherence. The very traits that make him a good family man – loyalty, keeping your word, sincere interest in the well-being of others – would hurt one in being a philanderer, which requires selfish manipulation of others for one's own pleasure. The good family man will be a bad philanderer and vice versa. To try to do both well involves a sure-loss contract. Such an individual will fail at both. This is what inductive incoherence means.

Third is *connection to a theory of the good – most prominent being ethics.*[42] The personal worldview imperative enjoins that we consider and adopt an ethical theory.[43] It does not give us direction, as such, about which theory to choose except that the chosen theory must not violate any of the other three conditions (completeness, coherence, and practicability). What is demanded is that we connect to a theory of ethics and use it to guide our actions.

The final criterion is *practicability.* It is important that the demands of ethics and social/political philosophy (including human rights) be doable and its goals be attainable. A *utopian* command may have logically valid arguments behind it but also be existentially unsound – meaning that some of the premises in the action-guiding argument are untrue by virtue of their being unrealizable in practical terms. If, in a theory of global ethics, for example, we required that everyone in a rich country gave up three-quarters of their income so that they might support the legitimate plight of the poor, then this would be a utopian vision. Philosophers are all too often attracted to tidy, if perhaps radical, utopian visions. However, unless philosophers want to be marginalized, we must situate our prescriptions in terms that can actually be used by policymakers. Philosophers involved in human rights discourse must remember that these theories are to apply to real people living in the world. In taxation policy, for example, at some point – let's say at the point of a 50 percent income-tax rate – even the very wealthy among us will feel unjustly burdened and will rebel and refuse to comply with the policy. Thus it is utopian to base a policy upon the expectation that the rich will submit to giving up 75 percent of their income. An *aspirational* goal (by contrast) is one that may be hard to reach but is at least possible to achieve (it does not violate principles of human nature or structural facts about the communities that inhabit the world). For the purposes of this book, the aspirational perspective will be chosen over the utopian.

---

[42] Other aspects of the good can include commitments to aesthetics and to religion.

[43] My take on the various real and anti-real theories is generally set out in my text, *Basic Ethics,* Part Two.

The purview of the personal worldview imperative is the individual as she interacts with other individuals in the world. Each of us has to do as much as possible to take stock of who we are and what we think we should be. Our personal consciousness is in our power to change. Though factors of environment and genetics are not to be dismissed, in the end it is the free operation of our will that allows us to confront the personal worldview imperative as a challenge for personal renewal. The acceptance of the personal worldview account means that it is in our power to create our ethical selves. The personal worldview imperative thus grounds my theory of personhood that is part of the foundation of natural human rights.

6.3.2 The Community Worldview Imperatives

Since we are not people who live in a vacuum, the next piece of the natural human rights puzzle concerns the various communities in which we are members. After all, it is within the context of communities that rights are recognized and duties are undertaken. Writers such as Michael Sandel and Amitai Etzioni have in their own various ways recognized the role of the community in morality and justice.[44] There is some overlap in their concerns for community and my own approach.

The first community that most of us know is the family. In the family, we are bound by filial ties of love and shared sacrifice for common goals.[45] This is the smallest and often the most effective of all communities in setting out social and political institutions that are of critical importance in human rights recognition and enforcement. However, in aggregate, there is perhaps no more powerful pro-community-force in the world.

Other communities substitute friendship and mutual understanding built through one-on-one interpersonal activity. These communities may center around where one lives (the neighborhood), where one works (the business), where one worships (the church, temple, mosque, et al.), and so on. There is often a political institutional structure at this level.

---

[44] For a taste of the general direction of Sandel, see Michael Sandel, *Liberalism and the Limits of Justice,* 2nd ed. (Cambridge: Cambridge University Press, 1998), and *Democracy's Discontent: America in Search of a Public Philosophy* (Cambridge, MA: Harvard University Press, 1998). For Etzioni, see Amitai Etzioni, Ronald Bayer, Benjamin R. Barber, and Daniel Bell, *The Essential Communitarian Reader* (New York: Rowman and Littlefield, 1998), and Amitai Etzioni, *The New Golden Rule* (New York: Basic Books, 1998).

[45] Of course, many families fall short of this goal, but the description I present is at least aspirational as defined earlier.

In some villages it is the town government. In larger cities it is often the precinct. Generally, this intimate committee of the whole can exist up to around 500 people. Let's call these the *micro communities.*

Larger groups of people we will call *macro communities.* When there is some proximate connection to the larger groups due to locale or other marks of similarity, the individuals in the macro community identify as being members of that community and cite it as a part of their personal identity. The largest macro community would be the nation itself. From the macro community various institutional structures are created so that the business of the community gets done. (Other sorts of communities are set out following.)

The essential unit in either sort of community is the people who make up the community. My model sets out the people as the sovereign who, in turn, legitimate institutions to advance their interests. In the case of a micro community, the governmental structure is often carried on by designated representatives along with the advice and consent of the micro community as a whole. This is what gave rise to the town meeting style of New England polity. In the case of the macro community, the government structure is carried on by surrogates (elected in a democracy) who are charged with representing the people. If they do not, then (in a democracy) they will be discharged from office.

Though most countries in the world are not effective democracies, this does not mean that other forms of government cannot engage in a social dialogue that allows the wishes of the people to be represented to their leaders in some way and that affords some real interchange. This may occur in various settings, but the accountability factor in these non-democratic nations is certainly lower. Because of this, autocratic regimes can often trample upon human rights until the status quo is intolerable and an armed or unarmed revolt is the outcome.

But it is possible for a lower level of accountability to exist among some autocratic societies. This occurs when nonpolitical social institutions, such as the church, are able to exert a counterbalancing force against the government. In other instances, business interests can also exert such a force. The point is that the model advocated for best advancing human rights from an internal vantage point of the nation is democracy, and lacking that, strong, independent social institutions that represent the interests of their members.

Both micro and macro communities develop social and cultural worldviews that affect life in those communities. These shared community worldviews have normative character so that they also need some structural guidance through an imperative aimed at the community: the shared community worldview imperative.

Each agent must contribute to a common body of knowledge that supports the creation of a shared community worldview (that is itself complete, coherent, and good) through which social institutions and their resulting policies might flourish within the constraints of the essential core commonly held values (ethics, aesthetics, and religion).

There are five important parts of this imperative that deserve attention. The first criterion is *agent contribution*. This means that members of a community have responsibilities to be active members. One cannot ethically shift this responsibility completely to others. Even in communities in which there are elected officials, each person in the community has an obligation periodically to check to see whether she thinks the community is doing what it says it is doing and whether what it says it is doing is proper policy (meaning here that it is supportive of human rights within the community). When either of those conditions is not being met, members of the community have an obligation to engage whatever institutional mechanisms of protest and change are open to them.

The second criterion is the reference to the *common body of knowledge*, which represents what is culturally accepted to be good, true, and beautiful about the world (discussed earlier). Many communities (especially most macro communities) are diverse. In order to create acceptance within some community, it is necessary to recognize the nonmoral character of these differences. Because natural human rights depend upon justice and morality, it is important to differentiate these outcomes. Sometimes the moral and the nonmoral become confused. In these situations, one must refer back to the personal worldview and the relevant theory of ethics that have been embraced in order to separate an ethical from a nonethical practice.[46] It is easy to be prejudicial against what is new or unfamiliar, but when the unfamiliar is merely different and nonethical, then the common body of knowledge must expand to accommodate it. However, when the unfamiliar is immoral, then the common body of knowledge should give direction for the proper way to exclude such an input to the community (for example, the Ku Klux Klan terrorist cult).

The third criterion of the shared community imperative describes common traits shared by the personal worldview imperative: *complete, coherent*, and *connected to a theory of good*. As per our discussion of the

---

[46] It is important to distinguish a nonethical (nonmoral) practice from an unethical (immoral) practice. The former does not concern ethics while the latter is judged to be wrong by some theory of ethics.

common body of knowledge, these pivotal criteria allow the members of the community to evaluate new members to the community so that they might be accepted or not. New doesn't necessarily mean bad (as per the fifth criterion discussed later).

The fourth criterion enjoins that the *creation of social institutions* occurs within the guidelines set out by the imperative. The way communities act is via the operation of social and political institutions that represent the worldview of the micro or macro group. It is important that the institutions that are so created actually represent the sense of the shared worldviews of the group's members. It is certainly possible for an institution to be created that loses its original mission and strays in the way that it operates. When this occurs, it is the community's responsibility to put the institution back on course (revise it) or eliminate it.

Finally, the last part of the imperative is an acceptance of the *diversity of the community in terms of core values: ethics, aesthetics, and religion.* The acceptance of diversity is very important. People are different. Embracing these differences and allowing institutional space for them is morally and practically important if we want to protect natural human rights. Though there is a limit to this acceptance, the default position in the shared community worldview imperative is that diversity is a *pro tanto* good and a healthy state of affairs for the micro or macro community. The burden of proof to the contrary is upon those who believe that such behavior is unethical.

It is the position of this author that these five aspects of the shared community worldview imperative lay the groundwork for ethical communities that operate in a way that protects the natural human rights for all its members.

The Extended Community Worldview Imperative

The next level of imagining the community is a construction that extends human community membership to those beyond the conventional boundaries of our micro and macro groups (ending at the state). To intellectually grasp this aspect of community membership we need to import a new concept: the *extended community.* The extended community is one in which the agent is remotely connected. For example, I live in suburban Maryland just outside Washington, DC. I am a member of various micro communities (such as my college and my son's school parents group, and so on) and macro communities (such as my city, county, state, and nation). In each of these I have some direct or indirect contact that is proximate and tangible. I can go into the District of Columbia. I can write my congressperson or senator. I can get into my car or travel via public transit directly to the physical domains of the state or national capital. Each of these is connected proximately to me through a tangible, operational, institutional structure that operates (in theory) under the principle of sovereignty set out earlier.

Now the extended community is a little different. Even though I travel there by rail, sea, or air, I do not have immediate access. I must present a passport. I can be denied entrance. I have fewer tangible institutional rights in the foreign country than I do at home. The foreign culture is different from my national culture. In some cases I may be completely ignorant about its customs, government, and social circumstances. The media often make it more difficult for me to find out facts on many foreign nations – particularly those that are poor and don't seem to fit our perceived national interest. Because of these aspects of remoteness, there may be a famine occurring in Mali or severe storm damage on one of the islands of Indonesia that many in the United States (for example) don't even know about.

International ignorance is a large cause of international apathy. We cannot engage in public dialogue about the world's problems if we do not possess accurate information about situations in various societies and the relevant history and social conditions that situate them. To address a background condition necessary for morality and global human rights we must embrace a third sort of worldview imperative: the *extended community worldview imperative:*

> *Each agent must educate himself and others as much as he is able about the peoples of the world – their access to the basic goods of agency, their essential commonly held cultural values, and their governmental and institutional structures – in order that he might create a worldview that includes those of other nations so that individually and collectively the agent might accept the duties that ensue from those peoples' legitimate rights claims, and to act accordingly within what is aspirationally possible.*

The extended community worldview imperative has three principal parts. The first has to do with *self* and *micro community education*[47] about the peoples of the world. This educational exercise should include important facts like geographical situation, political and institutional structures, culture, and how the people fare with respect to the basic goods of agency (Table 6.3; see p. 186). This education process should be ongoing. The point is to

---

[47] Of course, if one is in the position to influence the macro community via the media or public lectures, this would be helpful, too. However, this is a position open to only a few. The general duty for all is to educate themselves about the plight of especially distressed regions of the world and to work individually and collectively to be positive agents of change.

allocate space in one's consciousness and in the consciousness of those in your micro community to the existence and lives of others remote from you. Because this is an imperative, obedience is not optional.

The second feature has to do with the way you *incorporate others into your worldview.* Fulfilling this has to do with the operation of one's imagination. The imagination is the power of the mind that makes real and integrates what is abstract into lived experience and vice versa. When one educates himself about the lives of others, the imagination steps in and makes possible rational and emotional applications of the good will in assessing one's duties in response to others' valid rights claims, and in creating an extended style of sympathy. Normally, sympathy requires two people in direct contact. In the extended variety of sympathy, the knowledge gained through self and micro community education is put to work by the imagination to construct an image of some typical person living in another country, such that the vividness of that individual's imagined situation sparks an approximation of direct person-to-person sympathy. In this way, the rational and affective good will act together to exhort one to a caring, loving attitude.

The third feature refers to an *action response.* Those in other countries who have legitimate rights claims are entitled to our responding via our correlative duties. Ignorance of their plight does not absolve us from our responsibility. What often gets in the way is that we view those in the extended community as having their own society (that is viewed as the proximate provider of goods and services). Because our world is set up on the model of individual, sovereign states, it seems to many that each country should take care of its own. The community model offers some support to this analysis. However, in the end this sort of parochialism fails because the boundaries of states are not natural facts but socially constructed conventions. Where one country ends and another begins is an artifact of history and military conquest. The boundaries of states are artificial and do not indicate natural divisions (even when the boundary between states is a mountain range or a river).

Thinking in this way is important because it shows that the manner we parse ourselves (via geography, language, or culture) is rather arbitrary. There is a much stronger sense (based upon human biology) that our existence as *Homo sapiens* is the only real robust boundary that counts among our species.[48] However, there is much truth in the old adage "out of sight, out of mind." When we are ignorant of the plight of others and when we

---

[48] Of course, the existence of other species poses other problems. For an example of this sort of analysis, see Thomas White, *In Defense of Dolphins* (Oxford: Blackwell, 2008).

haven't undergone the imaginative connection of the other to ourselves, then it is certainly the case that we will be less likely to be moved to action.

The extended community worldview imperative exhorts us all to educate ourselves about the plight of others in the world (their unmet valid rights claims) and then to respond with individual and corporate action according to our abilities to act effectively. It must become a top priority issue for all of us.

Eco-Community Worldview Imperative
Though the shared community worldview and the extended community worldview exhaust the human communities of the world, there is also a further understanding of how we are situated and that is as part of nature. Too often in the last hundred years or so, nature was seen to be opaque and utterly resilient. We could do anything to nature and it would bounce right back. Species could be hunted to extinction without consequence. We could dump garbage wherever we wanted. We could burn various carbon-based fuels at reckless levels and only talk of *development*. At the writing of this book, the folly of such an attitude is evident to most people (particularly to almost every scientist who studies ecology). The average temperature has risen in the past century .08 degrees centigrade. It has generally been thought that a rise of 2 degrees centigrade would bring about a radical alteration of life as we know it on earth with entire geographical regions changing character.[49] We steadily are moving in that direction. This reality along with other alterations in ecosystems from the "top-down" or from the "bottom-up" has put the entire ecosystem at risk.[50] It is for this reason that I have brought nature into the focus of community membership which humans have duties to protect.[51] The eco-community worldview imperative runs like this:

> *Each agent must educate herself about the proximate natural world in which she lives relating to her agency within this ecosystem: (a) what her natural place in this order is vis-à-vis her personal agency; (b) how her natural place (vis-à-vis her personal agency) may have changed in recent history; (c) how her social community's activities have altered the constitution of the natural order and how this has effected community agency; (d) the short-term and long-term effects of those changes vis-à-vis agency; and*

[49] These statistics are from the United States' National Aeronautics and Space Administration (NASA): http://www.nasa.gov/topics/earth/features/rapid-change-feature.html (accessed 11/11/12).
[50] Carl Zimmer, "Ecosystems on the Brink," *Scientific American* **307**.4 (2012): 61–65.
[51] My arguments for this are found in my essays "Worldview and the Value-Duty Link" and "The Self-in Context: Grounding for Environmentalism," both in *Environmental Ethics*, 2nd ed., ed. Michael Boylan (Oxford: Wiley-Blackwell, 2013): 95–108; 14–24.

(e) what needs to be done to maintain the natural order in the short and long term so that the ecosystem might remain vibrant.

Let's examine the various parts of this worldview imperative. First there is a requirement for people to educate themselves as much as is practically possible about the proximate environment in which they live. This will require some attention to the three parts of the environment: the land, the plant life, and the animal life. In the age of the Internet, most people in countries that have widespread digital access can view reports by national and international agencies. Satellite data gathering is very accurate. In countries that do not have this access, then the individual herself must make continued personal surveys of the area in which she lives.

Second is an admission that we live in a natural context that is interactive. All people should assess how this context affects them personally and how they are actors that affect nature. It is a mutual relation.

The third requires a sense of recent history. How has the natural context changed and who is responsible for that change? This is a factual search that will be more exact in richer countries (such as the G-20 nations). But it will still be possible in the rest of the world, albeit at a more anecdotal, less precise level. Once we know what has happened and what parties are to blame, then the political community is in a position to call for change.

The fourth and last point is to form an action plan for the short and long term with a sustainability sensibility in mind. Sustainability is a pivotal concept in environmental ethics. It gives recognition to the dynamic reality of natural systems. A natural system is a robust interactive collection of animate and inanimate objects geographically proximate. Though there are different ways to parse such collections, this treatise will rely on a three-fold classification: ecosystems, watersheds, and biomes (in ascending size).[52] In order for a natural system to be sustainable it must exhibit feedback loops that interact to protect the existence of the natural system. A natural system that is sustainable can thus adapt to changes in the inanimate and animate elements of the system. When a

[52] My account of these collections follows Robert L. Smith (*Elements of Ecology*, 3rd ed., [New York: Harper Collins, 1992], G 12), who defines watershed as an "entire region drained by a waterway that drains into a lake or reservoir; total area above a given point on a stream that contributes water to the flow at that point; the topographic dividing line from which surface streams flow in two different directions"; and Elizabeth Tootill (ed., *Dictionary of Biology* [Maidenhead, Berkshire, UK: Berkshire Intercontinental Kook Productions, 1980], 29), who defines biome as a "major regional community of plants and animals with similar life forms and environmental conditions. It is the largest geographical biotic unit, and is named after the dominant type of life form, such as tropical rain forest, grassland, or coral reef."

natural system fails to be able to adapt, its very existence is threatened. The eco-community worldview imperative seeks to involve people in the task of maintaining sustainability at the ecosystem level. It is the proximate level at which we live.

Extended Eco-Community Worldview Imperative
It is one thing to create ethical duties based upon our proximate community membership. Communities that touch us each day capture our attention. But larger and extended communities are important to recognize as well. The problem is that they are remote. Just as we saw with the shared community worldview, the problem with "remote" is *out of sight, out of mind.*[53] Most of us respond more readily to problems that confront us head-on where we live. Thus, it may be the case that readers will support the eco-community worldview imperative because it affects them personally. In this way, it is a manifestation of psychological egoism: people are only out to advance what they perceive to be their personal self-interest. I have argued in the past that basing communal public policy upon the self-interest of powerful people in the community is unjust.[54] Thus, I believe that social and political public policy should follow my The Moral Status of Basic Goods argument (see later). This argument suggests that various goods of human agency (that are hierarchically ordered in the table of embeddedness [Table 6.3]) are given rigorous status as natural human rights that incur correlative duties that must be met with the "ought implies can" caveat. The idiosyncratic preferences of the marketplace are overridden by these strict entailed duties. This is because the marketplace should be viewed as opportunity neutral: accidental economic circumstances that exist at some particular time and place (the preferences of the marketplace can be understood much like the changing environments of evolutionary theory). If a variegated-patterned moth prevails in an unpolluted forest and the black-colored moth prevails in a polluted forest, this is considered to be a simple fact.[55] Neither moth coloring is *better,* as such. But in an environment with high

---

[53] This dynamic has been discussed by Peter Unger (1996, chps. 1 and 2) in relation to human duties to other humans who live in remote communities.
[54] Boylan, *A Just Society* and *Morality and Global Justice.*
[55] This, of course, follows H. Kettlewell, *The Evolution of Melanism* (London: Oxford University Press, 1973); cf. George Williams, *Adaptation and Natural Selection* (Princeton, NJ: Princeton University Press, 1966); Michael Ruse, "Charles Darwin on Group Selection," *Annals of Science* **37** (1980): 615–630; for an opposing view, cf. N. Eldredge and S. Gould, *The Units of Evolution: Essays on the Nature of Species* (Cambridge, MA: MIT Press, 1992). A good discussion of the present state of the debate can be found in Robert A. Wilson, ed., *Species: New Interdisciplinary Essays* (Cambridge, MA: MIT Press, 1999).

evolutionary pressures, one is better in environment$_1$ and the other is better in environment$_2$ where "better" is functionally defined.

In an analogous way, the "preferences" of the market are also contextually linked. If a group of people having a particular trait – such as the ability to focus on one particular task – have an advantage in one social/economic environment, then they will flourish. However, in another environment (such as one that rewards multi-tasking) they might founder. Thus, in the same way that moth color does not assign moral merit, economic advantage is similarly restricted to functional criteria.

If this reasoning is correct, then success is at least somewhat accidental. One way to react to this is to say, "well that's the way it is: let it be – it is the way of evolution." Those who take this approach will view remote ecosystems, watersheds, and biomes as, at most, a fact to stimulate intellectual speculation. isn't It interesting that the hundred square mile wetland in Thailand dried up and the flora, fauna, and the historic water table that sustained the wetland is no more. Curious that!

To avoid this sort of reaction, I believe that another kind of worldview imperative is called for:

EXTENDED ECO-COMMUNITY WORLDVIEW IMPERATIVE:

Each agent must educate herself about the world's biomes: freshwater, saltwater, arid regions, forests, prairies and grassland, tundra, and artic regions. This education should be ongoing and should include how the relative stability and natural sustainability is faring at various points in time. This knowledge will entail a factual valuing that also leads to an aesthetic valuing. Since all people seek to protect what they value, this extended community membership will ground a duty to protect the global biomes according to what is aspirationally possible.

What this worldview imperative prescribes is first to educate oneself about the scientific *facts* of the world. This doxastic responsibility is primary. Far too often people create beliefs that are unsupported by hard data. This is irresponsible and immoral.[56] As the late U.S. New York senator, Daniel Patrick Moynihan, is reputed to have said, "We are all entitled to our own opinions, but not our own facts." What this means is that each individual, according to his or her own abilities, should seek *objective scientific facts* about the global environment. This fact-searching should be in the context of what will be sustainable for the distant ecosystem, watershed, or biome. Such a project will involve some education in geography as well as the physical and biological systems that exist globally.

---

[56] See Julie Kirsch's take on this ("When Is Ignorance Morally Objectionable?" in *The Morality and Global Justice Reader*, ed. Michael Boylan (Boulder, CO: Westview, 2011): 51–64.

Now some will say that I'm asking too much of people. But I don't think so. Remember, I couch my duty upon the caveat of what each person is capable of learning. I must admit that I think the bell curve shifts more to the right than many other academics admit – meaning that I think more people have a higher intellectual capability than many of my colleagues do. I base my belief on nearly forty years of teaching at all levels in the educational hierarchy. What is often the case among those in lower socioeconomic groups is that they have internalized the low expectation levels that others have projected on them. I say give them a challenge and they will respond to it if they believe they are capable and they feel a responsibility to do so.

Statistically, I think it is correct that many do not fire themselves up to the task of surveying a variety of sources to ascertain the facts about the environment in which they live or the extended environment. As a result, many take their lead from politicians who often have a self-interested motive in espousing opinions that do not coincide with widely accepted scientific findings such as whether there is global warming (regardless of the cause). A 2009 *Washington Post* poll found that 28 percent of the general public and 46 percent of Republicans doubted that there was global warming (regardless of the cause).[57] This contrasts to virtually unanimous consensus by scientists who compare composite and disparate biome readings by mechanical measuring devices that have been in place for a century. My only account for this is that many people skip ahead to the policy responses. If certain deleterious states of affairs are accepted as true, then something needs to be done. If the respondents don't like the resultant policy response, then they will decry the facts as well. Such reactions are prohibited by the extended eco-community worldview imperative.

A second consequence of the extended eco-community worldview imperative is to transition from factual understanding to aesthetic valuing. It is my contention that this is a seamless process.[58] Understanding the operation of a complex natural system will result in an intellectual valuing of that system. To value a system is to undertake a duty to protect said system. Thus, the second part of the extended eco-community worldview imperative is to undergo this process. It all begins with education and it ends with an intellectual cum aesthetic appreciation that translates into a duty to protect.

57 Eilperin, Juliet, "Fewer Americans Believe in Global Warming, Poll Shows," *Washington Post*, November 25, 2009. http://www.washingtonpost.com/wp-dyn/content/article/2009/11/24/AR2009112402989.html (last accessed February 7, 2014).
58 Boylan, *Environmental Ethics*: 100.

At the end of day, the extended eco-community worldview imperative is a duty to protect all of the world's natural systems according to our resources.

All of these worldview stances – the contiguous and extended human community and the contiguous and extended natural community – focus on people viewing themselves within a context. The underlying understanding is that we must accommodate and fit into our communities. We should not look at those people and living organisms outside our proximate geographical situation as being ripe for our personal domination. Rather, we should work within these contexts to build up institutions that are responsive to community needs and the flourishing of the community.

Now I want to be clear that I do not think that communities themselves possess natural human rights. Communities are abstractions made up of real, existing individuals and real, existing organisms. Only *humans* have rights according to my formula (set out in the next section). This is due to the argument that grounds natural human rights. Because of the structure of agency rights justification, the model of correlative model human rights/duties (set out in Chapter 1) is only expressed in the human communities. Duties to nature originate within particular existing humans who band together to value and respect nature: an anthropocentric justification. This is an example of a duty arising without a claimant who possesses a natural right. The origin of natural human rights springs from my conception of personhood via the personal worldview imperative and continues through the human community worldview imperatives. From this standpoint, there is a valuing of nature, and that valuing incurs a duty to protect it.[59] This is, in short, the schema of rights and duties as they arise from human and natural communities.

6.3.3 The Moral Status of Basic Goods

Readers can clearly see that I think one ought to adopt the logically strongest fundamental justification for human rights as is possible. As I have set out earlier, the author who most closely meets this requirement with a deductive argument is Alan Gewirth. However, though I applaud his goal, I believe that there are shortcomings to his approach. My deductive argument that grounds natural human rights shares some features with Gewirth, but on several key levels is significantly different.

59 Michael Boylan, "Worldview and the Value-Duty Link," in *Environmental Ethics,* 2nd ed. (Malden, MA: Wiley Blackwell, 2013): 95–108.

ARGUMENT 6.3: THE MORAL STATUS OF BASIC GOODS

1. All people, by nature, desire to be good – Fundamental Assertion
2. In order to become good, one must be able to act – Fact
3. All people, by nature, desire to act – 1, 2
4. People value what is natural to them – Assertion
5. What people value they wish to protect – Assertion
6. All people wish to protect their ability to act – 3–5
7. Fundamental interpersonal "oughts" are expressed via our highest value systems: morality, aesthetics, and religion – Assertion
8. All people must agree, upon pain of logical contradiction, that what is natural and desirable to them individually is natural and desirable to everyone collectively and individually – Assertion
9. Everyone must seek personal protection for her own ability to act via morality, aesthetics, and religion – 6, 7
10. Everyone, upon pain of logical contradiction, must admit that all other humans will seek personal protection of his or her ability to act via morality, aesthetics, and religion – 8, 9
11. All people must agree, upon pain of logical contradiction, that since the attribution of the basic goods of agency are predicated generally, that it is inconsistent to assert idiosyncratic preference – Fact
12. Goods that are claimed through generic predication apply equally to each agent and everyone has a stake in their protection – 10, 11
13. Rights and duties are correlative – Assertion

   ———

14. Everyone has at least a moral right to the basic goods of agency and others in the society have a duty to provide those goods to all – 12, 13

(*Note:* This is set out in more detail in Michael Boylan, *A Just Society* (Lanham, MD: Rowman and Littlefield, 2004): chapter three.)

The argument begins with an assertion about human nature: all people, by nature, desire to be good. What does this mean? By all people, I am referring to the highest sense of Aristotle's *epi to polu*. For the most part (statistically between 95% and 99.5%)[60] the population wishes to act in a way such that they approve of what they are doing on some primary level (or else they wouldn't ceteris paribus) be doing it. People are purposive

———

[60] I use these figures because in the present context of inductive logic as applied to modern day science in the United States, proving the null set between .5% and 5% is the standard for cogent results. I am following these figures.

agents who intend certain outcomes of their actions and these are outcomes that they (for the most part) agree with. They believe the outcomes to be good (as judged by their personal worldview).

Now some people make bad assessments about their outcomes. For
example, some may think that getting the most money possible is good.
So they go into the most profitable of all industries: crime. They buy
and sell drugs, or do other illegal acts. They do this not to be bad, but
because they think this is good – since getting the most money possible
is the driving end. Thus, my assessment follows Augustine and Plato as
setting out evil as ignorance.

Once we have established that all people (understood generally at the
species level) desire to act (because it is only by action that anybody can
hope to fulfill his vision of what he takes to be good), then the exami
nation moves to what are the general preconditions of action. Whatever
they are, *Homo sapiens* (as a species) will logically possess them as a
claim.[61] This is because only by doing this can anyone fulfill his human
nature (acting to achieve what he takes to be good). Since this purports
to be a factual assessment of what it means to be human, it is a factual
claim that has embedded normative implications (this mirrors Griffin's
assessment of is-ought, described earlier). As a consequence of the factual claims assessment, the normative implications become evident and
the inference to normative human rights results. This argument is my
fundamental justification for the natural right claim to the basic goods
of agency.

The most controversial premises in this argument are #8, #11, and
#13. It is here that proponents and objectors will focus. In premise #8
the rather scientific induction about the relation of goods to action and
the fact that this might be viewed equally at the level of the individual or
at the level of the group requires an acceptance of moral realism based
on the nature of human action, generally understood. Objectors would
be the anti-realists who would deny that human action has a natural,
normative character.

Premise #11 is somewhat less controversial because it purports to be
about the nature of subsumption in axiomatic systems. For example, if

---

[61] It is important to note that this formulation does not create a fictive situation in which
some random x is actually in the position of *claiming*. Rather, it is more like a scientific
description of the operation of human digestion. Alan's or Tanisha's digestion may alter
from the species description but these alterations are viewed as aberrations (diseases).
The move in science to the individual is one of logical subsumption. This intentional
direction makes this account a "top-down" account.

a general law said that no citizens in society x may commit murder, then it would be illogical for Juan (a citizen in society x) to assert that he had permission to murder. Objectors would be those who don't believe that ethics or social/political philosophy can ever be formulated in a nested axiomatic system. The ethical particularists fall into this camp.[62]

Premise #13 is the least controversial of all. It asserts merely that there is a well-accepted relation between valid rights claims holders against some group of people such that they incur a duty to justified right claim holders (be it an individual or another group). Detractors would be those who disagree with any but legal rights claims – that is, those who disagree that there are any valid *moral* right claims (some overlap here with objectors to premise #8).

The obvious question that arises from this argument is *what are* these so-called basic goods of agency? There are many ways to respond to this question. Some will want to limit the discussion to one master good (such as liberty). Others create a long list of goods that are on a par (such as the United Nations Universal Declaration of Human Rights). My own understanding of this question is really about creating a scale of goods that are instrumental to action (since this is at the heart of the fundamental justifying argument on agency). If it is the case, that human nature is all about acting so that we can try to move toward our vision of what we perceive to be good, then what is necessary to get there? Enter the table of embeddedness.

6.3.4 The Table of Embeddedness

Like Nussbaum, I think that creating a table of specific goods does much to advance the discussion of what people, as such, may legitimately claim as a human right. Whereas Nussbaum gives us a group of goods that have emerged from her various intercultural discussions over the years, I base my table upon my basic justifying argument: "The Moral Status of Basic Goods." Everything on my table is driven by what it means to be able to execute voluntary action. I see this as a gradated process following from the most minimal levels of purposive action to more fully realized circumstances. I call these gradations "embeddedness." Some good is more embedded than another if it is more proximate to the most minimal

---

[62] A key proponent of this position is Jonathan Dancy, *Ethics without Principles* (Oxford: Oxford University Press, 2006).

conditions for human agency – that is, every human's right according to the argument for the moral status of basic goods.

Now I do believe that others might create empirically based research that might add or move around certain goods on the table. This would entail a biological or psychological assessment of what we need to execute purposive action. Another sort of objection might come from those who for reasons besides simply allowing for basic conditions of action add certain other considerations – such as liberty being the most valuable to human agency.[63] However, what I think is most important in my theory of natural human rights is that we all agree that a table is a useful device for clarity and for giving direction in public policy. We must also agree that a hierarchical table (Table 6.3) helps practitioners to make tough decisions when we perform a social triage of goods that affect action. When that triage formula follows directly from a primary argument on the logical justification of a claims right, then the hierarchy is not seen to be arbitrary but rather one that follows from a foundational principle that undergirds all human rights claims. This table begins with level-one basic goods. These are embedded above any other goods. These are necessary to stay alive. If we are dead we cannot act. If we are dead we cannot move toward our vision of the good.

But the bare minimum is not enough. If we are ultimately concerned with public policy and how we will enable the people of the world to achieve their natural human design (to act in order to achieve their own vision of the good), then it is important to make some gradations in the goods (resources) put forward. For ease in discussion, let us agree to call the most basic goods necessary for human action the most *embedded*. Other goods/resources are also necessary but they may be rated lower in the hierarchical order according to their functional, instrumental value of furthering human action. The table of embeddedness shows one possible hierarchy of such goods.

The import of the table of embeddedness is that it identifies the strength of agents' claims to various sorts of goods (according to the proposed good's degree of indispensability to human agency – here called *embeddedness*). In cases of conflict between claims for different goods, the agent's (or group's) claim to more-embedded goods trumps the claim that logically can be made on behalf of those who desire less-embedded

---

[63] A proponent of putting liberty before all other goods on my table of embeddedness is Marcus Düwell, "On the Possibility of a Hierarchy of Moral Goods," in Gordon, ed., *Morality and Justice: Reading Boylan's A Just Society* (Lanham, MD: Lexington Books, 2009): 71–80.

TABLE 6.3. *The Table of Embeddedness*

Basic Goods

Level One: *Most Deeply Embedded* (That which is absolutely necessary for human action): food and clean water, clothing, shelter, protection from unwarranted bodily harm (including access to basic health care and adequate sanitation)

Level Two: *Deeply Embedded* (That which is necessary for effective basic action within any given society)

- Literacy in the language of the country
- Basic mathematical skills
- Other fundamental skills necessary to be an effective agent in that country, e.g., in the United States some computer literacy is necessary
- Some familiarity with the culture and history of the country in which one lives
- The assurance that those you interact with are not lying to promote their own interests
- The assurance that those you interact with will recognize your human dignity (as per above) and not exploit you as a means only
- Basic human liberties such as those listed in the U.S. Bill of Rights and the United Nations Universal Declaration of Human Rights

Secondary Goods

Level One: *Life Enhancing*, Medium to High-Medium on Embeddedness

- Basic societal respect
- Equal opportunity to compete for the prudential goods of society
- Ability to pursue a life plan according to the personal worldview imperative
- Ability to participate equally as an agent in the shared community worldview imperative

Level Two: *Useful*, Medium to Low-Medium Embeddedness

- Ability to utilize one's real and portable property in the manner one chooses
- Ability to gain from and exploit the consequences of one's labor regardless of starting point
- Ability to pursue goods that are generally owned by most citizens, e.g., in the United States today a telephone, television, and automobile would fit into this class

Level Three: *Luxurious*, Low Embeddedness

- Ability to pursue goods that are pleasant even though they are far removed from action and from the expectations of most citizens within a given country, e.g., in the United States today a European vacation would fit into this class
- Ability to exert one's will so that one might extract a disproportionate share of society's resources for personal use.

Note: Embedded in this context means the relative fundamental nature of the good for action. A more deeply embedded good is one that is more primary to action.

goods. One consequence of accepting my natural human rights theory would be a realignment of income in most societies and between societies when applied to the whole world. Advocates of this position are those who think that there should not be such a large gap between the "haves" and "have nots." Detractors would be those who think that whatever one acquires according to rules of his society belong to him in a very strong sense and thus are his to use as he wants to regardless of what others have. These detractors at the extreme would be against any redistribution of wealth to the poor by government policy.

However, I demur. This is because once again, I see human rights as largely justified through a vision of justice.

6.3.5 Desert Theory

One of the most controversial arguments of John Rawls's *A Theory of Justice* is his argument on moral desert.[64] In that argument, Rawls questions the prevailing meritocratic understanding of desert. Rawls's argument is that when assessing a moral desert claim one ought to consider natural talents and other undeserved preferment as a mitigating factor in assessing claims for societal distribution of goods and services. One should not benefit or be penalized for that which is not in one's power. The target audience, of course, is the least advantaged. Thus this maxim follows from the difference principle.

My take on moral deserts builds upon Rawls's initial insights. I take his point about natural talents and societal preferment and develop them in a different fashion. We can begin my take on this problem by examining the most common objectors to any larger contextual reading of social and economic desert. The objectors say that the individuals who do not achieve college admission, professional school admission, or employment in desirable jobs do not merit it.[65] They are losers in the competition of life. They *deserve* to fail. Those promoting this position often say that merit[66] must be based on past actions and not on some sort of social, utopian goal. Who do you want holding the scalpel (in the case

---

[64] John Rawls, *A Theory of Justice* (Cambridge, MA: Harvard University Press): 103–105, 310–315.

[65] Michael Boylan, "Affirmative Action: Strategies for the Future," *Journal of Social Philosophy* **33**.1 (2002): 117–130.

[66] The reader should note that 'merit' (often referred to in the literature of philosophy as 'deserts') refers to a theory of what agents can justifiably claim on the basis of their achievements; a further expansion of this argument can be found in Michael Boylan, *A Just Society* (Lanham, MD: Rowman and Littlefield, 2004), ch. 7.

of medical school admissions) – a person whose actions have shown his excellence or some other individual who acquired his position based on some sort of legalistic quota? For simplicity's sake, let us label this position as merit$_1$ (m$_1$).

Proponents of my theory also support desert-based criteria. My version of desert-based criteria agrees that merit should be based on past actions. However, where I differ from the m$_1$ account is the method of assessing these past actions. M$_1$ asserts that they are interested in actual work outcomes to judge an individual's merit. This *work* is generally measured by a standardized test (like the MCAT in the United States for medical school admissions) and by the background of the candidate (the B.S.-granting school – again following the medical school example). More prestigious schools hold more sway. Really, what m$_1$ wants to assert is that some sort of positioning on the majority population's recognized achievement grid marks work performed. For the m$_1$ advocates, this is the way the *right* to be admitted to medical school (a level-one secondary good) should occur.

However, I think that the m$_1$ advocates have it wrong. To explain this, let us examine the problem via the model of the puzzle-maker.[67] In this thought experiment, any given period of life (a subcategory – such as preparing for one's life profession as an orthopedic surgeon – or the whole of one's life) can be thought of as putting together a puzzle. Now as anyone who has worked at puzzle-making knows, the early stages of puzzle creation are the hardest. One has to assemble the border and then organize the thematic and color combinations in a general, holistic fashion. This is very time-consuming. Most aspiring puzzle-makers fail during this stage. As one progresses in the puzzle-making process things become easier. The final 10 percent is really a breeze.

Now, what if life were really like puzzle-making? Some people enter life with very little if any of the puzzle completed for them. In these situations, most fail. Others are given a 40 percent, a 60 percent, or even an 80 percent completed puzzle. This dynamic means that these privileged individuals must complete only a small portion of the puzzle.

Now, let us try to compare two individuals at the extremes who are applying to college (Figure 6.2). Person A was given only 10 percent of her puzzle at birth and when she finished high school she had completed 50 percent of the puzzle. She is up against Person B who was given

---

[67] By "puzzle-maker" we mean the person who puts a puzzle together, not the one who manufacturers it.

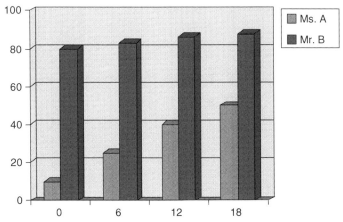

FIGURE 6.2. Merit Measured by the Puzzle-Making Thought Experiment (y axis = percentage of the puzzle completed, x axis = ages of Ms. A and Mr. B)

an 80 percent completed puzzle at birth. B had a calm and supportive domestic life, two hard-working, supportive parents, comfortable income, and a biological makeup that was free from chemical imbalanced mental afflictions. Person B's parents are both physicians and *know* faculty at prominent colleges. They are part of a several-generation good old boys' (and girls') network. With so much oversight and so many environmental and natural advantages, it's no wonder that B went from 80 percent to 87.5 percent in his pre-medical school years. However, when evaluating the two candidates, which one really *did* more?

The m_1 group would say Mr. B. They would point to the differential between 50 percent and 87.5 percent on society's grid (standardized test scores, prestige of schools attended, connections to the inner workings of the system, legacy connections, and basic net monetary worth). However, my theory construes things differently. I contend that Ms. A has demonstrated greater merit because she went from 10 percent to 50 percent. This indicates that by her own actions alone she accomplished 40 percent whereas B, by his own actions, achieved only 7.5 percent.

Obviously, this is a case at the extremes. However, it is put forth to make an abstract point about merit. Some people have advantages of natural and social environment that can include some or all of the following when it comes to the ability to enter a profession:

- Adequate food, clothing, shelter, and protection from unwarranted bodily harm
- Basic educational opportunity

- Being treated with dignity and love for who you are
- A nurturing home environment
- Parental models for patterning behavior (that the society views positively)
- Freedom from disabling disease whether it be mental or physical
- Inside connections affecting admission to universities and to the professions
- Affluence
- Connections to decision makers via one's parents

Obviously, this list could go on and on. But when Mr. B speaks with hubris about how he has become a partner in the accounting firm at the age of twenty-five, it may be important to know that Mr. B's father is the senior partner in the firm and got B his job in the first place (and has been holding B's hand all his life). This is the arena of preferment that allows parents to present to their children, ceteris paribus, a puzzle that is 80 percent complete. All the child has to do is not to screw up too badly and he's set for life.

This preferment list need not merely include socioeconomic factors. Race and gender are also factors. For example, in a profession that is not representative of society's diversity, one will (by definition) find an over-representation of some other group. Let it be assumed that this over-represented group in the United States comprises white males. And let it further be assumed that unreflective members of that group, without actual malice, simply imagine that the typical member of said profession is a white male. In this case, a clique is created that seeks its own continuation (as all cliques do). Thus, the practitioners of the profession put up barriers that create "old boys' club" expectations that have the effect of excluding all others outside of that model. If such assumptions are correct, then on the puzzle-maker example, being a white male seeking to enter that profession is to possess (whether one seeks it or not) a preferment: a significant part of the puzzle completed for him. My theory of natural human rights (here interpreted) would say that this is *not* success by merit; it is success by unmerited preferment.

What I offer as an alternative to m_1 is an alternative model, m_2. Under m_2 merit is a more inclusive concept. It includes the *road traveled* by the individual in question. What part of the puzzle did she complete by herself (or largely by herself)? What is the probable trajectory of her development from here on out? In Figure 6.2 Ms. A looks to outpace Mr. B in fifteen years. If each were to apply to medical school (four years in the United States after college) and complete a rigorous residency program (three to seven years in the United States at this writing), then this trajectory would put Ms. A above Mr. B at 0–4 years into practice as an attending physician (a doctor who is board certified and has completed her residency). When I worked with the Academy of Orthopedic Surgeons in the United States on their code of ethics, members of the ethics board asked me the question of who I wanted to hold the scalpel under my puzzle-maker model; I replied, Ms. A. This is because were there to be a problem in the surgery, Ms. A rather than Mr. B would (measured by probability) be more able to adapt since that was what she had had to do most of her life, whereas Mr. B followed the prescribed road that was paved with preferment.

It is significant here to note that levels of competence are notoriously difficult to assess. Sure, there are standardized tests, but it is unclear how accurate they are in predicting how excellent an individual will be.[68] In the end, the m_2 model suggests that the way we should think about merit is to ask these questions: *What has this person done to get where she is? What is the story of her journey?* This is the only way that I know of to recognize the level-one secondary goods:

- Basic societal respect
- Equal opportunity to compete for the prudential goods of society
- Ability to pursue a life plan according to the personal worldview imperative
- Ability to participate equally as an agent in the shared community worldview imperative

Of course, I have been attacked for this position.[69] The attack says that I penalize people who are born into a situation of preferment. These individuals didn't choose to be born in this way so why am I penalizing them? This is an interesting objection since it takes my own argument (that one should not be penalized for being born with little of the puzzle completed) and turns it to say *why should one be penalized for being born into advantage?*

---

[68] Ben Carson is an excellent example of this dynamic. He was not the best test-taker and came from an African American background. Early indicators did not look good on the m_1 model. But he traveled a long road as per my m_2 model. In the end, my conjecture of graph extension was correct in his case. He is one of the premier neurosurgeons in the country. His story can be found in Ben Carson and Cecil Murphy, *Gifted Hands* (Grand Rapids, MI: Zondervan, 2011).

[69] John-Stewart Gordon makes this claim against my desert theory in "On Justice," in *Morality and Justice: Reading Boylan's A Just Society*, ed. John-Stewart Gordon (Lanham, MD: Lexington/Roman and Littlefield, 2009): 121–133.

This is an interesting objection. Structurally, they seem the same, but the key difference is *cui bono?* The one born into preferment gains. And this makes all the difference. If we are committed to the argument for the Moral Status of Basic Goods and the table of embeddedness, then the human rights claim of the person from preferment translates to a claim for level-two secondary goods (keeping up with your peer group) or even level-three secondary goods (exceeding your peer group). These claims are trumped by a level-one secondary goods rights claim to gain respect for the road you have traveled. This theory is not about putting incompetent people into jobs they cannot perform. It is simply recognition that we have poor measures for desert and that *the road traveled* via the puzzle-maker model should be a key ingredient in assessing merit and moral desert.

6.3.6 The National Perspective versus the Cosmopolitan Perspective

In the book *Morality and Justice: Reading Boylan's A Just Society,* Gabriel Palmer-Fernandez queried why I set my theory within the confines of the nation-state.[70] Others (like Thomas Pogge) made the same query to John Rawls. This is a good line of inquiry. In the case of Rawls, his original position seems better suited to a nation-state than to a cosmopolitan perspective. This is because the contractarian outcome seems better suited to a more homogeneous community (like the nation-state). In the *Law of Peoples* he tries to replicate the original position within an international context.[71] This has led commentators to mixed reactions. At best, it seems to be a bit of a squeeze.

I think I am on better footing. The reason is that unlike Rawls whose essential justificatory mechanism seems best suited to the national model, my three essential elements – (1) the personal and community worldview imperatives, (2) the argument for the moral status of basic goods, and (3) the table of embeddedness – are all set in a non-national framework. It was because of this that I responded to Professor Fernandez that I intended to do just what he suggested and was (at that time) already contracted to write a book to that effect.[72] This current book is a further

---

[70] Gabriel Palmer-Fernandez, "Public Policy: Moving toward Moral Cosmopolitanism," in John-Stewart Gordon, ed., *Morality and Justice: Reading Boylan's A Just Society* (Lanham, MD: Lexington/Roman and Littlefield, 2009): 147–160.

[71] John Rawls, *The Law of Peoples* (Cambridge, MA: Harvard, 2001): 30–37.

[72] Michael Boylan, *Morality and Global Justice: Justifications and Applications* (Boulder, CO: Westview, 2011).

extension of this effort. The context here is human rights as opposed to global justice, but as I have indicated, I believe that the best theory of human rights focuses on an ethically based theory of justice. Since I depict rights claims as having differential strength according to the good involved in the rights claim, level-one basic goods trump all other claims and level-three secondary goods are only valid when there are no other more embedded (to the possibility of human action) claims.

Now since the world is divided into nation-states that view their sovereignty as paramount, the way that the cosmopolitan perspective gets developed is by attention to the extended community worldview and the extended eco-community perspectives. This works out in policy terms in this way: (a) individual governments providing foreign aid to those in the world lacking level-one and level-two basic goods (for the moment, level-one secondary goods will be left to individual states for implementation since they are not significantly resource-driven initiatives); (b) public international organizations (such as the United Nations and its various subsidiary units) that are titular world governments without strong enforcement mechanisms; (c) non-governmental charitable organizations; and (d) wealthy individuals. These are the entities that can make the critical difference in fulfilling the duties that the cosmopolitan rights claims demand. There are not enough resources in the world to fulfill these rights claims in every instance. Therefore, under the table of embeddedness triage strategy, those suffering a lack of level-one basic goods are at the front of the line. We all must do as much as possible to satisfy these valid rights claims first before all others. Level one is a very resource-intensive category. Food and clean water, clothing, shelter, protection from unwarranted bodily harm (including basic health care and adequate sanitation) are not cheap. But the rights claim that belong to those suffering is the strongest possible attributable human rights claim. It makes no difference whether they cry out for it or not. This is because the argument for the moral status of basic goods is grounded in the species. The claim is against all *Homo sapiens* living on earth. This is what it means to ascribe rights that are viewed as natural human rights.

6.3.7 WHAT MAKES THIS A THEORY OF NATURAL HUMAN RIGHTS?

The theory that I have described in this chapter is a theory that sets out the strength of various rights claims that agents might make for every sort of good. For the purposes of my argument, goods can be parsed according to their proximity to the possibility of human agency. Because of the argument for the moral status of basic goods, a strong duty is incurred by everyone on earth to all others on earth to provide level-one basic goods. This is not negotiable. If it is possible to do, then it must be done. The only barrier is whether it is possible. This separates the utopian from the aspirational. My theory sides with the latter because I am not engaged here in spinning a bedtime story. Those souls around the world who are dying every minute of the day have a right to minimum nutrition, protection, clothing, lodging, sanitation, and health care. By setting the argument at the species level, the ensuing duty is against everyone else on earth.

The level-two basic goods are not as embedded to the foundations of action but are necessary nonetheless. *After* we have provided everyone level-one basic goods, we next have a responsibility to provide them level-two basic goods. Prominent among these goods are basic liberties. Most of the activity surrounding human rights has been at this level. However, my account broadens the perspective because behind my account of possessing a right is a theory of distributive justice. I have set out an argument to show how the goods associated with agency should be parsed out (distributive justice) according to their proximity of agency. Liberty is not as necessary as food to agency, but it is very important. Just because these goods are at level two does not mean that people around the world don't have a strong claims right for them – just not the strongest of their claims rights.

Finally, at level-one secondary goods we have the goods of opportunity that would permit people to integrate fairly into their communities and have a *desert-based* opportunity (as I have defined it) for success. Again, though this is an essential category of human rights, it is not as important as the two levels of basic rights.

The final two levels of secondary goods characterize an economic system in which people may possess private property that they can accumulate to maintain an even level with those like themselves (level two) or to exceed others in accumulating a surplus (level three). These two levels of economic rights to private property and a path to personal wealth are also important, but whenever there is a conflict with more embedded individuals' rights claims, then the more embedded rights claim trumps and a social redistribution of wealth is justified. Again, justice supports human rights claims.

At both the basic and secondary goods levels we are talking about rights claims. This is why my theory is about human rights. Because the justification of the rights claim follows from natural facts about humans and the preconditions necessary for human action (biological and social facts from the world), the theory is also *natural*. The ontological status of this claim is examined in the next chapter.

6.4 THE AGENCY PERSPECTIVE ON HUMAN RIGHTS

This chapter has been all about the agency approach to justifying human rights. If one can find natural criteria for this exercise (such as Griffin's interest approach or the agency approaches set out here), then we will be talking about natural human rights. There are certainly several candidates that can fit this bill. I put forward my own proposal because it incorporates what I think are important criteria in this project without the various drawbacks that I have set out with the other approaches. Let me be clear: I think that my approach is the best of the agency approaches, and I think that the agency justification strategy is the superior one for setting out the groundwork for natural human rights.

7

Ontology, Justice, and Human Rights

As I have argued from the beginning of this book, talk of human rights means something quite different when one believes that human rights are *natural* as opposed to being *conventional*. In *the first case,* human rights would apply to all people on earth from the time (at least) of the appearance of *Homo sapiens* until they become extinct or until they cease to be essentially rational/emotive creatures who primarily seek to act in order to realize their vision of what is good. As we have seen in Chapters 2 and 3, much of the historical understanding of morality, justice, and some shared community worldview (that is at least consistent with human rights) has been viewed in just this way in Europe and in China (emblematic of the West and the East). This chapter explores this and other ontological issues as they affect my general argument.

7.1 REALISM AND ANTI-REALISM IN HUMAN RIGHTS DISCOURSE

In *the second case* (human rights as conventional), the currency of human rights will be of much less national and cosmopolitan value. This is because it has lost its necessary universality. Instead, it will depend on social and political forces that will shape and respond to changing conditions within global regions and within countries. And the results may be various – as in the case of women's rights (for example). Some countries of the world might afford women the same legal rights as men while others do not. If human rights are only conventional, then the picture of human rights is merely one of politics and public relations.

To think about this distinction with greater clarity, let us introduce the notions of moral realism and anti-realism into the discussion. Since I have contended from the start that theories of human rights are conceptually connected with theories of justice and that theories of justice are based on theories of morality, then the transitive move is to also link theories of human rights to morality. In morality, anti-realism is connected to the conventional standpoint.

There are many ways to characterize ethical anti-realism. The method that I have set out in the past depends upon reference to the correspondence theory of truth.[1] In this theory, people can hold true beliefs about objects just in case there is fidelity between the belief and true perceived properties of the object (determined via empirical intersubjective agreement including a critical scientific method). When the belief matches the actual properties of the object, then the belief is judged to be true. When the belief does not match the actual properties of the object, then the belief is judged to be false. The anti-realists hold one of two positions: (a) because there are no real ethical objects, one cannot create a fidelity relationship; thus there can be no belief that can be judged to be true or false – this leads to ethical noncognitivism; and (b) people may form beliefs about what they take to be ethical objects, but because there are no ethical objects, their beliefs are mistaken.[2]

Let us briefly examine these in order. First, among the ethical noncognitivists there are various strains I have dealt with elsewhere.[3] Because the ethical noncognitivists deny that moral claims express beliefs, they must express something else. The most popular candidate is the expression of feelings.[4] This can vary from any form of feeling evocation as per Charles

[1]   Michael Boylan, *The Good, The True, and The Beautiful* (London: Continuum, 2008): ch. 5; Michael Boylan, *Basic Ethics*, 2nd ed. (Upper Saddle River, NJ: Prentice-Hall, 2009): ch. 5.
[2]   Sometimes this second sort of anti-realism is called "error theory" after J. L. Mackie, *Ethics: Inventing Right and Wrong* (Harmondsworth, UK: Penguin, 1977): ch. 1. My understanding of this second tack goes beyond Mackie's analysis.
[3]   Boylan, *Basic Ethics*, 2nd ed. (Upper Saddle River, NJ: 2009): ch. 9.
[4]   Contemporary accounts of the relation of emotion to ethics include Annette Baier, "What Emotions Are About," *Philosophical Perspectives* **4** (1990):1–29; Annette Baier, *Moral Prejudices: Essays on Ethics* (Cambridge: Harvard University Press, 1995); Jonathan Bennett, "The Conscience of Huckleberry Finn," *Philosophy* **49** (1974): 123–134; Simon Blackburn, *Ruling Passions* (Oxford: Oxford University Press, 1998); Donald Davidson, "How Is Weakness of Will Possible?" in *Essays on Actions and Events* (Oxford: Oxford University Press, 1980): 21–43; Simone de Beauvoir, *The Second Sex*, ed. and trans. H. M. Parshley (New York: Bantam, 1952); Jon Elster, *Alchemies of the Mind: Rationality and the Emotions* (Cambridge: Cambridge University Press, 1999); Sigmund Freud, *Project for a Scientific Psychology*. Vol. 1 of *Standard Edition of the Psychological Works*, ed. and trans. James Strachey (London: Hogarth Press, 1895); Allan Gibbard, *Wise Choices, Apt Feelings: A Theory of Normative Judgment* (Cambridge, MA: Harvard University Press, 1990); Patricia Greenspan, *Emotions and Reasons: An Inquiry into Emotional Justification* (New York: Routledge, Chapman and Hall, 1988); Patricia Greenspan, *Practical Guilt:*

L. Stevenson,[5] which can include advertising and propaganda to more subtle treatments of espressivist quasi-realism as per Simon Blackburn.[6] Blackburn agrees that moral discourse seems to possess a realist surface because we speak of moral beliefs and moral characteristics such as "good" to express agreement with a moral claim and thereby claim that it is "true." But he says that this process is not authentic and thus invalidates the beliefs as really being proper beliefs. This is because they are not centered upon viewing the empirical world in one particular way as opposed to another (such that it could be judged and authenticated to be true or false).

This first form of ethical anti-realism carries considerable weight in the Anglo-American-Canadian-Australian philosophical world. It is my contention that this first form of anti-realism leads to a shared community worldview that is especially subject to nonlogical vehicles of persuasion – such as mass media entertainment and advertising. It is all about creating various attitudes on the part of the populace. By using imagery that is associated with emotional responses, skillful advertisers can emotionally turn individuals toward action-guiding responses – such as voting, buying a product, or signing onto a social movement. If human

---

Moral Dilemmas, Emotions and Social Norms (New York: Oxford University Press, 1995); Patricia Greenspan, "Emotional Strategies and Rationality," *Ethics* **110** (2000): 469–487; William James, "What Is an Emotion?" *Mind* **19** (1884):188–204; Anthony Kenny, *Action, Emotion and Will* (London: Routledge and Kegan Paul, 1963); Martha Nussbaum, *Love's Knowledge* (Oxford: Oxford University Press, 1990); Martha Nussbaum, *The Therapy of Desire: Theory and Practice in Hellenistic Ethics* (Princeton, NJ: Princeton University Press, 1994); Martha Nussbaum, *Upheavals of Thought: The Intelligence of Emotions* (Cambridge: Cambridge University Press, 2001); Justin Oakley, *Morality and the Emotions* (London: Routledge and Kegan Paul, 1992); Jean-Paul Sartre, *The Emotions: Outline of a Theory,* trans. Bernard Frechtman (New York: Philosophical Library, 1948); Robert Solomon, *The Passions: The Myth and Nature of Human Emotions* (New York: Doubleday, 1984); Bernard Williams, "Morality and the Emotions," in *Problems of the Self: Philosophical Papers 1956–1972* (Cambridge: Cambridge University Press, 1973): 207–229; Ludwig Wittgenstein, *Philosophical Investigations,* trans. G. E. M. Anscombe (New York: Macmillan, 1953); Richard Wollheim, *On the Emotions* (New Haven, CT: Yale University Press, 1999).

5 Charles L. Stevenson, *Ethics and Language* (New Haven, CT: Yale University Press, 1944), and "The Emotive Meaning of Ethical Terms," in C. L. Stevenson, *Facts and Values: Studies in Ethical Analysis* (New Haven, CT: Yale University Press, 1963): 10–31. This work gave rise to contemporary expressivism. Examples include Simon Blackburn, *Spreading the Word* (Oxford: Oxford University Press, 1984); Simon Blackburn, *Essays in Quasi-Realism* (New York: Oxford University Press, 1993); Alan Gibbard, *Wise Choices, Apt Feelings: A Theory of Normative Judgment* (Cambridge, MA: Harvard University Press, 1990); and Alan Gibbard, *Thinking How to Live* (Cambridge, MA: Harvard University Press, 2008).

6 Simon Blackburn, "Anti-Realist Expressivism and Quasi-Realism," in *The Oxford Handbook of Ethical Theory,* ed. David Copp (New York: Oxford University Press, 2006): 146–162. See also Simon Blackburn, "How to Be an Ethical Antirealist," *Midwest Studies in Philosophy* **12** (1988): 361–375; and Blackburn, *Essays in Quasi-Realism.*

rights are like this, then it is about creating attitudes that are based on stirring up emotions that are not tied to some ulterior object that can be separately verified to exist. The river flows, and changes occur. And so does emotively based public opinion. That's all there is.

The second form is more enticing. This is because it includes ethical intuitionism and contractarianism. This variety of anti-realism allows for beliefs about moral principles, but because there are no real moral objects, the beliefs are mistaken. It is a theory based, on the one hand, on sincerely held beliefs, and on the other hand, on beliefs based on no objective truth. In ethical intuitionism, the agent immediately forms an opinion that justifies her belief, and that belief is the basis of action. In contractarianism there is a social event that constructs a reality grounded on consensus. Like ethical intuitionism, the consensus is premised on a worldview that is largely supported by intuitionism. Contractarians (such as Rawls and Scanlon) take as irreducible the intuitions that justify the worldviews of those who enter a contract. For example, in Rawls's original position, the author encourages this intuitive tack through the notion of the reflective equilibrium. But what tilts the agent in the reflective equilibrium? It is merely his experience in the world. If the agent were a party to Fagin's band of child thieves, then the way to the good would be to steal a pocketbook or two. "Conscience" (*con-scientia*) is merely the bringing together of various "understandings" into the personal worldview in a nonreflected fashion. When an agreement is reached, it means nothing more than "birds of a feather flock together." It is a fact about social grouping. Since *agreement* is connected to autonomy and since autonomy is generally held to be a personhood condition of high ethical importance, then the proponents of contractarianism contend that what they set out as a justification is firmly grounded. However, since there is nothing behind the agreement but intuition based upon conscience (that, in turn, is merely based upon one's random experiences in life), contractarianism's contribution to human rights is to refer to randomly constructed societal worldview understandings that can vary widely.[7] Because of this there is ultimately nothing to tell for and against

---

[7] It is true that Rawls intends that this conventionality can be countered by his veil of ignorance that is meant to block out social randomness. However, if this is carried out in a thoroughgoing fashion, then what is left by which one can center an anti-realist intuition? I would contend that the answer is "nothing." The only way around this problem would be to posit a realist-based intuitionism so that conscience is formed from some parallel universe of the Forms. But this is certainly not the tack that Rawls would embrace.

any sensibility on human rights. It's all a process of political power that exerts the will of the dominant community upon subordinate *others*.

In contrast to the anti-realists there are the moral realists. These also can be parsed into two groups: the naturalists and the non-naturalists. Under the naturalist category there must be empirical objects by which one may form moral beliefs that can be judged to be true or false (in this case via intersubjective criteria akin to those of natural science). One must stop for a moment here because of a problem that many philosophers have with naturalist theories based on there being a clear distinction between empirical "facts" and nonempirical "values."[8] Under this account there could be no naturalist theories of values because in the realm of nature there are facts that are understood via scientific laws and their applications. Values are of a different sort. They are either exhortations of emotion (as per the anti-realists) or they come from some non-natural source (a separate realm akin to Platonic Forms). This understanding gave way to the "is-ought" question (also known as the fact-value dichotomy). However, as set out by James Griffin earlier, I would reject this traditional paradigm.[9] This is because many scientific facts (on conceptual analysis) are found to have normative dimensions. They are intrinsic to one's understanding of the object itself. Thus, by this ontological paradigm, there is no chasm between facts and values in many natural objects. An example of this is the groundwork for my theory of natural human rights: the foundational conditions that are necessary to allow human action.

Biology, psychology, and anthropology can discuss various physical and social conditions that can facilitate action in a hierarchical ordering.[10] For example, on the table of embeddedness, "food" is listed among level-one basic goods. What does this mean? How many calories do we need for the very minimum level of action? What about another level of low-level action? What about the average level? What about the flourishing (nonexcess) level? The United Nations, citing scientific studies, answers these questions at 500, 750, 1,000, and 2,000 calories, respectively

---

[8] Cf. David Hume, *An Enquiry Concerning Human Understanding*, ed. Eric Steinberg (Indianapolis, IN: Hackett, 1977 [1748]): 112–115, and David Hume, "Of The Standard of Taste" [1757], in *The Philosophical Works of David Hume* (Edinburgh: Black and Tait, 1826): 4–6.

[9] Another objector on different grounds is Hilary Putnam, *The Collapse of the Fact/Value Dichotomy and Other Essays* (Cambridge, MA: Harvard University Press, 2004).

[10] Some commentators have made analogical comparisons to Abraham Maslow, *Toward a Psychology of Being*, 2nd ed. (New York: Van Nostrand, 1968).

(depending upon body mass index).[11] Thus, the food calorie requirement for basic human action at various levels is a matter of scientific fact. Embedded within this requirement belongs the conclusion of the conceptual analysis of action found in the argument on behalf of the moral status of basic good. Together, there is a (fact + value) irreducible object that is both found in nature and is the basis of a belief about its application – that is, no one could deny it as applying to all without logical contradiction. This is one example of the foundation of the most fundamental of human natural rights claims. It comes from a merging of a seminal argument about action, human nature, and normativity and the scientific facts that fills in the blanks.

The same sort of exercise could be made for clean water (what level of water purity is necessary to fulfill our need for water and our need to avoid disease [sanitation]); shelter (what level of protection from natural elements is necessary to allow human health so necessary for action); protection from unwarranted bodily harm (what general conditions are necessary structurally to allow for safety from assault and to avoid PTSD [post-traumatic stress disorder] and to be protected from the attack of viruses and bacteria). Again, the answers to all these questions come from scientists, psychologists, and anthropologists. They are based on *facts in the world* that, in turn, *are normatively seeded when seen in the context of the role of human action.*

Thus, I would put forward the combination of the conceptual argument on the moral status of basic goods along with the table of embeddedness as representing the shared duality of fact and normative value that supports a general theory of justice and natural human rights.

The second area of ethical realism concerns non-natural objects. Now, non-natural objects are socially troublesome. This is because they cannot be demonstrated empirically via intersubjective criteria as naturalistic objects can be. They are separate. G. E. Moore famously set 'good' to be among these objects.[12] I concur with Moore that 'good' is a non-natural object. However, I am not so skittish as many are about believing in non-natural objects so long as we agree that "objects" includes both physical objects and once-removed theories about their interaction (natural science) as well as the second-removed foundational principles that allow these investigations to exist in the first place. This is what I call "meta-ethical" investigations. Elsewhere I have characterized the difficulty

---

[11] United Nations, *The 2013 Human Development Report* (New York: United Nations, United Nations Development Program): part one.

[12] G. E. Moore, *Principia Ethica* (Cambridge: Cambridge University Press, 1903): ch. 4.

of accepting these once and twice removed objects as being largely epistemological. The ground of such objections stems from what I call the rationality incompleteness conjecture.[13] Any correspondence theory that is grounded in empirical, intersubjective justification criteria will fall short at the generating first principles – such as the law of noncontradiction, the law of the excluded middle, the law of identity, numerical succession, the truth and operation of laws of inference, and so on. All of these objects lie in the non-natural epistemological realm. Thus, from an epistemological standpoint among correspondence theory advocates, it seems clear to me that unless one wants to assert that there is no firm basis for anything (ultimate radical skepticism), we must mine this realm for some critical posits. This really is a form of epistemological intuitionism. At the level of principles, I have argued elsewhere that there is no alternative. This sort of intuitionism connects with non-natural, real objects necessary for any coherent experience whatsoever. But this should be distinguished from the anti-realist form of intuitionism that is only a summary of one's lived experience in the world.[14]

7.2 WHAT DOES IT MEAN TO INCLUDE ONTOLOGY IN RIGHTS TALK?

If the reader will commit to my form of realistic moral naturalism, then the following consequences will occur. First, rights talk is *not* about individual or statistical group preference. When national bodies debate about granting various goods to petitioners, there is a *correct answer*. It is not merely a matter of feeling or taste. Instead, it is grounded in a scientifically based understanding of human nature as a nested set of goods that can make human action possible. All people have an equal claim to be able to commit purposive action simply by being a member of the species. The claims are necessary relative to the personhood account, the argument for the moral status of basic goods, and the table of embeddedness.

Could one imagine a possible state of affairs in which there were rational people who could not act? Not very easily, but I have been in discussions with some AI (artificial intelligence) engineers who sometimes discuss "backing up" one's mind onto a consciousness-enabled computer so that one might exist in the memory bank of some giant hard drive.

---

[13] Boylan, *The Good, the True, and the Beautiful*, 33, 70, 76.
[14] This dual nature of intuitionism is discussed in Boylan, *Basic Ethics*, ch. 8.

One would have all one's memories and sense of self, but be unable to communicate with anyone else or unable to *do* anything. It is possible that these memory banks might be rational, but because they cannot act, it is possible that their only need is to have the computer that gives them "life" not to be destroyed.

The point of such fanciful reveries is merely to underscore that the ontology of the naturalistic moral claim being made is that it is dependent upon some existing *Homo sapiens* – not any rational being whatsoever.[15] Following Aristotle's account I believe that when primary substances cease to be (because their species no longer is), then the former primary substances exist in nature only as an abstract concept: a historical record. At this point, there would no longer be any natural human rights because there would no longer be any existing humans in nature.[16] The origin of the natural human rights claim lies in actual people in the world striving to commit purposive action to bring about their vision of the good. This empirical reality grounds the associated human rights claims and their correlative duties.

7.3 INDIVIDUALS AND GROUPS

Another key ontological issue is the relative status of individuals and groups. There has been much talk in this book about both. I set out that individuals are the primary substances in the world. They exist in the most real way. The personhood account that is described by the personal worldview imperative supports the existence of people (one example of a primary substance).[17] Other natural objects also exist as primary substances, but because we rarely assign a proper name to rocks, branches, or grains of sand, their individualistic status is frequently lost to most people.

Collections operate differently. They are assortments of primary substances that are not primary substances themselves. They can have a real character based on the interactions of the actual members of the group. For example, four men who have high singing voices can form a tenor

---

[15] This distinguishes my brand of deontology from Kant's, which does indeed ground morality and duty in rationality, as such.

[16] Here it should be noted that non-natural moral realists might be able to assert the existence of human rights if they were grounded in a realm that was not affected by whether *Homo sapiens* (as we know them) ceased to exist in nature. This is another difference between natural and non-natural moral realists.

[17] My use of *primary substance* follows Aristotle's usage in the *Metaphysics*.

quartet: the Four Tenors. This group is marked by the pitch, quality, and style of their singing voices. As the Four Tenors practice together group dynamics will emerge. These properties exist solely because of the individual members of the community viewed in their collective interactions. This is why an individual's community participation is of utmost importance (as per the shared community worldview imperative). The community is nothing but the members who make up the community and their shared interactions along with the resulting institutions that arise.

Some view this group dynamic as indicating that the group has an existence akin to the individual. For example, Jeremy Waldron sets out a well-known example of evaluating various dinner parties on the basis of a group trait of *conviviality*.[18] Conviviality seems to be a property of the group, the party at x's place versus the party at y's place, and since properties generally attach themselves to real objects, it would seem that the convivial group exists on a level akin to individuals.

However, I would disagree with this line of analysis. This is because I see the party example to be just like the tenor quartet example. Certainly the Four Tenors as a named singing group produce a unique sound. It is like no other. The Four Tenors possess a property such that they could be evaluated in singing competitions and similar forums. But how are we to understand this? Do all properties suggest attachment to a proximate primary substance that would verify their existence as primary substances: Fx (x has property F)? No. There are relational truth functional attributions as well. These bring to bear the *relation*, for example, of every tenor in the Four Tenors to each of the other tenors. If we name them Abe, Bill, Cal, and David, then Abe's singing relates to Bill's in a particular way producing an effect of Abe-Bill together. The effect is joint, and that joint effect has an existence but *not as a primary substance* because it is dependent upon Abe and Bill for its existence. It has no existence on its own.[19] We can go through the rest in the same way with the binary, ternary, and quaternary relations. The result is that groups *do* exist in a real way. But they *do not* exist in a primary way. They are not substances. Their existence depends upon the existence of their members.

[18] Jeremy Waldron, "Can Communal Goods Be Human Rights?" in *Liberal Rights* (Cambridge: Cambridge University Press, 1993): section iv.

[19] Going back to Gilbert Ryle's thought experiment in the last chapter, one would say that Ryle was *right* about the primary substances involved: the dons, students, library, and so on. What he was *wrong* about is that there is an Oxford that does possess interactive properties, *esprit de corps*, that really exist. It's just that they are not *primary*. If one were to kill all the students, dons, and administrators at Oxford, then there would be *no Oxford*.

The membership in a collection can be described extensionally as a list of the members. This begs the question of how they got to be members of the community – except, perhaps, by chance. More interesting are intensional definitions that generally posit some membership criterion (such as family resemblance) that allows them to be placed within the community.[20] Because of this, individuals can assert identity both via reference to themselves as primary substances and through their membership in communities (that owe their own existence to their constituent members).

Only individuals possess human rights. This is because only individual people fundamentally are defined as desiring to execute purposive action in order to fulfill their vision of what is good. Communities do not act in a proper sense.[21] Instead, both micro and macro communities decide through some political process to do either x or y. What does this mean? It means that the individuals who are politically vested (first in creating a decision-making procedure and second in executing the decision) are individuals who reside in particular social/political roles that give them powers to act in proxy for others. This is a social/political process necessary for any community or institution to effect the interests of its members. (Autocratic communities operate with a rather more limited decision-making mechanism, though the execution function may be similar.)

Because of these ontological differences, one cannot talk accurately about denying human rights to African slaves, for example. This connects us to another argument that is put forth for groups existing on the same level as individuals. It is associated with the moral argument of recognizing and affirming oppressed peoples. Will Kymlicka makes just this sort of argument.[22] He argues that unless we recognize a culture as a natural unit that exists (as a primary substance, though Kymlicka does not use this terminology), great injustice will befall members of

---

[20] Ludwig Wittgenstein, *Philosophical Investigations* (Oxford: Blackwell, 1953): sects. 320–343.

[21] This would put my position against viewing institutions as individuals. Corporations and other collective entities are not natural kinds. They need to be analyzed in terms of the actions of their directors and officers (who *are* individuals). The same holds true of governmental agencies. It is the individuals involved in wrongdoing or right actions who should receive blame or praise. Under this analysis, it is not Germany (for example) that is responsible for the Holocaust, but rather the Nazi leaders and those who carried out their policies who are responsible. Likewise, the United States is not responsible for rebuilding Europe after World War II under the Marshall Plan, but rather Secretary of State George Marshall and his deputies William L. Clayton and George Keenan.

[22] Will Kymlicka, *Multicultural Citizenship* (Oxford: Clarendon Press, 1995): ch. 3

that community. "Loss of cultural membership, therefore, is a profound harm that reduces one's ability to make meaningful choices."[23] I agree with Kymlicka that recognizing community membership and maintaining various long-standing cultural units is important. My only qualm is *how we should describe* the dynamics of this question. The ontology is important. It can have policy ramifications (see Part Three).

When we talk in sociological or anthropological terms, we are moving into a scientific/social-scientific domain. In this domain, the very coin of the realm is the description of the group. I believe that the community worldview is *real*, but it isn't primary. It is shorthand for talking about denying human rights to a list of individuals who can be grouped together as suffering similar atrocities.

The same dynamic is true in the eco-communities discussed in Chapter 6. We can talk about the destruction of rain forests, but this again is shorthand for talking about the destruction of tree #1 and tree #2 and ... tree #n. A set is a collection of members. What is most real for my theory of human rights is the existence of each individual entity in the set that so-collected can be seen as a sort of community that anthropocentrically is connected with natural human rights (as per the last chapter).

This sort of distinction can make a difference when we discuss policy responses to various human rights dilemmas that face the world today.

7.4 HOW CHOICE ILLUMINES ONTOLOGY'S ROLE FOR NATURAL HUMAN RIGHTS

Another way to think about how ontology intervenes in human rights talk is to follow one model of what discussion would be like on human rights when moral realists are at the table and when anti-realists are there. To set this out briefly, let us assume that there are two orders of the political process: a primary judgment (about what is right or wrong) and a secondary judgment (about what is possible to bring about the right within some social/political setting: creating policy). Both are necessary to bring about aspirational ends. The secondary judgment phase

[23] Will Kymlicka, "Individual and Community Rights," in *Group Rights*, ed. Judith Baker (Toronto: University of Toronto Press, 1994): 25; cf. sentiments by Joseph Raz and Avishai Margalit, "National Self-Determination," in *Ethics in the Public Domain*, ed. Joseph Raz (Oxford: Clarendon Press, 1994): 133–134; Alan Buchanan, "Liberalism and Group Rights," in *In Harm's Way: Essays in Honor of Joel Feinberg*, ed. J. L. Coleman and A. Buchanan (Cambridge: Cambridge University Press, 1994): 1–15; and Charles Taylor, "The Politics of Recognition," in his *Multiculturalism: Examining the Politics of Recognition*, ed. Amy Gutman (Princeton, NJ: Princeton University Press, 1994): 32–36.

is of equal interest to both moral naturalists and anti-realists with respect to creating policy and bringing about change. These two orders of judgment structure Chapters 8–10. In the Afterword, some general thoughts about political change are raised.

Thus, to get a more detailed understanding of the primary phase, let us examine an example from the international sphere. The United Kingdom (which has recognized universal female suffrage since 1928) has a representative who is sitting at the table with a representative of a country that does not allow women to vote. The primary judgment phase of discussion must occur first, however; it is liable to result in dissonance and rejection (see Table 7.1). A second step would be to find some overlap in worldviews so that the question could be engaged further at the primary judgment level.

This process occurs as shown in Table 7.1. Let's examine two examples to better understand how this process works. Since *Coinciding and Amplification* is not problematic, there is no need for an example here. In *Dissonance and Rejection*, the best example is Zeno's paradoxes of motion.[24] To the ancient Greeks these are powerful arguments that, if accepted, would imply that our empirical sensations (that report to us that there is motion in the world) are false. If motion is false, and our senses are mistaken, then the sources of knowing what is true and good would lie elsewhere.

Did the ancients simply accept Zeno's argument and agree that "what is" consists of a motionless and static One? The answer is largely, "no!" Why is this? The reason is that when confronted with a theory that describes or prescribes propositions that are different from our worldview, we act cautiously. The inclination in *Dissonance and Rejection* is to reject the new theory. The most obvious way to do this is to provide an internal refutation. But in the ancient world this was not so easy. Indeed, it was not until the development of transfinite numbers and the resultant application of transfinite sums (in the latter nineteenth and early twentieth centuries) that Zeno's Paradoxes were refuted to most people's satisfaction.[25] But even in the ancient world there were attempts

[24] The four paradoxes of motion can be found in Aristotle: (a) The Stadium – *Phys.* Z9, 233a 21ff; *Topics* 160b7ff.; (b) The Achilles – *Phys.* Z9 239b 14ff; (c) The Flying Arrow – *Phys.* Z9 239b 30ff.; (d) The Moving Rows – *Phys.* Z9 239b 33.

[25] See especially G. E. L. Owen, "Zeno and the Mathematicians," *Proceedings of the Aristotelian Society* **58** (1957–1958): 199–222; J. F. Thomson, "Tasks and Super-Tasks," *Analysis* **15** (1954): 1–13; Gregory Vlastos, "A Note on Zeno's Arrow," *Phronesis* **11** (1966): 3–18; Gregory Vlastos, "Zero's Race Course," *Journal of the History of Philosophy* **4** (1966): 95–108; James Watling, "The Sum of an Infinite Series," *Analysis* **13**.2 (1952): 39–46.

TABLE 7.1. *The Way We Confront Novel Normative Theories*

Stage I: Overview and Rational Justification

1. *Considering the Theory.* When we consider a claim about human rights, both *its justification* and *our understanding* of its application need to be considered (i.e., the kind of world that would be created if we accepted the theory). If the theory (and its underlying assumptions about justice and morality) is sufficiently interesting in these ways, we create a favorable overview of the theory. This prompts more careful, formal analysis.

2. *Justifying the Theory.* We logically justify the theory by testing the theory on its own terms for logical validity, soundness, and cogency. If the theory passes our test(s) we move to Stage II.

Stage II: Dialectical Understanding through Personal Worldview Examination

1. *Reflecting on Our Own Worldview.* We entertain our own worldview with all its various components including our metaphysical, epistemological, ethical, and personal convictions and judgments. This stage should resonate against both our rational and emotional goodwill (the completeness component of the personal worldview imperative).

2. *Comparing Our Worldview to the New Theory.* This involves an interaction between the two stages. From this comparison one of three things will happen: (a) *Coinciding and Amplification:* The model and one's worldview will coincide and the model will enhance one's worldview by giving it additional structure; (b) *Dissonance and Rejection:* The model and one's worldview will be far apart and we will reject the model (in this case we may return to *Justifying the Theory* for a time and then possibly onto Stage III – although complete theory rejection is more likely); and (c) *Worldview Overlap and Modification:* The model and one's worldview will not be identical, but there is at least some consonance so that one continues a more complicated examination that will identify anomalies in either the theory (in which case we may modify the theory or reject it) or our worldview (in which case we may modify our worldview because of the theory – assuming we are a seekers of truth). In most cases *Worldview Overlap and Modification* will cause us to move to Stage III.

Stage III: Resolution and Change

This stage is a rather long process of dialectical interaction between the agent's worldview and the theory itself. As in Hegelian dialectic, both poles cannot be viewed *simpliciter,* but only mediately through the other at the same time. As we progress through these dialectical moments, we observe a modification of the theory along with the worldview until an equilibrium is achieved. The result is a transformation in which both the novel theory and the old worldview are discarded. In their place is a new amalgam that owes its origins to the generating poles, but like any offspring, although it may display various resemblances of the old and the new, the resolution is its own entity.[a]

[a] This entity may exhibit more traits of one or the other progenitor. Just because the offspring is born of dialectic does not mean there is equal mixing.

at dealing with infinitesimals through the theory of exhaustion. As Ian Mueller points out, Euclid XII. 2 suggests the groundwork for such a theory that was also used to "square the circle."[26]

The point is that though many thinkers could not come up with an adequate refutation of Zeno, they did not simply *accept* Zeno either. The reason for this is that Zeno's theory and the consequences it suggested did not square with their robust personal worldview. This larger picture suggested that though one *could not* come up with an adequate argument to prove Zeno wrong, still one was not prepared to accept the theory, either.

Now some might argue that *Dissonance and Rejection* will lead to blind prejudice. A person hears a logically persuasive position and though he cannot come up with a rejoinder, he will nonetheless reject the theory.

Descriptively I believe this to be true.[27] Much of the work over the last thirty-five years on so-called revolutions in the history of science documents that theory changes do not come easily.[28] In fact, Hilary Putnam has suggested that the more reasonable approach to a theory replacement situation is to "fix" the old theory rather than adopt a new one.[29] This is because without proven anomalies in the existing theory (in our case the subject's worldview), there is no reason to change. "If it ain't broke, don't fix it" is the old adage. *Dissonance and Rejection* describes

---

[26] Ian Mueller, *Philosophy of Mathematics and Deductive Structure in Euclid's "Elements"* (Cambridge, MA: MIT Press, 1981): 234; cf. T. L. Heath, "Greek Geometry with Special Reference to Infinitesimals," *Mathematical Gazette* 11 (1922–1923): 248–259; Simplicius, *Commentary on Aristotle's Physics,* ed. H. Diets, 2 vols. (Berlin: G. Reimeri, 1882, 1895). Simplicius gives an account of Antiphon's reasoning on pp. 54.2–55–8. Of course, Aristotle gives a rather conceptual refutation in *Physics* 4.2 and 6.2, 6.9. Aristotle's view is that the paradox works only when the two infinities involved view reality differently (discrete v. continuous). If both time and space are continuous, then the paradox vanishes.

[27] It is my opinion that prejudice is *unfortunately* a very real fact of *Homo sapiens's* behavior. This does not mean that I condone it in any way. It *does* mean that it is not surprising that so much prejudice exists all over the world. From the United States, to the Congo, to Cambodia, the history of the world reflects this prejudice. What we must therefore do, as moral thinkers, is to think of ways to alleviate this natural inclination. The only hope for change is in the mode of overlap and modification.

[28] The classic example, of course, is Thomas S. Kuhn, *The Structure of Scientific Revolutions,* 2nd ed. (Chicago: University of Chicago Press, 1970).

[29] Hilary Putnam, "The 'Corroboration' of Theories," from the Library of Living Philosophers, vol. xiv, *The Philosophy of Karl Popper,* ed. Paul A. Schilpp (LaSalle, IL: Open Court, 1974): 221–240. Putnam is arguing against Popper's thesis in *The Logic of Scientific Discovery* by discussing the actual behavior of scientists when Uranus's orbit was found to be incorrect (before the discovery of Neptune). This behavior was directed at modifying existing theories rather than discarding them. Thus the goal of "all or nothing" does not describe the way scientists act.

a situation in which one is inclined to remain in his existing worldview even when confronted with a logically sound argument.

Does this mean that the dynamics of *Dissonance and Rejection* are always arbitrary and prejudicial? I don't think so. There are some ontological touchstones of value that are independent of the proposition at hand. These touchstones come from our other core values that, in turn, arise from the personhood account through the personal worldview imperative. For example, in the case of Zeno's paradox, one may have a core value in a realist epistemology that is offended by Zeno's contention that empirical data are somehow illusions.

Still another person may have a core value in religion. In this situation let us imagine a religious philosopher who believed that his God was not a trickster. Thus, it would be impossible (given that belief) for God to create an intricate set of illusions meant to test humankind's faith.

A third person might be a devoted artist whose mission in life is to imitate nature for the purpose of conveying truth. If nature, itself, were merely an elaborate ruse, then his entire stock of values would be wholly misplaced.

In each of these three cases, it is the core understanding of the facts and values of the world in the context of the rational and emotional goodwill that serve as a check upon untenable theories and occasion the reaction of *Dissonance and Rejection.*

It is also possible that an irrationally based value comes into play that most would judge to be evil. For example, when discussing female suffrage, a diehard objector might claim something like the following before going to the table of negotiation.

"I don't believe that women should have the vote."

"Why not?"

"Women are just too emotional. They need a man's guidance in forming their personal worldview. They should model themselves on the man in their life – such as their father, brother, or husband. A strong hand of discipline must always rule."

"This seems like a bizarre attitude. Women score higher on tests for intellectual aptitude in Western countries that compile such statistics. It seems to me that the men should be molded by the women in their lives."

"This isn't America or some other decadent Western Culture. Tradition is clear. Every woman's worldview should be directed by the men in her life."

When this sort of dynamic occurs within the shared community worldview, then it is the responsibility of the other community members to cite concrete scientific facts about female capability to refute these objectors. This is an example of intersubjective use of scientifically based understanding of objects in the world that can be measured and defended (i.e., female capability).

Change is constrained by individuals and their spokespersons as they seek to relive the past. It is an inherent conservative philosophy that is frightened by reflection. Those in power *got into their position of power* via a paradigm that they are terrified to tamper with. They will do everything that they can to stop change.

On the other hand, when there is some connection between the presented theory and the worldview of the person considering the novel human rights claim, then the interplay of *Worldview Overlap and Modification* and Stage III dialectical interaction becomes possible. A good example of this can be found in the Reverend Dr. Martin Luther King Jr. The proposition that Dr. King was trying to get white America to accept was that African Americans were living under oppressive Jim Crow laws in the South and vicious de facto apartheid in the North. His enormous human rights task was to alter the shared community worldview and thereby create acceptance of racial equality that would accept the human rights claims of African Americans.

This was not an easy task.

What Dr. King did was to bridge the two worldviews of black and white America. On the side of black America, King (like his father before him) ministered daily to black victims of racial oppression. On the white side, King was a Christian minister (Christianity being the principal religion of white America) and held a Ph.D. in divinity from Boston University (white America respects those educated in its own institutions). In this way, Dr. King had enough commonalities with white America that when white people turned on the evening news and saw peaceful African American protesters singing Christian hymns while being beaten by police, knocked down by fire hoses, and attacked by fierce police dogs, the television watchers were confronted with cognitive dissonance. On the one hand, they honored the police and the white power structure that ruled the nation – because that's the way it always had been. On the other hand, they sang hymns in church each Sunday about a peaceful God who loves all people. Who did they want to identify with: peaceful black folk or overzealous white policemen bent on cruelty? Their own personal worldviews eventually dictated the former. Their own personal worldviews said that Dr. King's logical and emotional arguments for racial equality were valid. But it took the Stage III dialectical process occasioned by worldview overlap and modification for any real progress to be made in the *actual* acceptance of King's ideas. And though the struggle for racial equality isn't over by a long way (more than forty-five years since King's assassination), most people who lived through that era would agree that Dr. King, over time, won over a majority of white America. The process of theory acceptance depends on more than a strong logical argument for its justification. It also requires the dialectical interactions brought about by worldview overlap and modification.

It is the contention of this book that the described process of overlap and modification constitutes the way we actually accept novel normative theories concerning human rights. Certainly, there is a stage of deductive and inductive argumentation. But then, there is the inevitable sorting of those predisposed to be in favor of the novel theory (coinciding and amplification) and those predisposed to be against (dissonance and rejection).[30] When either of these alternatives results, then the existing worldview and not the argument at hand decides whether the agent will accept the human rights claim put before him. In the vast majority of cases, this is the end of the story. But there is also that glimmer of hope that the purveyor of the new theory can find enough common ground to initiate the sort of dialectical worldview interactions that Dr. King was able to initiate.[31] This constitutes the end of the primary judgment phase.

The primary judgment phase is necessary, for without it, we are left merely with one group or country exerting its will upon another. This process is different for moral realists and for anti-realists. This is because moral realists assert that there are real, natural (or non-natural) objects that support criteria by which argument can be engaged. This is why we need theories of natural human rights that can be discussed with the touchstone of moral realism (an ontological position). Once there has been some movement away from the original stance (in our generating example of women's suffrage), then one can engage in the secondary judgment phase of initiating change. This can become a practical process of carrots and sticks that must recognize that the tactics employed must be proportional to the goal. Sometimes this can involve stages of engagement. Using the terminology of Table 7.1, the initial stage is to put forth realistically based moral claims for first considering the novel

---

[30] There is also, of course, those who properly use dissonance and rejection as in the earlier example involving Zeno's paradoxes.

[31] This is also the model of Plato's depiction of Socrates as well as most other philosophers who have chosen the dialogue form to express their philosophy.

understanding of human rights and then secondarily their rational justification. This can take some time. In woman's suffrage in the United States the process took almost a century. The next stage (dialectical understanding) is to engage the personhood account of those who can effect the change. This stage involves both the rational and the emotive goodwill. The goal is to reach the *overlap and modification* position so that there is real engagement. This is the messiest stage. It involves real change in the personal worldviews of the decision makers and of the communities they represent. The worldview of the leaders (especially in democracies, but also to some degree in autocracies as well) often follows the people. Sometimes quick and dramatic changes can occur.

Finally, there is the stage of resolution and change. This stage can take a long time. The basic premise of African American emancipation from slavery required a hundred years or so before real human rights equality was able to be moved forward through effective policy responses (this after three hundred years of de jure servitude).[32] When we look at challenges to natural human rights around the world, we should acknowledge this important process of change.

The next three chapters focus on three critical challenges to natural human rights using this model to suggest the way forward via the model of primary and secondary phases. Finally, in the Afterword, we briefly look at the notion of political change, as such.

---

[32] This path is not always forward. For example, the United States Supreme Court (June 2013) in *Shelby County v. Holder* struck down section 5 of the 1965 Voting Rights Act. This changed the burden of proof from having prior approval by the Justice Department (for voting law changes proposed by traditionally racist areas of the country that had a history of denying voting rights to African Americans) to making the Justice Department prove that any new voting rights law change is discriminatory – such as requiring birth certificate-based voter ID (very expensive to obtain for poor populations). In the subsequent two months, several states previously under federal scrutiny have now passed laws that will guarantee a lower vote among poor African Americans (thus denying them their opportunity to vote). This represents a step backward in rights for African Americans. The road to progress is not always straight and positive.

PART THREE

APPLICATIONS OF HUMAN RIGHTS

Scherzo

"Straight to the Top"

I have a dream that my four little children will one day live in a nation where they will not be judged by the color of their skin, but by the content of their character.
– Reverend Doctor Martin Luther King Jr.

His appointment was for four o'clock. David Balfour opened the door that advertised itself in gold letters against the dark mahogany door: Ebe Balfour. The brass doorknob was round and oversized. He needed a little push to open the door as it was set with a very heavy hinge spring. Once inside, David proceeded to the young blonde, blue-eyed secretary, Mary Lou Sue Palmer.

"I have a four o'clock appointment with Mr. Balfour," said David to Mary Lou Sue. The gatekeeper to the regional sales manager turned off her I-pod, removed the ear buds, and picked up her smart phone.

Then she slid the gum she was chewing to the side of her mouth with her tongue and replied, "Oh, yeaaah. You're down all right. I'll text Mr. Balfour and let him know."

David sat down on the stiff, brown leather couch that sported inch-wide buttons, focusing on one of the pictures on the walnut-paneled walls: it was of the vice president for sales at Leopard Insurance, Abdullah Sa'id. As David gazed at the unyielding face of the vice president, he returned mentally to the meeting with Ebe Balfour that had started all the trouble – six weeks before.

David had been summoned to his Uncle Ebe by an urgent text message. It was mid-February in what had been a difficult winter in the Washington, D.C., metropolitan area. David had braved the snow for weeks as he headed over to Bethesda – headquarters of the Marriot Corporation. He had used a referral from a current client to get the request for proposal (RFP) for Marriot's self-insured employee benefits package and had been awarded the contract. It had been a tremendous project that had required David to work 100-hour weeks largely on this new case. But his hard work and imagination proved effective. Right now he was assembling the paperwork for the Marriott account that he had just closed this morning: employee benefits for a self-funded plan with low claims administrative fees and a wellness program that might cut usage from the previous "big name company's plan" by 6 percent – more if the wellness program worked as designed. David's annual fee for the account would be $60,000. That was four times more than any commission or fee that he had ever earned selling insurance. Marriott had plunked down $50,000 as earnest money for the deal. Everything was set except for the details. David couldn't wait to tell his partner, Alan, who would be so happy for him.

When David got to Ebe's office he was shown right in. Ebe didn't get up from his plush ergonomic chair but waved his hand for David to sit down. "You wanted to see me, Mr. Balfour?"

"Oh, c'mon, David. I'm Uncle Ebe to you." Ebe Balfour was a stout man just under six feet tall and around two hundred and seventy-five pounds. He wore off-the-rack Brooks Brothers suits – generally in bright colors. Today he was dressed in a light tan suit, powder blue shirt, and a solid red tie.

"Yes sir, Uncle Ebe."

Ebe guffawed. In the company Uncle Ebe liked to send out broadcast video memos in which he was frequently laughing. They generally ended with his epithet, "Honest Ebe is out for us!" The pronunciation of "Ebe" was drawled to sound like "Honest Abe." David's uncle thought of himself as Abraham Lincoln.

"Say, I just heard that you closed the Marriott deal!"

David nodded.

"That's wonderful. According to the paperwork that was forwarded to me on my e-mail sales account, you also negotiated a $60,000 annual fee."

"Yes sir."

"Why that will make you our top salesman for the year for sure. That trip to Puerto Rico will be yours, for sure."

"Thank you, Uncle Ebe." David had qualified for trips before but he never went. He couldn't go with Alan, and he didn't want to go without him.

"You betcha. They've got the sun and the beach there. And the girls! Wow those little ladies wear practically nothing, and you can believe me that they're not ladies when the sun goes down!"

David laughed perfunctorily but without enthusiasm.

"Well, David, now that I have you here there's something I want to go over with you."

"What is that?"

"It's a little arrangement that I have with the top producers in the region." Ebe leaned forward on his sizable teak desk that sported a gilded brown leather blotter built into the top. It was remarkable how clean Ebe kept his desk. At the far left corner was a foot-high bronze sculpture of a leopard who was in the process of leaping forward. The lead leg was bent up in a posture that suggested a leap forward to the path ahead.

"Yes, Uncle Ebe."

"Now that you are breaking out of the main pack of $50–$100,000 producers, your book will need more support from me."

"Support?"

"Oh yes – with the home office, with Mr. Sa'id, for example. You understand that as a captive agent with Leopard all the business you produce belongs to the company. If they think that you aren't servicing the account correctly, they'll come in and take over your business."

David didn't like the tone of this, but he tried to keep a straight face and nodded.

"So what I do for the top producers is I intervene on your behalf to keep the business in your book. I will personally make sure that any problems that arise are handled at the highest level."

"You mean *you?*"

Ebe slapped his hands together. "You betcha!" Then he licked his lips.

"How much is this going to cost me?"

"A flat 25 percent on national cases (anything over $30,000 in commission)."

"I have to pay you $15,000?"

Ebe let out one of his famous laughs, "No, it's nothing like that. This is pre-tax. Everything is legit. I have payroll take care of it. It never even hits your pay. It's treated like a split-commission case. Easy as pie, David."

David pursed his lips and looked down at his shoes. His left shoe had a long scuff mark on it. Then he looked back to his uncle.

"Oh, I understand what you're feeling, David. You're thinking that $60,000 is a hell of a lot more than $45,000. But you know on big cases we don't annualize commissions so that what we're really talking about is pre-tax of $5,000 versus a pre-tax of $3,750 monthly. That's only $1,250 less for the assurance that you won't be losing this baby in a month or two when something unforeseen hits. Better to have some protection – insurance, you know." Ebe laughed again as he slapped his hands together once more.

David forced a smile. "Well, when you put it that way …" His voice fell off. Again he looked down at his shoes. "Do I have to sign something?"

"Naw. Not necessary. I just wanted to call you in here to set you straight."

"Let me think this over Uncle Ebe. I'll come back in tomorrow. What time will work for you?"

"Tomorrow, I'm booked. But if you come in early – say around eight – I'll see you then."

David stood up and left without shaking his uncle's hand.

"And he wants *what?*" Alan asked in his "high voice." David told him. Then Alan Stewart arose and started pacing around the living room of their apartment. When Alan got excited his voice would climb to a higher pitch. He couldn't control it. It was one of the things that kept him out of courtroom law. Alan was one of those lawyers who worked behind the scenes with an investigating team. It was a skill that he had learned when he was on the staff of Edward Kennedy during the 1990s.

"This sounds like an illegal shakedown to me. And you say that this guy is your uncle?"

"Yeah. My dad's brother. My dad used to work at Leopard, too. That was when I lived in Seattle. They have a big branch office there. Then dad's health went bad in a hurry and suddenly he was dead. My uncle got me a spot in big accounts, but it meant that I'd have to move to Virginia. So I did."

"I don't like the sound of this, David." Then Alan walked over to David who was sitting on the couch and put his arm around his shoulders. "Hey, don't be so glum. It's not your fault that your uncle is strong-arming you."

"I wanted you to be happy for me, Alan. You're so successful, and I'm just an also-ran. I really want our relationship to be more on an equal level."

Then Alan gave David a hug and kiss on the cheek. "This will work out. Go to the meeting tomorrow and see what Ebe has to say. He wants you there before his secretary gets in so that 'just in case' there's a scene he can't control, he will have his privacy. This guy is cunning. I'll give him that."

It's about a seventy-minute commute by public transportation from Adams-Morgan, District of Columbia (where David and Alan lived) to Ballston (Arlington, Virginia). It requires taking the L-2 bus to Woodley

Park Metro and then a change of trains at Metro Center. At the end of the commute there is a half-mile walk to the office. David liked public transport. (He drove a company car for insurance appointments.) To make his appointment with Uncle Ebe it meant he had to be up at 5:15AM and out the door at 6:35AM.

On the way to the bus, David saw a man sleeping on the sidewalk. The man was in his twenties, black with knotted hair. David stopped, bent down, and put his hand on the man's shoulder. The young man was breathing irregularly. David knew the signs. His mother had died of apnea. He pulled out his cell phone and dialed 911. In twenty minutes an ambulance arrived to take the man to an emergency room, and David proceeded to his bus stop.

When David arrived fifteen minutes late to the appointment, he didn't even have to knock on the door. This disconcerted him. Could Uncle Ebe hear him walking on the plush carpet or did he have security cameras in the hall?

"Come on in, David," said the regional sales manager. He put his arm around David's shoulder and hurried him into his office (shutting doors as they went). Ebe was wearing a black suit, white shirt, and a gray tie.

They took their places and the drama began. "Now David, I took it that after our chat yesterday you seemed a little bent out of shape about my service override of your commission."

"Yes, Uncle Ebe, I was – and am. I was discussing it with my legal counsel on this topic and he advised me – "

" – Your legal counsel? And who might that be, David? That fag lawyer you play house with?"

David was suddenly confused. How did he – how could he –

"Oh, that surprises you, eh? Didn't know that I knew about your tawdry little secret? I had a private investigator check you out. I check out everyone in big accounts." Then Ebe took out a file folder and handed it over to David. Inside was a report and pictures. It included conversations that had to have been either the result of a bug or a remote listening device. What it did show was that David was a homosexual who was living with another man. David was confused. He didn't know if he was mad as hell or simply pained because his privacy had been violated.

"Don't try to rip them up. I've got the whole thing on disk. And the disk is backed up. Now David, I'm sure that you know the laws of Virginia. Homosexuals can be fired at will for no cause. Your Marriott account would then come to me and I'd have 100 percent of the commission."

It was all David could do just to sit there. He thought about lifting the statue of the leaping bronze leopard and hurtling it his uncle's head. But David didn't move. His uncle's life wasn't worth it.

"And don't think about going above me. Abdullah Sa'id, our vice president of sales, was born in Saudi Arabia. You know what they do to fairies there? They behead them publicly. I don't think he'll have much sympathy for an uppity faggot salesman."

David grimaced and got up. "You seem to be holding all the cards, Uncle Ebe. I guess I have no choice but to march to your orders."

Ebe let out another of his famous guffaws. "I'm glad you understand the real world. Let's just go forward and make some money."

David nodded his head.

During the next five weeks (of what should have been the happiest period of his professional life) existence for David had become unbearable. Alan tried to assuage him, but to no avail. David began to second guess the prowess of his life partner. Sure Alan had gone to Harvard and served on Kennedy's staff, but when you look at what he *did*, Alan had always ended up on the losing side. First there was the defense of the Glass-Steagall Act. Alan was point person against repeal and yet it was repealed anyway. Then there was the Gramm-Leach-Bliley Act which Alan worked against and it was passed, nonetheless. Finally there were the Bush tax cuts and the resolution on the War in Iraq before the United Nations weapons inspectors could finish their report. Once again Alan was a loser. That's why he left Kennedy and did a stint at the Center for American Progress before signing on to Billings, Stevenson, and Smith (a public interest law firm). David couldn't help but think that David and his problems were also testaments to Alan's losing ways.

It was early April. Spring was in the air. Alan roused David to make their annual pilgrimage to the zoo. It was a fifteen-minute bus ride on the L-2 to the Woodley Park Zoo. David swallowed a couple cups of coffee and a yogurt before he was ready to dress himself for the outing. It was a bright day already in the low 60s. The bus let them out in front of the thirty-yard-wide crosswalk that marks the entrance to the zoo. The couple took their usual route beginning in the panda house, then followed the Asia Trail. They were impressed by the new elephant center and then headed to the great ape house. Alan especially liked to spend time watching the chimps and apes.

The lighting in the great ape house is rather dim. There are several glass protected areas in which different sorts of primates eat and sleep in their captive environment. The visitors had long benches that they could sit on while studying their primate brethren.

In front of David and Alan was a cage with three chimps who seemed rather active. One of the chimps took some of the food from chimp #2 while #2 was gesticulating at #3 who was on the highest branch. Then #2 jumped to a branch to swing behind #1 and took the scarf that #1 had been playing with.

"Did you see that, David?"

David nodded. "You mean about the communication between the chimp on the ground and the one on top of the tree?"

"No, the way the one chimp paid back the one who stole some of his food. He took his scarf as payback."

"Payback? You think that chimps know payback?"

Alan put his hand on David's shoulder. "Every creature in nature understands payback. It's one of those unwritten laws that apply to everything."

David shrugged his shoulders. He was thinking about the Reptile Discovery Center since this was one of the feeding times. During feeding time one could see the normally dormant snakes wake up to devour rodents.

"I know what you're thinking, David. Let's go, but I want to tell you about payback. It may interest you more than watching those snakes consume helpless rats."

And it worked. David smiled as he sat in Uncle Ebe's office staring at the portrait of Abdullah Sa'id on the wall and listening to Mary Lou Sue chomping on her gum. After a forty-five-minute wait, the secretary got a text from her boss. It was time to show David in. Ebe was dressed in a deep burgundy suit, matching shirt (two shades lighter), and a yellow necktie.

"Hello, Uncle Ebe." David took a chair even as his uncle was starting to say, "Please sit down."

"I've got a proposition for you, Uncle Ebe. I want you to change your instructions to payroll that puts part of my money in your bonus pool."

"Why should I do that? I thought we went over all that, David."

"That's what you *thought*, wasn't it? Well, that's before I got some information on *you*, Uncle Ebe." David leaned forward even as Ebe leaned back.

"That's right. I did some detective work of my own and I discovered that you have been cheating the IRS. That shakedown money you get from the guys in big accounts amounts to a couple hundred grand a year. It's put into your bonus account and is paid through negotiable stock options which you sell for a big loss to a Cayman Island shell corporation that you own. You deduct the loss on your taxes and you get the principal tax free. It's quite a little trick. The former IRS agent I contacted said that it was very clever. You know these agents do appreciate a good job even as they are clicking on the handcuffs."

Ebe hit his desk hard with his closed fists. He wasn't laughing anymore. "You filthy fairy, I should have never hired you."

"You hired me as part of an arrangement with my father – your brother – who I've recently learned you compromised in order to assist your rise to the top."

David was wondering whether there might be a gun in Ebe's desk. "Before you do something that you'll regret, I want to let you know that the evidence is in the hands of a lawyer friend of mine who has instructions to turn you in should anything happen to me. He knows about this meeting and is waiting for me on this floor even while we speak."

"What do you want?"

"Restitution to me and to everyone in big accounts whom you have been stealing from. Then I want you to quit the company. My career is too important to have it jeopardized by the likes of you."

"And the IRS?"

"I advise you to turn yourself in. They tell me you can cut a better deal that way."

David then got up and left. As he departed he happened to glance at the bronze leopard lying down on his side – its leading leg bent sideways by the fall: a casualty of Ebe's temper.

It was the last anyone heard of Ebe Balfour. He was reported to have left the country. David and the rest of the big accounts insurance agents found their paychecks 25 percent higher in May. The new regional sales manager brought a different, more cooperative tone to the office. Morale was better, though David and Alan still couldn't go to Puerto Rico together with the year's top salespersons and their families.

The leopard's advancing leg bent forward. He was now prepared to leap into the future.

8

War Rape

War rape is one category of denying individuals their level-one basic good of "protection from unwarranted bodily harm." This chapter examines war rape, in particular, as an instance (in general) of sexual violence against women (though war rape also occurs against men albeit to a much lesser extent). This treatment serves as a paradigm of widespread denial of the most fundamental of all natural human rights: level-one Basic Goods – protection from unwarranted bodily harm.

8.1 THE FACTS IN THE WORLD TODAY

From the beginning of time, war rape has existed. The Trojan War occurred on some accounts in the abduction and rape of Helen (wife of Menelaus) by Paris (son of Priam). We remember accounts of the sack of Troy, the rape of the Sabine women, and a few other accounts in the ancient and medieval world (though there are not too many, because it's not a very comfortable topic for male historians). Michael Walzer reports that Mussolini bought mercenaries from North Africa to fight for him, and part of the deal was total amnesty for war rape.[1] In our current era (the last seventy years), we have seen widespread war rape in World War II by all parties. There have also been documented war rape allocations against combatant troops in Vietnam, the war in Bosnia, and the civil conflict in Rwanda.[2] This is not to suggest that these are the only

---

[1] Michael Walzer, *Just and Unjust Wars,* 4th ed. (New York: Basic Books, 2006): 133–136.
[2] Gina Marie Weaver, *Ideologies of Forgetting: Rape in the Vietnam War* (Albany: State University of New York Press, 2010); Jonathan Shay, *Achilles in Vietnam: Combat Trauma and the Undoing of Character* (New York: Simon and Schuster, 1995); Inger Skjelsbaek, *The Political Psychology of War Rape: Studies from Bosnia and Herzegovina* (New York: Routledge, 2011); Linda Melvern, *Conspiracy to Murder: The Rwanda Genocide and the International Community* (New York: Verso, 2004).

conflicts in which war rape has occurred. Instead, it is my contention that war rape has occurred in virtually every conflict in the world's history: international, and intranational. Why is this?[3]

A number of factors contribute to war rape. The most prominent is the perception males have of women's position in the world.[4] Women are objectified and seen as set on earth for men to dominate. This is true in war and peace. But in most wars today there are two sorts of predators: (a) government-sponsored army forces and (b) rebel insurgents. In the first case, some restraint often comes from the military's public institutional structure. Because of the patriarchal linear organization of most official military units, there is at least the pretense of a code of conduct and penalties for those who break it (rarely observed).[5] In the case of rebels this code of conduct is not there. Rebel insurgents are really a class that is characterized by the frenzy of killing in war. This frenzy cuts out the inhibition that stops most men from raping in peacetime. One study of college males in the United States claims that 35 percent of all college-aged men would rape their classmates if there were no consequences (such as jail time).[6] If this is correct, then it shows a very high number of males whose personal worldview accepts rape as a valid option for them – so long as they can get away with it. In war, you can get away with it.

Others who might not be inclined to rape in peacetime are desensitized to their actions by the violence and mayhem of war. For these individuals, rape becomes a new possibility because of their current horrific lifestyle as killers.[7] A number of cases have shown that group pressure

---

[3] There is certainly a growing literature on war rape; see the comprehensive bibliography given in Laura Sjoberg and Sandra Via, eds., *Gender, War, and Militarism: Feminist Perspectives* (Santa Barbara, CA: Praeger, 2010). In addition, see also Susan Brownmiller, *Against Our Will: Men, Women, and Rape* (New York: Penguin, 1976); Claudia Card, "Rape as a Weapon of War," *Hypatia* **11**.4 (Fall 1996): 5–18; Nicola Henry, Tony Ward, and Matt Hirshberg, "A Multifactorial Model of Wartime Rape," *Aggression and Violent Behavior* **9** (2004): 535–562; Kathryn Farr, "Extreme War Rape in Today's Civil-War-Torn States: A Contextual and Comparative Analysis," *Gender Issues* **26** (2009): 1–41; and Elizabeth D. Heineman, ed., *Sexual Violence in Conflict Zones: From the Ancient World to the Era of Human Rights* (Philadelphia: University of Pennsylvania Press, 2011).

[4] Brownmiller, *Against Our Will*; Card, "Rape as a Weapon of War"; and Henry et al., "A Multifactorial Model of Wartime Rape." This is a widely held view.

[5] Farr, "Extreme War Rape."

[6] N. M. Malamuth, "Rape Proclivity among Males," *Journal of Social Issues* **37** (1981): 138–157.

[7] T. Ward and S. Hudson, "The Construction and Development of Theory in the Sexual Offending Area: A Metatheoretical Framework," *Sexual Abuse: A Journal of Research and Treatment* **10** (1998): 47–63.

on soldiers on the edge has made the difference in whether they participate in group rape. This peer pressure can also include the possibility that any reluctant soldiers could themselves be killed if they do not join group rape situations.[8]

There are no good data on just how prevalent war rape is because no party wants to admit to this shameful action. It is as invisible as the women victims. The data we do have generally come from NGOs. Here are some estimates: (a) at least 50,000 rapes occurred in the 1990s conflict in Bosnia; (b) between 100,000 and 1,000,000 German women were raped by Soviet soldiers at the end of World War II; (c) 250,000 were raped in Sierra Leone in the 1990s; (d) 500,000 rapes were committed in a few weeks of the Rwanda genocide; and (e) 200,000 Chinese women were kidnapped and forced to work as "comfort women" (forced prostitutes) by the Japanese army in World War II.[9] There are many more examples.

Though precise statistics are hard to come by, we do know that of all deaths that occur in contemporary conflicts, civilians account for as many as 75 percent (of the total number of fatalities), and among these, women and children account for 75 percent of the civilian deaths. This means that around 56 percent of the total casualties are women and children.[10] Thus, if we want to get a quick view of where war rape is occurring, we need only look at where war is occurring (generally known as intranational war since the end of World War II). This is

[8] Henry et al., "A Multifactorial Model of Wartime Rape"; cf. J. L. Janis, *Victims of Groupthink: A Psychological Study of Foreign Policy-Decisions and Fiascoes* (Boston: Houghton Mifflin, 1973); D. Lang, *The Casualties of War* (New York: McGraw Hill, 1969); and A. N. Groth, *Men Who Rape: The Psychology of the Offender* (New York: Plenum, 1979).

[9] Valerie Oosterveld, "The Special Court for Sierra Leone's Consideration of Gender-Based Violence: Contributing to Transitional Justice?" *Human Rights Review* **10** (2009): 73–98; Laura Flanders, "Rwanda's Living Women Speak: Human Rights Watch – Rwanda's Living Casualties," in *War's Dirty Secret: Rape, Prostitution and Other Crimes against Women,* ed. Anne Llewellyn Barstow (Cleveland, OH: Pilgrim Press, 2000): 95–100; Chunghee Sarah Soh, "Human Rights and the 'Comfort Women,'" *Peace Journal* **12** (2000): 123–129; Alexandra Stiglmayer, ed., *Mass Rape: The War against Women in Bosnia-Hertzegovina* (Lincoln: University of Nebraska Press, 1994); Anonyma, *Eine Frau in Berlin: Tagebuchaufzeichnungen vom 20 April bis zum 22 Juni 1945* (Frankfurt: Eichborn, 2003); Antony Beevoir, *The Fall of Berlin 1945* (New York: Viking, 2002); and Norman Naimark, *The Russians in Germany: A History of Soviet Zone Occupation 1945–1949* (Cambridge, MA: Harvard University Press, 1995).

[10] M. Vlachova and L. Biaso, eds., *Women in an Insecure World: Violence against Women, Facts, Figures, and Analysis* (Geneva: Geneva Centre for the Democratic Control of Armed Forces, 2005), and Z. Salbi, *The Other Side of War: Women's Stories of Survival and Hope* (Washington, DC: National Geographic Society, 2007).

first in sub-Saharan Africa (Burundi, Chad, Côte d'Ivoire, Democratic Republic of the Congo, Somalia, Sudan, Angola, Liberia, Rwanda, Sierra Leone, and Uganda).[11] Next is Asia (Myanmar, Nepal, Sri Lanka); then North Africa and the Middle East (Afghanistan, Algeria, Iraq); then the Americas (Colombia, Haiti); and Europe (Chechnya [Russia]). There is also lingering war rape in countries previously at war but now at peace – for example, Rwanda.

When we speak of war rape, there are various instantiations. Most often rape is committed by men against women – though this is not always the case. The American-led torture and sexual violence in Abu Ghraib prison in Iraq is an example of sexual violence against men (with men and women perpetrators).[12]

When we speak of sexual violence we must include any sort of sexual violence – including but not limited to sexual degradation, forced intercourse, forced fellatio or cunnilingus, penetration of bodily orifices by various objects, mutilation, and murder. These acts are committed in several ways: one man against one woman, many men against one woman, and many men against many women. The assaults can be private or public. They can be committed haphazardly (as it strikes some military unit) or they can be the result of a planned strategy – such as entering various small villages and raping the wife of the leader in a public setting. The aftermath of the rape can include disfigurement and murder. A short list of these extreme forms of violence include amputation, stabbings, cuttings, long-term sexual enslavement, kidnapping and killing of family members, and forced intra-family rape.

The planned strategic rape can have several motives: (a) breaking the morale of the town involved; (b) creating a new source of children who resemble the opposite side (often associated with ethnic cleansing); (c) kidnapping individuals for forced labor or prostitution (so-called army comfort women), and others. These attacks occur within villages, detention facilities, border checkpoints, and refugee and IDP (internally displaced persons) camps.

Victims are frequently scorned for having been raped. They lose social status and are often exiled (many times with their children who are also

[11] Farr, "Extreme War Rape," 4.
[12] An account of female involvement via a feminist lens can be found in David Levi Strauss, Charles Stein, Barbara Ehrenreich, John Gray, Meron Benvenisti, Mark Dannner, and David Matlin, *Abu Ghraib: The Politics of Torture* (New York: North Atlantic Books, 2004). A more general account can be found in Justine Sharrock, *Tortured: When Good Soldiers Do Bad Things* (Hoboken, NJ: Wiley, 2010).

tainted by the mother's victimhood). It is indeed an illogical shared community worldview that treats the victim as a culpable perpetrator.

What sort of profile fits the male war rapist? There is no single list of characteristics, of course, but among the most commonly cited traits are these: (a) a mind-set of hyper-sexuality that expresses itself in exaggerated "stereotypically masculine" swaggering behavior; (b) lack of human empathy that allows one to dehumanize another without experiencing cognitive dissonance; (c) upbringing in a family where violence is prevalent; and (d) youth. In the first case, the hyper-sexuality is thought to be a response by some males to compensate for feelings of inferiority and insecurity.[13] By performing as if they were powerful and in complete control, these individuals are compensating through bravado and random acts of violence for what they deeply lack. In the second case, when the experience and pain of others does not personally resonate, the natural prohibitions against causing pain to others never kicks in.[14] In the third case, early family interactions – especially family violence and sexual abuse – can permanently affect cognitive/attachment and behavior responses.[15] In the last case, age is critical. Sexual over-aggressiveness and general delinquency factors (associated with anti-social behavior) are highly correlated first with males between the ages of sixteen and twenty-five, then twenty-six to thirty. After that, there is a general decline in anti-social sexual crime.[16] When you consider that most combat military troops are younger than thirty, this coincides with the general period of increased socially pathological sexual aggressiveness.

What environmental conditions contribute to war rape? To begin with the obvious, war is about killing people to gain strategic advantage. When this is done according to the international conventions on war,

[13] Groth, *Men Who Rape.*

[14] W. L. Marshall and H. E. Barbaree, "An Integrated Theory of the Etiology of Sexual Offending," in W. L. Marshall, D. R. Laws, and H. E. Barbaree, eds., *Handbook of Sexual Assault: Issues, Theories, and Treament of the Offender* (New York: Plenum, 1990): 257–275.

[15] N. M. Malamuth, R. J. Koss, M. Koss, and J. S. Tanaka, "Characteristics of Aggressors against Women: Testing a Model Using a National Sample of College Students," *Journal of Consulting and Clinical Psychology* 59 (1991): 670–681; K. D. O'Leary. "Physical Aggression between Spouses: A Social Learning Theory Perspective," in *Handbook of Family Violence,* ed. V. B. Van Hasselt, R. L. Morrison, A. S. Bellack, and M. Hersen (New York: Plenum, 1988): 31–55; and K. A. Dodge, J. E. Bates, and G. S. Pettit, "Mechanisms in the Cycle of Violence," *Science* 250 (1990): 1678–1683.

[16] C. R. Bartol, *Criminal Behavior: A Psychosocial Approach,* 3rd ed. (New York: Simon and Schuster, 1991); S. S. Ageton, *Sexual Assault among Adolescents* (Lexington, MA: Lexington Press, 1983); and Malamuth et al., "Characteristics of Aggressors against Women."

then the only other combatants are properly subject to harm, and the harm is identified as minimal force necessary to achieve a military, tactical objective. Sometimes this means that people will be killed. Rape is not specifically addressed, as such, but since it is almost always against civilians, it is *always* unjustified. However, in the environment that sanctions "force in the field of combat is permitted," it is easy to see how this environmental factor might promote other uses of force (even those that are not permitted).[17] Other situational or triggering disinhibitors include the issue of prejudicial loyalty: "*us* versus *them*." This group orientation creates a perversion of the shared community worldview. The *ad populum* influence initiates a sense of the group working together. This can spawn a sensibility of anonymity for the individual who does not really feel accountable for what he does individually.[18] When you also insert alcohol and drugs, the combination can create a situation in which it seems that the amorphous group acts as one and will sanction anyone who fails to go along. Lang (1969) tells a story of a former private in the Vietnam War, Sven Eriksson, and the "Incident on Hill 192." Eriksson and four other enlisted men were on reconnaissance when they kidnapped Phan Thi Mao. The sergeant said they "would get the woman for the purpose of boom boom, or sexual intercourse, and at the end of 5 days ... would kill her" (p. 26). The reason given was for the morale of the squad. When Eriksson refused to take part in the rape, the sergeant told Eriksson that if he took this stance, then he would likely become a victim of *friendly fire*. Eriksson was also taunted by the other men as a "queer" and a "chicken." Eriksson did not take part in the rape. When they returned to base he reported his group and they were court-martialed. During the trial, the others (the enlisted men under the sergeant) cited that they were "afraid of being ridiculed." It is clear that the perverted community worldview can be a force for evil when divorced from the shared community worldview imperative.

The environment of war is unlike that of civilian life. Henry et al. (2004) states that Japan as a peacetime society has a very low level of civilian rape, yet during World War II in Nanking, Japanese soldiers committed widespread rape and abduction of females who were held as "comfort women."

Finally, there is the case of war rape in sexually integrated armies. By some accounts in the U.S. military during the Iraq War, U.S. military

[17] B. Reardon, *Sexism and the War System* (New York: Teachers College Press, Research Centre, 1985).

[18] Marshall and Barbaree, "An Integrated Theory of the Etiology of Sexual Offending."

males raped U.S. military females at a rate approaching 33 percent.[19] To say this is a serious problem is a huge understatement. It paints the picture outlined earlier of males within a shared community worldview that is patriarchal, krateristic, and for whom women are objectified as rewards with euphemistic language like "boom, boom." This last trend broke into the public consciousness during the 1991 Tailhook Scandal in which 100 men sexually assaulted 83 women and 7 men during a two-day debriefing in Las Vegas, Nevada, after the short "Desert Storm" intervention. Though this was not on the battlefield, many of the same dynamics were probably at work. Since then (despite efforts to ensure secrecy) there have been numerous reports, from the military academies to the battlefield, demonstrating that U.S. male armed forces not only engage in wartime rape of others but also of their own female comrade soldiers (and there have been few consequences for these crimes).

8.2 THE PRIMARY JUDGMENT PHASE (WHAT IS THE RIGHT THING TO DO?)

Obviously, rape is wrong. It deprives individuals of a level-one basic good: protection from unwarranted bodily harm. But as the preceding subsection has argued, the causes for war rape are deeply embedded in perverted tenets within the shared community worldview. The challenge is to reverse this – a monumental task. Using the methodology from Chapter 7, let us consider Stage I: consideration and justification. Many will give pyrrhic assent against the personal and community worldviews that objectify and marginalize women and put them at tremendous risk for war rape, but then they enter into dissonance and rejection when it comes to the Stage II dialectical understanding phase. They retreat to their closely guarded worldview, which amounts to the status quo. How do we traverse this seemingly wide chasm?

It seems to this author that the real answer is the full gender integration of the military around the world. Now, as shown in the case of Abu Ghraib, women can become complicit in rape just like their male counterparts. However, since rape overwhelmingly occurs by males

[19] *Military Sexual Trauma (MST) – Report of the Defense Task Force on Sexual Assault in the Military Services, December, 2009 – Military Sexual Assault, Harassment, Rape* (Palm Harbor, FL: Progressive Management, 2010). Cf. Terri Spahr Nelson, *For Love of Country: Confronting Rape and Sexual Harassment in the U.S. Military* (New York: Routledge, 2002). The 2012 documentary "The Invisible War" also explores this outrage within the U.S. Military.

committing violence against females, the shared community worldview of fighting forces would change significantly if women were to approach parity in the combat front-line forces around the world. It is this author's conjecture that the "Incident on Hill 192" would never have occurred if half of the soldiers had been female. At the very least, far fewer of these incidents would occur. This because (a) women are biologically more empathetic than males – especially to those of their same sex; and (b) women do not fit the profile of the aggressive young male.[20]

It is also possible that working alongside women will make the males lessen their basic objectification/subordination attitude. If this conjecture is correct, then we would move a step toward the overlap and modification response in the Stage II dialectical understanding phase of the way we confront novel normative theories (Chapter 7).

Changing deeply held attitudes does not come easily (as we have seen with racial integration). But positive steps can be made so long as there is a vision of the endpoint to be achieved. The road is long but it can be traveled to its terminus.

8.3 THE SECONDARY JUDGMENT PHASE (POLICY RESPONSES)

When we set out policy responses to ensure the realization of human rights, we first have to consider the aspirational goal of the primary judgment phase. In this case it is the elimination of war rape by achieving parity in fighting forces between males and females. This is a very long-term goal for every nation on earth. But this author does believe it is possible.

However, in the short term, we must consider the safety of women in the army. We must protect these female soldiers from becoming victims of war rape. The long-term path must be pursued prudently with safeguards for our emerging female fighting force.

There are also other short-term responses to war rape that are essentially stopgap measures. These include (a) increased surveillance of

---

[20] Two psychology studies on men versus women on empathy include B. J. Carothers and H. T. Reis, "Men and Women Are from Earth: Examining the Latent Structure of Gender," *Journal of Personality and Social Psychology* **104**.2 (2013): 385–407, and J. W. Chun, H. J. Park, and J. J. Kim, "Common and Differential Brain Responses in Men and Women to Non-Verbal Emotional Vocalizations by the Same and Opposite Sex," *Neuroscience Letters* **515**.2 (2012): 157–161. An application to the field of battle can be found in Kathleen Lois Barry, *Unmaking War, Remaking Men: How Empathy Can Reshape Our Politics, Our Soldiers, and Ourselves* (Gilbert, AZ: Phoenix Rising Press, 2010).

war zones (using new technology including cell phone video and the upcoming advent of mini-drones)[21] to record information (to act against the trigger of *anonymity*) and actually bring war rape perpetrators to justice (via reliable evidence); (b) continuous video surveillance at checkpoints so that these cease to be stations of rape; (c) integration of the International Red Cross and Red Crescent or Doctors without Borders into refugee camps to provide safety and medical attention for the women in the camps; and (d) better intelligence on the mercenaries who are in the field of conflict (this is often most important among the rebel forces). On a different front, efforts must be made to reintegrate rape victims and their children into society. Such efforts can include moving victims to a different part of the country (sometimes with a new name), job training, and a new start for the family with temporary subsidies for food and housing. This is crucial because it is the only way that victims can move forward.

To back up these short-term solutions we also need a more straightforward designation of rape within a theater of war as a war crime punishable by the International Court of Justice. Before World War II, discussion of rape in war did not occur as a matter of judicial interest. The post–World War II Nuremburg Trials (a famous institutional originator for war crimes) did not cite war rape. Since then, various ways have been used to add it to a list of other factors that can constitute a war crime. But what we need *right now* is to make rape a war crime, *simpliciter.* And we need aggressively to prosecute the crimes with speedy procedural justice so that the time between the crime and its punishment is shortened.

Pavlov proved in his work with canines that conditional stimulus is a powerful motivator. If we can get enough good information about perpetrators and develop a real zeal to prosecute war rape, then it is possible that we can eliminate these rapist dogs from the fields of war.

---

[21] Mini-drones represent an upcoming technology that has been approved for testing in the United States. These mini-drones (that are the size of a box of cornflakes) can fly at altitudes of up to 200 feet and record in real time actions on the ground – see the article from the *Los Angeles Times* on the British use of these devices that resemble a child's toy but are effective at gathering intelligence: http://www.latimes.com/business/money/la-fi-mo-mini-drone-battlefield-20130204,0,4050682.story (accessed March 1, 2013).

9

Political Speech

Freedom of speech – especially political speech – is not widely allowed around the world. On the table of embeddedness it constitutes a level-two basic good. This chapter first briefly examines the problem and then applies the natural human rights theory that I have presented to suggest worldview alteration and policy responses.

9.1 THE FACTS IN THE WORLD TODAY

Li Tiantian knows firsthand how the state can use video images against people it doesn't like. Li, 46, is an outspoken human rights lawyer in Shanghai.

Police watch Li so closely, it's best to visit her after dark and use a grove of trees behind her apartment building as cover. Once inside, she'll tell you to turn off your cellphone and put it in another room.

"People with technological know-how all said the cops can use cellphones to monitor people, track your location, even use cellphones as a listening device," Li explains, as dumplings she has prepared bubble in a pot. "People have reached a consensus that when we chat together, we put cellphones away."

Li Tiantian, a human rights lawyer, is under heavy surveillance by Chinese authorities. She says police tried to get her boyfriend to break up with her by showing him photos of other men she had been involved with.

Sound paranoid?

It isn't.[1]

Across the world freedom of speech on matters relevant to the state is often under attack. From across the world stage there are countless

[1] http://www.npr.org/2013/01/29/170469038/in-china-beware-a-camera-may-be-watching-you, National Public Radio broadcast, January 29, 2013, Frank Langfitt/NPR.

A	B	C
No suppression	Maximum allowable suppression	Open rebellion

FIGURE 9.1. The Dictator's Dilemma

examples of governmental affronts to political speech. From Saudi Arabia, to Syria, to Uganda, to Ethiopia, to Azerbaijan, to Burma, to China (to name a few among many), political speech is under attack by autocratic governments.[2] There are various ways to think about this. One approach that is attractive to this author is to focus on individuals who hold governmental positions and believe that it is in their best interests to compromise privacy and freedom of speech – especially when it concerns political matters. Why is this? It generally begins in autocratic states. Leaders wish to maintain control of their states and so they crack down on any dissent that might lead to protest and eventually to revolution. This is the concern of those who believe that without such measures the result would be destabilizing to the state. Under this worldview, a tight, restrictive environment is the only one in which the status quo might continue. However, there is considerable research to suggest that crackdowns can go too far.[3] In Figure 9.1, one begins with a state without suppression of the political speech (including all sorts of communication) and moves toward censorship.

Between points A and B, the autocrat can effectively use suppression (via arresting people, torturing them, imprisoning them, mutilating

[2] Amnesty International, *Saudi Arabia: Dissent Voices Stifled in the Eastern Province* (London: Amnesty International Publications, 2012); Amnesty International, *The Spring that Never Blossomed: Freedoms Suppressed in Azerbaijan* (London: Amnesty International Publications, 2011); Amnesty International, *Stifling Dissent: Restrictions on the Rights to Freedom of Expression and Peaceful Assembly in Uganda* (London: Amnesty International Publications, 2011); Human Rights Watch, *Uganda: Media Minefield: Increased Threats to Freedom of Expression* (New York: Human Rights Watch, 2010); Human Rights Watch, *A Wasted Decade: Human Rights in Syria during Bashar al-Asad's First Ten Years in Power* (New York: Human Rights Watch, 2010); Ben Rawlence and Leslie Lefkow, *One Hundred Ways of Putting Pressure: Violations of Freedom of Expression and Associations in Ethiopia* (New York: Human Rights Watch, 2010); Maureen Aung-Thwin, "Freedom of Expression around the World: Burma," *World Literature Today* 83.6 (2009): 54–62; "China Asserts Sovereign and Other Rights to Control Internet," *Tibetan Review: The Monthly Magazine on all Aspects of Tibet* 45.7 (2010): 33–34.

[3] See James Davies, "The J-Curve of Rising and Declining Satisfaction as Cause of Some Great Revolutions and a Contained Rebellion," in *Violence in America*, ed. H. D. Graham and Ted Robert Gurr (New York: Praeger, 1969): 690–730; Ivo K. Feierabend and Rosaline L. Feierabend, "Aggressive Behaviors within Politics, 1948–1960: A Cross-National Study," *Journal of Conflict Resolution* 10 (1962): 249–271; and Ted Robert Gurr, *Why Men Rebel* (Princeton, NJ: Princeton University Press, 1970).

them, and killing them) to maintain their control of things (the personal cost of resisting is seen to be too high). Between B and C the equilibrium begins to decay. At point C open rebellion occurs. The perfect autocrat would situate himself on the continuum between A and B stopping just short of the B-point. Sounds easy, right? Well, recent history has shown that it is not. This has sometimes been called the Dictator's Dilemma.[4] On the low end (closer to A), people within an autocratic regime have recourse to some positive institutional responses when corruption and ineffectiveness present themselves. This would be a mistaken version of the democratic shared community worldview imperative. However, when people cease to have an assurance that their institutional participation in the community is viable, then a line is crossed (the "B-point") that will create an escalation of state violence and a counter response by the population.[5]

It should not be supposed that restrictions on political speech occur only within autocracies. It is well known that when Richard Nixon was president of the United States he created an enemy's list that sought to suppress the activities of the U.S. news media. Some have alleged that Nixon had the support of the Federal Bureau of Investigation (FBI) on this project.[6] And in the aftermath of the 2001 terrorist attack on the World Trade Center and the Pentagon, there is some evidence that the Central Intelligence Agency (CIA) was ordered to engage in a policy known as extraordinary rendition that involved kidnapping individuals within the United States and in the Middle East and taking them to remote locations in Eastern Europe where they were subsequently subject to torture. This was under the guise of *obtaining* information but it also had the intended effect of restricting political speech within the United States.[7] To oppose such measures was said to be *unpatriotic*. In fact, one act that passed the U.S. Congress called "The Patriot Act" allowed the government to get fast-track (nonjudicial) authority to monitor phone

---

4   Ronald A. Francisco, "After the Massacre: Mobilization in the Wake of Harsh Repression," *Mobilization: An International Quarterly* **9** (2005): 107–126.

5   Robert W. White and Terry Falkenberg White, "Repression and the Liberal State: The Case of Northern Ireland, 1969–1972," *Journal of Conflict Resolution* **39** (1995): 330–352; John L. Olivier, "State Repression and Collective Action in South Africa 1970–1984," *South African Journal of Sociology* **22** (1991): 109–117; and Karl-Dieter Opp and Wolfgang Roehl, "Repression, Micromobilization and Political Protest," *Social Forces* **69** (1990): 521–547.

6   Don Fulsom, *Nixon's Darkest Secrets* (New York: St. Martin's Press, 2012).

7   Alan W. Clarke, *Rendition to Torture (Genocide, Political Violence, and Human Rights)* (New Brunswick, NJ: Rutgers University Press, 2012).

calls and even to monitor what books an individual might have checked out from her local library.

In these cases (Nixon with the Vietnam crisis and Bush with the 9-11 crisis) democratically elected governments responded to popular unrest by curbing political speech. In democracies, this generally involves secrecy so as not to upset the general population (who falsely believe that because they are a democracy they are immune to such state suppression of speech). In autocracies the state overtly presents a violent response to political speech – often promoted in the spirit of making the state better (as opposed to specific personal interest). Recent examples of this are most evident in the Arab Spring and its violent second chapter in Syria and Egypt (2013).

The attitude from the point of view of the regional governments was that free media would be a threat to their countries. The Ibn Khaldun Center for Development Studies said in 2010:

> All Arab countries continue to criminalize press offences – where offences are interpreted expansively. Thus Egypt, Libya, Saudi Arabia, Syria, Tunisia, and to a slightly lesser degree, Algeria, Jordan, Morocco, and Yemen, are all zealously hauling journalists to court where they are sentenced to prison terms for having spoken out freely criticizing the regime or the ruling elites. As noted by Freedom House the "media in the region is constrained by extremely restrictive legal environments in which laws concerning libel and defamation ... hamper the ability to report freely." Of particular concern in this regard are Egypt, Libya, Syria, Tunisia, and Saudi Arabia.[8]

Further the Ibn Khaldum Center observes in the same report that at the end of 2010, (a) political regimes in the region vary but there is very restricted citizen participation in the political process; (b) no Arab parliament has the ultimate power of the purse (thus rendering it politically impotent); and (c) human rights institutions are very weak.

It is clear that autocracies are intimidated by political expression executed individually and writ large (the media). In the recent Arab Spring, the autocracies had control over traditional print media and television.

---

[8] M. Zaki, "Civil Society and Democratizing in the Arab World," in *Ibn Khaldun Center for Development Studies Annual Report 2010* (Cairo: Ibn Khaldun Center for Development Studies, 2010): 9; cf. C. D. Johnston, *Global News Access: The Impact of New Communications* (Westport, CT: Praeger, 1998); and Stephen Quinn, Tim Walters, and John Whiteoak, "A Tale of Three (Media) Cities," *Global Media Journal* **3**.5 (2004): online journal – http:// lass.purduecal.edu/cca/gmj/fa04/gmj-fa04-quinn-waters-whiteoak.htm (accessed March 20, 2013).

This power was disrupted by cell phones (principally) and the social media (secondarily).[9]

Nonetheless, this did not stop governments in the region from trying to shut down the new media. In Egypt, the government tried to ban Facebook, Twitter, and video sites such as Daily Motion and YouTube. However, within a few days people achieved a workaround as SMS (short message service) networks became the organizing tool of choice.[10] Since a very high number of Egyptians had cell phones, these became the most effective media device. Still, the government tried setting up firewalls and *denial of service attacks*. With outside help, the activists shared new software that circumvented government efforts. With all the submarine cables that run from Europe to North Africa, it is impossible for the governments of the region to be able to pull the plug totally as they were used to doing in the era of traditional television and print media. Sami ben Gharbia, a Tunisian exile, monitored online censorship attempts and alerted the world about the situation. "This self-styled middle class rapper streamed digital soundtracks for the revolution."[11] In the battle of the media, the cell phone was not to be censured.

Another trigger is similar to the first. It rests in the popular reaction to national and local political corruption. Corruption is endemic to most dictatorial regimes.[12] This is because the dictatorships are all about secrecy in state-run affairs. Secrecy creates a mighty temptation to take advantage of the "Ring of Gyges protection" and commit evil deeds.[13] If this

---

[9] According to the Arab Social Media Report, 2011, in spring 2011 Facebook had a penetration rate of 22.49 percent in Tunisia and 7.66 in Egypt. Twitter had a penetration rate of 0.34 in Tunisia and 0.15 in Egypt. www.dsg.ae/en/ASMRHome1.aspx (accessed March 19, 2013); cf. Nawaf Abdelhay, "The Arab Uprising 2011: New Media in the Hands of a New Generation in North Africa," *Aslib Proceedings: New Information Perspectives* **64**.5 (2012): 529–539.

[10] Philip N. Noward and Muzammil M. Hussain, "The Role of Digital Media," *Journal of Democracy* **22**.3 (2011): 35–48; cf. "International: Reaching for the Kill Switch: Internet Blackouts," *The Economist* **398**. 8720 (February 12, 2011): 87–88.

[11] Noward and Hussain, "The Role of Digital Media," 37.

[12] Hank Johnston, "State Violence and Oppositional Protest in High-Capacity Authoritarian Regimes," *International Journal of Conflict and Violence* **6**.1 (2012): 55–74.

[13] In book two of Plato's *Republic*, the Ring of Gyges story is told. This story sets the structure for the entire work of Plato's *Republic*. According to the story, Gyges of Lydia was a shepherd; after an earthquake revealed an old tomb, he entered it and found a magic ring that would render him invisible. Gyges took the ring to the palace and used his power to seduce the queen and murder the king. Thus Gyges supplanted the king. The question that Plato poses is whether this was in Gyges' best interest. In other words, are there intrinsic reasons for acting ethically that would make ethical action the most

conjecture is correct, then dictatorships have a strong incentive toward corruption built into their very structure. For example, at the upper levels there is widespread competition for power over certain sectors as the one who succeeds is in position to obtain lucrative corporate bribes.[14] This upper-echelon struggle creates *space* for opposition to grow.[15] By "space" two meanings are intended: $space_a$ as a conceptual arena in which various ideas go back and forth, are debated, and ultimately lead to commonly held conclusions; and $space_b$ as a practical venue in which these conversations can occur (such as a tea shop, someone's home, a back alley, et al.), resulting in action response. Using these two senses of space together with the causal force – that $space_a$ creates urgency for $space_b$ – then the activities of the upper-echelon members of the dictatorship (as remotely understood) create some space for protest.

The more forceful causal factor that creates space is at the local level. It is here that the functional bureaucracy is located and works among actual people. Since these functionaries are paid very poorly, yet possess local power, they are subject to bribes – in fact, they generally demand them. For example, in Tunisia Mohamed Bouazizi was a street vendor with a pushcart. He was constantly harassed for bribes of ten dinars (almost seven dollars – or several days' wages) or he would be forced to abandon his cart and stock.[16] The man became outraged with corruption at the local level. On December 17, 2010, Bouazizi refused to yield and was severely beaten. Bouazizi's consequent public, self-immolation precipitated general protest that brought down the Ben Ali government. It's all about space. In Tunisia it was a slap to an ordinary man's dignity that set off the cascading series of events.

Dictatorships present a front indicating that they have everything under control. Adolph Hitler, Joseph Stalin, and Chairman Mao are the poster boys for this vision of complete state domination. It is true that during their eras there were fewer opportunities for $space_b$. Various devices, such as an informant network and use of emerging technology

---

choiceworthy? Plato's book is an argument that there are such intrinsic reasons. However, the point in this text is that some use the guise of secrecy to commit evil deeds. I refer to this dynamic by referencing the Ring of Gyges myth.

[14] Doug McAdam, Sidney Tarrow, and Charles Tilly, *Dynamics of Contention* (New York: Cambridge University Press, 2001).

[15] Edwin Amenta and Michael Young, "Democratic States and Social Movements: Theoretical Arguments and Hypotheses," *Social Problems* **46** (1999): 153–172.

[16] Kareem Fahim, "Slap to a Man's Pride Set off Tumult in Tunisia," *New York Times* (January 21, 2011) online at http://www.nytimes.com/2011/01/22/world/africa/22sidi.html? pagewanted=all&_r=0 (accessed March 20, 2013).

to spy on others, seemed to give them an unassailable advantage. With the advent of a communications network that may be beyond national control, this advantage may no longer exist. With the exception of North Korea (which does not [at the writing of this book] have widespread cell phone ownership), most of the world's autocracies have lost their absolute advantage. This presents an interesting possibility for the future.

Harsh repression of political speech by dictators creates space$_a$, which desperately seeks an outlet for organizing a response, space$_b$. The greater the oppression (at the upper level) or the greater the corruption (at the local level), the greater the need for space by the people. The new technology creates a new venue for space$_b$. This accentuates the dictator paradox. Creating space$_b$ requires ingenuity. For example, Hank Johnson describes a case in the former Soviet Union in which a Soviet censor took annual vacations. The people within space$_a$ would take that opportunity to publish uncensored writings.[17] Likewise, it is well known that when Mubarak in Egypt tried to outlaw the Muslim Brotherhood, they found a way to create space$_b$ by doing charitable work among the poor (Hamas has employed the same strategy). Within Communist Poland, the Roman Catholic Church offered space$_b$ opportunities to Solidarity for its mobilization.

Sometimes space$_b$ opportunities come about via code language. For example, in China, reference to the Tiananmen Square Massacre is made by using the date, June 4 (6–4 or 64).[18] The creation of space$_a$ stimulates creativity among the cohort to find ways for laying out a space$_b$.

Thus the bad news is that throughout the world today there are severe restrictions on free speech. The good news is that both from the national and the local levels these activities must be seen within the context of the dictator's paradox such that overreach will have unintended consequences for the autocrats responsible.

9.2 THE PRIMARY JUDGMENT PHASE (WHAT IS THE RIGHT THING TO DO?)

In the primary judgment phase there needs to be a plausible worldview response that can change things. In the case of political speech, the worldview response has to be the creation of responsive governments and communities. This is the imperative that rulers around the

[17] Hank Johnston, "State Violence and Oppositional Protest in High-Capacity Authoritarian Regimes," *International Journal of Conflict and Violence* **6**.1 (2012): 55–74, 64.
[18] Edward Wong and David Barbosa, "Wary of Egypt Unrest, China Censors Web," *New York Times* (January 31, 2011): A4.

world must consider. The justification is the acceptance of the shared community worldview imperative that all members of any community (micro or macro) must be afforded an opportunity to bring forth suggestions to improve and reform the community. This is largely what the shared community worldview imperative is all about. Now I am confident that a few will disagree from the standpoint of a normal citizen of some state. This is because it flows naturally from rational consideration of one's place in a community that is a first-order meta-ethical principle enunciated by the shared community worldview imperative.[19] But it has been my experience that, for the most part, those in power are rather diminished in their ability to think speculatively – especially when self-interest is involved.[20] If my experience is representative, then promoting the concept of real popular input into the political process will be a very hard sell.

The story that controls these autocrats' personal worldview is the myth of total state domination as an achievable goal. And though they might dream of the powerful Stalin, Hitler, and Mao in their misguided vision of totalitarian perfectionism, their dream is really false and unachievable because of the dictator's paradox. If these autocrats can move to the second stage of dialectical understanding, and if they look about them (especially to the brief Arab Spring phenomenon), they *might* (via self-interest) ease up on the control of political speech. For example, perhaps they could use political speech within a blogosphere in which they were an engaged partner. In China, there is currently a limited (though inauthentic) experiment with this approach.[21]

One need not hold out for full-blown democracy for real progress to be made. If autocracies could get to the overlap and modification stage under the dialectical understanding phase, then real resolution and change might occur. But since these individuals are kraterists, and since kraterists act *only* when it is to their perceived advantage, it is important

---

[19] I remind readers I contend that there are two flavors of meta-ethics: (a) the realistic flavor that views this domain as containing the presuppositions necessary to create either a naturalistic or non-naturalistic realism, and (b) an anti-realistic flavor that sees this domain as self-referential talk about the talk of moral language. I am of the first flavor, which I tag as first-order meta-ethics.

[20] I am speaking primarily from my personal experience as a policy fellow at the Center of American Progress where I had the opportunity to chat with members of the U.S. Congress and a few foreign government officials. It surprised me that the individuals with whom I conversed were almost unable to think speculatively – at all. Their practical agenda and political talking points controlled their personal worldview.

[21] This trend is noted by Guobin Yan, "The People's Standoff: China's Twitter Generation Squares Off against the 'Great Firewall,'" *Scientific American* **308**.4 (April, 2013): 14.

to emphasize the dynamics of the dictator paradox within this new age of cell phone communication that may belie governmental censorship.

Within democracies, the problem is different. Democracies often perform as if they exemplified completely free political speech, and then they hypocritically act on the secret side and work the other way. For example, in the 2012 presidential election in the United States, there was a concerted effort by Republicans to suppress the vote among poor people by creating new restrictions requiring everyone to get an official voting identification and by installing only a few voting machines in those locales that had predominantly poor populations (often causing six-hour waits). This is because the poor overwhelmingly vote for the Democratic Party. In contrast, the local state Republican Party functionaries assigned a full complement of voting machines in wealthy areas (presumed to vote Republican – fifteen-minute waits).[22] It was only by publicity and an independent judiciary that this tactic was derailed. In the end, for democracies, transparency (to defuse the Ring of Gyges problem) has to be enforced by an independent judiciary for any lasting protection of political speech to endure.

9.3 THE SECONDARY JUDGMENT PHASE (POLICY RESPONSES)

Short-term policy responses that aim at increasing the opportunity for political speech around the world should center on creating spaces$_b$ for communication. When the government suppression level passes the B-point in Figure 9.1 (either from central governmental action or local corruption), there is a natural urge in all people to respond. As mentioned, the model of Tunisia and Egypt suggests that this can be successful – especially when there is outside help in the event that the government tries to shut down these lines of communication. The modes of communication include (in order of importance) cell phone conversations and the sharing of text and video cell phone data; Twitter and micro blogs; and the Internet (including social networking).[23] It should be the business of the international

---

[22] The news media reported alleged efforts by the Republican Party to suppress the vote within probable Democratic voting groups in an effort to win the 2012 election. See *Salon. com*, – http://www.salon.com/2012/07/27/fla_republican_we_suppressed_black_votes/; *New York Times* – http://www.nytimes.com/2012/09/10/us/politics/legal-battles-on-voting-may-prove-a-critical-issue-in-election.html?pagewanted=all&_r=0; and *Washington Post* – http://www.washingtonpost.com/wp-dyn/articles/A707-2004Oct26.html.

[23] These avenues are discussed in Hu Yong, "Spreading the News," *Index on Censorship* 41.4 (2012): 107–111; Philip N. Howard and Muzammil M. Hussain, "The Role of

community to create communication response plans for countries around the world that have been hovering around the B-point. Depending upon the locale, keeping communications open might include workaround networking through neighboring countries (as happened in Tunisia and Egypt). In more remote locations such as China, emergency, subsidized satellite hookups might be the backup plan of choice.

What makes the social communication approach so attractive for dissemination of information and protest is that it is so decentralized. In the past, the creation of spaces involved getting groups together in secret gatherings in which someone emerged as a leader. All that was necessary for dismantling this communication mode was a spy who could betray the leader. The group would be intimidated into believing the myth of governmental invincibility, and as a result, would probably dissolve. However, when thousands of people are connecting to a video that is shared person to person (in the case of cell phone only communication), then there is very little the state can do to disrupt this communication.

Of course, we have to consider cases in which the tyrant in question has complete control of the military (not the case in Tunisia or Egypt). In these cases (such as Libya and Syria) there may still be a prolonged insurgency that will also require international support for airspace and tactical weapons. This is a battle that the insurgents must fight themselves, but they should be afforded a more equal venue of conflict.

Not every country has enough cell phone users to make a difference, but at the writing of this book over 150 countries in the world have significant cell phone ownership (exceeding 20 percent of the population).[24] If political responsiveness by the general population is the long-term goal of our primary judgment phase, and if enabling decentralized communication among the general population during cases in which the B-point has been reached is one step in that direction, then a short-term policy strategy among G-6 nations to enable cell phone access (primarily) and Internet access (secondarily) will move the world in the direction of enabling political speech as an essential level-two Basic Good that everyone on earth should enjoy.

Digital Media," *Journal of Democracy* **22**.3 (July 2011): 35–48; Nawaf Abdelhay, "The Arab Uprising 2011: New Media in the Hands of a New Generation in North Africa," *Aslib Proceedings: New Information Perspectives* **64**.5 (2012): 529–539; Rodolfo Diaz, "From Lambs to Lions: Self-Liberation and Social Media in Egypt," *Harvard International Review* **33**.1 (2011): 6–7; Evgeny Morozov, "Technology's Role in Revolution: Internet Freedom and Political Oppression," *Futurist* **45**.4 (2011): 18–21.

[24] *CIA World Factbook* (New York: Skyhorse, 2013).

10

LGBT Rights

Lesbians, gays, bisexuals, and transgendered (LGBT) human beings seek the acceptance that will allow them to pursue their dreams and participate openly in the communities in which they live. This can involve many levels of natural human rights. Acceptance itself would be a level-one secondary good. The opportunities denied to individuals because they fit into the LGBT group constitute a level-two basic good. Finally, the violence perpetrated against LGBT individuals constitutes a level-one basic good. This chapter first briefly examines the problem and then applies the natural human rights theory that I have presented to suggest worldview alteration and policy responses.

10.1 THE FACTS IN THE WORLD TODAY

So how is it to be LGBT in the world today? The answer is mixed. It's generally bad. There are some countries and regions in which real progress is being made in social recognition of the legitimate human rights claims for LGBT individuals. Most of the buzz has been about homosexuals, but transgendered individuals have, perhaps, the hardest road to travel and are among the least protected groups in the world. Consequently, they have one of the highest suicide rates.[1] For example:

> On April 18 [2011] a transgendered woman named Chrissy Lee Polis went to the women's bathroom in a Baltimore County McDonald's. When she came out, two teenage girls approached and spat in her face. Then they

---

[1] For an excellent presentation of some of the medical and psychological issues facing transgendered children and adolescents, see Simona Giordano, "Ethics of Management of Gender Atypical Organization in Children and Adolescents," in *International Public Health Policy and Ethics,* ed. Michael Boylan (Dordrecht: Springer, 2008): 249–272.

threw her to the floor and started kicking her in the head. As a crowd of customers watched, Polis tried to stand up, but the girls dragged her by her hair across the restaurant, ripping the earrings out of her ears. The last thing Polis remembers, before she had a seizure, was spitting blood on the restaurant door. The incident made national news – not because this sort of violence against transgender people is unusual, but because a McDonald's employee recorded the beating on his cell phone and posted the video on YouTube.[2]

Violence against the LGBT community varies from official death penalties in Iran, Saudi Arabia, Yemen, United Arab Emirates, Sudan, Nigeria, and Mauritania to active official persecution in Bulgaria, Brazil, Iraq, Senegal, South Africa, Uganda, and Colombia.[3] Unofficial violence against the LGBT community occurs in virtually every country on earth.[4]

---

[2] Eliza Gray, "Transitions," *New Republic* **242**.10 (2011): 10–18, 10.

[3] *Changing Laws, Changing Minds: Challenging Homophobic and Transphobic Hate Crimes in Bulgaria* (New York: Amnesty International Publications, 2012); Neal Broverman, "Fighting Back in Brazil," *Advocate* **1065** (2013): 15; Jack Healy et al., "Threats and Killings Striking Fear among Young Iraqis, Including Gays," *New York Times* (March 11, 2012): A4; Scott Long et al., *They Want Us Exterminated: Murder, Torture, Sexual Orientation and Gender in Iraq* (New York: Human Rights Watch, 2009); Dipika Nath et al., *Fear for Life: Violence against Gay Men and Men Perceived as Gay in Senegal* (New York: Human Rights Watch, 2010); Dipika Nath, *We'll Show You a Woman: Violence and Discrimination against Black Lesbians and Transgender Men in South Africa* (New York: Human Rights Watch, 2011); Sigrid Rausing, "Uganda Is Sanctioning Gay Genocide," *New Statesman* **138**.4976 (2009): 22; Julieta Lemaitre Ripoll, "Love in the Time of Cholera: LGBT Rights in Colombia," *Sur-International Journal of Human Rights* **11** (2009): 73–89; and Joanna Sadgrove et al., "Morality Plays and Money Matters: Towards a Situated Understanding of the Politics of Homosexuality in Uganda," *Journal of Modern African Studies* **50**.1 (2012): 103–129.

[4] Though every country can tell its own story, one historical account about the United States sets out some critical common body of knowledge factors: Krystal Noga-Styron, Charles E. Reasons, and Derrick Peacock, "The Last Acceptable Prejudice: An Overview of LGBT Social and Criminal Injustice Issues within the USA," *Contemporary Justice Review* **15**.4 (2012): 369–398. Also of note is employment discrimination: András Tilcsik, "Pride and Prejudice: Employment Discrimination against Openly Gay Men in the United States," *Journal of Sociology* **117**.2 (2011): 586–626. Tilcsik presents the first large-scale audit of employment discrimination against gay men. Fictitious resumés were sent to 1,769 job postings in seven states. On one group of resumés, applicants listed experience in a gay campus organization; in the other group, there was no listing for this. The first group did significantly worse than the second group in the job search. A predicting factor of a company's response to the job applications was the language it used in the job ad. Companies that incorporated macho language discriminated at a higher rate than those with more neutral language in the ad. In the workplace itself (as in the *Scherzo* short story, Part Three) there is pervasive discrimination as per Jennifer C. Pizer et al., "Evidence of Persistent and Pervasive Workplace Discrimination against LGBT People: The Need for Federal Legislation Prohibiting Discrimination and Providing for Equal Employment Benefits," *Loyola of Los Angeles Law Review* **45**.3 (2012): 715–779.

Clearly, homosexuals and transgendered individuals have been picked out for much ill treatment. One expression of this discrimination as a worldview construct can be found in Marcel Proust's *Sodome et Gamorrhe:*

> [A comment about Baron Monsieur de Charlus by one who doesn't know him] "Ah now! There is a happy man.... If I had a daughter to marry and was one of the rich myself, I would give her to the Baron with my eyes shut." ... [the narrator speaks:] These descendants of the Sodomites, so numerous that we may apply to them that other verse in Genesis: "If a man can number the dust of the earth, then shall their seed also be numbered" have established themselves throughout the entire world; they have had access to every profession, and pass so easily into the most exclusive clubs that, whenever a Sodomite fails to secure election, the blackballs are, for the most part, cast by other Sodomites, who are anxious to penalize sodomy having inherited the falsehood that enabled their ancestors to escape from the accursed city ... but I [utter] a provisional warning against the lamentable error of proposing to create a Sodomist movement and to rebuild Sodom.[5]

Thus wrote Marcel Proust in the early twentieth century examining pre–World War I attitudes among the upper class in France about a gay man living a dual existence: (a) passing as heterosexual so as to avoid the sort of social stigma that put Oscar Wilde in prison, and (b) seeking love among those who were also homosexual – though often finding them to be equally prejudicial. This is all tied up in the religion of the Torah (viewed from the Catholic perspective).

This obviously seems like an example of inductive incoherence within the personal worldview imperative. Such incoherence leads to a sure-loss contract. And indeed, at the end of the book, Baron Monsieur de Charlus does find himself balancing on a precipice. The reason for this worldview crisis is the way society treats individuals who do not fit the concept of standard heterosexual identity. What lies behind this social prejudice is the community worldview understanding of sexual orientation – as set out in Argument 10.1.

ARGUMENT 10.1: THE ARGUMENT AGAINST LGBT RIGHTS

1. All human action is freely undertaken by an act of the will – Fact
2. Sexual orientation (homosexual or transgender) is an action that is more properly termed "sexual preference" – Fact

---

[5] Marcel Proust, *Sodome et Gomorrhe* (Paris: Nouvelle Revue Française, 1921–1922), trans. F. Scott Moncrieff as *Cities of the Plain* (New York: Random House, 1927): ch. 1, 24–25.

3. Sexual preference is freely undertaken – 1, 2
4. All sexual activity must follow the general social norms as agreed upon by a given society – Assertion
5. In every nation of the world the general social norm of sexual activity is heterosexual – Fact
6. What societies agree upon is the proper ground of a human right – Assertion
7. The only sexual activity that an agent has a right to is heterosexual – 4–6
8. [Sexual activity contrary to socially based rights is a perversion] – Assertion
9. Rights-perversions should be punished – Fact

---

10. All nonheterosexual sexual preferences and activity should be punished – 3, 7–9

Argument 10.1 has several controversial premises beginning with premise #2. Though science has not discovered a "homosexual gene" or a "transgender gene," there seems to be a consensus that there is a biological basis for sexual orientation.[6] It is not a choice. It is therefore

---

[6] There is still some debate on the biology of how someone becomes LGBT. Most of the research has been done on gay men. The old theories of citing nurture as the cause are now a minority, but are still around. An example of this debate can be found in Qazi Rahman, Stanton L. Jones, and Alex W. Kwee, "Is Homosexuality Biologically Based?" in *Clashing Views on Psychological Issues,* ed. Brent Slife (New York: McGraw-Hill, 2010): 89–108. Rahman takes the view that there is a biological cause while Jones and Kwee claim that "twin studies" point to an environmental cause based on a particular learning model. A sample of the proponents of the biological causation include Francesca Iemmola and Andrea Camperio Ciani, "New Evidence of Genetic Factors Influencing Sexual Orientation in Men: Female Fecundity Increase in the Maternal Line," *Archives of Sexual Behavior* **38**.3 (2009): 393–399 (the authors solve the so-called Darwinian objection to there being a genetic basis to male homosexuality by empirically demonstrating that females in the line that produces homosexual males are significantly more fertile than females without a homosexual male in their genetic line); David P. Barash, "The Evolutionary Mystery of Homosexuality," *Chronicle of Higher Education* (2012): B4–5 (a great introduction to some of the broad issues involved – especially interesting is his discussion of the Xq28 gene that may be partially responsible as well as notions concerning group selection theories); William J. Jenkins, "Can Anyone Tell Me Why I'm Gay? What Research Suggests Regarding the Origins of Sexual Orientation," *North American Journal of Psychology* **12**.2 (2010): 279–295 (the author examines the genetic and epigenetic factors that affect prenatal development and the stability and plasticity of sexual orientation); and William R. Rice, Urban Friberg, and Sergey Gavrilets, "Homosexuality as a Consequence of Epigenetically Canalized Sexual Development," *Quarterly Review of Biology* **87**.4 (2012): 343 (discusses the role of DNA markers that act in the monogenetic changes in DNA, epigenetics, to develop a new model for homosexuality). Finally, a very

not a preference. It is a phenotypical expression that is not subject to individual control.

The second key area to be examined is set out in premise #6. Along with the sociological fact of premise #5, it creates a case that minority right claims are really *perversions* (when they go against the common body of knowledge). This is consistent with the anti-realist position on human rights. Whether the justifying theory is legal, contractarian, or interest-based, the theories cannot escape agreeing with premise #6 and coming to the conclusion that nonheterosexual "preference" should be punished.[7] This social reality has been very strong in some societies for hundreds of years and is even interpreted (by some) to be linked to prohibitions in religious holy books.[8]

This is why we should prefer a natural theory of human rights: it is realist and not derived "from the bottom up" by examining the practice of various sociological groups.[9] The first step here is to determine why people are sexually oriented as they are. This is behind premise #2. As noted earlier, the contemporary evidence does not match the assumptions of premise #2. If we accept an alternate premise – "Sexual orientation is biologically based and is not under the control of the agent" – then an alternative argument is generated.

---

thorough book makes the case that sexual orientation is based upon endocrine expression: Jacques Balthazart, *The Biology of Homosexuality* (Oxford: Oxford University Press, 2012): chs. 8 and 9.

[7]   One possible exception to this categorization of the interest-based approach is the naturalistic inclinations of James Griffin. It is possible that through his "autonomy" super right provision, he could reject premise #6.

[8]   Among many of those who attack LGBT individuals, a substantial number bring forth arguments based on religion. An overall guide to these arguments and responses can be found in Jeffrey S. Siker, ed., *Homosexuality and Religion: An Encyclopedia* (Westport, CT: Greenwood, 2006); for a historical examination of Christian attitudes until the fourteenth century that support an attitude of tolerance, see John Boswell, *Christianity, Social Tolerance, and Homosexuality; Gay People in Western Europe from the Christian Era to the Fourteenth Century*, 8th ed. (Chicago: University of Chicago Press, 2005); for a look behind the veil of contemporary Islam, see Shereen El Feki, *Sex and the Citadel: Intimate Life in a Changing Arab World* (Westport, CT: Pantheon, 2013); and for a general work that encompasses religion and other social factors, see Louis Crompton, *Homosexuality and Civilization* (Cambridge, MA: Cambridge University Press, 2006).

[9]   This is in contrast to James Griffin, *On Human Rights* (Oxford: Oxford University Press, 2008): 29, and Charles Beitz, *The Idea of Human Rights* (Oxford: Oxford University Press, 2009): 8, who espouse a bottom-up approach. This creates an inductive logic that is first descriptive. The aim is to be *scientific* in the approach. The moral realism approach demurs.

ARGUMENT 10.2: THE ARGUMENT SUPPORTING LGBT RIGHTS

1. All natural rights are grounded in realistic naturalism (with respect to one's ability to commit purposive action to achieve his or her vision of the good) – from the Argument for the Moral Status of Basic Goods (see Chapter 6, this volume)
2. All people's sexual orientation is a hardwired natural, genetic expression – Fact
3. One's ability to commit purposive action in behavior concerned with sexuality (one subcategory of a person's vision of the good) is made within the context of one's natural sexual orientation (either heterosexual, homosexual, bisexual, or transgendered) – Fact
4. There is a natural right to commit purposive action in behavior concerned with one's sexuality, ceteris paribis,[10] according to that person's hardwired sexual orientation – 1–3
5. Rights and duties are correlative – Fact

_____

6. There is a natural right to pursue, ceteris paribis, actions in accord with one's natural sexual orientation, and others in the community have a duty to make that possible – 4, 5

Argument 10.2 begins with rejecting the idea that sexual orientation is about *choice*. The proponents of Argument 10.1 believe that all people are made the same genetically with respect to sexual orientation. This is an odd belief given that evolutionary theory (regardless of the version of evolutionary theory you choose) is all about variation within the species. Strict *homogeneity* is part of some essentialist pre-1850 biology. Diversity is now the watchword. This permits greater fitness in a world of changing natural environments: meteorological or social.

The deeper point behind Argument 10.2 is that people come into the world constructed in a certain way. Maybe they are extra tall or very

_____

[10] The ceteris paribus condition refers here to actions that have no harmful effects upon others. Among heterosexuals, for example, this caveat would exclude nonconsensual sex (rape), or sexual behavior that would damage another within the given norms of that society (such as heterosexual "seduction and abandonment" in cultures in which this causes the partner to lose social status). Just because one has a biological, hardwired inclination is not, in itself, sufficient to permit unbridled expression. For example, one might contend that *pedophilia* is a natural hardwired orientation, but because there is a nonconsenting minor involved, expression of that natural inclination is not permitted. The same point can be made about people with genetic anger management problems or other severe anti-social tendencies. These actions are wrong – not because they are natural, but because they involve hurting others who are not consensual actors in their drama.

short. Did those people have any control over their height? No. Should people be discriminated against for something over which they have no control? No.

Moral merit and demerit should be about what people *do*. This is the basis of *deserts* (see my discussion in 6.3.5). There I argued that one should not suffer or be rewarded for something that is an accident of birth. This includes being the child of a drug addict or child abuser or the child of a president or a billionaire. Accidents of birth or circumstance are not deserved. All people should be judged on what they do within the circumstances presented to them. A person born as a heterosexual should not be applauded or punished for acting within that context. The same holds true for homosexuals, bisexuals, or transgendered people. So long as the ceteris paribus clause is adhered to, nature's rendering of one's sexuality should be respected as a human right that incurs a duty among others to respect and defend it.

10.2 THE PRIMARY JUDGMENT PHASE (WHAT IS THE RIGHT THING TO DO?)

When we look at the severe violations of the human rights to express one's natural sexuality, ceteris paribus, it appears necessary to get individuals to the very beginning of Stage One: Consideration and Justification. This is the problem of getting people whose worldview is expressed in the Argument 10.1 mind-set to even question the truth of premises #2, #5, and #6. This is a tough task because the truth of those premises has been in the consciousness of most people around the world, unchallenged, for such a long time (in some cases, centuries). There are two ways to change this worldview (both community and individual). First, the common body of knowledge has to be altered. This can be done by continued scientific studies on biological mechanics of how sexuality is expressed in the phenotype. There may be several accounts as there are with the expression of "blue eyes," for example.[11]

Once the full mechanics have been established scientifically, then those individuals within the community who are swayed by science will put pressure on the common body of knowledge to change the attitude about "choice" (premise #2) and at least there will be a debate in the

---

[11] Phenotypic expression is often the result of several biological inputs that work together in different stages of development. For a discussion of this in the context of male homosexuality, see Emmanuele A. Jannini et al., "Male Homosexuality: Nature or Nurture?" *Journal of Sexual Medicine* 7.10 (2010): 3243–3253.

general community about what epistemological realistic naturalism says about sexual orientation.

However, the scientific approach is not sufficient. This is because such a large number of individuals in communities around the world distrust science. This is generally because of a lack of scientific education. For example, in the United States, there is a sizable minority opinion that human action – such as driving cars and using coal power plants, with their resulting harmful gaseous emissions – does *not* have any effect on global warming (and this group is goaded on by financially interested corporate agents).[12] It could be the influence of corporate money or it could be the ignorance of many people who don't know enough science to be able to form an opinion about whether they trust its almost unanimous findings. It is probable that these individuals never took introductory physics or chemistry in which a common lab exercise is to introduce CO_2 into a bell jar filled with the prevailing atmosphere. With no other action, the temperature rises within the bell jar. If people were more scientifically literate, their attitudes might be different. Science should have a key impact on the common body of knowledge – including sexual orientation. This can move people quickly through Dialectical Understanding and the outcome of Overlap and Modification and the prospect of a real worldview change.

The second way to change worldview attitudes is for heterosexuals to get to know individuals in the LGBT community and to recognize their humanity (i.e., that they are not the *other*). For such a long time in the United States and most other countries, the LGBT community felt the environmental threats of the violent, intolerant society. As we have seen, around the world it is not safe to be homosexual or transgendered. For this reason, individuals with nonheterosexual orientation have been forced to hide who they are for their own protection. Thus, many individuals did not personally know people who publicly represented themselves as nonheterosexual, as they often created a false sense of who they were for their own personal protection (like the fictional Baron de Charlus and the real-life Rock Hudson). This reality created a false understanding among many about the total numbers of individuals who are LGBT.[13] Generally, this false understanding greatly undercounts

[12] Riley E. Dunlap and Aaron M. McCright, "Climate Change Denial: Sources, Actors, and Strategies," in Constance Lever-Tracy, *Routledge Handbook on Climate Change and Society* (New York: Routledge, 2011): 240–259.

[13] It is difficult to get an accurate accounting of the number of LGBT individuals there are within a given population. This is partly due to the definition used and partly to the way it

the numbers of LGBT individuals. For example, Iranian president Mahmoud Ahmadinejad said in 2007 at a forum sponsored by Columbia University, "In Iran, we don't have homosexuals like in your country. In Iran, we do not have this phenomenon. I don't know who has told you we have that."[14] These are the comments of the Argument 10.1 individuals. It also reflects a society that treats homosexuality as if it were a crime. When people are persecuted for who they naturally are, ceteris paribus, then it is no surprise if those individuals live a life in the shadows.

For people who are unconvinced by science, having a nonsexual friendship with a nonheterosexual will go a long way to demystifying the "unspeakable." This, in turn, can lead to Stage Two Dialectical Understanding and hopefully Overlap and Modification on the way to Resolution and Change.

10.3 THE SECONDARY JUDGMENT PHASE (POLICY RESPONSES)

Short-term policy responses follow from the second method of worldview change set out above: exposing people to homosexuals as real people and not as the *other*. When people cannot meet people individually in real life, the next best thing to do is to introduce them via public media. This is one of the two policy responses that I put forth for the short-term solution (that synergizes with the long-term solution). For example, this strategy was successfully used during the late 1960s through the 1980s in

is measured. For example, for years people cited the Kinsey report's finding that 10 percent of the population was homosexual (based on interviews with World War II servicemen asked whether they had ever had sexual activity with another man): Alfred Kinsey, Wardell Pomeroy, et al., *Sexual Behavior in the Human Male* (Philadelphia: Saunders, 1948). Kinsey's methods and statistical analysis were later called into question: William G. Cochran et al., *Statistical Problems of the Kinsey Report on Sexual Behavior in the Human Male: A Report of the American Statistical Association, Committee to Advise the National Research Council, Committee for Research in Problems of Sex* (Washington, DC: American Statistical Association, 1954). Others have said that because there was such a social stigma about being gay, Kinsey actually *undercounted* his sample population. A more recent ongoing study at the Williams Institute at the UCLA School of Law puts the entire LGBT population at 3.5 percent of the U.S. population based on data gathered during the 2010 census: Gary J. Gates, "How Many People Are Lesbian, Gay, Bisexual or Transgender?" (Los Angeles: Lilliams Institute, UCLA School of Law, April 2011): 1–8. The report can also be found online: http://williamsinstitute.law.ucla.edu/research/census-lgbt-demographics-studies/how-many-people-are-lesbian-gay-bisexual-and-transgender/ (accessed April 2, 2013).

[14] ABC News, September 24, 2007, http://abcnews.go.com/US/story?id=3642673#. UVdJWpOG2po (accessed April 2, 2013).

the United States for introducing an isolated population to mainstream America.[15] The population was African Americans. With leadership from the government, the FCC (Federal Communications Commission) asked television stations to feature African Americans in positive roles and in a proportionate degree to their numbers in the general population (10%–12% at the time). This included advertisements, weekly television shows (dramas and comedies), and television movies. Moral suasion was also employed to convince print advertising and the Hollywood movie industries to use this approach.

And it worked. Though many European-descent Americans did not know an African American personally, they did know Sidney Poitier or some other actor chosen for a role. This had an analogous effect to meeting the *other* in person. True, the media campaign is ersatz and removed from real human interaction, but still it breaks down some barriers that can bar people from even entering the Stage One phase: Consideration and Justification. Actors such as Denzel Washington, Morgan Freeman, Samuel L. Jackson, James Earl Jones, Ruby Dee, Cicely Tyson, Angela Bassett, and Viola Davis (to name a few) allowed those European-descent Americans who lived in racially homogeneous communities to "safely" interact with African Americans and move to Overlap and Modification in Stage Two and eventually to Resolution and Change in Stage Three. Does this mean that America is "post-racial prejudice"? Of course not. However, it does mean that the country has come a long way since the findings of the National Advisory Commission on Civil Disorders (also known as the Kerner Commission Report of 1968) that described the United States as a very racist society.[16]

Now, there is a significant difference between race and sexual orientation. With race, you can look at someone and instantly classify him or her. No one wears a sign around her or his neck that says, "Hello: I'm LGBT!" This makes the task a little more difficult but not impossible. In advertisements, one can feature same-sex marriage families for products having to do with families – such as diaper sales, bicycles, skateboards, and computer games. These would not take the place of ads featuring heterosexual marriage families but would reach out to another segment of the population (and perhaps make the company sponsoring the ad

---

[15] A portion of this story of increasing the appearances of African Americans on television as part of the civil rights movement is set out by Aniko Bodroghkozy, *Equal Time: Television and the Civil Rights Movement* (Urbana: University of Illinois Press, 2012).

[16] Otto Kerner et al., *National Advisory Commission on Civil Disorders* (Washington, DC: U.S. Government Printing Office, 1968).

some additional money – especially for the early responders). For television shows in the United States, already a number have featured LGBT characters in a positive light, shows such as *Queer Eye for the Straight Guy, Girl Play, The New Normal,* and *Will and Grace.* And of course there was the well-received Hollywood movie *Brokeback Mountain.* These efforts have had an effect on the shared community worldview via the common body of knowledge such that young people (the demographic target for these shows) overwhelmingly support gay marriage (among 18–29-year-olds it is 73% according to a USA Today/Gallup Poll).[17]

Many other parts of the world have not moved very much in recognizing the LGBT group as acceptable members of the social community. Often, LGBT individuals are subject to severe danger. In these countries, the media strategy won't work because the old media – radio, print, and television – are tightly controlled by the state. This means that the short-term policy goal of promoting indirect access to positive role models who are LGBT in the context of a normal and natural life will be much more difficult to promote. During the Cold War, the United States tried to bridge a different gap (concerning Democracy versus Communism) with Radio Free Europe and other outlets devoted to reaching people where they lived and creating a space beyond censorship. If the countries around the world who may be making positive steps toward recognizing LGBT rights would mimic that tactic through radio outreach in the most rural and oppressed regions of the world and with short video clips (à la You Tube) that could be downloaded to smartphones in more technologically advanced countries, it is possible that real change might result. These dramatic vignettes would feature characters who were LGBT and are depicted as acting within the society's cultural milieu that has been modified in such a way that it accepts diversity.

A second short-term solution (in countries where the LGBT are far less oppressed) is to appeal to another already accepted tenet within the shared community worldview – in this case, marriage equality.[18] At first,

---

[17] Susan Page, "USA's Shifting Attitudes toward Gay Marriage," *USA Today* (December 5, 2012), http://www.usatoday.com/story/news/politics/2012/12/05/poll-from-gay-marriage-to-adoption-attitudes-changing-fast/1748873/ (accessed April 6, 2013).

[18] In a few countries the issue of marriage equality has proved to be a pivotal policy for getting people to move toward further worldview reflection. For a discussion of this, see Joseph Chamie and Barry Mirkin, "Same-Sex Marriage: A New Social Phenomenon," *Population and Development Review* **37**.3 (2011): 529–551; Emily R. Gill, *An Argument for Same-Sex Marriage: Religious Freedom, Sexual Freedom, and Public Expressions of Civic Equality* (Washington, DC: Georgetown University Press, 2012); and Kenneth W. Krause, "What Next for Gay Marriage?" *Humanist* **71**.1 (2011): 41–43. In the context of the United

this public policy proposal was very polarizing in the United States,[19] but then the discussion turned away from "gay and lesbian marriage" to "marriage equality." *Conceptually*, many people are very positive toward the idea of *equality*. This move allows certain worldview Dissonance and Rejection roadblocks to be detoured. Thus, many may find a way to move into the Second Stage of Dialectical Understanding. This is an important small step in the right direction for a broader, more inclusive set of human rights.

The implementation of LGBT rights is an extremely difficult journey for much of the world. But if we think as cosmopolitans, we cannot be content if the LGBT community is making progress only in our own regional community. We must move forward with a dual consciousness of our own: (a) do not rest until full legal and social rights are given to LGBT individuals (partial successes are only that – *incomplete*), and (b) do not rest until we can move the rest of the world via some media exposure to the real, positive images of LGBT individuals within each country's own cultural setting and show how the LGBT population can fulfill and advance the shared community worldview of that region. Once some progress has been made, the issue of marriage equality may help people go the rest of the way past the Consideration and Justification phase into the Dialectical Understanding stage.

At the very least, in much of the world, perseverance is necessary just to move to the Stage One – Consideration and Justification phase. It may not seem like much, but it is a striking advance in the right direction.

States, Laurence H. Tribe and Joshua Matz have made a strong argument from the legal realism perspective that marriage equality will happen throughout the United States: Laurence H. Tribe and Joshua Matz, "The Constitutional Inevitability of Same-Sex Marriage," *Maryland Law Review* 71.2 (2012): 471–489.

[19] Daniel C. Lewis, "Direct Democracy and Minority Rights: Same-Sex Marriage Bans in the U.S. States," *Social Science Quarterly* 92.2 (2011): 364–383.

Rondo

"The Game"

It was early in the afternoon one day when Henry came to the park. We were just a bunch of guys engaged in our weekly game. The air was chilly, but not cold – you know, late October before the grip of winter has taken hold: the end of autumn. Each Saturday, after our chores were done – around noon – a few of us from the neighborhood would head over to the park, which lay just across the freeway, to play touch football. Sometimes we'd see some people already there and invite them to play in our game. At other times it would be just the six or seven of us.

But none of us, save Mucho Pani, had ever seen Henry before.

On this particular day, Eddie Meyer was already running routes with Billy Washington. Billy is the only black guy in the neighborhood. He teaches up at Jefferson High. Eddie was, I guess you could say, the best friend Billy had in the neighborhood. Eddie didn't have any pretensions. He said what he thought and was not self-conscious about living in the smallest house while having the largest family on the block. He was a foundry worker, I think, and I'm quite sure he never finished high school. Still, there was something dependable about Eddie.

I came down to the park with Lincoln McCrae and Angelito Dominguez. We were going via the northern bridge over the freeway. It's only three blocks to the park, but you have to enter it from one of two gates. The rest of the park has a high fence around it for security. The park itself is about two miles around with a lake in the middle. It is pretty nice, I guess, for an urban park. There isn't much violence, and there are often games of baseball in the summer, and soccer and football in the early fall. Lots of kids use our park. Why there's even a group of Latinos (our area has the second highest concentration of Latinos in the city) who play a game that resembles volleyball except they kick a small wicker ball over the net.

On this day there wasn't anyone in the park except Eddie and Billy. We could see them from atop the hill that overlooks the north gate to the park. What an odd combination. Fat little Eddie was running out for passes while the tall, nearsighted teacher (who never wore his glasses to our games) tossed him arching offerings. I almost laughed aloud except that I didn't know what Lincoln might say. Lincoln was always so involved with things, you know: serious. Lincoln had been a member of the civil rights commission and the ACLU so that I didn't feel comfortable making light around him.

Angelito didn't say much.

I began to wonder if we would have enough for a game. We always needed at least three-on-three. It made for a better afternoon. There didn't appear to be any people in the park this afternoon we could ask to play with us. At that moment we only had five.

"Maybe we won't have a game," I ventured to Lincoln.

"Don't forget Mucho and Tattler. One of them is bound to show. Those two egos couldn't both miss together."

Angelito nodded and so we made our way down the hill. The field on which we played was field number one. It was designed for both soccer and football. On each side were smaller fields that served the same purpose. On Friday afternoons there were always three games going on from two until seven. Our park gets lots of use.

As we made our way down the hill I saw no one. The lowland basin, with its two baseball backstops and five-tiered bleachers, looked as bare as the trees were becoming. There was a "nippiness" to the air, but it wasn't cold. At least not yet.

"Hi Eddie," I yelled when we got to the bottom of the hill.

"Send one over here," cried Lincoln to Billy Washington who had the ball. Billy sent a wobbling pass to the senior member of our group.

Lincoln muffed it, but laughed it off as he generally did by declaring that it took his forty-five-year-old-bones awhile to warm up. Lincoln was like that. Said that a person should bide his time and wait for the opportunities. Who am I to disagree? Lincoln was a lawyer and I didn't even finish college.

Soon the four of us were tossing around the pigskin (or more precisely *cowskin*) and were feeling the sweat begin to flow when we heard the loud car stereo of Jimmy Tattler. Jimmy, who hated any other appellation, was perhaps the richest among our group. I use the superlative guardedly because though Jimmy certainly wanted us all to believe this about him, I'm not altogether sure that this was actually true. What a man wears and what he drives can often be deceiving. Revolving charge plans on credit cards make it easy to become overextended. I never use credit cards.

We were tossing the ball pretty well. It was time to begin the game. But even as we were dividing up, suddenly at the top of our natural green amphitheater stood Mucho Pani and another, unknown man. I don't know why, but we all looked up at the same time. They hadn't called attention to themselves. But for some reason we were all transfixed.

"Have you started yet?" yelled Mucho as he glided easily down the hill. And without waiting for a response he added, "We would have been here sooner, but we tried to get through the south gate. It's closed. Some road work, I guess."

Mucho walked with the confident stride of a man who felt he was among friends. I think Mucho always feels he is among friends – wherever he is. Anyway, as the two approached, Angelito turned away and began to pace off the field. We usually do this as a group after the teams are formed, but the rest of us were still standing there and Angelito wanted to get things going.

"Where'd you pick up that one?" began Jimmy in a needling tone.

I laughed, though no one else did. Jimmy was right that the stranger had a peculiar look about him. He reminded me more of a machine – a computer perhaps – than a being of flesh and bone. Though flesh and bone he had in abundance. He must have outweighed any of the rest of us by forty pounds. I was glad we were playing a friendly game of "touch."

"This is Henry," said Mucho. "He's going to play with us today."

There was a note of authority in Mucho's voice. Mucho was the manager at the supermarket on Capitol Court. He sometimes forgot who he was talking to. I suppose it's easy to mistake your friends for a couple of stock boys.

Everyone except Lincoln and I walked away to help Angelito. It was up to the four of us to choose teams.

I suggested that Eddie, Billy, Lincoln and I stand Angelito, Jimmy, Mucho and Henry. The others agreed except Henry. He scowled.

The first two possessions went all right except that Henry didn't seem to be doing much. He appeared to be studying us. At the time I thought he was trying to get the hang of our style of football. I wouldn't find out until later that I was totally wrong.

The score was one touchdown to none when we had the ball about midfield with a good chance to increase our lead. It was then that Henry declared sharply, "Rule change!"

"What's the matter?" asked Lincoln.

"The defense should be able to use their hands," was his mechanical reply.

"There's nothing against that," said Lincoln, "provided that you don't grab someone and that it doesn't get too rough."

Henry muttered something and the game went on. We had driven down near to the other team's goal when Billy Washington went out for a pass and Lincoln threw him a perfect strike. Billy had it for a touchdown when suddenly Henry sent his hands, as though propelled by pistons, into Billy's back. The play should have been over. Billy was unprepared for the blow and was thrown to the ground.

All of us were stunned except Tattler and Pani who chuckled at Billy's misfortune. I think Tattler is a closet racist.

"What you think you're doing?" cried Billy as he pugnaciously arose. "The play was over. You don't hit a man after he has made a touchdown."

"All I did was 'two-hand-touch.'"

"It was pretty hard for two hand touch. Besides, that was a late hit."

Henry didn't respond but walked down to the other end of the field with his team for the kickoff. Billy was muttering to himself. I was in some confusion. Billy never played roughly at all. He was a finesse player depending upon speed and agility. To change the style of our game would not be to his advantage. But there was more to it. This outsider was coming in and trying to run our game for us. I resented this. I also resented Mucho for bringing us this bore. He made Mucho seem like a decent kind of guy. Still, no one wanted to make a big thing of it, so we went on.

In the next series the other team had gotten halfway down the field when Henry picked up the snap himself and ran right over Lincoln and Billy. Lincoln was knocked over by Henry's shoulder hitting his ribs. Billy had taken the full brunt of Henry head-on.

Billy lay flat on his back. The soft-spoken schoolteacher looked hurt. A bunch of us ran to his aid. But Henry kept us away.

"I'll see to this," he said in a flat voice. There wasn't any great loudness to his speech, but somehow it seemed to carry great authority.

Henry helped Billy to his feet. He only had the wind knocked out of him. None of us did anything. All we did was stand there and watch.

"Billy better play on my team for a while," he concluded.

This seemed like a logical arrangement so we left it at that. We got Jimmy Tattler in the exchange. In the next play Henry gave Billy the ball.

The nearsighted schoolteacher followed Henry's block which flattened me and Jimmy.

I felt something hot and flowing. I had a nosebleed.

"I think this is getting a little rough," said Jimmy.

Billy, who had just made a touchdown, said, "How does it feel being on the other side of it? You seemed to think it was pretty funny when I got it."

"Get screwed, sambo," said Jimmy quietly, but so that Billy could hear.

Henry didn't say anything. He gathered his men and kicked off. The kick was right to Jimmy who got it and was instantly flattened by Billy.

"What in the name of shit are you doing?" yelled Jimmy as he got up hot and ready to punch Washington. "You nearly ripped my $300 Carabinni body suit."

Billy's eyes flashed. He wouldn't have minded laying into Jimmy right there. Then Henry intervened.

"Rule change," proclaimed Henry. "From now on tackling is allowed."

"Just a minute," Lincoln put in. "We play touch here. We've never played tackle."

Henry stepped up to the lawyer. "We're playing tackle now."

"I'm not. I'm leaving." Lincoln turned around to go when Henry stretched out his left arm and grabbed Lincoln by the shoulder and turned him around. The lawyer's eyes showed a fear which I had never seen. He had faced many important cases and had stood up to all odds, but now the threat was physically immediate.

"Let me go. I don't want to play anymore."

"You have to play. The game depends upon your presence." Henry's voice seemed almost to echo. There was a quality to it which reminded you of a loudspeaker system sending out its message to some crowd.

Then Eddie Meyer stepped forward. "You can't do this. If Lincoln wants to go, then so be it. I've had enough of this myself. This isn't football; it's butcher ball." Eddie stood up to Henry. There were two of them in front of this man and his dictatorial output. If only we had all taken that opportunity to rush him just then. We had our chance, but we muffed it. We just watched – myself included.

Henry wheeled and stared at Eddie a moment, and then with a terrible swing, he knocked Eddie's head at the temple with such a force that the stocky foundry worker fell to the ground. Eddie didn't get up. I rushed to Eddie's aid, but Henry told me to get back in my place.

Why hadn't we done something? Even then the six of us could have subdued him. But even Lincoln seemed impressed with what Henry could do if he wanted to. Henry could kill, and none of us wanted to be next.

"The game goes on. We play tackle."

None of us wanted to continue. Even Mucho seemed to lose that air of self-confidence he always tries to effect. But continue we did.

It was with a different feeling that we resumed. Henry was now making more and more changes in the rules. Lincoln whispered to me that we should watch for our chance to jump Henry and so effect our escape.

This seemed like a good idea, but I could not help going over in my mind the fact that we had had the opportunity to jump Henry and we hadn't taken it.

Henry was now making up all the plays. He assigned Mucho and Angelito to tackle Lincoln. When the lawyer had taken several jarring tackles he began to send sharp punches to the bodies of his hunters. After this had occurred three times Angelito sent a fierce blow to Lincoln's jaw. The lawyer went reeling. Angelito didn't stop there. He tackled the former civil rights activist attorney, and pushed Lincoln's face into the dirt. Lincoln fought back.

Jimmy yelled to Lincoln, "Take care of that wetback, Link. It's time we got the garbage out of here anyway." As he said this he looked back to Billy who responded by putting the salesman and his designer athletic costume down to the ground. Mucho went in to help Jimmy against Billy. I didn't like to see two against one so I got in to help Billy.

I'm not sure how long we were on the ground, but it wasn't long. Soon Henry stopped it. We had fought with passion, but for some reason we did not turn our violence against Henry. He had intervened. We obeyed.

"The game must proceed," he said.

We stopped fighting. Billy had a puffy ear and a cut over his left eye. Jimmy was suffering from abdominal pains. Mucho seemed pretty good except for shoulder stiffness. My nose was bleeding again. This time it was broken.

The teams were rearranged again. Lincoln, now without two teeth, was playing alongside Angelito. No one seemed to care. We just kept doing what Henry said.

I looked around hoping someone would come and rescue us. The park is normally very busy. But today it was completely vacant. I hoped someone would come and stop Henry. If only we had acted earlier when we had had the chance.

Now Henry ran every play. We did what he told us to do. I kept waiting, as Lincoln had suggested earlier. But now, none of us were allowed to talk to each other so that organization would be difficult. The only one we could talk to was Henry. I felt he could be stopped, but I couldn't do it alone. I needed help. But how could I get it when everyone was so badly divided? No one was himself anymore.

If only someone would come. We continued with the game. Each of us waited – waited for a way out. In the center of the field was the body of Eddie. It was getting stiff by now. Strange, we all seemed to ignore it. We shut it out. We played the game. We waited, and we played the game.

Afterword: The Politics of Change

Our symphony began by setting out the disparate voices involved with human rights and their traditions. We then transitioned to means of justifying human rights and then proceeded according to the model of normative worldview change and short-term policy solutions particularly related to the principal concerns of the table of embeddedness: level-one basic goods, level-two basic goods, and level-one secondary goods. One needs a vision of how the theory comes-to-be in the world. This is not an easy process. One could approach such a question from the point of view of political dialogue. In Chapter 1 several promising approaches were highlighted along that line. The key ingredient in most accounts of political dialogue is the Overlap and Modification dynamic. This is connected to effecting real change in personal worldview that collectively understood will change both the common body of knowledge as well as the shared community worldview. As was argued earlier, this Overlap and Modification dynamic can take a long time. In the interim, short-term policies are needed to move us in that direction. However, it should also be emphasized that not any direction will do. This book has supported an agency approach that is based on (a) a personhood account via the personal worldview imperative; (b) the argument for the moral status of basic goods (this makes the theory a *natural* theory of human rights); and (c) the table of embeddedness (based on a hierarchical ranking of goods necessary for human agency) that lays out a pattern for political triage in policymaking. In the process of change all three elements must work together.

How does one alter normative beliefs within the personal worldview of a large number of people? Traditionally, philosophers have offered tight logical analysis in order to bring about such a change. Under the quasi-axiomatic model, logical analysts believed that they could achieve a certainty in their results that approached the certainty of mathematics. Certainly, much of the appeal of Single Principle Theories (especially Kant's first formulation of the categorical imperative) seems to be their affinity to closed logical systems and the formal necessity attributed to them. One might be led to the conclusion that if one provides *a justification* within the style of a closed, deductive system, he or she has done enough. Once the reader logically accepts the argument as presented, and has exhausted her rebuttals, then she must accept and act upon the conclusions of such a system.

There is something very reassuring in single principle theories to those enamored of deductive logic. However, it is my contention that such single principle theories leave out the affective goodwill (see Chapter 6). Rather, I would suggest something like the process set out in Chapter 7 concerning the way we accept novel normative theories. There, a general structure of the underlying mechanism is set out; however, the details are likely to vary in individual cases. Application of this mechanism facilitates the presentation in Chapters 8 to 10.

What is essential is that each person undergo the examination individually and then seek out space to engage in the social dialogue that is aimed at Stage One (Consideration and Justification) and aimed at worldview change (as an end goal) and incremental policy change (as a short-term objective). This process has to occur from the bottom up by invoking principles from the top down. Sometimes a society gets lucky. This is when a charismatic leader emerges like Gandhi or King. In most other cases, there needs to be a broad effort by many like the unheralded negotiators who fashioned the Northern Ireland Peace Accord or the many volunteers who worked for civil rights for women. Often the actors are ordinary people. At other times they are politicians (like Anwar Sadat, Menachem Begin, and Jimmy Carter) and sometimes they are religious leaders (like the Dalai Lama and his work for the people of Tibet or John Paul II and his use of the Catholic Church to give space for the restoration of freedom in Poland). Whoever they are, we need a combination of ordinary citizens who recognize what must be done and leaders who will take the risk to move us into the mode of Overlap and Modification in the practical realm of acknowledging and supporting natural human rights at all relevant levels on the table of embeddedness (level-one and level-two Basic Goods and level-one Secondary Goods). We need to do this, desperately. We cannot be content to let the fictional Henry call the rules and set out (according to his autocratic command) what our rights should be. We cannot allow this outcome: "Strange, we all seemed to ignore it. We shut it out. We played the game. We waited, and we played the game."

We all need to take risks to bring the recognition of and the implementation of the natural human rights we all possess. It's a dangerous game, but it there is no other way to live sincerely and authentically.

Glossary

Aspirational perspective on human rights: The perspective that promotes human rights goals that can be achieved without violating principles of human nature or the structural facts about the various communities that populate the world; see also utopian perspective on human rights.

Authenticity: In the context of rights, engaging in a sincere quest via a reliable process that one has consciously and reflectively chosen via rational and emotional good will. This book recommends the structure of the personal worldview imperative as a general guide; see also sincerity.

Common body of knowledge: The background conditions concerning facts and values about the world. Some agents accept these uncritically. The personal worldview imperative assumes a critical evaluation of these background conditions via reliable epistemological criteria.

Communitarianism: The view that individuals should modify their personal inclinations when they come into conflict with community standards (so long as those standards conform to the shared community worldview imperative).

Community worldview: The shared understandings within a micro or macro community that are expressed via the common body of knowledge. See also shared community worldview imperative.

Conventional human rights: The view that human rights are justified and achieve their ontological status via one of the versions of ethical anti-realism—especially ethical noncognitivism, ethical intuitionism, and contractarianism.

Eco-community worldview imperative: The command that each agent must educate herself about the proximate natural world in which she lives relating to her agency within this ecosystem: (a) what her natural place in this order is vis-à-vis her personal agency; (b) how her natural place (vis-à-vis her personal agency) may have changed in recent history; (c) how her social community's activities have altered the constitution of the natural order and how this has effected community agency; (d) the short-term and long-term effects of those changes vis-à-vis agency; and (e) what needs to be done to maintain the natural order in the short and long term so that the ecosystem might remain vibrant.

Emergent human rights: Particular human rights that exist only when there is a society that recognizes that right; see also conventional human rights.

Extended communities: Communities that extend beyond the nation-state to embrace peoples and nature around the world; see also extended community worldview imperative.

Extended community worldview imperative: The command that each agent must educate himself and others as much as he is able about the peoples of the world – their access to the basic goods of agency, their essential commonly held cultural values, and their governmental and institutional structures – in order that he might create a worldview that includes those of other nations so that individually and collectively the agent might accept the duties that ensue from those peoples' legitimate rights claims, and to act accordingly within what is aspirationally possible.

Extended eco-community worldview imperative: The command that each agent must educate herself about the world's biomes: freshwater, saltwater, arid regions, forests, prairies and grassland, tundra, and arctic regions. This education should be ongoing and should include how the relative stability and natural sustainability is faring at various points in time. This knowledge will entail a factual valuing that also leads to an aesthetic valuing. Since all people seek to protect what they value, this extended community membership will ground a duty to protect the global biomes according to what is aspirationally possible.

Hard communitarianism: A form in which the community is the primary unit. It exists naturally. The individuals that make up the community have the right to find out how they can successfully contribute to the mission of the natural unit (the community). To move outside the natural unit by any individual is to undermine the mission of the community (regardless of the normative mission of the community) and has to be suppressed. The sovereign is the community.

Hard individualism: A form of liberalism in which the individual, alone, is the primary unit. It exists naturally. A community only exists at the permission of the individuals. The size of the community and its influence should be as minimal as possible. The sovereign is the individual, separately.

Human rights: Classified according to the ground of their justification that reveals the state of their ontology: conventional (anti-realist) or natural (realist).

Individual (personal) worldview: The structure of personal consciousness as it pertains to what we hold to be factual and normatively true about the world; see also personal worldview imperative.

Legal rules: Classified by type: first-order rule covers the rule-making function. It concerns the process of making rules in the society. A second-order rule concerns the rules of recognition, rules of change, and rules of adjudication. Meta-foundational rules concern justification that the legislators or sovereign uses to give authority (second-order rule recognition) to the rules that are set out. This justification can be an abstract moral principle or an appeal to a historical community worldview with its attendant institutions and the procedures that can bring about rational understanding and consensual acceptance of first-order rules in the given domain (e.g., the state or the world). In either case, it is assumed that meta-foundational rules exhibit more authority than first- or second-order rules. This is because meta-foundational rules condition first- and second-order rules and not vice versa. Observance must be maintained via specified sanctions.

Legal system: Consists of governmental orders backed up by threats. The basis of the orders or legal rules refers to first- and second-order legal rules. The grounding of the second-order rule recognition is the meta-foundational rules. The threats should be proportional to the gravity of the obligation incurred.

Macro communities: Communities of 501 people or more. The governing principle is either democratic or autocratic. In the democratic form, the sovereign is the collection of all the individual people. The sovereign selects individuals to represent their interest in governing. In autocracy, the sovereign is the ruler who acts as he or she sees fit.

Micro communities: Communities of 500 or fewer people who govern by the principle of the committee of the whole (in cases of democracy). Large units subsume smaller units ascending to the nation-state; see also extended communities.

Natural communities: Communities consisting of all living organisms within some given geographical boundary condition.

Natural human rights: Human rights that are properly justified from a moral realist perspective—either via approaches grounded proximately in some objective discoverable fact in nature or via a rationally apprehended existence of some non-natural property. The complementary position is conventional human rights that are justified from a moral anti-realist perspective.

Natural law perspective: Background conditions that validate understanding the human condition (considered collectively and normatively) and nature (considered as a realm separate from human agreement).

Novel normative theories, how we confront them: Occurring in three stages: Stage One: Overview and Rational Justification (a. considering the theory, and b. justifying the theory); Stage Two: Dialectical Understanding through Personal Worldview Examination (a. reflecting on our own worldview, and b. comparing our worldview to the new theory); Stage Three: Resolution and Change.

Objective and subjective senses of natural law/rights: Natural law/rights viewed as adjectives in the objective sense: "It is right of me to act in this way"; opposed to the *subjective* sense in which 'right' becomes a noun, "It is my right to act this way" (cf. Henrik Syse, *Natural Law, Religion, and Rights*). Under the objective sense, citizens have the right to recognize, decide, and act upon the law or not (to their peril).

Ontology of ethical/political/legal natural law: Assumes that (a) the natural law exists as *other* that abides in our own natural realm (the realist naturalism assumption); (b) the natural law exists because of *another* existent entity in a different realm that is immanent with this world (the realist non-natural assumption).

Ontology of the natural law as science perspective: Assumes a mechanical approach consistent with "when the gods leave." This means that those laws exist as *other* that abides in our own realm (the realist assumption).

Orders of the political process: A primary judgment (about what is right or wrong) and a secondary judgment (about what is possible to bring about what is right within some social/political setting). Both are necessary to bring about aspirational ends; see also novel normative theories, how we confront them.

Personal worldview imperative: Command that all people must develop a single comprehensive and internally coherent worldview that is good and that we strive to act out in our daily lives; see also individual worldview.

Scientific revolution on human rights: A movement away from the teleological approach (final causes) to make the inquiry more empirically concrete (efficient causes).

Shared community worldview imperative: Command that each agent must contribute to a common body of knowledge that supports the creation of a shared community worldview (that is itself complete, coherent, and good) through which social institutions and their resulting policies might flourish within the constraints of the essential core commonly held values (ethics, aesthetics, and religion).

Sincerity: Practiced by someone who puts forth an individual commitment toward using his highest capacities to examine the questions raised concerning his understanding of facts and commitment to values in his life via the personal worldview imperative; see also authenticity.

Single principle moral theories: "Top-down" theories that argue for a supreme principle of morality. Application of most single principle theories is by deductive subsumption so that the outcomes acquire logical necessity. A well-known proponent of a single principle moral theory is Immanuel Kant.

Soft individualism/communitarianism: Embracing both the personal worldview imperative and the shared community worldview imperative. It sees both the individual and the community as socially bound together as a natural unit with each dialectically informing upon the other and this amalgam is the sovereign.

The two foci of natural law: (a) Ethical/political/legal and (b) scientific (natural philosophy).

Two perspectives of natural law in the ancient, medieval, and modern realms: The ethical/political/legal approach versus the natural philosophy approach.

Utopian perspective on human rights: A set of prescriptions that is entirely unworkable given the facts of human nature and cultures living in the world; see also aspirational perspective on human rights.

Worldview: Can be parsed into personal and community. The personal worldview consists in one's understanding of the facts and values about the world. It is chosen by the agent against the background of the dominant common body of knowledge. The community worldview comes in several strains: human communities (consisting of *Homo sapiens* and their understanding about the facts and values that inhere in the community via the common body of knowledge), and natural communities (consisting in all living fauna and flora within a given geographical area); the worldview here is an anthropocentric, scientific understanding of this community and an action component of valuation and protection; see also eco-community worldview imperative, extended community worldview imperative, extended eco-community worldview imperative, personal worldview imperative, and shared community worldview imperative.

Bibliography

Abdelhay, Nawaf. "The Arab Uprising 2011: New Media in the Hands of a New Generation in North Africa." *Aslib Proceedings: New Information Perspectives* 64.5 (2012): 529–539.

Ageton, S. S. *Sexual Assault among Adolescents*. Lexington, MA: Lexington Press, 1983.

Akerlund, Erik. "Suárez's Ideas on Natural Law in the Light of His Philosophical Anthropology and Moral Psychology," in Virpi Mäkin, ed., *The Nature of Rights: Moral and Political Aspects of Rights in Late Medieval and Early Modern Philosophy* (Helsinki: Philosophical Society of Finland, 2010): 165–196.

Althusser, Louis. "Ideology and Ideological State Apparatuses," in Louis Althusser, *Lenin and Philosophy, and Other Essays*. New York: Monthly Review Press, 1971: 127–186.

Amenta, Edwin, and Michael Young. "Democratic States and Social Movements: Theoretical Arguments and Hypotheses." *Social Problems* 46 (1999): 153–172.

Amnesty International. *Saudi Arabia: Dissent Voices Stifled in the Eastern Province*. London: Amnesty International Publications, 2012.

The Spring that Never Blossomed: Freedoms Suppressed in Azerbaijan. London: Amnesty International Publications, 2011.

Stifling Dissent: Restrictions on the Rights to Freedom of Expression and Peaceful Assembly in Uganda. London: Amnesty International Publications, 2011.

Angle Stephen C. *Human Rights and Chinese Thought*. Cambridge: Cambridge University Press, 2002.

Sagehood: The Contemporary Significance of Neo-Confucian Philosophy. Oxford: Oxford University Press, 2012.

Angle, Stephen C., and Marina Svensson. *The Chinese Human Rights Reader*. London: M.E. Sharpe, 2000.

Annas, George J. "The Emerging Stowaway: Patient's Rights in the 1980's," in Bart Gruzalski and Carl Nelson, eds., *Value Conflict in Health Care Delivery*. Cambridge, MA: Ballinger, 1982: 89–100.

Anonyma. *Eine Frau in Berlin: Tagebuchaufzeichnungen vom 20 April bis zum 22 Juni 1945*. Frankfurt: Eichborn, 2003.

Aquinas, Thomas. *Summa Theologica*. Rome: Typographia Forzani, 1894.

Arendt, Hannah. *The Origins of Totalitarianism*. New York: Harcourt, Brace, Jovanovich, 1973 [1951].

Aristotle. *Ethica Nicomachea*, ed. I. Bywater. Oxford: Clarendon Press, 1920 [1894].

"On Interpretation" translated by E. M. Edghill in *The Works of Aristotle*, ed. W. D. Ross and J. A. Smith. Oxford: Oxford University Press, 1928.

Categoriae et Liber de Interpretatione, ed. L. Minio-Paluello. Oxford: Clarendon Press, 1936.

Physica, ed. W. D. Ross. Oxford: Clarendon Press, 1956.

Metaphysica, ed. Werner Jaeger. Oxford: Clarendon Press, 1957.

Arnim, Hans von. *Stoicorum Veterum Fragmenta in Four Volumes*. Leipzig: Teubner, 1903–1924.

Asmis, Elizabeth. "Cicero on Natural Law and the Laws of the State." *Antiquity* 27.1 (2008): 1–33.

Audi, Robert. *Epistemology: A Contemporary Introduction to the Theory of Knowledge*. New York: Routledge, 2011.

Augustine of Hippo, Saint, in Jacques Paul Migne, ed., *Patrologia Latina*, vol. 35. Paris: Garnieri Fratres,1844–1855.

Aung-Thwin, Maureen. "Freedom of Expression around the World: Burma." *World Literature Today* 83.6 (2009): 54–62.

Aurelius, Marcus Aurelius. *Meditations*, trans. Robin Hard. New York: Oxford University Press, 2011.

Austin, John. *The Province of Jurisprudence Determined*, 5th ed. vol. 2, ed. Robert Campbell. London: John Murray, 1885.

Baber, H. E. "Worlds, Capabilities and Well-Being." *Ethical Theory and Moral Practice* 13.4 (2010): 377–392.

Baier, Annette. "What Emotions Are About." *Philosophical Perspectives* 4 (1990): 1–29.

Moral Prejudices: Essays on Ethics. Cambridge, MA: Harvard University Press, 1995.

Baker, Jean H. *Sisters: The Lives of America's Suffragists*. New York: Hill and Wang, 2006.

Balthazart, Jacques. *The Biology of Homosexuality*. Oxford: Oxford University Press, 2012.

Barash, David P. "The Evolutionary Mystery of Homosexuality." *Chronicle of Higher Education* (November 19, 2012): B4–5.

Barry, Kathleen Lois. *Unmaking War, Remaking Men: How Empathy Can Reshape Our Politics, Our Soldiers, and Ourselves*. Gilbert, AZ: Phoenix Rising Press, 2010.

Bartol, C. R. *Criminal Behavior: A Psychosocial Approach*, 3rd ed. New York: Simon and Schuster, 1991.

Bassford, H. A. "The Justification of Medical Paternalism." *Social Science and Medicine* 16.6 (1982): 731–739.

Beagon, M. *Roman Nature*. Oxford: Oxford University Press, 1992.

Beard, Charles. *Martin Luther and the Reformation in Germany until the Close of the Diet of Worms*. Cornell, NY: Cornell University Press, 2009 [1889].

Beauchamp, Tom L. "The Promise of the Beneficence Model for Medical Ethics." *Journal of Contemporary Health Law and Policy* 6 (Spring, 1990): 145–155.

Beauvoir, Simone de. *The Second Sex*, trans. and ed. H. M. Parshley. New York: Bantam, 1952.

Beevoir, Antony. *The Fall of Berlin 1945*. New York: Viking, 2002.

Behuniak, James Jr. "Naturalizing Mencius." *Philosophy East and West* 61.3 (2011): 492–515.

Beitz, Charles. *The Idea of Human Rights*. Oxford: Oxford University Press, 2009.

Bennett, Jonathan. "The Conscience of Huckleberry Finn." *Philosophy* 49 (1974): 123–134.

Bentham, Jeremy. "Nonsense on Stilts," in P. Schofield, C. Pease-Watkin, and C. Blamires, eds., *Jeremy Bentham: Rights, Representation and Reform*, in *The Collected Works of Jeremy Bentham*. Oxford: Clarendon Press, 2003.

Berger, J. "Paternalistic Assumptions and a Purported Duty to Deceive." *American Journal of Bioethics* 9.12 (2009): 20–21.

Berges, Sandrine. "Why the Capability Approach Is Justified." *Journal of Applied Philosophy* 24.1 (2007): 16–25.

Berlin, Isaiah. *Four Essays on Liberty*. Oxford: Oxford University Press, 1969.

Bernecker, Sven. "Davidson on First-Person Authority and Externalism." *Inquiry: An Interdisciplinary Journal of Philosophy* 39.1 (1996): 121–139.

Beyleveld, Deryck. *The Dialectical Necessity of Morality: An Analysis and Defense of the Principle of Generic Consistency*. Chicago: University of Chicago Press, 1992.

Blackburn, Simon. *Spreading the Word*. Oxford: Oxford University Press, 1984.

"How to Be an Ethical Antirealist." *Midwest Studies in Philosophy* 12 (1988): 361–375.

Essays in Quasi-Realism. New York: Oxford University Press, 1993.

Ruling Passions. Oxford: Oxford University Press, 1998.

"Anti-Realist Expressivism and Quasi-Realism," in David Copp, ed., *The Oxford Handbook of Ethical Theory*. New York: Oxford University Press, 2006: 146–162.

Bodroghkozy, Aniko. *Equal Time: Television and the Civil Rights Movement*. Urbana, IL: University of Illinois Press, 2012.

Boswell, John. *Christianity, Social Tolerance, and Homosexuality; Gay People in Western Europe from the Christian Era to the Fourteenth Century*, 8th ed. Chicago: University of Chicago Press, 2005.

Boyd, Richard. "On the Current Status of Scientific Realism." *Erkenntnis* 19 (1983): 45–90.

Boylan, Michael. "Seneca and Moral Rights." *New Scholasticism* 53.3 (1979): 362–374.

"Henry More and the Spirit of Nature." *Journal of the History of Philosophy* 18.4 (1980): 395–405.

Method and Practice in Aristotle's Biology. Lanham, MD: Rowman and Littlefield/UPA, 1983.

"Galen's Conception Theory." *Journal of the History of Biology* 19.1 (1986): 44–77.

"The Abortion Debate in the 21st Century," in Michael Boylan, ed., *Medical Ethics*. Upper Saddle River, NJ: Prentice Hall, 2000: 289–304 (rpt. Wiley-Blackwell, 2013).

"Worldview and the Value-Duty Link," in Michael Boylan, ed., *Environmental Ethics*. Upper Saddle River, NJ: Prentice Hall, 2001: 180–196 (rpt. Wiley-Blackwell, 2013).

"Affirmative Action: Strategies for the Future." *Journal of Social Philosophy* 33.1 (2002): 117–130.

"Aristotle's Biology." *Internet Encyclopedia of Philosophy*. 2004. www.iep.utm.edu/.

"Galen." *Internet Encyclopedia of Philosophy*. 2004. www.iep.utm.edu/.

"Hippocrates." *Internet Encyclopedia of Philosophy*. 2004. www.iep.utm.edu/.

A Just Society. Lanham, MD: Rowman and Littlefield, 2004.

"Michael Oakeshott," in Donald M. Borchert, ed., *Encyclopedia of Philosophy*, 2nd ed. Farmington Hills, MI: Macmillan, 2006.

"Niccolo Machiavelli," in Donald M. Borchert, ed., *Encyclopedia of Philosophy*, 2nd ed. Farmington Hills, MI: Macmillan, 2006.

"Galen on the Blood, Pulse, and Arteries." *Journal of the History of Biology* 40.2 (2007): 207–230.

The Good, the True, and the Beautiful. London: Continuum, 2008.

"Medical Pharmaceuticals and Distributive Justice." *Cambridge Quarterly of Healthcare Ethics* 17.1 (Winter, 2008): 32–46.

Basic Ethics, 2nd ed. Upper Saddle River, NJ: Prentice-Hall, 2009.

"A Reply to My Colleagues," in John-Stewart Gordon, ed., *Morality and Justice: Reading Boylan's "A Just Society."* Lanham, MD: Lexington Books, 2009: 179–220.

Critical Inquiry: The Process of Argument. Boulder, CO: Westview, 2010.

"Duties to Children," in Michael Boylan, ed., *Morality and Global Justice*. Boulder, CO: Westview, 2011: 385–404.

Morality and Global Justice. Boulder, CO: Westview, 2011.

"Ethical Limitations on Scientific Research," in Simonna Giordano, John Coggon, and Marco Cappato, eds., *Scientific Freedom*. London: Bloomsbury, 2012: 149–161.

"The Moral Right to Healthcare—Part Two," in Michael Boylan, ed., *Medical Ethics*, 2nd ed. Oxford: Wiley-Blackwell, 2013.

"The Self in Context: A Grounding for Environmentalism" in Michael Boylan, ed., *Environmental Ethics*, 2nd ed. Oxford: Wiley-Blackwell, 2013.

The Origins of Ancient Greek Science: A Philosophical Study of Blood. Forthcoming. London: Routledge.

Boylan, Michael, ed. *Gewirth: Critical Essays on Action, Rationality and Community*. Lanham, MD: Rowman and Littlefield, 1999.

ed. *The Morality and Global Justice Reader*. Boulder, CO: Westview, 2011.

ed. *Environmental Ethics*, 2nd ed. Oxford: Wiley-Blackwell, 2013.

Boylan, Michael, and Alan Gewirth. "Marsilius of Padua," in Donald M. Borchert, ed., *Encyclopedia of Philosophy*, 2nd ed. Farmington Hills, MI: Macmillan, 2006.

Brandt, Richard. *Ethical Theory*. Englewood Cliffs, NJ: Prentice Hall, 1959.

Brett, Annabel S. *Liberty, Right, and Nature: Individual Rights in Later Scholastic Thought*. Cambridge: Cambridge University Press, 1997.

Bridgman, Percy. "The Operational Character of Scientific Concepts," in Percy Bridgman, *The Logic of Modern Physics*. London: Macmillan, 1955: 1–32.

Broverman, Neal. "Fighting Back in Brazil." *Advocate*. 1065 (2013): 15.

Brownmiller, Susan. *Against Our Will: Men, Women, and Rape*. New York: Penguin, 1976.

Buchanan, Alan. "Liberalism and Group Rights," in J. L. Coleman and A. Buchanan, eds., *In Harm's Way: Essays in Honor of Joel Feinberg*. Cambridge: Cambridge University Press, 1994: 1–15.

Buchanan, D. R. "Autonomy, Paternalism, and Justice: Ethical Priorities in Public Health." *American Journal of Public Health* 98.1 (2008): 15–21.

Buchler, Justus. *The Philosophical Writings of Pierce*. New York: Dover, 1955.

Bullard, Sara. *Free at Last: A History of the Civil Rights Movement and Those Who Died in the Struggle*. Oxford: Oxford University Press, 1994.

Burgers, J. H. "The Road to San Francisco: The Revival of the Human Rights Idea in the Twentieth Century." *Human Rights Quarterly* 14 (1992): 447–477.

Cantor, Chris, and John Price. "Traumatic Entrapment, Appeasement, and Complex Post-Traumatic Stress Disorder." *Australian and New Zealand Journal of Psychiatry* 41.5 (2007): 377–384.

Capps, John. "Dewey, Quine, and Pragmatic Naturalized Epistemology." *Transactions of the Charles S. Peirce Society* 32.4 (1996): 634–668.

Card, Claudia. "Rape as a Weapon of War." *Hypatia* 11.4 (Fall 1996): 5–18.

Carnap, Rudolf. "Empiricism, Semantics, and Ontology," in Rudolf Carnap, *Meaning and Necessity*, enlarged ed. Chicago: University of Chicago Press, 1956: 205–221.

Carothers, B. J., and H. T. Reis. "Men and Women Are from Earth: Examining the Latent Structure of Gender." *Journal of Personality and Social Psychology* 104.2 (2013): 385–407.

Carson, Ben, and Cecil Murphy. *Gifted Hands*. Grand Rapids, MI: Zondervan, 2011.

Chamie, Joseph, and Barry Mirkin. "Same-Sex Marriage: A New Social Phenomenon." *Population and Development Review* 37.3 (2011): 529–551.

Chan, Wing-tsit Chan, trans. *A Sourcebook in Chinese Philosophy*. Princeton, NJ: Princeton University Press, 1963.

Chang, Carsun. *The Development of Neo-Confucian Thought*, 2 vols. New Haven, CT: College and University Press, 1963.

Changing Laws, Changing Minds: Challenging Homophobic and Transphobic Hate Crimes in Bulgaria. New York: Amnesty International Publications, 2012.

Childress, James F. *Who Should Decide? Paternalism in Health Care*. Oxford: Oxford University Press, 1982.

Childress, James F., and Mark Siegler. "Metaphors and Models of Doctor-Patient Relationships: Their Implications for Autonomy." *Theoretical Medicine* 5 (1984): 17–30.

"China Asserts Sovereign and Other Rights to Control Internet." *Tibetan Review: The Monthly Magazine on All Aspects of Tibet* 45.7 (2010): 33–34.

Chomsky, Noam. *New World of Indigenous Resistance.* San Francisco: City Lights, 2010.

Christie, Niall. *Noble Ideals and Bloody Realities: Warfare in the Middle Ages (History of Warfare,* vol. 37). Leiden: Brill, 2001.

Christofides, Emily, Amy Muise, and Desmarais Serge. "Information, Disclosure and Control and Facebook." *Cyberpsychology and Behavior* 12.3 (2009): 341–345.

Chun, J. W., H. J. Park, and J. J. Kim. "Common and Differential Brain Responses in Men and Women to Non-Verbal Emotional Vocalizations by the Same and Opposite Sex." *Neuroscience Letters* 515.2 (2012): 157–161.

Churchill, Robert Paul. *Human Rights and Global Diversity.* Upper Saddle River, NJ: Prentice Hall, 2006.

CIA World Factbook. New York: Skyhorse Publishing, 2013.

Cicero. *De re Publica and De Legibus,* ed. and trans. Clinton Walker Keyes. Cambridge, MA: Harvard University Press, 1928.

Claassen, Rutger. "Making Capability Lists: Philosophy versus Democracy." *Political Studies* 59.3 (2011): 491–508.

Clarke, Alan W. *Rendition to Torture. Genocide, Political Violence, and Human Rights.* New Brunswick, NJ: Rutgers University Press, 2012.

Cmiel, Kenneth. "The Recent History of Human Rights." *American Historical Review* 109.1 (2004): 117–135.

Cochran, William G., et al. *Statistical Problems of the Kinsey Report on Sexual Behavior in the Human Male; A Report of the American Statistical Association, Committee to Advise the National Research Council, Committee for Research in Problems of Sex.* Washington, DC: American Statistical Association, 1954.

Cohen, Jean. "Whose Sovereignty? Empire v. International Law." *Ethics and International Affairs* 18.3 (2004): 1–24.

Coleman, Lee. *The Reign of Error.* Boston: Beacon Press, 1984.

Confucius. *Analects,* trans. D. C. Lau. New York: Penguin Books, 1979.

  Analects, trans. Roger T. Ames and Henry Rosemont Jr. New York: Ballantine Books, 1998.

  Analects, trans. William Cheung. Hong Kong: Confucian Publishing, 1999.

  Analects, trans. Arthur Waley. New York: Everyman's Library, 2000.

  Analects. trans. Edward Slingerland. Indianapolis, IN: Hackett, 2003.

Copernicus, Nicolaus. *De revolutionibus orbium coelestium.* Nurenberg: Johannes Petreius, 1543.

Coulmas, Florian, ed. *Linguistic Minorities and Literacy: Language Policy in Developing Countries.* New York: Mouton, 1984.

The Council on Foreign Relations. *The 2010 Annual Report.* New York: Council on Foreign Relations, 2010.

Cranston, Maurice. "Human Rights, Real and Supposed," in Morton E. Winston, ed., *The Philosophy of Human Rights.* Belmont, CA: Wadsworth, 1989.

"The Creation Hymn," in *Rig Vedas,* trans. Wendy Doniger. New York: Penguin, 2005.

Creuzer, F., and G. H. Moser, eds. *M. Tulli Ciceronis de legibus libri tres, cum Adriani Turnebi commentario ejusdemque apologia et ominum eruditorum notis.* Frankfort: E. Typ. Broeneriano, 1824.

Crompton, Louis. *Homosexuality and Civilization.* Cambridge, MA: Harvard University Press, 2006.

Cummiskey, David. *Kantian Consequentialism.* Oxford: Oxford University Press, 1996.

Dancy, Jonathan. *Ethics without Principles.* Oxford: Clarendon, 2006.

Davidson, Donald. *Essays on Actions and Events.* Oxford: Clarendon Press, 1980.

Davies, James. "The J-Curve of Rising and Declining Satisfaction as Cause of Some Great Revolutions and a Contained Rebellion," in H. D. Graham and Ted Robert Gurr, eds., *Violence in America.* New York: Praeger, 1969: 690–730.

Deacon, Robert. "Human Rights as Imperialism." *Theoria* 50.102 (2003): 126–138.

De Bary, William Theodore. *Neo Confucian Orthodoxy and the Learning of the Mind-and-Heart.* New York: Columbia University Press, 1981.

    The Message of the Mind in Neo-Confucianism. New York: Columbia University Press, 1989.

    Learning for One's Self: Essays on the Individual in Neo-Confucian Thought. New York: Columbia University Press, 1991.

De Bary, William Theodore, and Irene Bloom, eds. *Principle and Practicality: Essays in Neo-Confucian Practicality.* New York: Columbia University Press, 1979.

de Vivo, Filippo. *Information and Communication in Venice: Rethinking Early Modern Politics.* Oxford: Oxford University Press, 2009.

Diamond, Jared. *Guns, Germs, and Steel: The Fates of Human Societies.* New York: Norton, 2005.

Diamond Sutra, trans. A. F. Price. Boston: Shambhala rpt. 2005 [1974].

Diaz, Rodolfo. "From Lambs to Lions: Self-Liberation and Social Media in Egypt." *Harvard International Review* 33.1 (2011): 6–7.

Dierenfield, Bruce J. *The Civil Rights Movement,* rev. ed. Boston: Longman, 2008.

Dodge, K. A., J. E. Bates, and G. S. Pettit. "Mechanisms in the Cycle of Violence." *Science* 250 (1990): 1678–1683.

Dogan, Aysel. "Confirmation of Scientific Hypotheses as Relations." *Journal for General Philosophy of Science* 36.2 (2005): 243–259.

Donnelly, Jack. "Recent Trends in U.N. Human Rights Activity: Description and Polemic." *International Organization* 35 (Autumn, 1981): 633–655.

    Universal Human Rights: In Theory and Practice. Ithaca, NY: Cornell University Press, 2003.

Dubois, Ellen Carol. *Feminism and Suffrage: The Emergence of an Independent Women's Movement in America 1848–1869.* Ithaca, NY: Cornell University Press, 1999.

Dumont, Louis. *Essays on Individualism.* Chicago: University of Chicago Press, 1992.

Dunlap, Riley E., and Aaron M. McCright. "Climate Change Denial: Sources, Actors, and Strategies," in Constance Lever-Tracy, ed., *Routledge Handbook on Climate Change and Society.* New York: Routledge, 2011: 240–259.

Düwell, Marcus. "On the Possibility of a Hierarchy of Moral Goods," in John-Stewart Gordon, ed., *Morality and Justice: Reading Boylan's A Just Society.* Lanham, MD: Lexington Books, 2009: 71–80.

Dworkin, Gerald. *The Theory and Practice of Autonomy.* Cambridge: Cambridge University Press, 1988.

Dyck, A. R. *A Commentary on Cicero, De legibus.* Ann Arbor: University of Michigan Press, 2004.

Eilperin, Juliet. "Fewer Americans Believe in Global Warming, Poll Shows." *Washington Post.* November 25, 2009. http://www.washingtonpost.com/wp-dyn/content/article/2009/11/24/AR2009112402989.html (last accessed February 7, 2014).

Eldredge, N., and S. Gould. *The Units of Evolution: Essays on the Nature of Species.* Cambridge, MA: MIT Press, 1992.

Elster, Jon. *Alchemies of the Mind: Rationality and the Emotions.* Cambridge: Cambridge University Press, 1999.

Etzioni, Amitai. *Rights and the Common Good: The Communitarian Perspective.* Belmont, CA: Wadsworth, 1994.

  The New Golden Rule. New York: Basic Books, 1998.

Etzioni, Amitai, ed. *The Essential Communitarian Reader.* Lanham, MD: Rowman and Littlefield, 1998.

Fahim, Kareem. "Slap to a Man's Pride Set Off Tumult in Tunisia." *New York Times* (January 21, 2011): A-2.

Farr, Kathryn. "Extreme War Rape in Today's Civil-War-Torn States: A Contextual and Comparative Analysis." *Bender Issues* 26 (2009): 1–41.

Feierabend, Ivo K., and Rosaline L. Feierabend. "Aggressive Behaviors within Politics, 1948–1960: A Cross-National Study." *Journal of Conflict Resolution* 10 (1962): 249–271.

Feki, Shereen El. *Sex and the Citadel: Intimate Life in a Changing Arab World.* Westport, CT: Pantheon, 2013.

Feyerabend, Paul. *Against Method.* New York: Verso, 1975.

Fine, Arthur. "The Natural Ontological Attitude," in L. Leplin, ed., *Scientific Realism.* Berkeley: University of California Press, 1984: 83–107.

Finnis, John. *Natural Law and Natural Rights.* Oxford: Clarendon Press, 1980.

Flanders, Laura. "Rwanda's Living Women Speak: Human Rights Watch—Rwanda's Living Casualties," in Anne Llewellyn Barstow, ed., *War's Dirty Secret: Rape, Prostitution and other Crimes against Women.* Cleveland: Pilgrim Press, 2000: 95–100.

Fletcher, Holly Berkeley. *Gender and the American Temperance Movement of the Nineteenth Century.* London: Routledge, 2007.

Fossier, Robert, ed., and Sarah Hanburg-Tenison, trans. *The Cambridge History of the Middle Ages: Volume III: 1250–1520.* Cambridge: Cambridge University Press, 1986.

Foucault, Michel. *Les Mots et les Choses.* Paris: Gallaimard, 1966.

  "The Archeology of Knowledge," in *The Archeology of Knowledge and The Discourse on Language*, trans. A. M. Sheridan Smith. New York: Pantheon, 1972.

  "What Is an Author?," trans. Josué Harari, in David H. Richter, ed., *The Classical Tradition*, 3rd ed. Boston: Bedford/St. Martins, 2007: 904–914.

Fraasen, Bas van. "To Save the Phenomena," *Journal of Philosophy* 73.18 (1976): 623–632.

Francisco, Ronald A. "After the Massacre: Mobilization in the Wake of Harsh Repression." *Mobilization: An International Quarterly* 9 (2005): 107–126.

Franco, Paul. "Michael Oakeshott as Liberal Theorist." *Political Theory* 18.3 (1990): 411–436.

Frankfurt, Henry. "Meaning, Truth, and Pragmatism." *Philosophical Quarterly* 10 (1960): 171–176.

French, R. *Ancient Natural History.* New York: Routledge, 1994.

Freud, Sigmund. *Project for a Scientific Psychology,* vol. 1 of *Standard Edition of the Psychological Works,* ed. and trans. James Strachey. London: Hogarth Press, 1895.

Fulsom, Don. *Nixon's Darkest Secrets.* New York: St. Martins, 2012.

Gates, Gary J. "How Many People are Lesbian, Gay, Bisexual or Transgender?" Los Angeles: Lilliams Institute, UCLA School of Law, April 2011: 1–8.

Gerson, Jean. *De vita spirituali animae in Oeuvres completes,* ed. P. Glorieuvx, vol. 3. Paris: Palémon Glorieux, 1965.

Gewirth, Alan. *Reason and Morality.* Chicago: University of Chicago Press, 1978.

The Community of Rights. Chicago: University of Chicago Press, 1996.

Self-fulfillment. Princeton, NJ: Princeton University Press, 1998.

Gibbard, Allan. *Wise Choices, Apt Feelings: A Theory of Normative Judgment.* Cambridge, MA: Harvard University Press, 1990.

Thinking How to Live. Cambridge, MA: Harvard University Press, 2008.

Gill, Emily R. *An Argument for Same-Sex Marriage: Religious Freedom, Sexual Freedom, and Public Expressions of Civic Equality.* Washington, DC: Georgetown University Press, 2012.

Giordano, Simona. "Ethics of Management of Gender Atypical Organization in Children and Adolescents," in Michael Boylan, ed., *International Public Health Policy and Ethics.* Dordrecht: Springer, 2008: 249–272.

Giradet, K. M. *Die Ordnung der Welt: Ein Beitrag zur philosophischen und politischen Interpretation von Ciceros Schrift De legibus.* Wiesbaden: Franz Steiner, 1983.

Glendon, Mary Ann. *A World Made New: Eleanor Roosevelt and the Universal Declaration of Human Rights.* New York: Random House, 2002.

Gordon, John-Stewart, ed. *Morality and Justice: Reading Boylan's A Just Society.* Lanham, MD: Lexington Books, 2009.

"On Justice," in John-Stewart Gordon, ed., *Morality and Justice: Reading Boylan's A Just Society.* Lanham, MD: Lexington, 2009: 121–133.

Gramsci, Antonio. *Selections from the Prison Notebooks,* trans. Quintin Hoare and Geoffrey Nowell Smith. London: Lawrence and Wishart, 1971.

Gray, Eliza. "Transitions." *New Republic* 242.10 (2011): 10–18.

Greenspan, Patricia. *Emotions and Reasons: An Inquiry into Emotional Justification.* New York: Routledge, Chapman and Hall, 1988.

Practical Guilt: Moral Dilemmas, Emotions and Social Norms. New York: Oxford University Press, 1995.

"Emotional Strategies and Rationality." *Ethics* 110 (2000): 469–487.

Grene, David, and Richard Lattimore, trans. *Antigone.* Chicago: University of Chicago Press, 1954.

Grenoble, Lenore A., and Lindsay J. Whaley, eds. *Endangered Languages: Language Loss and Community Response.* Cambridge: Cambridge University Press, 1998.

Griffin, James. *On Human Rights.* Oxford: Oxford University Press, 2008.

Grimshaw, Patricia, and Andrew May, eds. *Missionaries, Indigenous Peoples and Cultural Exchange.* Eastbourne, UK: Sussex Academic Press, 2010.

Groth, A. N. *Men Who Rape: The Psychology of the Offender.* New York: Plenum, 1979.

Grotius, Hugo. *De jure belli et pacis,* Prolegommena, 2 vols., trans. Francis W. Kelsey et al. Oxford: Oxford University Press, 1925.

Gurr, Ted Robert. *Why Men Rebel.* Princeton, NJ: Princeton University Press, 1970.

Habermas, Jurgen. *On Pragmatics of Communication.* Cambridge, MA: MIT Press, 2000.

Hall, Stuart. "The Local and the Global: Globalization and Ethnicity," in Anthony King, ed., *Globalization and the World System: Contemporary Conditions for the Representation of Identity.* Binghamton, NY: Macmillan, 1991: 19–39.

Hampton, Harry, Steve Fayer, and Sarah Flynn. *Voices of Freedom.* New York: Bantam, 1991.

Hart, H. L. A. "Are There Any Natural Rights?" *Philosophical Review* 64 (1955): 176–177.

The Concept of Law. Oxford: Oxford University Press, 1961.

Hawthorne, Geoffrey Hawthorne. *Enlightenment and Despair.* Cambridge: Cambridge University Press, 1987.

Healy, Jack, et al. "Threats and Killings Striking Fear among Young Iraqis, Including Gays." *New York Times* (March 11, 2012): A4.

Heath, T. L. "Greek Geometry with Special Reference to Infinitesimals." *Mathematical Gazette* 11 (1922–1923): 248–259.

Hegel, G. W. F. *Werke. vol. 8 Grundlinien der Philosophie des Rechts,* ed. E. Gans. Berlin: Duncker and Humblot, 1833; T. M. Knox, trans., *Hegel's Philosophy of Right.* Oxford: Clarendon Press, 1942.

Heineman, Elizabeth D., ed. *Sexual Violence in Conflict Zones: From the Ancient World to the Era of Human Rights.* Philadelphia: University of Pennsylvania Press, 2011.

Hennig, Christian. "Falsification of Progensity Models by Statistical Tests and Goodness of Fit Paradox." *Philosophia Mathematica* 15.2 (2007): 1666–1692.

Henry, Nicola, Tony Ward, and Matt Hirshberg. "A Multifactorial Model of Wartime Rape." *Aggression and Violent Behavior* 9 (2004): 535–562.

Hofstader, Albert. "The Myth of the Whole: A Consideration of Quine's View of Knowledge." *Journal of Philosophy* 51 (1954): 397–416.

Hohfeld, Wesley. *Fundamentals of Legal Conception.* New Haven, CT: Yale University Press, 1919.

Holihan, Kerrie Logan. *Rightfully Ours: How Women Won the Vote.* Chicago: Chicago Review Press, 2012.

Hope, T., D. Springings, and R. Crisp. "Not Clinically Indicated: Patients' Interests or Resource Allocations." *British Medical Journal* 306 (1993): 379–381.

Howard, Philip N., and Muzammil M. Hussain. "The Role of Digital Media." *Journal of Democracy* 22.3 (July 2011): 35–48.

Hull, N. E. H. *The Woman Who Dared to Vote: The Trial of Susan B. Anthony.* Topeka: University Press of Kansas, 2012.

Human Rights Watch. *Uganda: Media Minefield: Increased Threats to Freedom of Expression.* New York: Human Rights Watch, 2010.

A Wasted Decade: Human Rights in Syria during Bashar al-Asad's First Ten Years in Power. New York: Human Rights Watch, 2010.

Hume, David. "Of The Standard of Taste," in *The Philosophical Works of David Hume.* Edinburgh: Black and Tait, 1826 [1757]: 4–6.

"Of the Original Contract," in Ernest Barker, ed., *Social Contract.* London: Oxford University Press, 1947 [1748].

An Enquiry Concerning Human Understanding, ed. Eric Steinberg. Indianapolis, IN: Hackett, 1977 [1748].

Hummer, Hans J. *Politics and Power in Early Medieval Europe: Alsace and the Frankish Realm, 600–1000.* Cambridge: Cambridge University Press, 2009.

Hwang, Philip Ho. "An Examination of Mencius' Theory of Human Nature with Reference to Kant." *Kant-Studien: Philosophische Zeitschrift der Kant-Gesellschaft* 74 (1983): 343–354.

Iemmola, Francesca, and Andrea Camperio Ciani. "New Evidence of Genetic Factors Influencing Sexual Orientation in Men: Female Fecundity Increase in the Maternal Line." *Archives of Sexual Behavior* 38.3 (2009): 393–399.

Ignatieff, Michael. *Human Rights as Politics and Idolatry,* ed. Amy Gutmann (Princeton, NJ: Princeton University Press, 2001).

"Is the Human Rights Era Ending?" *New Republic* 227 (2002): 18–19.

"International: Reaching for the Kill Switch: Internet Blackouts." *The Economist* 398.8720 (February 12, 2011): 87–88.

I Saw it with My Own Eyes: Abuses by Chinese Security Forces in Tibet, 2008–2010. New York: Human Rights Watch, 2010.

Israel, Jonathan I. *Radical Enlightenment.* New York: Oxford University Press, 2001.

James, William. "What Is an Emotion?" *Mind* 19 (1884): 188–204.

Janis, J. L. "*Victims of Groupthink: A Psychological Study of Foreign Policy-decisions and Fiascoes.* Boston: Houghton Mifflin, 1973.

Jannini, Emmanuele A., et al. "Male Homosexuality: Nature or Nurture?" *Journal of Sexual Medicine* 7.10 (2010): 3243–3253.

Jansen, L. A., and S. Wall. "Paternalism and Fairness in Clinical Research." *Bioethics* 23.3 (2009): 172–182.

Jasper, David. "Violence and Post-Modernism." *History of European Ideas* 20-4-6 (1995): 801–806.

Jenkins, William J. "Can Anyone Tell Me Why I'm Gay? What Research Suggests Regarding the Origins of Sexual Orientation." *North American Journal of Psychology* 12.2 (2010): 279–295.

Johnston, C. D. *Global News Access: The Impact of New Communications.* Westport, CT: Praeger, 1998.

Johnston, Hank. "State Violence and Oppositional Protest in High-Capacity Authoritarian Regimes." *International Journal of Conflict and Violence* 6.1 (2012): 55–74.

Kenny, Anthony. *Action, Emotion and Will.* London: Routledge and Kegan Paul, 1963.

Kerner, Otto, et al. *National Advisory Commission on Civil Disorders.* Washington, DC: U.S. Government Printing Office, 1968.

Kettlewell, H. *The Evolution of Melanism.* London: Oxford University Press, 1973.

Kinsey, Alfred, Wardell Pomeroy, et al. *Sexual Behavior in the Human Male.* Philadelphia: Saunders, 1948.

Kirsch, Julie. "When Is Ignorance Morally Objectionable?" in *The Morality and Global Justice Reader,* ed. Michael Boylan. Boulder, CO: Westview, 2011: 51–64.

Kohn, Margaret, and Keally McBride. *Political Theories of Decolonization: Post Colonialism and the Problem of Foundations.* New York: Oxford University Press, 2011.

Kon, A. A. "Silent Decisions or Veiled Paternalism? Physicians Are Not Experts in Judging Character." *American Journal of Bioethics* 7.7 (2007): 40–42.

Korsgaard, Christine M. "Ethical, Political, Religious Thought," in Christine M. Korsgaard, *Creating the Kingdom of Ends.* Cambridge: Cambridge University Press, 1996.

Krapp, George Philip, and Elliott van Kirk Dobbie, eds. *The Exeter Book.* New York: Columbia University Press, 1936.

Krause, Kenneth W. "What Next for Gay Marriage?" *Humanist* 71.1 (2011): 41–43.

Kuhn, Thomas S. *The Copernican Revolution.* Cambridge, MA: Harvard University Press, 1957.
  The Structure of Scientific Revolutions, 2nd ed. Chicago: University of Chicago Press, 1962.

Kymlicka, Will. "Individual and Commuinity Rights," in Judith Baker, ed., *Group Rights.* Toronto: University of Toronto Press, 1994: 17–33.
  Multicultural Citizenship. Oxford: Clarendon Press, 1995.

Lane, Mark N., and Olivia M. Little. "Defending Moral Particularism," in James Dreier, ed., *Contemporary Debates in Moral Theory.* Malden, MA: Blackwell, 2006.

Lang, D. *The Casualties of War.* New York: McGraw-Hill, 1969.

Lasee, John. *Theories on the Scrap Heap: Scientists and Philosophers on the Falsification, Rejection, and Replacement of Theories.* Pittsburgh, PA: University of Pittsburgh Press, 2005.

Lauren, Paul Gordon. *The Evolution of International Human Rights,* 2nd ed. Philadelphia: University of Pennsylvania, 2003.

Leger, James Saint. *The "Etiamsi Daremus" of Hugo Grotius: A Study in the Origins of International Law.* Rome: Pontificium Athenaeum Internationale, 1962.

Lehoux, Daryn. "Weather, When, and Why?" *Studies in History and Philosophy of Science* 35 (2004): 209–222.
  "Laws of Nature and Natural Laws." *Studies in History and the Philosophy of Science* 37 (2006): 527–549.

Lewis, Daniel C. "Direct Democracy and Minority Rights: Same-Sex Marriage Bans in the U.S. States." *Social Science Quarterly* 92.2 (2011): 364–383.

Liu, Qingping. "Is Mencius' Doctrine of 'Extending Affection' Tenable?" *Asian Philosophy* 14.1 (2004): 79–90.

Long, Scott et al. *They Want Us Exterminated: Murder, Torture, Sexual Orientation and Gender in Iraq.* New York: Human Rights Watch, 2009.

Luban, David. "The War on Terrorism and the End of Human Rights." *Philosophy and Public Policy Quarterly* 22 (September 2002): 9–14.

Luna, Florencia. "Paternalism and the Argument from Illiteracy." *Bioethics* 9.3/4 (July 1995): 283–290.

Luo, Shirong. "The Political Dimension of Confucius' Idea of Ren." *Philosophy Compass* 7.4 (2012): 245–255.

MacIntyre, Alasdair. *After Virtue: A Study in Moral Theory.* London: Duckworth, 1985.

Mackie, J. L. *Ethics: Inventing Right and Wrong.* Harmondsworth, UK: Penguin, 1977.

Macpherson, C. B. *The Political Theory of Possessive Individualism: Hobbes to Locke.* Oxford: Oxford University Press, 1962.

Mahowald, Mary B. "Against Paternalism: A Developmental View." *Philosophy Research Archives* 6.1386 (1980): 340–357.

Malamuth, N. M. "Rape Proclivity among Males." *Journal of Social Issues* 37 (1981): 138–157.

Malamuth, N. M., R. J. Koss, M. Koss, and J. S. Tanaka. "Characteristics of Aggressors against Women: Testing a Model Using a National Sample of College Students." *Journal of Consulting and Clinical Psychology* 59 (1991): 670–681.

Marshall, Peter. *The Reformation: A Very Short Introduction.* Oxford: Oxford University Press, 2009.

Marshall, W. L., and H. E. Barbaree. "An Integrated Theory of the Etiology of Sexual Offending," in W. L. Marshall, D. R. Laws, and H. E. Barbaree, eds., *Handbook of Sexual Assault: Issues, Theories, and Treatment of the Offender.* New York: Plenum, 1990: 257–275.

Marsilius of Padua: The Defender of the Peace, trans. Annabel Brett. Cambridge Texts in the History of Political Thought. Cambridge: Cambridge University Press, 2005.

Martin, Rex, and James W. Nickel. "A Bibliography on the Nature and Foundations of Rights, 1942–1977." *Political Theory* 6.6 (1978): 395–413.

Maslow, Abraham. *Toward a Psychology of Being,* 2nd ed. New York: Van Nostrand, 1968.

Mass, Peter. "How America's Friends Really Fight Terrorism." *New Republic* 227 (2002): 20–21.

May, Thomas. "Sovereignty and Internal Order." *Ratio Juris* 8.3 (1995): 287–295.

McAdam, Doug, Sidney Tarrow, and Charles Tilly. *Dynamics of Contention.* New York: Cambridge University Press, 2001.

McGrew, Timothy. "Confirmation, Heuristics, and Explanatory Reasoning." *British Journal for the Philosophy of Science* 54.4 (2003): 553–567.

McGuire, Danielle L. *At the Dark End of the Street: Black Women, Rape, and Resistance.* New York: Vintage, 2011.

Melvern, Linda. *Conspiracy to Murder: The Rwanda Genocide and the International Community.* New York: Verso, 2004.

Mencius, trans. D. C. Lau. New York: Penguin, 2005 [1970].

Military Sexual Trauma (MST)—Report of the Defense Task Force on Sexual Assault in the Military Services, December, 2009—Military Sexual Assault, Harassment, Rape. Palm Harbor, FL: Progressive Management, 2010.

Miller, Fred. *Nature, Justice, and Rights in Aristotle's Politics.* Oxford: Oxford University Press, 1995.

Minh, Ho Chi. "Declaration of Independence of the Democratic Republic of Vietnam," in Ho Chi Minh, *Selected Writings: 1920–1969.* Hanoi: University Press of the Pacific, 2001 [1973]: 53–56.

Mink, Louis. "Postmodernism and the Vocation of Historiography." *Modern Intellectual History* 7.1 (2010): 151–184.

Mitsis, Philip. "Natural Law and Natural Right in Post-Aristotelian Philosophy. The Stoics and Their Critics," in W. Hasse and H. Temporini, eds., *Aufstieg und Niedergang der römischen Welt II.* 36.7. Berlin: Walter de Gruyter, 1994: 4812–4850.

Moore, G. E. *Principia Ethica.* Cambridge: Cambridge University Press, 1903.

Mormann, Thomas. "A Place for Pragmatism in the Dynamics of Reason?" *Studies in the History and Philosophy of Science* 43.1 (2012): 27–37.

Morozov, Evgeny. "Technology's Role in Revolution: Internet Freedom and Political Oppression." *Futurist* 45.4 (2011): 18–21.

Morsink, Johannes. *The Universal Declaration of Human Rights: Origins, Drafting, and Intent.* Philadelphia: University of Pennsylvania Press, 2000.

Mueller, Ian. *Philosophy of Mathematics and Deductive Structure in Euclid's Elements.* Cambridge, MA: MIT Press, 1981.

Murray, James, ed. *Oxford English Dictionary.* Oxford: Oxford University Press, 1971.

Naimark, Norman. *The Russians in Germany: A History of Soviet Zone Occupation 1945–1949.* Cambridge, MA: Harvard University Press, 1995.

Nash, Kate. *Cultural Politics of Human Rights: Comparing the U.S. and U.K.* Cambridge: Cambridge University Press, 2009.

Nath, Dipika, et al. *Fear for Life: Violence against Gay Men and Men Perceived as Gay in Senegal.* New York: Human Rights Watch, 2010.

We'll Show You a Woman: Violence and Discrimination against Black Lesbians and Transgender Men in South Africa. New York: Human Rights Watch, 2011.

Negley, Glenn. "Values, Sovereignty, and World Law." *Ethics: An International Journal of Social, Political, and Legal Philosophy* 60 (1950): 208–214.

Neier, Aryeh. *The International Human Rights Movement: A History.* Princeton, NJ: Princeton University Press, 2012.

Nelson, Terri Spahr. *For Love of Country: Confronting Rape and Sexual Harassment in the U.S. Military.* New York: Routledge, 2002.

Nickelsen, Kärin, and Gerd Graßohoff. "In Pursuit of Formaldehyde: Causally Explanatory Models and Falsification." *Studies in History and Philosophy of Biological and Biomedical Science* 42.3 (2011): 297–305.

Noga-Styron, Krystal, Charles E. Reasons, and Derrick Peacock. "The Last Acceptable Prejudice: An Overview of LGBT Social and Criminal Injustice Issues within the USA." *Contemporary Justice Review* 15.4 (2012): 369–398.

Noward, Philip N., and Muzammil M. Hussain. "The Role of Digital Media." *Journal of Democracy* 22.3 (2011): 35–48.

Nussbaum, Martha. *Love's Knowledge.* Oxford: Oxford University Press, 1990.

  The Therapy of Desire: Theory and Practice in Hellenistic Ethics. Princeton, NJ: Princeton University Press, 1994.

  Women and Human Development. Cambridge: Cambridge University Press, 2000.

  Upheavals of Thought: The Intelligence of Emotions. Cambridge: Cambridge University Press, 2001.

Nuttall, Jenni. *The Creation of Lancastrian Kingship: Literature, Language, and Politics in Late Medieval England.* Cambridge: Cambridge University Press, 2011.

Oakeshott, Michael. "Introduction to *Leviathan*," in Michael Oakeshott, *Hobbes on Civil Association.* Berkeley: University of California Press, 1975: 15–28.

Oakley, Justin. *Morality and the Emotions.* London: Routledge and Kegan Paul, 1992.

Ogletree, Charles J. Jr., and Nasser Hussain, eds. *When Governments Break the Law: The Rule of Law and the Prosecution of the Bush Administration.* New York: New York University Press, 2010.

Ojike, Mbonu. *My Africa.* New York: John Day, 1946.

O'Leary, K. D. O. "Physical Aggression between Spouses: A Social Learning Theory Perspective," in V. B. Van Hasselt, R. L. Morrison, A. S. Bellack, and M. Hersen, eds., *Handbook of Family Violence.* New York: Plenum, 1988: 31–55.

Olivier, John L. "State Repression and Collective Action in South Africa 1970–1984." *South African Journal of Sociology* 22 (1991): 109–117.

O'Neill, Onora. *Towards Justice and Virtue.* Cambridge: Cambridge University Press, 1991.

Oosterveld, Valerie. "The Special Court for Sierra Leone's Consideration of Gender-based Violence: Contributing to Transitional Justice?" *Human Rights Review* 10 (2009): 73–98.

Opp, Karl-Dieter, and Wolfgang Roehl. "Repression, Micromobilization and Political Protest." *Social Forces* 69 (1990): 521–547.

Owen, G. E. L. "Zeno and the Mathematicians." *Proceedings of the Aristotelian Society* 58 (1957–1958): 199–222.

Palmer-Fernandez, Gabriel. "Public Policy: Moving toward Moral Cosmopolitanism," in John-Stewart Gordon, ed., *Morality and Justice: Reading Boylan's A Just Society.* Lanham, MD: Lexington, 2009: 147–160.

Pask, Colin. *Magnificent Principia: Exploring Isaac Newton's Masterpiece.* Amherst, NY: Prometheus, 2013.

Pearson, A. C., ed. *Sophoclis Fabvlae.* Oxford: Clarendon Press, 1924.

Peerenboom, Randall. "Human Rights, China, and Cross-Cultural Inquiry: Philosophy, History, and Power Politics." *Philosophy East and West* 53.2 (2005): 283–320.

Peppet, S. R. "Unraveling Privacy: The Personal Prospectus and the Threat of a Full Disclosure Future." *Northwestern Law Review* 105.3 (2011): 1153–1204.

Pinkus, Rosa. "The Evolution of Moral Reasoning." *Medical Humanities Review* 10 (Fall 1996): 20–44.

Pizer, Jennifer C. et al. "Evidence of Persistent and Pervasive Workplace Discrimination against LGBT People: The Need for Federal Legislation Prohibiting Discrimination and Providing for Equal Employment Benefits." *Loyola of Los Angeles Law Review* 45.3 (2012): 715–779.

Platonis Opera, ed. John Burnet. Oxford: Clarendon, 1900.

Pogge, Thomas. "Can the Capability Approach Be Justified?" *Philosophical Topics* 30.2 (2002): 167–228.

Popper, Karl. *The Logic of Scientific Discovery.* London: Unwin Hyman, 1987 [1959].

Power, Samantha. *A Problem from Hell.* New York: Harper, 2007.

Prestwich, Michael. *Armies and Warfare in the Middle Ages: The English Experience.* New Haven: Yale University Press, 1999.

Proust, Marcel. *Sodome et Gomorrhe.* Paris: Nouvelle Revue Française, 1921–1922. trans. F. Scott Moncrieff, *Cities of the Plain.* New York: Random House, 1927: chapter 1, 24–25.

Pufendorf, Samuel. *De jure naturae et gentium. Libri Octo. Lib. II. Cap 3. 19*, trans. C. H. and W. A. Oldfather, 2 vols. Oxford: Oxford University Press, 1934.
On the Law of Nature and Nations, trans. C. H. Oldfather. Oxford: Oxford University Press, 1934.

Pullman, Philip. *Golden Compass Trilogy.* New York: Knopf, 2006.

Putnam, Hilary. "Explanation and Reference," in G. Pearce and P. Maynard, eds., *Conceptual Change* (Dordrecht: Reidel, 1973): 199–221.
"The 'Corroboration' of Theories," in *The Library of Living Philosophers*, vol. 14: *The Philosophy of Karl Popper*, ed. Paul A. Schilpp. LaSalle, IL: Open Court, 1974: 221–240.
The Collapse of the Fact/Value Dichotomy and Other Essays. Cambridge, MA: Harvard, 2004.

Qian, Sima. *Records of the Grand Historian: Quin Dynasty*, trans. Burton Watson. Research Center for Translation. Hong Kong: Chinese University of Hong Kong and Columbia University Press, 1993.

Qizilbash, Mozaffar. "Sugden's Critique of the Capability Approach." *Utilitas: A Journal of Utilitarian Studies* 23.1 (2011): 25–51.

Rahman, Qazi, Stanton L. Jones, and Alex W. Kwee. "Is Homosexuality Biologically Based?" in Brent Slife, ed., *Clashing Views on Psychological Issues.* New York: McGraw-Hill, 2010: 89–108.

Rausing, Sigrid. "Uganda Is Sanctioning Gay Genocide." *New Statesman* 138.4976 (2009): 22.

Rawlence, Ben, and Leslie Lefkow. *One Hundred Ways of Putting Pressure: Violations of Freedom of Expression and Associations in Ethiopia.* New York: Human Rights Watch, 2010.

Rawls, John. *A Theory of Justice.* Cambridge, MA: Harvard University Press, 1971.
The Law of Peoples. Cambridge, MA: Harvard University Press, 2001.

Raz, Joseph. "The Internal Logic of the Law." *Materiali per Una Storia della Cultura Giuridica* 14 (1984): 381.
"Legal Rights." *Oxford Journal of Legal Studies* 4 (1984): I.

The Morality of Freedom. Oxford: Clarendon Press, 1986.

"The Trouble with Particularism." *Mind* 115.457 (2006): 99–120.

Raz, Joseph, and Avishai Margalit. "National Self-Determination," in Joseph Raz, ed., *Ethics in the Public Domain.* Oxford: Clarendon Press, 1994: 133–134.

Reader, Soran. "Does a Basic Needs Approach Need Capabilities?" *Journal of Political Philosophy* 14.3 (2006): 337–350.

Reardon, B. *Sexism and the War System.* New York: Teachers College Press, Research Centre, 1985.

Regan, Donald. "Gewirth on Necessary Goods: What Is the Agent Committed to Valuing?," in Michael Boylan, ed., *Gewirth: Critical Essays on Action, Rationality and Community.* Lanham, MD: Rowman and Littlefield, 1999: 45–70.

Reid, Charles J. "The Canonistic Contribution to the Western Rights Tradition: An Historical Inquiry." *Boston College Law Review* 33 (1991): 37–92.

Rhodes, Sinéad, and Fiona Jones. "Captivating Interest in Survival." *Psychologist* 22.12 (2009): 1008–1009.

Rice, William R., Urban Friberg, and Sergey Gavrilets "Homosexuality as a Consequence of Epigenetically Canalized Sexual Development." *Quarterly Review of Biology* 87.4 (2012): 343.

Ripoll, Julieta Lemaitre. "Love in the Time of Cholera: LGBT Rights in Colombia." *Sur-International Journal of Human Rights* 11 (2009): 73–89.

Ross-Nazzal, Jennifer M. *Winning the West for Women: The Life of Suffragist Emma Smith DeVoe.* Seattle: University of Washington Press, 2011.

Ruse, Michael. "Charles Darwin on Group Selection." *Annals of Science* 37 (1980): 615–630.

Rüsen, Jörn. "Jacob Burckhardt: Political Standpoint and Historical Insight on the Border of Post-Modernism." *History and Theory* 24.3 (1985): 235–246.

Ryle, Gilbert. *The Concept of Mind.* London: Hutchinson, 1949.

Sadgrove, Joanna, et al. "Morality Plays and Money Matters: Towards a Situated Understanding of the Politics of Homosexuality in Uganda." *Journal of Modern African Studies* 50.1 (2012): 103–129.

Salbi, Z. *The Other Side of War: Women's Stories of Survival and Hope.* Washington, DC: National Geographic Society, 2007.

Sandel, Michael. *Democracy's Discontent: America in Search of a Public Philosophy.* Cambridge, MA: Harvard University Press, 1998.

  Liberalism and the Limits of Justice, 2nd ed. Cambridge: Cambridge University Press, 1998.

  Justice: What Is the Right Thing to Do? New York: Farrar, Straus and Giroux, 2009.

Sartre, Jean-Paul. *The Emotions: Outline of a Theory,* trans. Bernard Frechtman. New York: Philosophical Library, 1948.

Scanlon, T. M. *What We Owe to Each Other.* Cambridge, MA: Harvard University Press, 1998.

Schlick, Moritz. "Positivism and Realism," trans. Peter Heath. *Erkenntis III* (1932–1933); rpt. *Moritz Schlick: Philosophical Papers II (1925–1936)* from *Vienna Circle Collection,* ed. Henk L. Mulder. Dordrecht: Kluwer, 1979: 259–284.

Schmidt, P. L. *Die Abfassungszeit von Ciceros Schrift über die Gesetze.* Rome: Centro di Studi Ciceroniani, 1969.

Sen, Amartya. *Inequality Reexamined.* Cambridge, MA: Harvard University Press, 1992.

———. *Development as Freedom.* New York: Alfred A. Knopf, 1999.

———. *The Idea of Justice.* Cambridge, MA: Harvard University Press, 2009.

Seneca. *Moral Essays,* vol. 3., trans. J. W. Basore. Cambridge, MA: Harvard University Press, 1935.

Sharma, Arvind. *Are Human Rights Western?* Oxford: Oxford University Press, 2006.

Sharrock, Justine. *Tortured: When Good Soldiers Do Bad Things.* Hoboken, NJ: Wiley, 2010.

Shay, Jonathan. *Achilles in Vietnam: Combat Trauma and the Undoing of Character.* New York: Simon and Schuster, 1995.

Short, Damien. *Reconciliation and Colonial Power: Indigenous Rights in Australia.* Farnham, UK: Ashgate, 2008.

Shue, Henry. *Basic Rights.* Princeton, NJ: Princeton University Press, 1980.

Sijie, Dai. *Balzac and the Little Chinese Seamstress,* trans. Ina Rilke. New York: Anchor, 2002; first published as *Balzac et la petite tailleuse chinoise.* Paris: Gallimard, 2000.

Siker, Jeffrey S., ed. *Homosexuality and Religion: An Encyclopedia.* Westport, CT: Greenwood, 2006.

Sim, May. "Rethinking Virtue Ethics and Social Justice with Aristotle and Confucius." *Asian Philosophy* 20.2 (2010): 195–213.

Simplicius. *Commentary on Aristotle's Physics,* ed. H. Diets, 2 vols. Berlin: G. Reimeri, 1882–1895.

Simpson, A. W. Brian. *Human Rights and the End of Empire.* Oxford: Oxford University Press, 2004.

Singer, Beth. *Operative Rights.* Albany: SUNY Press, 1993.

———. "Community, Mutuality, and Rights," in Michael Boylan, ed., *Gewirth: Critical Essays on Action, Rationality and Community.* Lanham, MD: Rowman and Littlefield, 1999: 145–154.

Singer, Marcus. *Generalization in Ethics.* New York: Athenaeum, 1961.

Sjoberg, Laura, and Sandra Via, eds. *Gender, War, and Militarism: Feminist Perspectives.* Santa Barbara, CA: Praeger, 2010.

Skjelsbaek, Inger. *The Political Psychology of War Rape: Studies from Bosnia and Herzegovina.* New York: Routeledge, 2011.

Smith, Robert L. *Elements of Ecology,* 3rd ed. New York: Harper Collins, 1992.

Snyder, Laura. "Confirmation for a Modest Realism." *Philosophy of Science* 72.5 (2005): 839–849.

Soh, Chunghee Sarah. "Human Rights and the 'Comfort Women.'" *Peace Journal* 12 (2000): 123–129.

Solomon, Robert. *The Passions: The Myth and Nature of Human Emotions.* New York: Doubleday, 1984.

Southern, R. W. *The Making of the Middle Ages.* New Haven, CT: Yale University Press, 1961.

Spinoza, Baruch. *Letters,* trans. Samuel Shirley. Indianapolis, IN: Hackett, 1995.

Stevenson, Charles L. *Ethics and Language.* New Haven, CT: Yale University Press, 1944.

"The Emotive Meaning of Ethical Terms," in C. L. Stevenson, *Facts and Values: Studies in Ethical Analysis* (New Haven, CT: Yale University Press, 1963): 10–31.

Stiglitz, Joseph. *The Price of Inequality: How Today's Divided Society Endangers Our Future.* New York: Norton, 2013.

Stiglmayer, Alexandra, ed. *Mass Rape: The War against Women in Bosnia-Herzegovina.* Lincoln: University of Nebraska Press, 1994.

Strauss, David Levi, Charles Stein, Barbara Ehrenreich, John Gray, Meron Benvenisti, Mark Danner, and David Matlin. *Abu Ghraib: The Politics of Torture.* New York: North Atlantic Books, 2004.

Strauss, Leo. *Natural Right and History.* Chicago: University of Chicago Press, 1953.

Sulmasy, Daniel. "Managed Care and the New Paternalism." *Journal of Clinical Ethics* 6.4 (Winter 1995): 324–326.

Summenhart, Konrad. *De contractibus licitis atque illicitis Tractatus.* Venice: Francesco Ziletti, 1580.

Sungmoon, Kim. "Mencius in International Relations and the Morality of War." *History of Political Thought* 31.1 (2010): 133–156.

Sunzi (Sun Tzu). *The Art of War*, ed. John Minford. New York: Viking, 2002.

Syrian Human Rights Committee. http://www.shrc.org/data/aspx/d5/2535. aspx (accessed May 1, 2012).

Syse, Henrik. *Natural Law, Religion, and Rights.* South Bend, IN: St. Augustine's Press, 2007.

Szabo, Arpad. *The Beginnings of Greek Mathematics.* Dordrecht: D. Reidel, 1978.

Tasioulas, John. "The Moral Reality of Human Rights," in Thomas Pogge, ed., *Freedom from Poverty as a Human Right: Who Owes the Very Poor?* Oxford: Oxford University Press, 2007.

Taylor, Charles. "The Politics of Recognition" in Charles Taylor, *Multiculturalism: Examining the Politics of Recognition*, ed. Amy Gutman (Princeton, NJ: Princeton University Press, 1994): 32–36.

Thavavel, V., and S. Sivakumar. "A Generalized Framework of Privacy Preservation in Distributed Data Mining for Unstructured Data Environment." *International Journal of Computer Science* 9.1 (2012): 434–441.

Thomson, J. F. "Tasks and Super-Tasks." *Analysis* 15 (1954): 1–13.

Tierney, Brian. *The Idea of Natural Rights: Studies on Natural Rights, Natural Law and Church Law 1150–1625.* Atlanta: Scholars Press, 1997.

Tilcsik, András. "Pride and Prejudice: Employment Discrimination against Openly Gay Men in the United States." *Journal of Sociology* 117.2 (2011): 586–626.

Tolley, Howard. *The U.N. Commission on Human Rights.* Boulder, CO: Westview, 1987.

Tong, Rosemarie. "Taking on the Big Fat," in Michael Boylan, ed., *Public Health Policy and Ethics.* Dordrecht: Kluwer/Springer, 2004: 39–58.

"A Feminist Personal Worldview Imperative," in John-Stewart Gordon, ed., *Morality and Justice: Reading Boylan's A Just Society.* Lanham, MD: Lexington, 2009: 29–38.

Tootill, Elizabeth, ed. *Dictionary of Biology.* Maidenhead, Berkshire, UK: Berkshire Intercontinental Kook Productions, 1980.

Tribe, Laurence H., and Joshua Matz. "The Constitutional Inevitability of Same-Sex Marriage." *Maryland Law Review* 71.2 (2012): 471–489.

Tsai, Denis Hsin-an. "On Mencius' Choice." *Philosophical Review* (Taiwan) 10 (1987): 137–175.

Tuck, Richard. *Natural Rights Theories.* Cambridge: Cambridge University Press, 1982.

Unger, Peter K. *Living High and Letting Die.* Oxford: Oxford University Press, 1996.

United Nations. *The 2013 Human Development Report.* New York: United Nations Development Program.

United States Commission on Civil Rights. *Under the Rule of Thumb: Battered Women and the Administration of Justice,* 2 vols. Ann Arbor: University of Michigan Library, 1982.

Viley, Michel. "La Genèse du Droit Subjectif chez Guillaume d'Ockham." *Archives de la Philosophie du Droit* 9 (1969): 97–127.

Vlachova, M., and L. Biaso, eds. *Women in an Insecure World: Violence against Women, Facts, Figures, and Analysis.* Geneva: Geneva Centre for the Democratic Control of Armed Forces, 2005.

Vlastos, Gregory. "A Note on Zeno's Arrow." *Phronesis* 11 (1966): 3–18.

"Zero's Race Course." *Journal of the History of Philosophy* 4 (1966): 95–108.

Waerdt, Paul van der. "Philosophical Influence on Roman Jurisprudence? The Case of Stoicism and Natural Law." *Aufstieg und Niedergang der römischen Welt* II.36.7: 4851–4900.

Waldron, Jeremy, ed. *Theories of Rights.* Oxford: Oxford University Press, 1984.

"Can Communal Goods Be Human Rights?" in Jeremy Waldron, *Liberal Rights.* Cambridge: Cambridge University Press, 1993: section iv.

Walzer, Michael. *Just and Unjust Wars,* 4th ed. New York: Basic Books, 2006.

Ward, T., and S. Hudson. "The Construction and Development of Theory in the Sexual Offending Area: A Metatheoretical Framework." *Sexual Abuse: A Journal of Research and Treatment* 10 (1998): 47–63.

Watling, James. "The Sum of an Infinite Series." *Analysis* 13.2 (1952): 39–46.

Weaver, Gina Marie. *Ideologies of Forgetting: Rape in the Vietnam War.* Albany: SUNY Press, 2010.

Wellman, Carl. *Welfare Rights.* Totowa, NJ: Rowman and Allanheld, 1982.

White, Robert W., and Terry Falkenberg White. "Repression and the Liberal State: The Case of Northern Ireland, 1969–1972." *Journal of Conflict Resolution* 39 (1995): 330–352.

White, Thomas. *In Defense of Dolphins.* Malden, MA: Blackwell, 2008.

Whitehead, Alfred North. *Process and Reality.* London: Macmillan, 1929.

Whorf, Benjamin Lee. *Language, Thought, and Reality,* edited with introduction by John B. Carroll. Cambridge, MA: MIT University Press, 1966 [1956].

Wicclair, Mark R. "Patient Decision-Making Capacity and Risk." *Bioethics* 5 (April 1991): 91–104.

Williams, Bernard. "Morality and the Emotions." In Bernard Williams, *Problems of the Self: Philosophical Papers 1956–1972.* Cambridge: Cambridge University Press, 1973: 207–229.

Williams, George. *Adaptation and Natural Selection*. Princeton, NJ: Princeton University Press, 1966.

Williams, Tennessee. *The Glass Menagerie*. New York: New Directions, 1999 [1945].

Wilson, Judith. *Discovering Species*. New York: Columbia, 1999.

Wilson, Robert A., ed. *Species: New Interdisciplinary Essays*. Cambridge, MA: MIT Press, 1999.

Witte, John. *The Reformation of Rights: Law, Religion, and Human Rights in Modern Calvinism*. Cambridge: Cambridge University Press, 2008.

Wittgenstein, Ludwig. *Philosophical Investigations*, ed. G. E. M. Anscombe, Rush Rhees, and G. H. von Wright; trans. G. E. M. Anscombe. Oxford: Blackwell, 1953.

   Das blaue Buch: Eine Philosophische Betrachtung. Hrsg. von Rush Rhees, G. E. M. Anscombe, and G. H. von Wright. Frankfurt: Suhrkamp, 1970.

Wolfe, Tom. *Bonfire of the Vanities*. New York: Bantam, 1988.

Wollheim, Richard. *On the Emotions*. New Haven, CT: Yale University Press, 1999.

Wong, Edward, and David Barbosa. "Wary of Egypt Unrest, China Censors Web." *New York Times* (January 31, 2011): A4.

Wood, Allen. "The Emptiness of the Moral Will." *The Monist* 72 (1989): 454–483.

Wu, Chengqiu. "Sovereignty, Human Rights, and Responsibility: Changes in China's Response to International Humanitarian Crises." *Journal of Chinese Political Science* 15 (2010): 71–97.

Wulff, Henrik. "The Inherent Paternalism in Clinical Practice." *Journal of Medicine and Philosophy* 20.3 (1995): 299–311.

Xingjian, Gao. *Soul Mountain*, trans. Mabel Lee. New York: HarperCollins, 2000; first published as *Linghan*. Taiwan: Linjing Chubanshe, 1990.

Yan, Guobin. "The People's Standoff: China's Twitter Generation Squares Off against the 'Great Firewall.'" *Scientific American* 308.4 (April, 2013): 14.

Yang-Ming, Wang. "*Inquiry on the Great Learning*," in Wing-tsit Chan, ed. and trans., *A Sourcebook in Chinese Philosophy* (Princeton, NJ: Princeton University Press, 1963).

Yin, Jing. "The Clash of Rights: A Critical Analysis of News Discourse on Human Rights in the United States and China." *Critical Discourse Studies* 4.1 (2007): 75–94.

Yong, Hu. "Spreading the News." *Index on Censorship* 41.4 (2012): 107–111.

Yoon, Kaesuk. *Naming Nature*. New York: Norton, 2009.

Young, Marilyn. "Preface," in Jeffrey Wasserstrom, Lynn Hunt, and Marilyn Young, eds., *Human Rights and Revolutions*. Lanham, MD: Rowman and Littlefield, 2000.

Zagorin, Perez. "History, the Referent, and Narrative: Reflections on Postmodernism Now." *History and Theory* 38.1 (1999): 1–24.

Zaki, M. "Civil Society and Democratizing in the Arab World." *Ibn Khaldun Center for Development Studies Annual Report 2010*. Cairo: Ibn Khaldun Center for Development Studies, 2010.

Zhong hua xue yi she, in *The Chinese Classics*, 4 vols. London: Trübner, 1875–1876; available online in Chinese and English from the University of Virginia at http://etext.lib.virginia.edu/chinese/ (accessed June 1, 2012).

Zimmer, Carl. "Ecosystems on the Brink." *Scientific American* 307.4 (2012): 61–65.

Zomorodi, Meg, and Barbara Jo Foley. "The Nature of Advocacy vs. Paternalism in Nursing: Clarifying the 'Thin Line.'" *Journal of Advanced Nursing* 65.8 (2009): 1746–1752.

Index

Made in the USA
Middletown, DE
21 January 2021